Whose Freud?

Whose Freud?

The Place of Psychoanalysis

in Contemporary Culture

Edited by Peter Brooks and Alex Woloch

Yale University Press

New Haven and London

Dominick LaCapra's essay "Reflections on Trauma, Absence, and Loss" appeared in an earlier and shorter version in Critical Inquiry 25 (Summer 1999). © 1999 by The University of Chicago Press.

Library of Congress Cataloging-in-Publication Data
Whose Freud? : the place of psychoanalysis in contemporary culture / edited by Peter Brooks and Alex Woloch.
    p.   cm.
Includes bibliographical references and index.
ISBN 0-300-08116-2 (cloth : alk. paper)
ISBN 0-300-08745-4 (pbk : alk. paper)
1. Psychoanalysis and culture—Congresses.   2. Freud, Sigmund, 1856–1939—Congresses.   I. Brooks, Peter, 1938–   II. Woloch, Alex, 1970–

BF175.4.C84 W46 2000
150.19'5—dc21   00-027261

A catalogue record for this book is available from the British Library.
The paper in this book meets the guidelines for permanence and durability of the Committee on Production Guidelines for Book Longevity of the Council on Library Resources.

10 9 8 7 6 5 4 3 2 1

Contents

Acknowledgments

We wish to thank all the contributors for their energetic participation in the "Whose Freud?" conference, held at the Whitney Humanities Center, Yale University, in April 1998, and for their patience as we translated the talks and discussions into their current form. The conference was originally conceived and organized by an interdisciplinary group brought together at the Whitney Humanities Center in 1997. Although the committee members make only brief appearances in the book, as session moderators, Esther de Costa Meyer, Katherine Kearns, Kevis Goodman, Elise Snyder, and Peter Gay were instrumental not just in selecting the participants in the conference but in formulating the very categories that underlie the book, the six different "places" where we investigate psychoanalysis in contemporary culture. We would also like to thank Laura Jones Dooley, at Yale University Press, for her efficient and supportive work on the manuscript. Finally we want to express our gratitude to the excellent staff of the Whitney Humanities Center: to Manana Sikic, administrator of the Center, for her grace and skill in handling all the complications involved in an international conference, and to Annette Myers, for her support at the original conference and in the production of this book.

Introduction

Peter Brooks

It was ninety-one years ago—in May 1909—that what Ernest Jones calls an "important Congress" of psychiatrists met in New Haven, Connecticut, to listen to talks by himself and James J. Putnam, professor of neurology at Harvard University. "Putnam and I read papers that provoked much discussion," Jones reports. The purpose of this "New Haven Congress" was to prepare for the American visit of Dr. Sigmund Freud. Freud himself arrived in September, accompanied by Carl Jung and Sandor Ferenczi, was met in New York by Jones and A. A. Brill, traveled by boat to New Haven, then on to Massachusetts to give his Clark University lectures, which marked the beginning of the pervasive influence of psychoanalysis in American culture.

The symposium held at the Whitney Humanities Center, Yale University, on April 3–4, 1998, was not an attempt to revive the New Haven Congress. Rather, it marked a recognition by the group of Yale faculty who planned the conference that we had reached a good moment, in fact a critical moment, to assess the place of psychoanalysis in our culture. The response to this idea, both from those we invited to participate in the symposium and from the public at large, was almost overwhelming: the largest and most attentive audience the Center has ever gathered. The response suggested that psychoanalysis is both bitterly contested and still a potent force. Freud, the *Times Literary Supplement* reported three years ago, remains the most frequently cited writer of our time—cited, I think, a bit like Jean-Jacques Rousseau two centuries ago: as the presiding genius of our culture and the author of its symptomatic illnesses.

The symposium aimed to assess the status of psychoanalysis as a discipline and discourse in contemporary culture. That we should be setting psychoanalysis in so broad, and so vague, a context as "culture" is of course itself significant and problematic: what was at first conceived as a therapy for neurotics has more than fulfilled its founder's most grandiose ambitions. It has become a theory of mind, a theory of human development, a theory of cultural history, a theory of interpretation. Freud noted that he owed as much to "the poets and philosophers" as to medical science, and it may be within domains that are broadly concerned with poetry and philosophy that his thought is most alive today.

The place of psychoanalysis is very much at issue. At one time firmly established within medical-therapeutic practices, especially in the United States, psychoanalysis has increasingly been contested by other forms of therapy: traditional psychoanalytic treatment is too long, too expensive, too uncertain in its outcomes; psychopharmacology is often held to be more effective. As a science of mind, psychoanalysis has been challenged by both philosophical analyses and neuroscientific advances—and yet it has recently been revived as a model of psychic functioning by some philosophers and neuroscientists. If psychoanalysis holds little prestige in most university departments of psychology, where it is disconsidered as outmoded and unscientific, it has been at the center of many debates in humanistic fields, including literary studies. Often rejected by feminism, it continues to figure in debates about sexual identity. As a cultural discourse, it has become commonplace but also has been challenged in its most basic assumptions, as the debates over "recovered memories," repression, and the law most dramatically suggest.

Here is something of a muddle. At one extreme, there is the claim (made by Jeffrey Masson) that every patient treated since the invention of psychoanalysis should be recalled, like the Ford Pinto. At the other end of the spectrum is the assumption made by many practitioners of cultural critique that the tools of psychoanalysis are not only valid but illuminating in the study of literature, film, biography, and history. If psychoanalysis, in its classic forms, seems to be losing adherents in the field for which it was first designed—the cure of neurotic patients—and has been contested as a model of the "psychic apparatus," should we happily, or resignedly, conclude that it has simply become one of the hermeneutic arts, useful—though perhaps ungrounded—to those who interpret literature, art, and cultural history? If this were to prove the case, would there not be a considerable loss: loss of the tension and discipline created when the importation of a science of mind into interpretive activity needs constant testing against the original uses and intentions of that science? That is, if you lose the base of psychoanalysis in clinical experience and theory of mental functioning, it may become simply one more hypothesis of reading, unanchored from any reality. Has this in fact already occurred? Have its applications in such fields as history, anthropology, art history, and literary and film criticism enriched psychoanalytic understanding—or trivialized and even parodied it? How does psychoanalysis contribute to cultural analysis? And does it still have validity as a theory of mind? What may now be our best model of the truth provided by psychoanalytic insight?

The present moment seems well chosen for a searching reassessment of how and where psychoanalysis survives in our culture. Our title *Whose Freud?* asks where psychoanalysis now belongs and where it is effectively and responsibly exercised. It asks whether there has in fact been a wholescale displacement of psychoanalysis from mental science into the human sciences, and if so, what are the consequences. And lurking somewhere behind *Whose Freud?* is its punning equivalent, "Who's Freud"—giving a place to radical dissent from the assumption that psychoanalysis can claim any interpretive validity at all.

These basic questions led us to six topics that focused the sessions of the symposium. We begin with "Psychoanalysis and Its Discontents," designed to open our discussions with an airing of the reasons psychoanalysis is now just as fiercely contested as at any other time in its contentious hundred-year history. Our title, echoing Freud's *Civilization and Its Discontents,* means to comprehend not only those who reject psychoanalysis totally (Frederick Crews) but also those who—as in the portrait of humanity given in Freud's essay—are living uneasily in a culture imposed upon them, which has certainly been the case of many feminist thinkers in regard to psychoanalysis. As it turns out, Frederick Crews's claim that "psychoanalysis has no more standing than astrology or palmistry" has no takers from his fellow panelists (Robert Michels, Judith Butler, and Juliet Mitchell). But his claim that Freud's ideas are now vanishing and that "academics, like bunkered troops on a remote island who haven't heard that the war is over," are the last to get the news, though intended as dismissive, in fact sets up complex resonances.

For the other panelists are all acutely aware of the belatedness of their relation to psychoanalysis, either through the revisionary lessons learned from therapeutic practice or through rethinking of fundamental theoretical premises.
And they are all conscious of the academic setting as the current and future testing ground of psychoanalysis. For Robert Michels, in fact, the academic culture
of research and testing is what has been most lacking in psychoanalytic training
and intellectual transmission. Judith Butler and Juliet Mitchell, in their very different ways, bring to psychoanalysis a critique developed from many sources—
feminism, anthropology, Lacan, gay studies—but it is one that accepts psychoanalysis as a necessary context of argument. They demonstrate that Crews's
claim of academics' belatedness can be reinterpreted, in a very Freudian gesture,
as a move of *Nachträglichkeit:* a later action or mental operation that retroactively modifies an earlier one. Psychoanalysis as it is known and practiced in
the academy partakes of this retroactive quality, perceiving and highlighting in
psychoanalysis the posing of issues in a form that was there but not in so per-
spicuous a form originally. Butler's reconsideration of the incest taboo is a dramatic instance of such retroactivity; Mitchell's rethinking of "the story" in relation to the construction of the unconscious is another. So that the discontent in
these cases, unlike Crews's, is within an acquired framework of psychoanalytic
thinking.

The second large topic, "Psychoanalysis: Between Therapy and Hermeneutics?" asks about the current place of psychoanalysis between its original, and
continuing, use as therapy and its also original, but now much extended, use in
cultural hermeneutics. If Freud often assumes the stance of humble medical-
scientific researcher, intent upon the cure of his patients and the extrapolation
of what they teach him into a theory of mental functioning, he also often describes himself as "conquistador," opening up all of human behavior, and human
cultural artifacts, to the kind of semiotic decipherment originally exercised upon
hysterics and upon dreams. Although practicing psychotherapists naturally continue to be interested in what interpretation can do to their patients' understanding of their lives—and to change their lives—the practitioners of psychoanalytic interpretation in cultural fields are cut loose from this responsibility.

The contributions here (from Toril Moi, Hubert Damisch, Peter Loewenberg, and Mary Jacobus) do not so much argue this question as do something
more convincing: they take up a place precisely in that between, producing a
rich variety of interpretive gestures applied to issues of cultural importance, all
the while maintaining a sense of the original use of psychoanalytic interpretation. As Mary Jacobus usefully points out, psychoanalytic therapy itself has a

theory of its practice, and this is very much demonstrated in the diverse approaches of the other panelists. Toril Moi's rereading of Freud's notorious use of the phrase "anatomy is destiny," reconfigured in its allusion to Napoleon's "politics is destiny," and Peter Loewenberg's stark evocation of the architecture of Auschwitz, enact, as Hubert Damisch puts it, a bridging of the gap between clinical practice and textual and cultural interpretation: the gap is bridged because the discourse of psychoanalysis in its extension to cultural fields remains resolutely psychoanalytic, subject to the constraints of the Freudian hermeneutic. That the discussion following the four presentations came to focus to so large an extent on the latrines of Auschwitz seemed at the time a bit strange, yet now I believe it testifies to the power of psychoanalytic thinking precisely to open up the repressed in history.

In addressing, in the third session—which concluded day one of the symposium—the issue of "Psychoanalysis and Sexual Identity," we confront psychoanalysis on what might be seen as both its strongest and its weakest ground. Some of the best-publicized attacks on Freud have come from feminist thinkers and from those who find his views of sexuality too narrowly normative, of a type that promoted in American psychotherapy, at least, the notion that homosexuality was a deviance to be "cured" by psychoanalytic treatment. And yet, it is difficult to conceive of any contestation of the Freudian understanding of sexuality that does not make use of Freud's own terminology and indeed of his entire conceptual apparatus. From the *Three Essays on the Theory of Sexuality* (1905) on, Freud simultaneously argues the deep structuration of human action, character, destiny in infantile sexual identifications and fantasmatic scenarios of satisfaction—reducing the whole of human culture, one might say, to an ultimately sexual matrix—and at the same time extends the notion of sexuality so broadly that it becomes, at least by the time of *Beyond the Pleasure Principle* (1920), the large dynamic, integrative force, Eros, that binds all living matter.

As the contributions here (by Paul Robinson, Kaja Silverman, and Leo Bersani) make clear, to think sexuality within Freud's terms is hardly the reductive enterprise it is often taken to be in popular views of psychoanalysis, and in polemical attacks (to which Freud certainly left himself open) on some of his pronouncements on feminine sexuality and on sexual normativity. On the contrary, any close attention to Freud's arguments, in the *Three Essays* and elsewhere, shows that human sexuality is never simple "genitality" but always what Juliet Mitchell has called "psychosexuality," a construction that is always "deviant" and "perverse" in relation to simple reproductive utility because it is based on infantile scenarios of lack and imaginary fulfillment, on original bisexuality and the oedipal imperative to choose (all the while refusing) a fixed sexual identity. Leo Bersani refers to his discovery, with his students, that the oedipal triangle activates eighteen partners in various permutations of positive and negative relation with one another. Any nonreductive reading of sexual identity truly faithful to Freud must come out with some similar view of the extraordinary complexity of psychosexual subject positions—as, for instance, in the famous essay "A Child Is Being Beaten"—that a human being in the world activates.

If the claims of psychoanalysis to understand human character, motives, desires, and even the drives that underlie living and dying—drives not directly observable but detectable through their products and representations—are valid, they ought to be testable not only in therapy with individual patients but also in the practice of biography and, more generally, in the interpretation of individuals and groups that we call history. In particular, the cataclysmic history of the twentieth century would seem to be a particularly apt testing ground for the psychoanalytic study of the havoc wreaked by group psychology at its most destructive. Psychobiography and psychohistory exist, in relatively pure and extremely diluted forms, in examples both successful and failed. Our fourth section, "Psychoanalysis and the Historiography of Modern Culture," addresses the uses of psychoanalytic interpretation in understanding the shape and meaning of historical event and narrative. The contributors here (Dominick LaCapra, Eric L. Santner, Meredith Skura, and Robert Jay Lifton) reach for various models in Freud (*Mourning and Melancholia,* the Schreber analysis, itself a psychobiography, among other sources) in an attempt to define what comes of a psychoanalytic approach to history.

Robert Jay Lifton's initial premises may pose the issues most starkly: without psychoanalysis, we don't have a psychology worthy of address to history; yet psychoanalysis in its traditional forms has tended to bracket history in favor of the case study of the individual. Perhaps only with Erik Erikson's *Young Man Luther* did we gain a model of how the individual case history illuminates and is illuminated by an entire historical epoch. Yet Luther is almost too good a case; it's not clear that one can find all that many other "cases" that illustrate to so high a degree the problematics of one person trying to solve for all his contemporaries what he could not resolve in his own life. The psychic collectivity remains elusive, and the history of collective acts of sadism, atrocity, and the breakdown of civilization obscure, despite Freud's incisive remarks in *Civilization and Its Discontents,* "Thoughts for the Time on Life and Death," and "Why War?"—remarks that attack the problems at too great a level of generality to be useful for the working historian. If only psychoanalysis is worthy of the address to history, it is nonetheless true that most history continues to be produced with only a commonsense, everyday psychology behind its insights. And psychoanalytic explanations of history often make us uneasy, perhaps because they appear to overexplain, to understand too much—and thus perhaps implicitly to explain away too much. The mediation of history through psychoanalytic interpretation remains in my view a task as daunting as it is necessary.

"Psychoanalysis and Theories of Mind," the next section, is to a nonscientist such as myself perhaps the most exciting and tantalizing of this volume. I think I had for many years believed, somewhat defensively, that neuroscience was working on hypotheses and concepts concerning the brain that had nothing to do with Freud's conception of mind. Freud himself of course frequently stated that he thought neurobiology would eventually make most of his discoveries obsolete. And certainly that seems to be the working assumption of most university departments of psychology, which regard Freud as superannuated. But then I became vaguely aware that some researchers in neuroscience and cognitive science were finding the Freudian models of psychic functioning congenial as research hypotheses. What the contributions to this section (by Morton F. Reiser, David V. Forrest, Arnold M. Cooper, and Robert Shulman) suggest is the tentative protocols of a dialogue between neuroscience and psychoanalysis.

Neuroscience, thanks to new and rapidly developing technologies of brain scanning, is now able to track, in noninvasive experiments, some of the physiological processes taking place in the brain, giving exceptional new insight into what "happens" in the brain when it accomplishes certain set tasks. The question then becomes: What interpretive model of mental functioning are we to call upon to make sense of these experimental observations? With varying degrees of certitude and optimism, all the contributions here suggest that psychoanalysis, perhaps alone among inquiries into mind, has developed postulates that conduce toward a valid and nontrivial modeling of brain function. For instance, Freud's initial insistence on the importance of dreams, and the "dreamwork," as the "royal way" to understanding of psychodynamic process has long offered a fertile research hypothesis to the study of mental activity during sleep. The postulate of the unconscious itself, and of the dynamics of repression in relation to memory, also suggest approaches to mind that may turn out to be empirically testable in terms of the dynamic functionings of the brain. It's as if Freud's very early *Project for a Scientific Psychology* (1895) were on the verge of being revived—not in its specific terms, limited by late nineteenth-century biology, but precisely in its project: tracking the functioning of the "psychic apparatus" (*seelischer Apparat*) in its neuronal manifestations. A decade hence, one will want to reconvene psychoanalysts and neuroscientists—those sympathetic to the possibility of a dialogue—to draw up a new balance sheet of what at present is a tentative groping toward common solutions.

Finally, the symposium concluded with an address to the question that had been latent throughout—and not entirely latent, since Frederick Crews addressed it at the outset, with entirely negative conclusions: What kind of truth claims are made by psychoanalysis? Much of the current well-publicized wholesale rejection of Freud and psychoanalysis, exemplified in the work of Crews, Masson, and Adolf Grünbaum, for instance, argues that psychoanalysis offers no basis for verifying its claims as science, that its hypotheses are circular and untestable, and that even as an interpretative discipline it relies on suggestion, rhetoric, and the logic of "heads I win, tails you lose" (as Freud himself characterized his practice in the late essay "Constructions in Analysis" [1937]). Argument continues about the "seduction theory": principally, the accusation that when Freud abandoned his belief that his patients had in actuality been childhood victims of sexual abuse and came to see "seduction" by an adult figure as instead a nearly universal fantasy, thus giving him a first delineation of the Oedipus complex, he turned away from his own best insights and from social reality. Reverberations of this debate continue in courts of law, where psychoanalytic conceptions of seduction, memory, and repression enter into an uneasy dialogue with legal standards of evidence and proof. The reality or fantasy of seduction, the nature of "recovered memories" as biographical events or as therapeutically constructed as-if explanatory narratives: these instances suggest how much the debate about the kind of truth psychoanalysis claims to deliver may be a dialogue of the deaf.

So it would be good to know what might be the status of truth in psychoanalysis—a question that Freud by no means makes wholly clear, since he vacillates so often (often, it seems, with a certain gusto) between declaring (I allude here to the ending of *Totem and Taboo*), "In the beginning was the act" and "In the beginning was the word"—where word may stand for everything that has active force through fantasy, belief, and ideology but has not necessarily occurred as historical fact. The contributors to the final section, "Psychoanalysis: What Kind of Truth?" (Richard Wollheim, Donald Davidson, Jonathan Lear, and John Forrester) variously address issues of "truth" and whether it can and should be qualified (as in "narrative truth"), and the peculiar practices of psychoanalysis in arriving at the results it holds in some sense to be true. Jonathan Lear points out, for instance, that an analysand's obsession with truth as correspondence to real historical event "can serve as a massive obstacle to psychoanalytic understanding," a resistance to meaning. And an insistence on tidy explanatory narratives, with all the pieces well linked together, can also be a resistance to the anxiety of a messier truth.

The defenders of psychoanalysis reply to its critics that psychoanalytic theory and practice are complex structures of theory and empirical experience that cannot be tested wholly outside clinical experience, while conceding that clinical experience by its nature—in contrast with the biologist's experiments with rats—does not lend itself to much scientific testing. The defenders' claim rests to a large degree on the idea that human mind and personality are highly complex systems that have not, not yet at least, been reduced to simpler, more readily explained and manipulated units. Moreover—and here defenders and critics both will find fodder for their conclusions—psychoanalytic practice works with the unconscious and works via a relationship of analyst to analysand characterized by transference and countertransference that, Freud often stated, constitutes both resistance to truth and a means to get at the truth.

The notion of the transference (including the countertransference) provides a curious model of the "participant-observer," as an anthropologist would call it. John Forrester notes the "performativity" of the analytic dialogue and the nearly universal conviction of analysts that "transference is the central organizing concept and experience in their everyday practices." The "performativity" of the transference is in many ways stagey, an as-if reenactment of the past within the context of what Freud calls an "artifical illness," one accessible to the analyst's interventions. This means that the attitudes, beliefs, and actings-out of the transference will usually bear a symbolic or fictional relation to historical or biographical truth. This is not to say that they are untrue, but rather that their truth hovers somewhere between that of, say, *Middlemarch* and a parliamentary report on the conditions of rural towns in Victorian England—and that one can rarely know which truth it is, and indeed that posing the question in that form makes no sense. As Forrester also suggests, the kind of truth enacted in Sophocles' *Oedipus* may be truer to psychoanalytic experience than the precise experiences of the banal life of a given individual.

For Jacques Lacan, it is precisely the transference that allows the work of truth to begin, since, as he sees it, the analyst must turn aside the address to his or her person, to make it im-personal, addressed in fact to the analysand's unresolved relation to desire, and in this manner enlist it in the desire for truth. As Lacan claims, in characteristically vatic utterance, the analyst must learn to occupy a place which is "vacant to the desire of the patient in order for it to be realized as the desire of the Other"—where the Other, as opposed to the mere human

other, is the order of language, of the law, of the truth. But the notion of psychoanalytic truth as transferential and dialogic, emerging from the work performed in the affective space created between analyst and analysand, will probably never satisfy Freud's detractors. It is too imprecise and too messy, too
rhetorical—by which I mean that the analyst's discourse on the analysand's discourse can always be accused of suggestion, seduction, rhetorical power play—
to allay the suspicions of those who reject the initial hypotheses of psychoanalysis: the unconscious, the importance of infantile sexuality, the workings of
psychic retroaction, the vast role of fantasy and fiction in our self-conceptions
as human beings. Sometimes I persuade myself that the world is simply divided
between those to whom the Freudian hypothesis makes sense—no doubt because it somehow echoes personal experience, including the experience of fantasy—and those to whom it seems a kind of blot on human reason.

The virulence of the Freud wars, more than sixty years after his death, suggests something akin to such a stark choice in one's conception of humanity.
The most startling example may be the attacks leveled at the 1998 Library of
Congress exhibit long before it opened, with the effect of making its curators
redesign the exhibit and delay its opening for a year. The notion that a library
exhibit of manuscripts, photographs, and curios could arouse a battle in which
some of Freud's detractors argued that his legacy was not worth preserving suggests that central unresolved issues of our culture, and indeed of our nature as
human beings, cluster around this name and the knowledge he proposed. I earlier compared Freud's legacy to that of Rousseau—a thinker in whose wake so
many of Freud's insights are inscribed. Like Rousseau, he proposed a large revision of ways to think about human character and its place in culture, with results that tend to divide sharply adherents from detractors.

Lacan has recounted an incident he claimed to have been told him by Jung.
As Freud arrived in New York harbor in 1909, in sight of the Statue of Liberty,
he turned to Jung, to say: "They don't know that we are bringing the plague."
The plague, one presumes, of psychoanalytic knowledge, or perhaps more accurately, of the psychoanalytic attitude, an attitude of suspicion toward human
behavior and ostensible motives, a semiotic postulate that in all action and
speech there are unavowed messages to be read, a generalized undermining of
claims to unalloyed virtue, disinterestedness, and civilization. It is too easy—
and too typical of much psychoanalytic polemic—to dismiss those who reject
the Freudian worldview as benighted examples of resistance to and repression
of insight. With more equanimity and justice, one should probably conclude
that at this moment in Freud's legacy, the "proofs" of Freud's worldview are ev-

ident only to those who already accept it as consonant with their experience of human character, history, and civilization.

What is clear, I think, is that Freud's legacy does propose a view of "character"—to use an old and complex term that refers to distinguishing human traits and to their ethical import—that has profoundly altered business as usual not only in the domain for which it was originally elaborated, the treatment of the neurotic character, but also in all those fields that deal with expressive products of the human mind and spirit. Freud's own essays on literature and art, such as "Creative Writers and Daydreaming," "The Moses of Michelangelo," "Leonardo da Vinci and a Dream of His Childhood," and "Dostoevsky and Parricide," are rightly considered to be reductive and of dubious accuracy. And yet they put the interpretive disciplines on the track of something of crucial importance. Literary critics, art and music historians, and film theorists have learned to move beyond some of Freud's questionable distinctions between manifest and latent content and to see how form itself can be read psychoanalytically. The postulates of Freudian interpretation—which the French linguist Emile Benveniste showed to be compatible with traditional rhetorical conceptions—have opened a rich domain of possible meaning, both formal and cultural. While inept, heavy-handed "Freudian interpretations" continue to make a bad name for themselves, much of the subtle and innovative work in the humanities today (some of it done by contributors to this volume) is inconceivable without psychoanalytic insight.

It could be said that the terms in which current debates about Freud's legacy are carried out are themselves formed by Freud's legacy: terms at issue, such as repression, the unconscious, and the transference, were given currency and force by Freud's thinking, and even those who reject them wholesale have been forced into a dialogue about their meaning and reality. To say this is not an attempt to co-opt Crews and other anti-Freudians by a rhetorical trick but simply to suggest that the posing of questions about some of the large unanswered questions concerning human character and its social relations almost inevitably pass through the Freudian worldview. Just as we cannot help being children of Rousseau, however much some may detest his legacy, we cannot entirely free ourselves of the Freudian paternity. At least, not now. In the century that has passed since Freud, in *The Interpretation of Dreams,* quoted Virgil to the effect that he would stir up the powers of the underworld—"Flectere si nequeo superos, Acheronta movebo"—those powers still are unleashed among us.

In closing, I want to refer to two moments in the discussions that took place at the symposium. One is a comment by Paul Robinson, who had undertaken a rereading of major Freud texts in preparation for the conference. He reported his reading experience: "It's like falling in love all over again. This guy is incredibly powerful. He's not going to go away. He always surprises you. There's a quality about these texts that is incredibly seductive." Whether one succumbs to the seduction or rejects it, the statement accurately reflects the experience of many generations of those who have not simply accepted a generalized popular image of Freud but have turned to his texts. They are indeed something to be reckoned with.

The other remark, in the context of the discussion of neuroscience in relation to psychoanalysis, comes from Arnold M. Cooper, who, from a long career as psychoanalyst, announced: "As far as I'm concerned, this is the headiest time in psychoanalysis since the early days of Freud. Ideas are now competing and ideas are being exchanged. And I think there will be some newer resolution out of this that will last for a while, perhaps providing a basis for other kinds of research." Cooper suggests that any new synthesis in the understanding of mind and brain will to some extent incorporate Freudian insight, that Freudian hypotheses will continue to prove fruitful in understanding crucial problems that have heretofore proved resistant to both psychology and biology. It is too early to know whether Cooper's optimism is justified. But at least his optimism suggests that it is far too early to bury Freud's legacy. It will continue to be fought over in the new century.

Part One **Psychoanalysis and Its Discontents**

Introduction

Our first topic is marked by an immediate and noticeable split. Does the title refer to discontents generated *within* psychoanalysis or discontent with the psychoanalytic enterprise itself? The section begins oddly—with Frederick Crews's proleptic rebuttal of the arguments he assumes will follow. Alone among the essayists Crews wants to consider not *what* place psychoanalysis has in contemporary culture but *whether* it should even have a place. Because his perspective leads him to reject the premises of the volume, he shrewdly uses the essays themselves as examples of the circular reasoning and methodological flaws he considers inherent to psychoanalysis. The speakers Crews anticipates (and then reexamines in an extended postscript) enact, in his view, the very flaws he finds within psychoanalysis itself: "the epistemic circularity of Freud's tradition," as a theory that justifies "itself by appeal to its own contested postulates."

Although the other essays do not revolve around psychoanalysis's validity, the pressure of Crews's interrogation of psychoanalysis is quite relevant to developments within psychoanalysis. Robert Michels, in fact, shares many of Crews's concerns, although he is at pains to draw an important distinction: "I'm not troubled by people who challenge the lack of proof [in psychoanalysis], as long as that challenge is a call for inquiry rather than a disparagement of interesting ideas." Michels is the first of many contributors who try to relocate the questions that Crews raises in order to think through problems from within a psychoanalytic perspective.

Michels focuses on the various discontents of different constituencies: philosophers, psychiatrists, patients, and psychoanalysts themselves. First, he distinguishes between the philosophical critique of psychoanalysis and the clinical one: "the truth of the theories used by psychoanalysts in guiding their clinical work is not that important. Analysts are concerned with helping patients, not with establishing the validity of psychological theories." The test that psychoanalysis *cannot* fail, in Michels's view, is its developing relation with clinical psychiatry. This has at least three components. First, psychoanalysis must submit to the "reliable and respectable methodology for comparing and evaluating therapies" that the medical community has developed in the past few decades. Second, it must produce more researchers "with the skills necessary to collaborate in sophisticated psychiatric therapy research." Last, it must restructure its system of training to build more viable lines of communication with "the modern research university" and its nexus of "cultural, humanistic, sociological, psychological, and scientific" inquiry.

Judith Butler's essay—a reappraisal of the incest taboo and kinship structure—also begins with the problem of epistemology. Butler suggests that psychoanalysis will *always* generate evidentiary discontents because of its willingness to consider what cultural theorist Cathy Caruth has called "unclaimable experience": experience constituted through our inability to directly represent or grasp it. Specifically, Butler highlights the problematic event-structure of incest; its occurrence as an actual event is paradoxically registered by the subject's "loss of access to the terms that establish [its] historical veracity." Blurring clear boundaries between external fact and psychic apprehension, and between memory and desire, this unrepresentable event creates discontents within psychoanalysis but also reaffirms the specific nature of psychoanalytic knowledge. Psychoanalysis is uniquely able to comprehend an event under such erasure because it has always shown that "what is constituted as the thinkable realm is predicated on the exclusion (repression or foreclosure) of what remains difficult or impossible to think."

This is only half of Butler's interest. Having established the unrepresentable event-structure of incest, she then shifts attention to the incest taboo and the way this *taboo* also constitutes a thinkable and unthinkable realm: on one hand, an "idealization and ossification" of heterosexual kinship norms and, on the other, the *derealization* of alternative kinship structures, such as lesbian and gay forms of parenting. Butler thus uses the optic of psychoanalysis to connect the experiential unintelligibility of incest, *as an event*, with the kinship structures that are rendered culturally unintelligible, *as forms of love*, by the incest taboo.

Juliet Mitchell also focuses on the centrality of trauma within psychoanalytic theory, using its "return in the past decade" to raise a classic problem, and discontent, within psychoanalysis: Is it a theory that applies to universal, or only pathological, human experience? Mitchell insists that we situate trauma in a universal (and transcultural) rather than clinical context. As Mitchell writes, "The trauma and its potential cure through the telling of it as a story are likely aspects of the human condition; they are not specifics of particular pathologies." Before the development of the unconscious through repressed desire, the structure of the unconscious is developed by an original, universal trauma: the dread "that the helpless, prematurely born human infant feels when its existence is threatened on the failure of a provision of its needs." This original trauma, in turn, gives rise to what we might call an original story—the "simple mimesis" that a newborn employs to get milk. As Mitchell describes this, "A baby will start to mouth the sucking and dream or 'hallucinate' the breast it needs, an infant will make the faces and sounds of its care-taker." The primary, biological need for the breast, Mitchell suggests, continually manifests itself in two different and related forms: on one hand, this original lack or need sets the form for "the many large and small traumas that everyone experiences"; on the other, the story that the infant tells to the provider becomes the model for transindividual relationships, for processes of "identification with the other's desiring self."

Frederick Crews's essay ends with a "postscript" which—unlike revisions made to other essays in the volume—centers on the conference itself. Using a transcript of the discussions, Crews comments on many of the other speakers— most prominently Robert Michels, Judith Butler, Leo Bersani, Meredith Skura, and Richard Wollheim. One panelist is accused of McCarthyism; another is linked to both witch-burning and the Gulf of Tonkin resolution. In a final flourish, the whole conference is compared with the *Titanic!*

This rebuttal might have generated a different format for the book—one we considered but ultimately rejected. Crews's heated opposition to other panelists, especially Judith Butler, would seem to merit, or demand, a response. And such a response—probably itself heated—would inevitably prompt a third response from Crews. Such a back-and-forth discussion would fall into a genre perhaps best characterized by the angry letters in *the New York Review of Books*. This form would suit the content of Crews's position: the repeated dead ends of mutual recrimination that characterize this kind of exchange rhetorically demonstrate the incommensurability of psychoanalysis with discourses outside the discipline. Certainly, Crews is fond of such a form; as he notes in his postscript about Michels: "he and I have crossed swords before, both in person and in print." Such a genre—letters back and forth, the ritualized crossing of swords—might be more important for what it does than for what it says. Although we solicited and still appreciate the polemical content of Crews's perspective, we resisted the incursion of a polemical *form* onto the manuscript as a whole. For this reason, we denied other panelists an opportunity to respond to Crews's response, allowing the postscript, and the essays, to speak for themselves.

Unconscious Deeps
and Empirical Shallows

Frederick Crews

When I was invited to participate in the symposium whose proceedings are recalled in this book, I accepted with alacrity. Here, I thought, lay the makings of a lively and fruitful debate not merely about *what* role psychoanalysis plays in "contemporary culture" but also about *whether it deserves* to play such a role. If, as I believe, Freudian ideas tell us nothing that is empirically warrantable about the mind but much about the pitfalls of question-begging discourse, then presumably the application of those same ideas to cultural problems will itself run the risk of overconfidence and even circularity. Some panelists, I told myself, will doubtless explain why they consider that worry misplaced or exaggerated, but if others—myself among them—can show that psychoanalysis has no more standing as knowledge than astrology or palmistry, then the perils of "applied analysis" will be made usefully clear.

So much for expectations. When I eventually retrieved the list of symposium participants from my mailbox, I could not recognize among the twenty-nine presenters and panel chairs the name of any critic of psychoanalysis except my own. Nor, in asking around informally among my fellow skeptics, did I discover that any of them had been asked to join in. Even Yale faculty members whose expertise lay precisely in the area of Freud's cultural significance were condemned to the role of spectators; yet their reservations about psychoanalysis were certainly milder than my own. I guessed, then, that the question "Whose Freud?" though by no means settled in advance, was to be negotiated among several schools of psychoanalytic thought, with my own predictable demurral counting as evidence of hospitality, however scant, to extreme perspectives.

Perhaps this was uncharitable on my part, but it was the view I took at the time. So be it, I said to myself. Even if I was being asked to play the token naysayer, I would go to New Haven and nail my theses to the door of the Whitney Humanities Center. I knew that my dissenting judgment stood no chance of giving pause to my fellow symposiasts, but I felt that it ought to be voiced. Thereby, any independent observers who might be present could weigh my reasoning against the justifications of Freudian hermeneutics that, I assumed, would be offered on all sides.

Again—so much for expectations! Even though psychoanalysis finds itself in dire straits everywhere *but* among humanists and a minority of "soft" social scientists, very little was said in defense of Freudian notions during our two-day conference. Apologetics were apparently deemed unnecessary among the like-minded. To my own discordant mind, however, this imperturbability mirrored the epistemic isolationism of the whole psychoanalytic tradition. Notoriously, Freudians have listened only to other Freudians, and they have been inclined to mistake the mere sharing of a controversial set of premises within their own circle for assurance that those premises have withstood all challenge.

Despite the near solidarity lasting through our weekend, I did succeed in provoking a handful of remarks that were intended as refutation of my errors. Those remarks typified attitudes I have encountered many times before. So, of course, I want to make an example of them here. But I will do so only in an extended afterword, leaving my original text exactly as I read it aloud—failed predictions and all. By this means, readers will possess the full basis for comments about my position made by other participants.

To the question posed in the title of this volume, *Whose Freud?* I can offer a simple reply: he's all yours. Take my Freud—please! But do you really want him—the fanatical, self-inflated, ruthless, myopic, yet intricately devious Freud who has been unearthed by the independent scholarship of the past generation—or would you prefer the Freud of self-created legend, whose name can still conjure the illusion that "psychoanalytic truth" is authenticated by the sheer genius of its discoverer?

Let me put this issue concretely by reminding you of the evocative passage in Freud's *History of the Psycho-Analytic Movement* in which he describes the hostility of his Viennese colleagues when he first lectured them on May 2, 1896, about "the part played by sexuality in the aetiology of the neuroses." Who among us hasn't been moved by the story of Freud's sudden realization on that day that he was "one of those who had 'disturbed the sleep of the world'"? It dawned on him, he recalls, that he would never be able to expect "objectivity and tolerance" from straw authorities who lacked his own "moral courage"; thenceforth he would have to pursue the hard path of scientific discovery in "splendid isolation."[1]

That persecuted but dauntless figure is the Promethean hero commended to us not only by Freud himself but also by the house mythographer of psychoanalysis, Ernest Jones, and by subsequent partisans to this day. And it is just the Freud whose borrowed glory can improve the likelihood that one's own broadly psychoanalytic speculations will be deemed valiant and canny rather than, say, politically and academically conformist. If, however, we approach Freud not as our great forebear and patron but as a historical agent like any other, we cannot avoid noticing that the thesis he proposed to that doubting audience in 1896 was the very "seduction theory" that he would privately repudiate sixteen months later. Privately but not publicly, for in that case he would have had to own up not only to his mistake about the causation of hysteria but also to the nonexistence of his boasted cures and, still more damagingly, to the unreliability of both the investigative method and the psychodynamic premises that he would continue to employ for the remainder of his career.

Mental inertia and a reluctance to admit error may help to explain why academic humanists give no heed to such deflationary facts. But by shielding Freud's "insight" from normal skepticism, they also grant *themselves* the luxury of playing the knowledge game with the net down. The most fundamental rule of that game is that a given theory or hypothesis cannot be validated by invoking "evidence" manufactured by that same supposition. The question-begging traits of psychoanalysis—the treatment of tendentious interpretations as raw data; the reflex negation of appearances in favor of reduction to the selfish, the sexual, and the infantile; the ample menus of symbolic meanings and "defense mechanisms" upon which the interpreter can draw to adorn prearranged conclusions; the ever handy wild cards of "the unconscious" and "overdetermination"—all of these constitute a scandal for anyone who subscribes to community standards of rational and empirical inquiry. Yet the very liberties that mark Freudianism as a pseudoscience render it irresistibly charming to humanists in search of instant "depth." (I ought to know; I used to be one of them!) And if, emulating Freud's tactic of pathologizing his critics, Freudian humanists can brand dissenters as suffering from resistance, repression, and denial—in short, from the obsessive-compulsive disorder of "Freud bashing"—then their hermeneutic freedom would appear to be absolute.

Of course, academic Freudians would prefer not to think of themselves as having resigned from the wider intellectual enterprise. More typically, they invoke psychoanalytic notions to address cultural and historical problems and then infer from the very ingenuity of their handiwork, just as Freud did, that the doctrine has thereby proved its fruitfulness. Or, if they have an activist bent, they recast Freudianism to purge it of its patriarchal and conservative implications and then "discover" psychoanalytically that society needs to be realigned in accordance with their ideology.

A bright high school senior could easily detect the fallaciousness of such maneuvers. Unfortunately, however, a bright graduate student in literature, imbued with what now passes for theoretical sophistication, would find nothing to complain about. Such is the intellectually corrupting effect of a self-validating and parochial system of thought. But it is not the antiquated doctrine per se that deserves reproach; the fault lies with professors who not only refrain from teaching standards of empirical adequacy but actively or implicitly denigrate them.

As the first scheduled panelist in this conference and, I gather, the only one who shares the wholly negative view of psychoanalytic theory that is now all but consensual in American psychology departments, I am poorly situated to rebut the more sanguine judgments that will be voiced by others. But at least I can ask uncommitted members of this audience to keep some questions in mind. I will close by commenting briefly on three lines of argument that cannot fail to be broached by later contributors:

1. You will be told that evidence-based objections to Freudianism are beside the point, since psychoanalysis isn't a body of propositions but merely a subtle dialogue that weaves a fictive story, thus honoring the sheer ambiguity of experience while enhancing self-awareness of an ineffable but precious kind. This would have come as a surprise to the author of the Oedipus and castration complexes, the ego, id, and superego, penis envy, the vaginal orgasm, the death instinct, the primal scene and the primal crime, and on and on. Psychoanalysis does traffic in subtly guided and indoctrinating dialogue, but its theory has been, and remains, largely a causal account of mental functioning and development.

As such, it cannot dodge the criteria of assessment that apply to every such theory. And, of course, it doesn't begin to satisfy those criteria; hence the retreat of latter-day Freudians into the absurd pretense of nonpropositionality.

2. Subsequent panelists will assure you that while Freud made some mistakes, modern psychoanalysis has long since corrected them. When you hear this, please raise your hand and ask which of the ever-proliferating schools of analysis the speaker has in mind and why those schools cannot agree on a single point of doctrine or interpretation. The answer is that the epistemic circularity of Freud's tradition, guaranteeing abundant "confirmation" of every proposed idea, has not been remedied in any degree. Analysts of every stripe still adhere to Freud's illusion that reliable knowledge of a patient's repressed complexes can be gleaned from studying free associations and the transference—even though such study is well known to produce only those revelations favored by the therapist's sect or local institute.

3. You will doubtless hear that objections to psychoanalytic theory stem from a shallow and outmoded positivism that insists on impossible standards of proof. Wrong again. No philosophy of science, positivist or antipositivist, is entailed in the elementary demand that a theory refrain from justifying itself by appeal to its own contested postulates. That is just everyday rational sense, intuitively grasped by fair-minded researchers in every field, though not by the pundits of postmodernism.

It is precisely because such rationality continues to be exercised with vigor that Freud's ideas, as Edward Shorter observes in his recent *History of Psychiatry,* "are now vanishing like the last snows of winter."[2] How ironic it is that well-traveled academics, like bunkered troops on a remote island who haven't heard that the war is over, should be the last to get the news! And now that the point is finally sinking in, how sad it is—and how symptomatic of all that is feeble and dismissible about the humanities today—that humanists can look upon the collapse of a would-be science within its proper domain as a fine opportunity to turn that same doctrine to their own hermeneutic ends!

POSTSCRIPT

In the excerpts of discussion that follow our four panelists' essays, readers will see that my epistemologically based reservations about psychoanalysis did prompt some commentary, not all of it sharply negative. Robert Michels, for example, dismayed some members of the audience by announcing that he and I "are in agreement about the big picture"—that is, about the impossibility of *verifying* a given theory by *appealing* to that same theory. I will return to that key point at the end of this afterword, since it was challenged head-on by one of the conference's final speakers.

In other respects, Michels and I could not find common ground. He thought, for instance, that he had caught me saying that any corroboration of a theory would have to come from outside what he (not I) called "one's own group," to which he replied, "That's patently untrue. In fact, one of the characteristics of modern science is that data often can't be understood by anyone who's not a member of a group that understands the methodology and the kind of data that it produces."

This, however, was a straw-man argument, imputing to me the bizarre view that only nonpsychologists are competent to judge psychological theories. Obviously, no one is better qualified to evaluate Freudian claims than are empirically scrupulous researchers within the field of psychology. Michels, however, in raising his meretricious objection, managed to imply that *psychoanalysts themselves* are best suited for this role—rather a different, and wonderfully convenient, proposition.

On this as on other occasions (he and I have crossed swords before, both in person and in print), Michels admitted that no credible support for psychoanalytic theory or for the differentially positive efficacy of psychoanalytic treatment has ever been presented. This concession places him in a small vanguard of enlightened Freudians who have perused the relevant literature and accepted its clear import. Well, *sort of* accepted it. For, regrettably, Michels always follows this obeisance to research with some very fast talk about where the *real* scientific issue lies—somewhere far removed from the vast terrain he has just ceded to the doubters. And so he gives an impression of being at once empirically scrupulous and upbeat about psychoanalysis.

Thus, in the panel discussion that follows, Michels says that "the scientific question"—as if the general cogency of Freudian theory weren't itself a scientific question!—is this: "Do interpretations based upon the model that the oral phase precedes phallic interests have a differential and preferable impact on patients when I make them? That's easily testable." Here Michels appears to have forgotten about the placebo effect, to say nothing of the confirmatory bias that makes all anecdotal reporting of "clinical results" a form of science fiction. We don't even know whether his patients improve at all, much less whether they do so at a better than average rate, and still less whether their progress can be credited to the brand of psychological dogma to which he makes them privy. Even if we supposed that all of those questions can be answered affirmatively, Michels's hypothesis would remain trivial, because we already know that *false* ideas, supportively presented, can have *positive* therapeutic effects. Thus Michels's "real scientific issue" is just a diversion from what he acknowledges to be the case: the complete failure of psychoanalysis to make good on its scientific boasts.[3]

I will also say a word about Michels's statement that he is "not troubled by people who challenge the lack of proof, as long as that challenge is a call for inquiry rather than a disparagement of interesting ideas." As Michels is well aware, many if not most of his fellow analysts point habitually to the "clinical proof" of their belief system.[4] He himself, however, grants that all such proof is chimerical. Indeed, he admits that psychoanalytic dogma has by now failed to impress non-Freudian assessors for a hundred years. How far into the future, then, does he think the patience of outsiders should extend? Indefinitely? That would enable him to finish his distinguished career without undergoing a crisis of faith, but from the standpoint of public welfare, no basis has been shown for treating psychoanalytic notions with any more indulgence than those of Scientology or the Unification church.

Let me turn now to my fellow panelist and sometime Berkeley colleague Judith Butler. In politely raising some questions about my position, Butler gave us to understand that I might profit from cultivating greater philosophical sophistication on one hand and less unsavory soulmates on the other. Her doubts focused on my reference to *community standards of empiricism*. Both terms, "community standards" and "empiricism," struck her as containing trapdoors that I had failed to notice. Let us first see what she said about "empiricism" and ask whether she had indeed located a fatal weakness in my stand.

Empiricism, Butler said, needs to be grasped in a spirit that makes allowance for the theory-laden nature of "facts." Hence she drew a careful distinction between two possible complaints against a theory: first, that it tautologically derives its conclusions from its own postulates, and second, that it makes use of a "prior conceptualization" in deciding what is to count as data. Butler thought she was agreeing with my appeal to the first complaint but rebuking my endorsement of the second, unreasonable, one. She was mistaken on both counts.

First, why *shouldn't* a theory "derive its conclusions from its postulates," if the postulates are themselves well founded? As postpositivist philosophers of science often remind us, we aren't entitled to care how a given conclusion was originally reached. Maybe it occurred in a dream or by a casting of the I Ching; that would still be none of our business. To complain that an idea wasn't derived inductively would be to exercise that same naive Lockean version of empiricism with which Butler is attempting to saddle me.

Epistemological concern properly arises only when *justifications* of a theory are put forward. My objection is to the notion that a theory can be *proven correct* by sole reference to features that it shares with no other well-regarded theory. If, for example, the proposition that childhood masturbation underlies adult hysteria is justified by citing Dora's fiddling with her purse, or if the castration complex is said to be supported by the fact that many people fear losing their eyesight, no non-Freudian needs to surrender his or her doubts, since in both cases the "proof" appeals to transformational rules unique to psychoanalysis.

Butler is equally wrong in depicting me as believing that a real fact will be found to be unpolluted by theory of any kind. On the contrary, she and I concur in holding that one never arrives at a pure fact in that sense—a fact, in other words, whose discovery hasn't been facilitated by theoretical expectations of one kind or another. We must ask, however, whether a given theory manages to justify itself in relation to facts *other than the ones it has produced for its own purposes*. If not, the theory is in big trouble; and that is exactly the plight of psychoanalysis.

The other term that raised a warning flag for Judith Butler was "community standards." To her ear, the term smacked of "a very interesting desire for respectability" on my part. This is not, I suspect, what most of the other conference participants might regard as my leading vice, but I could see that a concern of Butler's own—expounded in her conference paper—was paramount here. For her, a wish to be empirically respectable must entail a tendency to fall in line with social "normativity" in general, especially as it applies to the imposing of heterosexist values and rules on people who should be left in peace to pursue their own goals and pleasures. What was *very interesting*, then, about my statement of ordinary rational principles—and the point was not lost on Butler's audible rooting section in our conference hall—was my self-alignment with social oppression. The hint was planted deftly and inconspicuously, but there it was: "community standards" meant homophobia.

I take this imputation very seriously—indeed, more seriously than it was meant, for Butler was surely not implying that I had already joined forces with the Pat Robertsons of the world. Rather, she was admonishing me that, if I don't watch out, I may be mistaken for one of them. Nonetheless, there is something profoundly disturbing here. In a mild and cordial manner, Butler was indulging in a form of McCarthyism that has become routine in university life. For it is now considered acceptable and even chic to ascribe a backward, repressive sociopolitical attitude to those with whom we in fact disagree only intellectually. *That* trapdoor can be sprung at any time to make dissenters disappear, and not just for a day but for a career.

I won't pause here to protest that Butler would find nothing obnoxious in my social views if I were to submit them for her approval; that would be to play the very game I am deploring. But I will emphatically insist that the intellectual values invoked in my talk are not located anywhere at all on the spectrum of ideologies and lifestyles. They are the very values to which lesbian and gay scientists appeal when presenting and defending their hypotheses—hypotheses which will be accorded the same tough peer scrutiny as those emanating from any other quarter. Science cannot be practiced at all without such a tacit understanding that the playing field will remain level. In principle, moreover, the same concern for fairness—that is, for keeping our criteria of propositional adequacy distinct from our private tastes and affiliations—ought to prevail not just in science but in every academic field.

In making this point, which conveys the only thinkable basis for pursuing knowledge that is not corrupted in advance by partisanship, I am aware of sounding like a dinosaur. That is not a sufficient reason, however, for me to alter my conception of intellectual integrity and start trying to please—that is, not offend—those of my fellow humanists who apply political tests to knowledge. To be sure, my adamancy here is cost-free. If, instead of being comfortably pensioned, I were an untenured colleague of Butler's, I might want to sing a more prudent tune; my very livelihood might hang in the balance. But in that case, ought Butler to be implicitly charging *me* with exacting conformity?

Now, rejoining our common topic, I must ask whether Butler's equivocal stance toward knowledge has anything to do with her kindly feelings toward psychoanalysis. Assuredly it does. In her discussion of my essay, she expresses doubt as to "whether there could ever *be* an empirically adequate account of the unconscious." She and I agree that the answer is no. But what, then, should we conclude—that "the unconscious" is, as I am persuaded, not so much a region of the psyche as a blank check that every Freudian can fill out as he or she sees fit? No, according to Butler the fault must lie with empiricism itself. Because she won't regard such traits as untestability, absence of operational content, and self-contradiction as marks against a psychological notion that she can handily adapt to her own ends, the empirical criteria themselves must be downgraded to the status of prejudices wielded in the service of shady interests. This is just what I meant when referring, in my essay, to "the intellectually corrupting effect of a self-validating and parochial system of thought."

The connection, then, is not fortuitous: scratch any academic Freudian and you will find someone whose commitment to disinterested rational inquiry has been compromised to one degree or another. And, of course, the same was true of Freud, who felt entitled to make up his own biological laws and to regard seeming counterinstances as corroborative. Butler's subtle assault on "community standards" is only one, overtly ideological, instance of an anti-intellectual strain that runs through a century's-worth of psychoanalytic special pleading. For, whatever they may say when trying to appear philosophically rigorous, all Freudians behave in practice as if they accepted Freud's outlandish dictum that "applications of analysis are always confirmations of it as well."[5]

It is also possible, however, for an academic Freudian to take one extra step and abandon the whole pretense of "applying" knowledge about the mind to texts that are presumed to "contain" the sought-after psychological meaning. In this connection, I was fascinated by Leo Bersani's thoughtful and candid essay. Bersani has reached a point in his impressive career at which he feels ethically compelled to disavow any style of literary criticism that purports to honor "fidelity to the text." He now sees such intellectual monogamy as implicitly denigrating gay promiscuity, tolerance of which now serves as his test for any adequately ample vision of the good society. Thus Bersani is not even seeking some psychoanalytically grounded understanding of the text that will be more intimate, supple, and unbiased than that of a critical dogmatist. Rather—and this is my own gloss—the very idea of a nubile "object of knowledge" demurely awaiting Mr. Right, its critic-spouse-for-life, is to be eschewed.

Such epistemic radicalism naturally leaves us wondering where if anywhere, for Bersani, psychoanalysis will enter the picture. Feminist, gay, and lesbian theorists have long considered themselves licensed to rewrite Freud's system of thought so as to discount its bourgeois implications while retaining its heady negativity. Bersani, however, seems to be getting tired of the whole enterprise; now he wonders whether there may not be something inherently normalizing in the Freudian outlook.

Yes, of course, psychoanalysis always normalizes, but not always in the same way. It lends an appearance of deep psychological truth to gay and straight ideologies alike. Its cosmetic services are impartially available to pontificating soothers of the bourgeoisie like Erik H. Erikson and to orgasmic zanies like Wilhelm Reich; to the ultra-orthodox shrinks of Park Avenue and to Left Bank Lacanians in suede and sunglasses. Whatever lesson you want to teach, there will always be a Freudian way of putting it.

Psychoanalysis normalizes because, possessing only fake psychological knowledge that changes wildly from one Freudian pundit to the next, it has nothing better to do than to lend the moral inclination of the moment an air of being supported by "findings." You needn't take my word for it. Just read through the rest of this book, counting all the references to the psychoanalytic significance of *x* and what psychoanalysis tells us about *y*, and then ask yourself: if psychoanalysis "tells us" all of these contradictory things, does it tell us anything at all?

In the panel discussion, Leo Bersani expressed his growing awe for the way each of Freud's texts "enacts a particular relation of the mind to its own interpretations." Among the assembled company, this observation was received with uneasy puzzlement. Auditors could only hope that it might prove to be a compliment of some kind. I heard it quite differently, though, as a sign of crisis on Bersani's part; and I would like if possible to help the crisis along.

Bersani is just now registering the extent to which Freud's reports of patients' symptoms and of those symptoms' meanings unresistingly flatter his theoretical enthusiasms. His writings achieve a poetical density of texture by abolishing the boundary we might expect to find between the honest investigator's fantasy life and the material he is trying to explain. In order to cease being a Freudian, Bersani now needs only to allow this realization to sink in: Freud's "evidence" was conjured to meet the rhetorical need it was meant to fill. Everything fits "geniusly," as Bersani put it, because Freud is a writer of fiction.

Of course, one thing more is required for skeptical detachment from the discourse that famously "never lets go," and that is a resistance to being taken in. Commenting on Bersani's remark, Paul Robinson announced that he has "bad news for Fred Crews. . . . [Freud] is incredibly seductive." I already knew that, having been seduced by Freud myself around the age of thirty-two. But by thirty-seven I was over it, because by then I had been stymied by unanswerable empirical objections and had decided that a literary scholar ought to inquire how an unreliable narrator is accomplishing his seductive tricks. I invite Bersani and Robinson to do the same. They would soon discover, if they don't already know it, that Freud as literary magician is immeasurably more deft than Freud as mental lawgiver. Indeed, it is only when one has realized the capriciousness of his laws that one can grasp how every sentence in his complete psychological writings amounts to an act of cunning self-dramatization.

Meanwhile, of course, the path of least resistance is to remain inside Freud's scholastic universe of linked correspondences. There one can always count on the "aha!" effect, or the sense of confirmation that comes from meeting up with "psychoanalytic insight" that seems to verify one's hunches. As I mentioned in my essay, most Freudian academics "invoke psychoanalytic notions to address cultural and historical problems and then infer from the very ingenuity of their handiwork . . . that the doctrine has thereby proved its fruitfulness." It isn't easy to forswear this cheap thrill and its attendant promise of discourse (one's own) that will never run dry.

The feedback loop between exercising Freudian hermeneutic privilege and re-inforcing one's faith in psychoanalysis works best if one can remain distracted from its perfect circularity. To this end, even trained and certified psychoanalysts will sometimes deny that they have any particular commitment to Freudian ideas. Thus, in her essay, Meredith Skura writes that she generally eschews theory in her historical inquiries, preferring instead to conceive of psychoanalysis simply as a way of thinking and an attitude toward life. Theory enters her work, Skura says, only in the form of hypotheses that are to be tested by the "so what?" criterion, among others. If, for example, a particular Freudian tenet has helped her to "pull details together" in an illuminating way, she knows she was on the right track.

Alas, any theory whatsoever—phrenological, ufological, what have you—will confirm itself in just this specious manner. The creative rush that one feels as new data effortlessly adhere to old certainties is no substitute for the sober task of inquiring whether there may be other, less dogmatic, ways of making the facts cohere. And doesn't the global "psychoanalytic attitude toward life" amount to a partiality toward Freudian theory? To disavow explicit theory while implementing such an attitude is simply to disguise one's premises from oneself, a retrogressive step in any field.

No such pussyfooting could be charged, finally, against Richard Wollheim, who, in his essay, displays a self-assurance about theory that is meant to teach a lesson to fainter-hearted contributors. Wollheim begins by expressing displea-sure with the timidity of earlier essayists, who show too much deference to ob-jections that can, in his estimation, be easily neutralized. He throws down the gauntlet to my own contention that one can't prove psychoanalytic theory by merely exercising it. Oh, yes, one can, replies Wollheim, who deems it quite fea-sible to demonstrate the cogency of Freudian tenets from directly within a clin-ical context. The devolution of psychoanalysis from science to hermeneutic to mere occasion for "narrative truth," Wollheim says in effect, stops here.

In Wollheim's main example, the object of inquiry is the subtly uncoopera-tive behavior of an analyst-trainee's female patient. Disagreeing with the candi-date's first effort at explanation of that recalcitrance, her supervisor and confer-ring colleagues arrived at a better idea: the problem was traceable to the patient's early relations with her mother. Presumably, then, the doctrine of transference was proving its mettle here. For, according to that doctrine, noncooperation within the analysis is often traceable to a childhood attitude that is being reen-acted in the consulting room.

Wollheim is pleased to note that since the patient hadn't been involved in the review session, nobody was influencing her; hence the example is suggestion-proof. And he further observes that a lot of accumulated clinical experience must have gone into the group's solution. That fact seems to him to vouch for the explanation's plausibility. Because, in this triumph of carefully reviewed interpretation, "a small piece of psychoanalytic thinking helps us to comprehend the situation," the theory behind that thinking had supposedly received strong support.

But had it? In the first place, Wollheim overlooks the dubious impressiveness of a Freudian consensus reached by a group of psychoanalysts who belonged to the same institute. That is the kind of guarantee of sound thinking that has resulted, over time, in everything from witch burnings through the Edsel to the Gulf of Tonkin Resolution. Moreover, how can Wollheim assure himself that all of the assembled minds were independently converging on the right answer? Isn't it far more likely, given the Machiavellian group dynamics one finds in every analytic institute, that some members were just allowing the supervisor to strut?

More fundamentally, transferential theory is here being "validated" merely by its application to the case at hand, as if there were no conceivable non-Freudian reasons for the patient's stubborn behavior. There are many such possible reasons, beginning with irritants supplied by a clumsy or overbearing therapist. The theory of transference regularly acts to immunize the psychoanalyst against criticism, pushing the blame backward into the remote past and laying it on patients themselves and/or their parents. We can't say whether such a causal misattribution was involved in Wollheim's specimen case, but we can't exclude it, either.

Most fundamentally, the "evidence" Wollheim finds so persuasive is itself a Freudian interpretation. Only if we already agree with a broadly psychoanalytic account of mental development and structure can an instance of alleged transference be regarded as support for the theory's cogency. As a trained philosopher, one might think, Wollheim could have perceived what was the matter with this nonprobative question begging. The reason he didn't is that he has chosen to remain under the Freudian bell jar, whose stale and breezeless air comes after a while to feel like the atmosphere of reality itself.

I am grateful to Peter Brooks for welcoming and, with even greater tolerance, for publishing my animadversions. But I must say that the fiasco of Richard Wollheim's "proof," after so many contributors had dodged the whole issue of validation, strikes me as an ironically fitting coda to the volume. By my lights, the symposium that formed the basis for this volume was a two-day pleasure "cruise to nowhere" on the *Titanic*. Those who remain on board for the longer journey will find, I believe, that the iceberg is out there waiting in the dark, the welding is defective, and the lifeboats are all too few.

Notes

1. Freud, *History of the Psycho-Analytic Movement, S.E.,* 14: 21–22.
2. Edward Shorter, *A History of Psychiatry: From the Era of the Asylum to the Age of Prozac* (New York: John Wiley, 1996), vii.
3. Michels's hypothesis about the superior effect of his theory-based interpretations would not be testable unless, at a minimum, he and many other therapists of different schools, under strict experimental controls and close observation by non-Freudian evaluators over a period long enough for the improvement, deterioration, or unchanged condition of the patient-volunteers to be reliably ascertained, were all to impart, to socioeconomically comparable sets of clients harboring the same complaints with the same level of gravity, the theoretical mumbo-jumbo in which those therapists variously believed. But even then, there would be no way of ascertaining that the concepts and supposed laws themselves, and not some other feature of treatment, had been responsible for the differential results.
4. A fine example is provided in the essay by Arnold M. Cooper, a past president of the American Psychoanalytic Association. Cooper asserts that the hypothesis of a dynamic unconscious is "now evidentially well founded" and that Freud's basic method of "free association and analytic listening" has amply proved its worth. Using those tools, Cooper adds, "we have moved very far" from Freud's single model of the mind. Indeed we have. Now we are faced with an ever-expanding number of conflicting models and no agreed-upon way of choosing among them. Is that progress, or does it constitute an indictment of the very tools that Cooper regards as having been vindicated?
5. *S.E.,* 22: 146.

Psychoanalysis
and Its Discontents

Robert Michels

Many people are discontented with psychoanalysis. Four broad groups have made their discontents widely known—philosophers and scientists; psychiatrists; patients; and practicing psychoanalysts—and I shall explore those discontents here.

Let us start with philosophers and scientists. One of the most articulate, and noisiest, attacks from this group comes from Adolf Grünbaum and is largely reflected in Frederick Crews's essay in this volume. Both men seem to believe that they are challenging the methodology that is at the core of psychoanalytic thinking. Along with the vast majority of psychoanalysts, however, I find that their ideas don't have much relevance to what I do in my professional life. From the perspective of a contemporary practicing psychoanalyst, philosophers' complaints about the flawed epistemological basis of the original theories of psychoanalysis seem to miss the point. First of all, they are largely directed to Freud's thinking in the first twenty years of the discipline. Most psychoanalysts were born after the theories to which the philosophers object had already been discarded. The vast majority of patients treated by psychoanalysis have been treated after Freud's death sixty years ago. It is somewhat beside the point to attack contemporary psychoanalysis because of methodological problems in ideas that were popular eighty years ago and are no longer seen as central while ignoring the past half-century of the discipline's development. The result is a critique of Freud's thinking of eighty to a hundred years ago when measured by the standards of a contemporary philosopher of science, perhaps an interesting exercise, but not the way to assess psychoanalysis today.

Oddly enough, the truth of the theories used by psychoanalysts in guiding their clinical work is not that important. Analysts are concerned with helping patients, not with establishing the validity of psychological theories. They want to know whether a theory is useful in formulating interpretations or other interventions, whether the theory is effective in facilitating the therapeutic process in the consultation room, not whether it meets some philosophic or scientific criterion for truth. These are not the same. A theoretical model of pathogenesis or of the early development of personality may be useful in treating patients whether or not it passes muster in the empiric scientific studies of psychiatry or developmental psychology. It is just as I find Freud's insights into personality that stem from his reading of *Richard III* clinically useful and wouldn't be at all distressed if a scholar, even one of Frederick Crews's caliber, told me that *Richard III* was one of Shakespeare's poorer plays, not well dramatized or constructed, and further that the history it claimed to depict was all wrong. Fascinating though this critique might be, it would not affect the value of Shakespeare's psychological insight in my work with patients.

The analyst's selection of which theory to use is not in the realm of science but rather in the realm of pragmatics, a question of technique. Whether the psychoanalyst using a specific theory is successful as a therapist, whether a theory works in the consultation room, *is* a scientific question. In fact, it is the most old-fashioned positivist type of scientific question imaginable, easily represented by clearly defined, readily falsifiable hypotheses. The research required to test such hypotheses is difficult and expensive, and it has largely not yet been conducted. However, it is not inherently different from other problems in everyday clinical medical research. This is the only question within psychoanalysis that is scientific in the narrow positivist definition of science employed by these critics. There are many fascinating scientific questions in fields contiguous to psychoanalysis, among them developmental psychology and neurobiology. When ideas from these fields enter psychoanalysis proper, however, they enter as *ideas,* as metaphors useful in generating interpretations rather than as scientific hypotheses or theories, and they cannot be tested, neither proven nor disproven, by the psychoanalytic method. The only scientific propositions testable in the psychoanalytic situation have to do with whether the treatment works and if so, how.

Of course, a great many other fascinating questions about the nature of psychoanalytic discourse interest philosophers, the ideas used and developed by psychoanalysts, their application to studies of culture, of history, of social structure, of gender, and of literature, the issues that psychoanalysts term "applied" psychoanalysis. There is a rich and stimulating dialogue at the interface of psychoanalysis and these disciplines, with a great deal of criticism. For some, these dialogues are an important part of the universe of scientific discourse; for others they are better defined as another type of scholarly pursuit, but in either event there is little evidence of discontent.

A second group with discontent about psychoanalysis are psychiatrists. They see psychoanalysts as mental health subspecialists, practitioners of one of the several treatments today available for psychiatric disorders. A few decades ago, psychiatrists were enthusiastic about psychoanalysis. The field was seen as based on a fascinating set of theories, while most other psychiatric treatments were purely empirical; as offering help for those with problems in living who did not have major mental illnesses, while most other psychiatric treatments were useful only for the seriously mentally ill; and as suggesting important links and ties between medicine and psychiatry, and thus providing an antidote for the drift away from the core of medicine that had marked alienist psychiatry. Last, it was seen as raising the status of psychiatry in the world of medicine and science. Times change. Today psychiatrists view psychoanalysis as based on unproven theories, while they applaud the growing importance of treatments based on empirical data. They are concerned that psychoanalysts treat those who are medically unneedy, the so-called worried well, rather than those with real mental disorders. They see psychoanalysis as threatening the newly won medical identity of psychiatry, and as lowering psychiatry's status in the eyes of medical colleagues. As psychiatry has embraced genetic and biologic theories of etiology, phenomenological and descriptive nosologies, and medical models of diseases and pharmacologic treatments, and as psychoanalysts have increasingly disavowed the etiologic implications of their theories and no longer defend a distinction between medical and nonmedical psychoanalysis, psychiatry finds its already diminishing relationship with psychoanalysis increasingly embarrassing. In the past few decades psychiatrists have developed a reliable and respectable methodology for comparing and evaluating therapies. In order for psychoanalysis to remain linked to psychiatry, it will have to submit to and pass evaluation by these methodologies. If it is effective, it will remain part of psychiatry; if not, it will be divorced from it, regardless of the intellectual appeal of its theories.

The third group whose discontents I shall describe is patients. Generally speaking, patients don't worry very much about epistemology, and they are not particularly interested in professional turf battles. They want help, to feel better, to be happier. Psychoanalysis, however, is often not quite what they have in mind. For one, it takes a long time. Also, it costs them a lot. The cost issue is interesting—actually, psychoanalysis is not particularly costly. It is rather that unlike most other therapies or treatments in our society, patients have to bear the cost personally. Managed care organizations and insurance companies don't like to pay psychoanalysts' bills. Even more important for patients, however, it often seems as if psychoanalysis isn't even designed to help them. Patients want answers, whereas psychoanalysts ask questions. Patients want advice, but psychoanalysts are trained not to give advice. Patients want support and love. Psychoanalysts offer interpretations and insight. Patients want to feel better; analysts talk about character change. Although patients may not understand all the complaints that psychiatrists register against psychoanalysis, they often agree with the conclusion that other treatments promise more while costing less. Of course, there are also some patients who seek character change—who have had other treatments but found that their lives have not changed very much as a result or who recognize from the beginning that they must truly change themselves, rather than just relieve symptoms. For them, the question is not whether psychoanalysis is a good treatment, for it is often the only treatment there is.

The fourth group with discontents is psychoanalysts themselves. Their primary concerns are finding patients for their practices, finding candidates for their institutes, and making a living. Philosophic critiques and competing theories within psychoanalysis may fill psychoanalytic journals, but these aren't always broadly read or of great concern to practicing psychoanalysts. In fact there are more analytic patients today than ever before, but it doesn't feel that way to many individual practicing analysts. The field is more crowded than it used to be, particularly in the older cities on the coasts, where analysis got an early start. The growth of nonmedical analysis is no longer limited by administrative restrictions of the training institutes, and unlike the finite pool of psychiatrists, there is a virtually unlimited supply of nonmedical potential candidates.

As a result, although there are actually more psychoanalytic candidates in the United States than ever before, the rate of increase has slowed, the number of institutes has multiplied, and the opportunity for a given senior psychoanalyst to become a training analyst has diminished considerably. This creates morale problems for a field in which becoming a training analyst and training younger colleagues has long represented the major source of status.

There has also been an exponential growth of competing therapies. These include many psychotherapies, often derived from some aspect of psychoanalytic thinking, which are briefer and more direct, as well as pharmacological therapies. Although modern psychopharmacology goes back at least four decades, the early drugs were only relevant for more seriously disturbed patients, those rarely seen by psychoanalysts, or for patients who are distressed enough to tolerate major side effects. However, there has been a major recent breakthrough in the drugs available for the treatment of depressive disorders, particularly less serious ones. Within the last decade we have had a new group of antidepressant drugs which are user friendly, unobjectionable, and sufficiently easy to take that doctors prescribe them for patients with mild depression. These patients are among the most prevalent in psychoanalytic practice and these new treatments challenge the traditional hegemony of psychoanalysis over their treatment.

Are the discontents of philosophers, scientists, psychiatrists, patients, and psychoanalysts themselves a mixture of unrelated problems, or are there underlying common themes? Are they growing pains or symptoms of a major disorder? Are they the beginning of the end of a dying cult, or are they clues as to how to further strengthen a vigorous and important discipline? These are complex questions, but in one important way the very structure of the psychoanalytic profession has contributed to many of the discontents it has elicited.

Psychoanalysis is almost unique among the academic disciplines and professions in that its organizational structure is largely in the form of freestanding analytic institutes, in which analysts train other analysts, with no relationship to other schools, universities, or academic institutions. This structure reflects Freud's personal views and is the dominant model around the world. Psychoanalytic institutes have had little interest in generating new knowledge—that is, in research. They have largely consisted of colleagues, each of whom spends the great majority of his or her professional time in independent, solo, private clinical practice but who come together to teach, supervise, and give courses and seminars. Status is linked to teaching old knowledge rather than to developing new knowledge. Scholarship is often devoted to studying texts rather than patients or clinical data. The scientific questions that fall within the domain of psychoanalysis, such as whether the treatment works, have seemed boring to most psychoanalysts. The academic context of the modern research university in which such inquiry would develop and thrive has been separated from the dominant psychoanalytic community of freestanding, isolated institutes. The result is that the world of academia, of cultural, humanistic, sociologic, psychologic, and scientific inquiry, has an ambivalent relationship with psychoanalysis. It borrows and enjoys many psychoanalytic ideas while attacking psychoanalytic methods and deriding the academic, scientific, and methodologic shortcomings of the discipline. There have been few psychoanalysts with the skills necessary to collaborate in sophisticated psychiatric therapy research. Psychoanalysts who might have become interested have had little opportunity for career tracks other than that of clinician-teacher and therefore little hope of developing the skills necessary to respond to many of psychoanalysis's critics. Reassuringly, however, this structural problem reflects the early history of the discipline and is not an essential characteristic of psychoanalysis. It can be corrected as we enter the second century of psychoanalysis.

For this to occur, psychoanalysis needs from the academic community what it has long requested from its patients—skepticism, tempered by benevolence. Skepticism alone will lead to discarding much that is valuable. Benevolence alone will lead to preserving much that is worthless. Their blend will allow psychoanalysts to join their academic colleagues in fruitful collaboration, as institutes are linked with universities, and the discontents of all are transformed into constructive criticisms.

Quandaries of the Incest Taboo

Judith Butler

I would like to address two issues that have not only caused some discontent for psychoanalysis, but that seem to emerge internal to psychoanalysis as its own proper sphere of discontent: incest and normative kinship. They are related, most prominently through the incest taboo: what it forecloses on one hand, what it inaugurates and legitimates on the other. I would like to make two separate remarks about incest and kinship. The first concerns contemporary debates on incest and how, and whether, incest can be conceptualized; the second concerns the relation between the prohibition against incest and the institution of normative kinship arrangements that take a presumptively heterosexual form. What I hope to suggest here is that psychoanalysis as a theory and a practice might well be rejuvenated by returning to the questions of incest and kinship and their interrelation.

Psychoanalytic theory has assumed that the oedipal drama in which the son's incestuous love for the mother is fantasized and feared is followed by an interdiction that forces the son to love a woman other than his mother. The daughter's incestuous passion is less fully explored in the Freudian corpus, but her renunciation of her desire for her father culminates in an identification with her mother and a turn to the child as a fetish or penis substitute. In the context of structuralist linguistics, this primary incest taboo becomes the way in which sexual positions are occupied, masculine and feminine are differentiated, and heterosexuality is secured. Even as psychoanalysis has charted for us this path through the normalization of gender and sexuality, it has also insisted from the start that the "development" that is described is in no sense secure. As a result, psychoanalysis gives us, and perhaps enacts for us, something of this drama of sexual normalization as well as its inevitable deviations.

In the developmental study, incest is generally described as a punishable fantasy. And one of the main questions that emerges within the context of the contemporary social discussion of incest is whether it is real or fantasized and how one might be able to determine epistemologically the difference between the two. For some, the answer to the epistemological quandary lies in whether there can be false memories and what respect is to be given to first-person narrative accounts of experiences that are often attributed to early childhood. For others, the question of the "reality" of incest links up with broader questions in the historiography of memory, whether historical "events" can be confirmed apart from the interpretive field in which they appear, and whether, accordingly, something like the nondeniability of traumatic events, usually typified by the destruction of European Jewry, can be confidently asserted against revisionist historians.

These matters are complicated all the more since the emergence of trauma studies (Cathy Caruth, Shoshana Felman, Dori Laub), in which the argument prevails that trauma is, by definition, not capturable through representation or, indeed, recollection; it is precisely that which renders all memory false, we might say, and which is known through the gap that disrupts all efforts at narrative reconstruction.

With regard to incest, the question thus turns on the relations among memory, event, and desire: Is it an event that *precedes* a memory? Is it a memory that retroactively posits an event? Is it a wish that takes the form of a memory? Those who want to underscore the prevalence of incest as an abusive family practice tend to insist that it is an event and that, insofar as it is a memory, it is a memory of an event. And sometimes this takes the form of a dogmatic premise: for incest to be traumatic and real, it must be understood as an event. This view is confounded, however, precisely by the position taken by trauma studies mentioned above, in which the sign of the trauma and its proof is precisely its resistance to the narrative structure of the event.

Those who worry about false allegations and believe we are in the midst of a public rash of such false allegations can speak against a psychoanalytic perspective or for one; they can, for instance, insist that incest is either a memory induced by therapy or, less often, a wish transmuted into false memory. One psychoanalytic approach asks whether incest is merely a wish or, derivatively, a wish transmuted into memory. This view suggests that the narrative report of incest correlates with a psychic event, but not a historical one, and that the two orders of event are clearly dissociable. A third position, however, is possible within psychoanalysis and is suggested by the point of view that insists that trauma takes its toll on narrativity: insofar as incest takes traumatic form, it can be precisely that which is not recoverable as a remembered or narratable event, at which point the claim on historical veracity is not secured through establishing the event-structure of incest. On the contrary, when and where incest is *not* figurable as an event, that is where its very unfigurability testifies to its traumatic character. This would, of course, be "testimony" difficult to prove in a court of law, which labors under standards that determine the empirical status of an event. Trauma, on the contrary, takes its toll on empiricism as well.

Incestuous trauma, then, is variously figured as a brute imposition on the child's body, as the exploitative incitation of the child's desire, as the radically unrepresentable in the child's experience or, indeed, in the adult's memory whose childhood is at issue. Moreover, to the extent that psychoanalysis attributes incestuous fantasy and its prohibition to the process by which gendered differentiation takes place (as well as the sexual ordering of gender), it remains difficult to distinguish between incest as a traumatic fantasy essential to sexual differentiation in the psyche and incest as a trauma that ought clearly to be marked as abusive practice and in no sense essential to psychic sexual development.

The opportunities for divisive debate are rife. From a psychoanalytic view (which is, emphatically, not a unified and harmonious set of perspectives), the urgent question seems to be: How do we account for the more or less general persistence of the incest taboo and its traumatic consequences as part of the differentiation process that paves the way toward adult sexuality without demeaning the claims made about incestuous practice that clearly are traumatic in unnecessary and unacceptable ways?

The effort to reduce all claims about the reality of incest to the symptoms of disavowed fantasy is no more acceptable than the effort to presume the veracity of all incest claims. The task is to find out how the incestuous passions that are part of emerging childhood sexuality are exploited precisely through the practice of incest, which overrides prohibitive boundaries that ought to be kept firmly in place. To understand the trauma of that practice, moreover, it is important not to dismiss the psychic register of pain or to read the absence of empirical evidence or narratable history as a sign that this trauma exists purely as fantasy. If trauma theory is right to assert that trauma often leads to the impossibility of representation, then there is no way to decide questions of the psychic and social status of traumatic incest through direct recourse to its representation. One must become a reader of the ellipsis, the gap, the absence, and this means that psychoanalysis must relearn the skill of reading broken narratives.

In relation to this epistemological set of quandaries, we need to remind ourselves that the distinction between event and wish is not as clear as it is sometimes held to be. It is not necessary to figure parent-child incest as a unilateral impingement on the child by the parent, since whatever impingement takes place will also be registered within the sphere of fantasy. In fact, to understand the violation that incest can be—and to distinguish between those occasions of incest that are violations and those that are not—it is not necessary to figure the body of the child exclusively as a surface imposed upon from the outside. The fear, of course, is that, if it emerges that the child's desire has been exploited or incited by incest, this will somehow detract from our understanding of parent-child incest as a violation. The reification of the child's body as passive surface would thus constitute, at a theoretical level, a further deprivation of the child: the deprivation of psychic life. It may also be said to perpetrate a deprivation of another order. After all, when we try to think of what kind of exploitation incest can be, it is often precisely the child's love that is exploited in the scene of incest. By refusing to consider what happens to the child's love and desire in the traumatic incestuous relation with an adult, we fail to describe the depth and psychic consequence of that trauma.

One might be tempted to conclude that the event is always psychically registered and that as a result the event is not, strictly speaking, separable from the psychic staging of the event: what is narrated, if it can be narrated, is precisely the mix of the two. But this solution does not address the non-narratable, that for which there is no story, no report, no linguistic representation. For the trauma that is neither event nor memory, its relation to wish is not readily legible. To avow the seriousness of the violation, which is ethically imperative, it is not necessary to compel the subject to prove the historical veracity of the "event." For it may be that the very sign of trauma is the loss of access to the terms that establish historical veracity—that is, where what is historical and what is true become unknowable or unthinkable.

It is always possible, from a clinical perspective, to claim that it does not matter whether or not trauma happened, since the point is to interrogate the psychic meaning of a report without judging its reality. But can we really dissociate the question of psychic meaning from that of the "event" if a certain fuzziness about the event having taken place is precisely part of its traumatic effect? It may be that what is unthinkable is precisely a fantasy that is disavowed, or it may be that what is unthinkable is the act that a parent performed (was willing to perform), or it may be that what is unthinkable is precisely their convergence in the event.

What constitutes the limit of the thinkable, the narratable, the intelligible— indeed, what constitutes *the limit of what can be thought as true?* These are, I believe, questions that psychoanalysis has always interrogated precisely because it relies on a form of analytic listening and a form of "reading" that takes for granted that what is constituted as the thinkable realm is predicated on the exclusion (repression or foreclosure) of what remains difficult or impossible to think.

This is, of course, not to say that nothing is thought, that no story is told, and no representation is made, but only that whatever story and representation emerge to account for this event that is no event will be subject to this same catachresis that I perform when I speak about it improperly as an event: it will be one that must be read for what it indicates, but cannot say, or for the unsayable in what is said. What remains crucial is a form of reading that does not try to find the truth of what happened but, rather, asks, What has this non-happening done to the question of truth? For part of the effect of that violation, when it is one, is precisely to make the knowing of truth into an infinitely remote prospect; this is its epistemic violence. To insist, then, on verifying the truth is precisely to miss the effect of the violation in question, which is to put the knowability of truth into enduring crisis.

So I keep adding this qualification: "when incest is a violation," suggesting that I think that there may be occasions in which it is not. Why would I talk that way? Well, there are probably forms of incest that are not necessarily traumatic or that gain their traumatic character by virtue of the consciousness of social shame they produce. But what concerns me most is that the term *incest* is over-inclusive, that the departure from sexual normalcy it signifies blurs too easily with other kinds of departures. Incest is considered shameful, which is one reason it is so difficult to articulate, but to what extent does it become stigmatized as a sexual irregularity that is terrifying, repulsive, unthinkable in the ways that other departures from normative exogamic heterosexuality are? The prohibitions that work to prohibit nonnormative sexual exchange also work to institute and patrol the norms of presumptively heterosexual kinship. Interestingly, although incest is considered a departure from the norm, some theorists, Linda Alcoff among them, argue that it is a practice that generally supports the patriarchalism of the family. But within psychoanalysis, and structuralist psychoanalysis in particular, positions such as Mother and Father are differential effects of the incest taboo, although the very existence of a taboo against incest presumes a family structure, for how else would one understand the prohibition on sexual relations with members of one's family without a prior conception of family?

Within structuralism, however, the symbolic positions of Mother and Father are secured only through the prohibition, so that the prohibition produces both the positions of Mother and Father in terms of a set of proscribed endogamic sexual relations. Some Lacanian analysts treat these positions as if they are timeless and necessary, psychic placeholders that every child has or acquires through the entry into language. This is a complicated question that I pursue elsewhere but consider here that the symbolic status of this position is not considered to be equivalent to its social position, and that the social variability of parenting and family structure is not reflected in the enduring binarism of Mother-Father installed at the symbolic level. To insist that kinship is inaugurated through linguistic and symbolic means that are emphatically not social is, I believe, to miss the point that kinship is a contingent social practice. In my view, there is no symbolic position of Mother and Father that is not precisely the idealization and ossification of contingent cultural norms. To treat these variable norms as presuppositions of culture and of psychic health is thus to divorce the psychoanalysis of sexual difference fully from its sociological context. It is also to restrict available notions of normativity to those that are always already encoded in a universal law of culture.

Thus, the law that would secure the incest taboo as the foundation of symbolic family structure states the universality of the incest taboo as well as its necessary symbolic consequences. One of the symbolic consequences of the law so formulated is precisely the derealization of lesbian and gay forms of parenting, single-mother households, and blended family arrangements in which there may be more than one mother or father, where the symbolic position is itself dispersed and rearticulated in new social formations.

If one holds to the enduring symbolic efficacy of this law, then it seems to me that it becomes difficult, if not impossible, to conceive of incestuous practice as taking place. It also becomes difficult, if not impossible, to conceive of the psychic place of the parent or parents in ways that challenge heterosexual normativity. Whether it is a challenge to the universality of exogamic heterosexuality from within (through incest) or from rival social organizations of sexuality (lesbian, gay, and bisexual, as well as nonmonogamous), each of these departures from the norm becomes difficult to acknowledge within the scheme that claims that the efficacious incest taboo determines the field of sexual intelligibility. In a sense, incest is disavowed by the law on incest, and the forms of sexuality that emerge at a distance from the norm become unintelligible (sometimes, for instance, even psychosis-inducing, as when analysts argue in the structuralist vein that same-sex parenting risks psychosis in the children who are raised under such conditions).

One argument that psychoanalysts sometimes make is that although the incest taboo is supposed to facilitate heterosexual exogamy, it never quite works, and that the array of perversion and fetishism that populates regular human sexuality testifies to the failure of the symbolic law fully to order our sexual lives. By this argument we are supposed to be persuaded that no one really occupies that norm and that psychoanalysis makes perverts and fetishists of us all. The problem with this response is that the form of the norm, however uninhabitable, remains unchanged, and though this formulation would have us all be equally deviant, it does not break through the conceptual structure that posits a singular and unchanging norm and its deviant departures. In other words, there is no way that gay parenting or bisexuality might be acknowledged as a perfectly intelligible cultural formation and thus escape its place as deviance. Similarly, there is no way to distinguish, as there must be, between deviations from the norm such as lesbian sexuality and incestuous practice.

To the extent that certain forms of love are prohibited or at least derealized by the norms established by the incest taboo, both homosexuality and incest qualify as such forms. In the case of homosexuality, this derealization leads to a lack of recognition for a legitimate love; in the case of incest, it leads to a lack of recognition for what might have been a traumatic set of encounters, although it is important to note that not all forms of incest are necessarily traumatic (brother-sister incest in eighteenth-century literature, for instance, sometimes appears as idyllic). But whether the point is to legitimate or delegitimate a nonnormative form of sexuality, it seems crucial that we have a theoretical framework that does not foreclose vital descriptions in advance. For if we say that, by definition, certain forms of sexuality are not intelligible or that they could not exist, we risk duplicating in the very theoretical language we use the kind of disavowal that it is the task of psychoanalysis to bring to light.

For those within structuralist psychoanalysis who take Claude Lévi-Strauss's analysis as foundational, the incest taboo produces heterosexually normative kinship and forecloses from the realm of love and desire forms of love that cross and confound that set of kinship relations. In the case of incest, the child whose love is exploited may no longer be able to recover or avow that love as love. These forms of suffering are disturbances of avowal, and not to be able to avow one's love, however painful it may be, produces its own melancholia, the suppressed and ambivalent alternative to mourning. What, then, of the other ways that kinship, which forms the conditions of cultural intelligibility for the structuralist position, is abrogated by a love that breaks the boundaries of what will and should be livable social relations and yet continues to live? There, another sort of catachresis or improper speech comes into operation. For if the incest taboo is also what is supposed to install the subject in heterosexual normativity, and if, as some argue, this installation is the condition of possibility for a symbolically or culturally intelligible life, then homosexual love emerges as the unintelligible within the intelligible: a love that has no place in the name of love, a position within kinship that is no position. When the incest taboo works *in this sense* to foreclose a love that is not incestuous, it produces a shadowy realm of love, a love that persists in spite of its foreclosure in an ontologically suspended mode. What emerges is a melancholia that attends living and loving outside the livable and outside the field of love.

It might, then, be necessary to rethink the prohibition on incest as that which sometimes protects against a violation and sometimes becomes the very instrument of a violation. What counters the incest taboo offends not only because it often involves the exploitation of those whose capacity for consent is questionable but because it exposes the aberration in normative kinship, an aberration that might also, importantly, be worked against the strictures of kinship to force a revision and expansion of those very terms. If psychoanalysis, in its theory and practice, retains heterosexual norms of kinship as the basis of its theorization, if it accepts these norms as coextensive with cultural intelligibility, then it, too, becomes the instrument by which this melancholia is produced at a cultural level. Or if it insists that incest is under taboo and therefore that it could not exist, what forfeiture of analytic responsibility toward psychic suffering is thereby performed? These are both surely discontents with which we do not need to live.

The Vortex Beneath the Story

Juliet Mitchell

The widespread diffusion of psychoanalysis into myriad therapies co-incides with the relative weakening of its own center as a clinical prac-tice and theory that emanates therefrom. Psychoanalysis is a discipline that demands the hard work of fifty minutes of daily free association from the patient and the suspension of consciousness from the analyst in order to listen to unconscious effects that, despite all their differ-ences, somewhere as humans (as analyst and analysand) they share.

It would be to trivialize the problem, however, simply to suggest that the current discontents of psychoanalysis are due to its misuse and the consequent misunderstandings, although this is certainly part of the truth. More important is that if recovered or false memory syndromes and their therapies can be mistaken for psychoanalysis, something is clearly amiss in the house of Freud.

Psychoanalysis, as theory and practice, starts with the deliberate sup-pression of the story not because it was either true or false but because stories interfere with listening to the manifestations of unconscious processes. At the same time as psychoanalysis introduced the suppres-sion of the story, there was likewise a confinement to a particular place of the trauma as the initiating event of psychic pathologies. The trauma and its potential cure through the telling of it as a story are likely aspects of the human condition; they are not specifics of particular pathologies. Which is not to say that traumas do not have psychological effects—of course they do; it is simply to indicate that that is not the focus of psychoanalysis.

The return in the last decade of the twentieth century of the trauma and the story as cause and solution of psychic ill-being, rather than as aspects of the human condition, is the problem I wish to emphasize here. Both the trauma and the story have escaped their confinement to a specific place within psychoanalytic treatment and theory. This was perhaps a danger inherent in the original project; it may be one of the reasons why, for instance, Freud worried that his case histories read like stories without the serious stamp of science.

The object of psychoanalytic practice is the manifestations of unconscious processes, above all, in symptoms. The construction of the unconscious is a double process. Prohibited desires are repressed, forming what is generally thought of as "the unconscious" but which—though I dislike the term—I shall call for simplicity's sake "the repressed unconscious." Given that we have an energetic model of the mind, the hypothesis is that something draws these repressed ideas into unconsciousness: they are not only pushed, they are pulled. What pulls is what is known as "primary repression," something that has happened that sets up a sort of residual unconscious. The suggestion is that some effraction, or breaking in, of the neonate's protective shield is the condition of this primary repression. This effraction is an energetic force that sets up a vortex within the individual and then draws chaotic and primitive representations to it. Wilfred Bion calls this the nameless dread; another term is "primal anxiety," which the helpless, prematurely born human infant feels when its existence is threatened because of the failure of a provision of its needs.

Primitive identifications with what is needed start to fill this hole, which is the first condition of our psyche—a baby will start to mouth the sucking and will dream or "hallucinate" the breast it needs, an infant will make the faces and sounds of its caretaker. But the caretaker, probably because it has the same source for its own psychic being, will do the same—milk flows in relation to the baby's need, smiles, and grimaces; sounds and words match each other across the divide of infant and caretaker. This is the simple mimesis found in all higher mammals. The effraction caused in the protective shield is likewise probably markable on some evolutionary scale. So we have a gap followed by a fantasmatic and an identificatory filling of that gap. We might call this a model of human or mammalian protodesire.

Freud's great discovery in this connection was to understand that this mimesis also involved an identification with the other's desiring self (or preself). This desire or wanting is predicated on the emptiness of the void or gap caused by the effraction. The identification is brought about by the suction of the vortex in the other. Vortexes draw all in. In its turn, this then would be a protoseduction. So, as with the process of primary repression, one has a two-way movement of the draw and pull of emptiness and the attachment of identifications. One can see it at the individual level of anorexia among a group of adolescent girls, where the desire of one attracts the identificatory processes of the other, or, at the level of group psychology, of mass hysteria. It is the necessary emptiness of the charismatic figure that draws into it the identifications made from the emptiness of the group of people that will become the followers.

This play of attraction and identification, on one hand, and the draw of vortical emphasis, on the other, continues to be a possibility throughout life. It happens at the primitive level I have outlined and at a sophisticated level, which is where we find the interaction of the trauma and the story. The story fills the holes of subsequent traumas, stands in for death, as in the exemplary tale *One Thousand and One Nights.*

When the gap that is set up by the effraction is filled, it will have not only a quality of life but also, in the broadest sense of the term, one of sexuality. The welding of the one through fantasy into the gap of the other becomes a model for psychosexuality and sexual desire. Here it is easiest to see the process—which is not only normal but human—at its outer edges of strangeness or pathology. For us "possession cults" are strange, we are more used to thinking about abuse; I suggest that the same psychic process subtends both. The shaman self-traumatizes, producing thereby the effraction, the gap or emptiness into which the object that is to possess her or him must flow. The abused child has the breach done for it, but then something has to be drawn in. What we witness in the abused child is the filling of the breach with an intense sexualization of everything that can fill the traumatic gap. An abused child of six (in the portrait of a clinician from the days before abuse was thought to be the key to everything) demonstrated a horrendous degree of foot fetishism—she was a girl at a time when the theory argued that only males were fetishists.

The story, as I see it, is the culturally normal or normative (though different) and individually, developmentally necessary stage of this filling of the breach that constitutes the human psyche. It replaces the breast that the needy baby hallucinates. Everyone experiences many large and small traumas; these fall over the primary one, which provides the transindividual basis. When a psychoanalyst listens to a patient's story, instead of preventing the story in the interests of enabling manifestations of the unconscious to emerge, he or she is listening to the material that fills the gap. The story has the seductive qualities that mark its origin as the life-giving force that acts against the death-producing moments of the effraction. The vortex beneath the story draws the therapist in. This can also work the other way around. The therapist shares the human paradigm, and something in his or her vortical need can draw the patient into an identification with the analyst.

In so far as psychoanalysis has been drawn to its edges in various therapies, it is because it has failed to suppress the story—not any particular story, but the story as such, the story that fills the traumatic effraction. Psychoanalysis may sometimes have failed to suppress the story in its clinical work. If so, this will have opened the way to therapies as stories. Psychoanalysis has certainly often failed to tackle this in its theoretical presentation of itself as the case history. This may, as with other social sciences, be inevitable; one aspect of the presentation of the social sciences is that they are life-affirming, story-telling. We must not, however, allow this tendency to stand unquestioned either for psychoanalytic treatment or for its theory.

Discussion

Judith Butler: I have just a couple of comments. I was interested in my colleague Frederick Crews's remarks, and I appreciate his bravery in coming here and letting us know his views. I suppose I'm just going to take up the position of the adversary of a certain kind—and I hope of a friendly kind. I thought it might be useful—my Freud–your Freud, you know—to make a distinction between questions about Freud the man: was he a person of character? did he lie? did he cover up? did he not? was he doing the best he could under difficult circumstances? That's an important set of difficult questions. In the end it's very different than questions about the practice of psychoanalysis, and I appreciated that Robert Michels performed that shift of attention, asking about psychoanalytic practice as an evolving practice. I thought that might be one thing to mark.

The other thing that did surprise me a little was the invocation of community standards and standards of empirical adequacy. I haven't visited philosophy of science for some time, but I understand there to be conflicting standards within empiricism, on in what verifiability consists. Of course, one of the classic problems of empiricism is that it includes the question of experience. And the minute that we begin with that problem we are in a tricky domain. What is empirically verifiable? What is experientially verifiable? What can and does emerge as verification within the context of experience? And can something be indicated or attested to within experience that is not as it were given in experience? I believe that opens up the question of the unconscious. And whether there could ever *be* an empirically adequate account of the unconscious. I think there probably *couldn't* be, but the unconscious does emerge in the empirical field and "is there," as it were. The gaps, the inconsistencies are there, in the experiential field. And what does one make of that kind of evidence?

Finally, I thought that Juliet Mitchell's reminder that trauma is not just a particular pathology but part of the human condition itself was very, very useful. I took that as an important corrective to the focus of my own paper. I suppose what I want to know, though, is: if what we need to do is not suppress the story, and if the story is material that fills this primary gap, can we talk more about what stories do? If stories fill a gap, they don't just report on an event, they don't just tell us what happened, but they perform something, and they produce something as well. It may be that the linguistic materiality of the story is precisely what attempts to fill this lack. And I'd like to know a little bit more about how stories precisely do that, and how they fail, and what they are if they do perform that function.

Frederick Crews: Judy, I will respond to the point you made about philosophy of science. I think this is crucial, and it's on a lot of people's minds. The philosophy of science deals with a lot of fairly abstruse questions. Abstruse from the point of view of working scientists, of the garden-variety scientist. The philosophy of science asks whether there is such a thing as progress in science or whether there is incommensurability between paradigms in science. Or whether scientific knowledge is acquired inductively and how certain we can be about our knowledge.

My objection to psychoanalysis resides on a more nuts-and-bolts, down-to-earth level than any of these questions. My point was that working scientists, day to day, in the conduct of their own research and in the evaluation of each other's research, exercise certain rules of thumb which are not particularly controversial. And the principle which is perhaps most universal is that one is not allowed to cite as proof of one's theory interpretations that are derived from that same theory. If you want to establish the truth of a hypothesis or a theory, you need to relate your postulates to data that can be regarded independently as facts by people who are not already members of your group. But notoriously, in the history of psychoanalysis, psychoanalytic confirmations consist of the adducing of psychoanalytic interpretations. And to my mind this is beyond the pale, and I think any practicing scientist would also say it's beyond the pale.

Peter Brooks, Moderator: Could I just intervene here? Wouldn't what you're saying describe any hermeneutic discipline, as opposed to a discipline in the physical sciences? You talked in terms of mistake and error, in your description of psychoanalysis, whereas Dr. Michels talked in terms of insight. Now I wonder how one confronts those two concepts. And maybe before you reply, I'd ask Dr. Michels if he has anything to say.

Robert Michels: Professor Crews just shifted terms in the middle of his response. First he said that we'd all agree that you can't use something that's derived from a theory to verify the theory. I agree. He then went on to say that the things used to verify a theory can't be things that are only available to members of one's own group. That's patently untrue. In fact, one of the characteristics of modern science is that data often can't be understood by anyone who's not a member of a group that understands the methodology and the kind of data that it produces. Those two statements—that you can't use something derived from a theory to verify it, and that the community of those competent to verify it can't simply be members of the same group—are not related to each other. He moved from one to another in the middle of a paragraph.

It's clear that if psychoanalysis is concerned with verifying theories it needs data that can be looked at independent of the theories. But I think he's conflating two different kinds of issues in psychoanalysis. One issue is, does the oral phase precede phallic interests? Frankly, I don't care. The other issue is, do interpretations based upon the model that the oral phase precedes phallic interests have a differential and preferable impact on patients when I make them? That's easily testable, just as easy as finding out whether penicillin is better or worse than streptomycin in treating tuberculosis. The second question is a scientific question.

If it turned out that Fleming had a totally absurd theory about how penicillin worked, it wouldn't affect at all my interest in using penicillin when it works. Similarly, if Freud's inspiration came from a false scientific theory: so what? I don't care whether Kekulé's image of the benzene ring was based on an impossible gyration by a snake that can't actually gets its tale in its mouth. That doesn't influence the scientific value of the benzene model. Professor Crews is attacking the scientific basis of Freud's imagery, because Freud used the sciences that Crews is talking about as imaginative sources of inspiration for interpretive metaphors. The scientific question isn't was the imagery based on good science, but do those interpretations make a difference to patients? That's of immense importance to us. Easily testable. Forget whether you're a positivist or not. That's a positivist question.

Frederick Crews: If the question is whether a given interpretation has a desired effect on patients, then the question indeed is a very pragmatic one, very down-to-earth. But those of us who would contemplate extrapolating from the activities of therapists to a system of ideas that we want to apply in intellectual endeavors that are outside the therapeutic context, would surely want to know whether the concepts so manipulated in therapy have an evidential basis, have some kind of empirical respectability. The problem with restricting one's inquiry to the level that Dr. Michels has proposed to us is that any number of contradictory interpretations can produce positive therapeutic effects.

Juliet Mitchell: I'm always very surprised when this sort of conversation starts. Which scientists are you referring to? There is such a range of scientific methods and theories. It seems to me so specific and so historically and ethnocentrically limited a definition of science that we start using. There isn't just one method. It isn't about verifiability and evidence, though those of course come into it.

For instance, if you read a scientist like Lewis Thomas, something like *The Snail and the Medusa,* it sounds very like Freud, actually.[1] He talks about what we can learn as scientists from poets, who have been able to imagine things before we got there as scientists to understand it. There's a snail and a jellyfish in the Bay of Naples that have a completely symbiotic dependency on each other and can actually swim across the Bay of Naples and join up. And, he says, now how do you think that as a scientist. He talks about dreams and poets. It's absolutely like reading Freud. The same with somebody like Barbara McClintock, who everybody thought was mad, for years, until she got the Nobel Prize. If you actually look at her methodology, at the way she looked down a microscope and identified with a germ cell in a grain of maize in order to understand what the germ cell was doing, it's terribly like the practice of a psychoanalyst.

So there's a wide range of scientists and scientific practices, and there's a very, very specific, very ethnocentric perspective that we always drag it into when we get this sort of challenge to Freud from scientists. It's such an impoverishment of science. In a way, like Dr. Michels, I don't mind about Freud or psychoanalysis, we'll get on with it. But I do mind the impoverishment of the scientific method and theory, that's my chief objection.

Frederick Crews: I'd like to go back to the point I was making. We have over four hundred recognized psychotherapies in this country. There is no strong evidence that any one of them is more therapeutically effective than the others; and certainly psychoanalysis has not been shown to be more efficacious than the others. Yet all of these therapies seem to be more efficacious than no treatment at all. They are approximately as effective as placebo treatment; perhaps some of them are more effective than placebo treatment, but let's be charitable and say they have mildly positive effects. These therapies all assert different theories about how the mind works and different theories about curing the patient. If their effects are not differentiated, then it is strongly suggestive that the theoretical content of what is asserted within the therapy doesn't matter very much. And this is why I say to Dr. Michels: when he says, "The really important thing is, does a given proposal or hypothesis have a good therapeutic effect on the patient?" he's throwing away the particular game that psychoanalysis has always played, of saying, "We have a correct theory of the mind, and the correctness of this theory of the mind is demonstrated by the unique efficacy of our therapy."

Juliet Mitchell: You've just got it all back to front. It doesn't work like that at all, when you say there are myriads of different schools and different disciplines none of which agree. You don't have a theory that you then impose on your practice. What you have is a practice in which you observe certain things. Some of those things that you observe will confirm hypotheses that have been raised to the status of theories by earlier workers, some will not and you propose something rather different. And so you build a network of different, differentiating, and comparable theories. But you go from the observation to the hypothesis, you take your hypothesis back to your material, and you produce a theory. And they won't all be the same. Your material is in a sense the same, if you're all listening, or trying to listen to unconscious processes.

As for taking a theory and putting it on a patient, that's only while you're waiting to learn something. You know, when you're a student you have these theories and you think, "Oh, Oedipus complex! Phew, there it is." That soon goes. You don't bother about that very much. You observe your material; it may indeed confirm something at one moment that looks very oedipal, it may not, and then you think about it. Like any subject, that's how it works.

Frederick Crews: Are you suggesting that the American Psychological Association was mistaken in listing over four hundred recognized psychotherapies?

Juliet Mitchell: Well, I've no idea. I couldn't care less.

Robert Michels: At this point I'm largely in agreement with what I think Professor Crews has said. He said, if I understand him, that the critical question for a treatment such as psychoanalysis is: does it work? And he recognizes that the scientific evaluation of that question is totally independent of the scientific evaluation of whether or not the theory it's based upon is true. He goes on to say something I think is incorrect. Which is, if it does work, that supports the theory it's said to be based upon.

Frederick Crews: No.

Robert Michels: That just isn't so. A therapy that's based on a theory can be totally effective for some reason the therapist wasn't aware of. So we can't test the founding notions of psychoanalysis by whether the treatment works, either way. If it works, it doesn't validate them; if it doesn't work, it doesn't invalidate them.

Frederick Crews: We agree.

Robert Michels: But we can test whether or not the theory is effective. That's a very important question to me, because I'm a psychoanalyst. It's not important to Professor Crews. He's not an analyst. I presume he's not a patient. He's interested in culture—

Frederick Crews: Not yet.

Robert Michels: I'll see you tomorrow. I told you analysts are looking for patients. He's interested in the application of psychoanalytic notions outside of the clinical sphere. And here he gives a very important warning: their popularity, and I would add even their therapeutic efficacy in analysis, doesn't validate them for application outside of analysis. Whether or not they're useful has to be judged by the discipline to which they're being applied. Just as analysts may draw ideas from neurobiology and find them useful, not because they're useful in neurobiology but only because they're useful in analysis. Professors of English literature may draw ideas from analysis in looking at, let's say, Hawthorne. But they're not useful because analysts found them useful. They're useful because they give us an exciting, new insight in Hawthorne. Or they fail because they don't.

He and I are in agreement on the big picture. I would add a methodologic, positivist footnote: there has never been a test that has the power to answer the question of whether these four hundred different models, or the eight basic ones that there really are, have differential effectiveness. He's right that we don't know the answer. But don't infer from the fact that we don't know an answer that the answer is: there isn't a difference. That's not a good syllogism.

I want to move to psychoanalysis for a minute, rather than Methods of Science 101a. I think there's a very fundamental shift in psychoanalysis that isn't being recognized in our dialogue. In the beginning, Freud was excited by his discoveries of unconscious powers and unconscious forces. Psychoanalysis was the science of the unconscious, of the forces and activities that appeared in those gaps that were covered by stories. That's not what it's been about for the last seventy years. It's not about removing the story to find underneath it the seething cauldron of unconscious factors. If we do that, it's of no use to patients. What it's about is the interpenetration of irrational, unconscious factors with the *apparently* seamless, conscious, rational story that's on top. How they relate to each other, how they interact. To listen to the story without being sensitive for the unconscious forces that it's covering is to be a guidance counselor. To look at the unconscious forces without paying attention to the story is to be a professor of English literature. It's the relationship between them that's at the core of the clinical activity.

Judith Butler: I just want to say that over and against the question of empirically respectable standards, we might ask where is the place in this culture for unrespectable stories? Or where can the unrespectable story be risked? And I think that's a very different question. I also wonder about this desire to be in conformity with community standards, subjecting psychoanalysis to H. L. A. Hart's theory of law or something. It strikes me as a very interesting desire for respectability, and I think it does raise the question of whether psychoanalysis does not uncover and persist *in* the unrespectable, and how important that is, especially in relationship to the problem of the unconscious.

I just wanted to say briefly that it's one thing to argue that a theory derives its conclusions from its own postulates. That indeed would be a completely circular and tautological enterprise. It's another thing to argue that what counts as data for any given theory is only available through a prior conceptualization of what will count as data, what will be, in fact, *a fact*, what will be empirically recognizable. There is indeed a theoretical contribution to the determination of data, which is, to use Peter Brooks's term, the meaning of hermeneutics as I understand it—part of any hermeneutical enterprise. That the data of psychoanalysis is contaminated by the theory strikes me as absolutely true and inevitable. And I think making a distinction between what is theoretical and what is observed is a mistake. It's not possible to sustain that distinction in a rigorous way. And I also then wonder—as this discussion has moved between questions of empirical verifiability and the status of the story—what is the relationship of the story to empiricism? Does the story not emerge precisely at the *limit* of empirical verifiability? Is there some way of bringing these two questions together?

Peter Brooks: Good. Well, now we will try to have a debate with the floor.

Dominick LaCapra: I'd like to point out something that may require more reflection. It struck me as interesting that there's a kind of gendered chiasmus in the panel. The men transgressed the operating rule of ten minutes, and did not even mention it, and yet Professor Crews asserted what he believed to be a dominant normativity in science, which he wanted to affirm. And Professor Michels assumed, rather than asserted, a dominant normativity in society, when he used an unexplicated notion of effectiveness or "what works." Often what works in terms of practical clinical care, perhaps *per force,* is bringing a person back into a dominant normativity of one sort or another. The two women, on the other hand, really tried to abide by the operating rules and norms of this conference. And yet both challenged in their own way, theoretically, a dominant normativity and the conception of dominant stories, and perhaps at times elided dominant normativity with the issue of normativity in general.

Judith Butler: I appreciate your comments, Dominick. I just want to point out that although Juliet did say she was a woman, I did not.

Juliet Mitchell: I did. Which is a sign that I am.

Judith Butler: Sorry, that was a little levity, you know.

Questioner: I wonder if Professor Crews could say something about his forthcoming book?

Frederick Crews: In August, Viking will be publishing a book that I am editing called *Unauthorized Freud: Doubters Confront a Legend.* It's an anthology of critical Freud scholarship and scholarship on psychoanalysis, from about 1970 to the present. And the aim behind the book is to put into the hands of general readers the kind of material that it takes a very long time to dig out if you're a scholar. Incidentally, anticipating the fact that I would be very much a minority voice here today, I brought along a little bibliography, of twelve items that I think would constitute a good reading list for someone who wants to get up to speed on independent Freud scholarship. Its called "Freudianism: A Twelve-Step Cure Through Bibliotherapy." And you are welcome to take whatever copies I have.

Questioner: For Juliet Mitchell: could you speak a little about how you would understand the relationship between what you called vortical need or vortical emptiness and what Judith Butler talked about, ontologically suspended codes of life?

Juliet Mitchell: Yes. Neither Judith nor I had seen each other's papers beforehand, and, as she said, it was dense and there was a lot in it. But I think both of us felt that we wanted to exchange and that there was a lot of overlap in our thinking, even if we were going slightly different ways with it.

I'll let Judith speak about what her concept is. But when she talks about incest, and tries to actually ramify and sophisticate our concept of incest, she identifies some incest as traumatic—which causes what I would call that vortical hole in the psyche, that really *is* traumatic—and some which I would describe as ego or culturally syntonic. In other words, it's not necessarily the same relationship in every case.

We do have this notion that because child abuse is completely traumatic to white middle-class America, it is universally traumatic. Now I am not saying that child abuse is not wrong, brutal, violent, whatever it might be. But it's not necessarily the same sort of trauma if you're living together in an extended family network in which brothers and sisters share the same bed, and there's the sort of touching and playing with each other that you in America and we in Europe would call abuse.

It's not *necessarily* traumatic, and we have to be quite careful to keep the notion of trauma for something that causes a sort of break, just like a physical trauma. You know, if you have a leg amputated, which is a physical trauma, you will probably have a fantasy of a leg that is no longer there. You will have all sorts of psychological concomitants, because of this physical break in you. And I see psychological trauma in those same terms. It breaks through a necessary protection that every human infant has to have—from having its need satisfied by a caretaker, because it cannot survive alone, because we're born prematurely. And a trauma breaks through that shield. Now incest will sometimes—very often, probably—do that. But not inevitably. And only if it breaks through a completely protective shield, would I classify it as trauma.

So I completely agree with Judith that one has to diversify and think through what has been a monolithic concept of incest. Again, it's culturally absolutely incorrect to think that what we call incest is incest in all cultures. You know, for some groups incest is if you have intercourse in the bush. It's nothing to do with who the relation is, it's the place where you might have it. The wrong place would be the law that is being broken, and therefore would be what we would call the breaking of the taboo against incest. You know, we're far too culture-bound.

Judith Butler: I would just say that Juliet Mitchell's account is obviously taking as its point of departure the life of the infant. I don't know if it's exactly a developmental model, but certainly it goes back to the infantile scene as its point of departure. And I'm not doing that. I don't think I know how to do that and I'm not sure whether I would want to even if I knew how. Or could know how. For me what is most important is the way in which certain rules of kinship that govern cultural intelligibility actually persistently produce this sort of melancholic realm where a love can neither be avowed nor grieved. How do we think about these forms of love that are not legitimated by the incest taboo—the incest taboo that produces legitimate kinship—and that operate outside of the sign of legitimation? So my point of departure is this normative scheme of kinship. These are somewhat different ways of getting to perhaps related issues.

Mary Jacobus: I'm astonished by the delightful aura of agreement that reigns over this panel. It seems to me very interesting that the Kenneth Starr as it were, the independent prosecutor of Freud, Professor Crews, and Bob Michels are in such great agreement, and I wonder why this is. It seems to me that Professor Michels should be in *huge* disagreement with Professor Crews, not about the question of whether it works, but about what "*it*" is. Because if any therapy, well, anything goes. It seems to me that anything does *not* go, and that clinicians know that.

   The other question I want to raise is about the two other panelists, who are in the kind of agreement I find much more appealing, and no doubt that is a matter of gender. But it does seem to me that there is a great theoretical difference between focusing on the incest taboo and focusing on the influence, need, and dependence of the infant as traumatic. They are very different positions. It reminds me of a moment of the textbook definition of projection, in Laplanche and Pontalis, when one philosopher says to the other, "we're in complete agreement," and the other philosopher says "Absolutely not."[2]

Peter Brooks: Who wants to start? Bob?

Robert Michels: The first half of the question challenged the apparent community of agreement between Professor Crews and myself, and suggested that we ought not to so quickly assume that we agree on what psychoanalysis *is*. Freud, of course, said psychoanalysis was three things. He said it was a system of psychology, a method of investigation, and a treatment. In the early part of its history, Freud applied the system of psychology to the therapeutic situation and used this system as the scientific basis of the treatment. A widespread revisionist version of this says that the real knowledge of psychoanalysis has come *from* the clinical situation. And there has been a great deal of effort to find theories that can encapsulate, represent, and contain that knowledge. But the real contributions of psychoanalysis come from the consultation room and have frequently been applied in a variety of other settings.

As a therapy, our interest in psychoanalysis is the belief that it works. That it's helpful. That it's better than random therapies, or the average of the 399 or 441 other therapies. This then makes us curious about independent tests—which are outside of psychoanalysis—of some of the theories that have been constructed in response to the experiences in the consultation room. Ideas which emerge from the consultation room have also been borrowed in an incredible range of disciplines. That's why we're here today. We don't have conferences on modern otolarangology and its cultural significance. Because very few professors of French culture are interested in modern otolarangology. Psychoanalytic ideas have an apparent power and applicability outside of the consultation room. So besides validating the efficacy of the therapy, we can join with colleagues, in all kinds of disciplines, in evaluating the ideas as they work in these disciplines. That's occurred successfully in studies in infant development, for example, a field that was of no interest a hundred years ago and that has been importantly responsive to psychoanalytic notions which point to the significance of the psychology of infancy. It's true in studies of language and communication, studies of group process, in sociology and history. And that's what you want to have happen in an intellectual and cultural environment such as a university.

I'm not troubled by people who challenge the lack of proof, as long as that challenge is a call for inquiry rather than a disparagement of interesting ideas. We need more inquiry, and the fact that an idea is interesting is the start of inquiry, not the end of it. I don't know how much of that Professor Crews would agree with.

Frederick Crews: I think there is a very significant area of agreement between Dr. Michels and me, and it has to do precisely with his granting the point that the usefulness of any given idea in a therapeutic context does not validate the empirical basis of that idea. That's a statement that not every psychoanalyst would make, by any means. The history of psychoanalytic discourse, right up to the present, is replete with claims of clinical validation of ideas. A kind of kitchen testing of ideas through therapeutic efficacy on the one hand and confirmatory feedback from the patient on the other hand. Doctor Michels is not making the claim, and in that sense we're very close.

But he then goes on to say that these ideas, which he admits are not validated within the clinical setting, are nevertheless truthful and applicable in a number of other ways. And of course they are applicable, they're applied all the time. But the question is: are these the best ideas to apply, and if so, on what basis can we ascertain that they are the best? That's a question that really hasn't been addressed at all here today. And all I would say is that the mere fact that a set of ideas came out of a form of treatment that once had high cultural cachet, and now has somewhat less, is not a sufficient basis for using these ideas for investigative procedures and endeavors in quite unrelated fields.

Juliet Mitchell: Yes, I'm very interested in the agreement that Mary Jacobus pointed out. This is the other part of her question, that we seem to be in agreement, and they seem to be in agreement. And there's some truth to that.

In terms of the intellectual content of our work, I was very interested that Judith Butler started talking about incest and kinship, because when I wrote *Psychoanalysis and Feminism* at the very beginning of the seventies, exactly what I asked for at the end of the book was a critical study of incest and kinship, in order to try to understand contemporary society in these terms. We have it anthropologically, but we need one to understand gender differences.

So here, twenty-five years later, when that's not the way psychoanalytic studies have gone at all, anywhere, either in clinical practice or in universities and humanities departments, Judith was taking me back to my first project. And I was very interested and grateful for that. I trained as a psychoanalyst after writing the book, not before. And I trained in a system that took me in the area that Mary Jacobus pointed to, about very early development of the human infant and object relations theory. But I'm extremely interested in what Judith is doing. So, it's that pleasure of interest in a project, rather than total agreement. It may look like agreement, but it's just a shared interest, I think.

Judith Butler: Let me just briefly say, I have been returning to Juliet's 1974 work and teaching it very productively. And I think what's interesting for me is that there you actually are working much more in a Lacanian vein, and you talk about the symbolic domain as the domain that regulates kinship. And I believe you refer to the symbolic as "primordial law" at that point. It seems to me that you've shifted. And although you've shifted, the structuralist influence within psycho-analysis has gone on in other directions and within certain more orthodox Lacanian veins. This ossification of kinship into this quasi-timeless, symbolic realm has produced what I take to be a very conservative position, one that is not able to come to terms with radical shifts in contemporary kinship arrangements. And not just gay and lesbian kinship, but blended families and displaced children, and questions of exile and loss, which are being brought into the analytic scene and which pose a very serious theoretical challenge to the kinship presuppositions of the theory.

Questioner: My question is addressed to Judith Butler. I was really troubled by Professor Butler's apparent conflation of the incest taboo and the marginalization of homosexual love. It seems to me that propositions like these, if they're inadequately delineated and clarified, are rhetorically convenient but socially and politically dangerous. I want you to explain a little more about this premise in your paper, what I saw as a rhetorical gesture of conflating the marginalization of homosexual love and kinship with the incest taboo.

Judith Butler: Well, if saying that I think not all forms of incest are exploitation or abusive, if that's politically dangerous, then so be it. Because I would rather have a more nuanced political discussion of what we mean by incest, and where and when it is violation. And not, as it were, be stuck in intellectual paralysis because we're afraid to speak or think carefully or make distinctions on this issue. So it's a risk I'm willing to take. What I'm objecting to is the way in which some people *do* understand the incest taboo not simply to prohibit incest but also to mandate heterosexual forms of kinship. It is that conflation which I oppose. I oppose it. It would be great if we could de-link them in some way, so that we didn't have people arguing, as they do in the academy and as I'm afraid they may well be presupposing in the analytic hour, that the proper and normative solution to the incest prohibition is heterosexuality. So that's the link that I oppose, and I feel perfectly politically responsible in opposing it.

Notes

1. Lewis Thomas, *The Medusa and the Snail: More Notes of a Biology Watcher* (New York: Viking, 1979).
2. See Jean Laplanche and J. B. Pontalis, *The Language of Psychoanalysis,* translated by Donald Nicholson-Smith (New York: Norton, 1973).

Part Two **Psychoanalysis: Between Therapy and Hermeneutics?**

Introduction

The four essayists here come from and work between many disciplines, bridging psychoanalysis with literary interpretation, art criticism, history, and feminist theory. The eclecticism of the group stems from the eclectic texture of Freud's writing: while always maintaining a base in medical science and therapeutic technique, Freud's work comes to include an array of essays in interpretation and several monumental theories of history and culture. This part of the volume investigates the relation between the techniques of psychoanalysis as a medical therapy and the application of psychoanalysis as a mode of cultural interpretation, considering questions raised by the unique way psychoanalysis bridges and disrupts disciplinary boundaries. Because psychoanalysis can be integrated into so many interpretive methodologies, it calls attention to the process of interpretation itself.

Hubert Damisch demonstrates how interpretive practices in the humanities can be illuminated in dialogue with psychoanalytic therapy by focusing on an underlying, and thus often overlooked, tension within art criticism: its translation of images into words. Interpreting a painting is necessarily an incomplete rendition of the image's "muteness" into speech, and the explanation of a painting will always be partial, at best pointing to that "something more" which is latent within the object and cannot be fully communicated through a verbal paraphrase. Damisch turns to psychoanalysis to help think through this difficulty. The art critic must "listen" to the work of art in the same way as a psychoanalyst should listen to a patient: the gap between a verbal paraphrase and the surplus of meaning within the image itself parallels the gap between the decoding of "free association" and the full meaning of unconscious desire. Psychoanalysis thus allows Damisch to use the tension between image and text as a way to reconfigure the relationship between interpreter and object of interpretation: "I am no longer interested in working on the work of art. . . . I am interested in working with the work of art, in exactly the same way that an analyst works with an analysand."

The interpretive inspiration that Damisch draws from psychoanalysis revolves around the play of transference and countertransference in the analytic situation. Mary Jacobus also focuses on these aspects of the analytic relationship in her chapter, "The Pain in the Patient's Knee," an examination of a single psychoanalytic session discussed by the post-Kleinian analyst Wilfred Bion. Jacobus uses the session to succinctly, and precisely, illustrate the radical hermeneutic consequences of transference. On one hand, a patient's inchoate monologue "conveys a meaning not fully available to the patient himself" and, in fact, turns out to be a *dialogue,* as the patient has woven his own anticipation of the analyst's response into his litany of complaints. As Jacobus writes, by complaining of a pain in the knee, "the patient caricatures—with hostile and aggressive intent—the very psychoanalytic theory ('the theory of internal objects') by which the analyst tries to understand and alleviate his pain." The object of analysis thus anticipates and helps condition its own frame of interpretation: just as the image, in Damisch's chapter, helps condition the way we arrange the words through which we incompletely grasp it. Pursuing the pain in the patient's knee even further, Jacobus teases out currents of countertransference in this session; by carefully reading Bion's account of the case in relation to his autobiography, she shows how the symptom that the patient uses is also embedded in conscious and unconscious chains of association for Bion.

Peter Loewenberg, in the most wide-ranging essay in this section, summarizes the essential qualities of psychoanalytic hermeneutics and offers two strikingly different vignettes. Broadening Jacobus's close reading of a single session (and its representation by the analyst), Loewenberg insists on the centrality of the transference: "All the good kinds of therapy are reflective and self-reflective. They all use the transference as ubiquitous. In fact, we live in fields of transference whether we're in therapy or not and the psychotherapies interpret it." It is Freud's elaboration of both transference and countertransference that makes psychoanalysis a paradigm, Loewenberg argues, for twentieth-century hermeneutics. First, Freud's insistence on unconscious meaning in free association anticipates, and makes room for, the "close reading" of twentieth-century interpretation: Freud's case studies lead to Clifford Geertz's "thick description" in which "a single event, artifact, or ritual . . . is treated as a prism by which an entire culture" is exposed. Second, and just as essentially, the countertransference serves as a paradigm for twentieth-century self-reflexivity, anticipating Hans-Georg Gadamer's insistence that we "not allow the interpreter to speak of an original meaning of the work without acknowledging that, in understanding it, the interpreter's own meaning enters as well." The transference shows us that meaning cannot be seized from the object of inquiry without a full immersion into the situation of the object; the countertransference shows us that interpretation must also account for the situation of the interpreter.

Loewenberg also suggests a third distinctively modern aspect of psychoanalytic interpretation: the fluidity of the psychoanalytic process and its tolerance of ambiguity are grounded in its "primary engagement . . . with human beings in their own right," preserving "the ever-changing human person behind any diagnostic category." This attention to the sympathetic humanism that underlies psychoanalysis's interpretive practice finds resonance in Toril Moi's essay, which puts Freudian notions of the human body in dialogue with Simone de Beauvoir's situational definition of freedom and consciousness. If Hubert Damisch uses Freudian hermeneutics to help him out of an interpretive problem of criticism, Toril Moi returns the favor—using the practice of literary criticism to reflect back on Freudian hermeneutics. As Moi says during the discussion, "My paper didn't talk about interpretation, but it did practice interpretation, on a psychoanalytic text. . . . We have to have the patience to listen to the text for good and bad, what Professor Damisch has called 'the listening eye.' And if psychoanalysis teaches us to listen to the text, so that psychoanalytic listening is crucial to literary criticism, in the same way we have to bring that critical attention to bear on Freud's own texts." Specifically, Moi does an exemplary close reading of Freud's famous, or infamous, statement "anatomy is destiny." Most often this has been taken to imply a deterministic method of interpretation, where psychic consciousness can be read as the direct consequence of anatomic, or biological, categories. Moi slowly and rigorously brings out the complex philosophical implications of Freud's statement—tracing the polyvalent meaning of *Schicksal* in German; examining the parody of Napoleon's claim that "politics is destiny" that is implicit in Freud's comment; and finally focusing on the quite different appearances of the phrase in two essays from 1912 and 1924. Through this careful attention to the language and context of the statement, Moi shows that the common interpretation of the phrase misses how Freud has reconfigured the meaning of destiny. The redefinition is crucial: rather than suggesting a simplified hermeneutic of biological determination, Freud anticipates the interpretive strategies of someone like Beauvoir, in which biology "is the inescapable background of our choices and actions" and in which the relation between the body and subjectivity is complicated and necessary but not predetermined.

Is Anatomy Destiny? Freud
and Biological Determinism

Toril Moi

This volume invites us to consider the place of psychoanalysis in contemporary culture. In modern feminism debates pitting cultural against biological causation have played an important role. Such debates have also arisen in relation to research in biotechnology, neurobiology, sociobiology, and ethnomethodology. I think it could be shown that Freud thinks of the body in terms that undermine the opposition between natural causation and cultural meanings that have been with us since Kant first distinguished between the realms of necessity and freedom. If this is right, then Freud does have a philosophically original contribution to make to contemporary debates about the relation between body and mind, nature and nurture, genetic inheritance and social construction. I want to take a first step toward this larger argument by raising a question that has been important to feminists: is Freud a biological determinist?

Biological determinists believe that social norms are or ought to be grounded on biological facts. They also believe that no amount of social change will change the fundamental biological nature of human beings. As the late nineteenth-century determinists Patrick Geddes and J. Arthur Thomson put it: "What was decided among the prehistoric Protozoa cannot be annulled by Act of Parliament."[1] Many biological determinists believe that biological facts express themselves in the social roles prevalent in their own society and that any change would lead to a disastrous incapacity to reproduce. This was the view of W. K. Brooks, a professor of biology at Johns Hopkins University in the 1880s: "The positions which women already occupy in society and the duties which they perform are, in the main, what they should be if our view is correct; and any attempt to improve the condition of women by ignoring or obliterating the intellectual differences between them and men must result in disaster to the race."[2]

Freud's views on women have often been taken to be consonant with this. Given that Freud studied medicine at a time when determinism was widespread and started his scientific career in the late 1870s with research on the physiology of eels, it would hardly be surprising were we to find traces of it in his work. Read against this historical background, Freud's famous phrase "anatomy is destiny" appears to clinch the case. If he can say such a thing, he must be a biological determinist. No single sentence of Freud's has been more troublesome to feminists. Sooner or later, anyone who believes that Freud was not in fact a biological determinist will have to explain why this sentence does not undermine their claim. Usually this is done by writing it off as a casual witticism, not compatible with Freud's more thoughtful comments on the body. I don't think that argument is good enough. After all, Freud was sufficiently content with the formulation to use it twice, twelve years apart. The phrase "anatomy is Destiny" appears in 1912, in "On the Universal Tendency to Debasement in the Sphere of Love," and again in 1924, in "The Dissolution of the Oedipus Complex." Unless there is evidence to the contrary, the assumption must be that Freud actually meant what he said. The question to be answered is: what exactly *did* Freud mean when he claimed that anatomy is destiny?[3]

THE MEANING OF DESTINY

What Freud actually wrote was not, of course, "anatomy is destiny" but rather "die Anatomie ist das Schicksal."[4] There are some differences between the German *Schicksal* and the English *destiny*. *Schicksal* can be translated either as *fate* or as *destiny*. In English, *destiny* is linked to words like *destination:* the idea is that a certain outcome is bound to occur, regardless of human attempts to intervene. Oedipus will kill his father and marry his mother, whatever his own wishes and inclinations might be. According to the *Oxford English Dictionary*, *destiny* means "predetermined events; what is destined to happen to person, country, etc.; power that foreordains, invincible necessity." The difference between destiny and fate is that whereas fate more often is negative, associated with death and destruction, destiny can be quite positive. One can have a magnificent destiny but hardly a magnificent fate. Both words nevertheless carry connotations of preordination and inevitability.

The German word *Schicksal* is more imbued with metaphysical gloom than the English word *destiny.* In her extensive analysis of the cultural meanings of different words for fate and destiny in various European languages, Anna Wierzbicka writes that *Schicksal* has a "pessimistic orientation," that it has connotations of something "inevitable, superhuman and awesome," and that it "suggest[s] a mysterious and other-worldly power." In contrast, the English *destiny* has a less awesome and more upbeat ring, and the English *fate* comes across as more unambiguously fatal than *Schicksal.*[5]

In 1915 Freud gave the word *Schicksal* great prominence by putting it in the title of his important essay "Triebe und Triebschicksale," which literally means "Drives and the Destinies of Drives."[6] It is striking to note that he chose to put the word in the plural, thereby making it obvious that he did not intend to write a paper about "the one inexorable fate" or "the inevitable and unescapable outcome" of drives. Translating the title as "Instincts and Their Vicissitudes," James Strachey, the editor of *The Standard Edition,* shows himself to be sensitive to Freud's main point, which is to show that drives are subjected to transformation by three different "polarities," each functioning more or less independently of the other two.[7] Whatever happens to the drive—the outcome of the different and varying pressure of these factors—is what Freud calls its *Schicksal.* To translate this as "destiny," Strachey recognizes, would be to provoke quite the wrong associations in English-speaking readers.[8]

In *Freud and Man's Soul,* his scorching critique of the translation of *The Standard Edition,* Bruno Bettelheim, who considers that both "Instinct" and "Vicissitudes" utterly fail to convey Freud's thought, comments: "It is true that both 'fate' and 'destiny' carry the implication of inevitability, which neither the German *Schicksale* nor the English 'vicissitudes' does. And Freud certainly did not mean that there is any inevitability inherent in the changes our inner drives are subject to. But if the translators rejected 'fate' because of its implication of immutability, they could have used 'change' or 'mutability' instead. They could, for example, have translated the title as 'Drives and Their Mutability.'"[9] The very fact that Bettelheim can propose to translate *Schicksale* as *mutability* shows that the range of meanings clustering around the word in Freud's work hardly add up to conclusive evidence of determinism or a belief in predestination. The meaning of the phrase "anatomy is destiny," however, cannot be settled simply by examining dictionary definitions or by looking at how Freud uses the word *Schicksal* in other contexts. The question now is what meaning the sentence acquires in the two contexts where Freud actually uses it.

ATROPOS, THE INEXORABLE

I have said that *Schicksal* can be translated either as destiny or as fate. In its most traditional, mythological sense, "fate" is linked to the three fates (in Greek the *moira*), the three goddesses of destiny. Fate has thus come to mean the "impersonal power by which events are determined." Freud himself mentions the three fates in his essay "The Theme of the Three Caskets" (1913), where he suggests that the three caskets that occur in so many fairy tales stand for, among other things, the three fates. Hesiod represents them as three old women spinning the thread of life: Klotho ("the spinner") held the distaff, Lachesis ("the apportioner") drew off the thread, and Atropos ("the inflexible") cut it short. Freud focuses on the third sister, the goddess of death, whom he calls "Atropos, the inexorable."[10]

The mythological meaning of destiny or fate foregrounded by Freud himself is death. We are all inexorably subject to death because we have human bodies. The fact that all human beings without exception are destined to die has enormous consequences for every human practice and every social institution, as well as for our own lived experience. Yet nobody seems to believe that to say so constitutes politically unacceptable biological determinism or that it is evidence of an attempt to situate human existence outside history or discourse. My point here is simple: It is often assumed that when Freud says that "anatomy is destiny" he must mean that certain features of our anatomy lead to an inexorable fate, that whatever the individual subject does, he or she cannot escape the predestined outcome dictated by anatomy. It is also usually assumed that any thought along these lines is bound to be evidence of biological determinism and sexism. Yet if Freud were saying that the fact of having a human body destines us to death, this would at once be a true description of a biological fact and a statement devoid of politically controversial implications. In this context, the word *destiny* does refer to Kant's necessity, to the iron law of natural cause and effect, yet *this* natural necessity does not abolish freedom. Or rather: the meaning we usually give to the word *freedom* is not such that it is undermined or voided by the fact of death. (Simone de Beauvoir, to mention one feminist explicitly opposed to biological determinism, would go even further: for her, death is the very condition of human freedom.)[11]

"TO VARY A SAYING OF NAPOLEON'S"

When Freud writes "anatomy is destiny," the idea that the human body destines us to death may linger in the air. Yet this is most likely not the meaning he had uppermost in his mind when he wrote the sentence. In the two passages I am considering here, "anatomy" refers to the specific configuration or structure of the human body, not just the body in its widest, biological generality. Let me return to Freud's texts. The most striking thing about the saying is the fact that in both passages, in 1924 as well as in 1912, Freud introduces it as a self-conscious twist on a "well-known" saying of Napoleon's:

> One might say here, varying a well-known saying by the great Napoleon: "Anatomy is destiny." [1912]

> "Anatomy is Destiny," to vary a saying of Napoleon's. [1924]

The fact that neither Freud nor James Strachey, the meticulous editor of *The Standard Edition* of Freud's works in English, supply a reference to what Napoleon actually said suggests that at the time the saying must have been well known in the German- and the English-speaking world. This is hardly the case today.[12]

Freud, an avid reader of the German classics, is referring to a conversation that took place between Napoleon and Goethe in Weimar in September 1808. According to Goethe's account in his *Autobiographische Einzelheiten,* the subject of the conversation was literature and theater: "Then he got to the destiny plays [*Schickstalsstücke*], of which he disapproved. They had belonged to a dark age. 'What does one want destiny for now?' he said. 'Politics is destiny.'"[13] Then Freud writes "anatomy is destiny," he explicitly intends us to recall Napoleon's "politics is destiny."[14] Napoleon, the most powerful man in the world at the time, scoffs at destiny. Power is destiny, he says. But this puts the meaning of destiny under pressure. For the victorious armies of Napoleon invading Europe irrevocably shaped the lives of millions, and many of those who starved and died in the Napoleonic wars must have thought that such suffering was their fate. Yet Napoleon's armies were neither the agents of divine intervention nor the ineluctable effects of the laws of nature. Napoleon, the self-made man par excellence, is not saying that he, too, is the mere plaything of politics. He makes politics. If anything, Napoleon sounds a positively Nietzschean theme here: in a world dominated by power, we either grasp the opportunity to forge our own destiny or succumb to the slave morality of Christianity. What some weak souls experience as the blow of fate is actually the work of other, more energetic personalities.

Gustave Flaubert captures the irony implicit in Napoleon's point of view perfectly in his account of the last words of the broken Charles Bovary: "No, I am no longer angry with you," he says to Rodolphe, Emma's first lover. The passage continues:

> He even added a grand phrase, the first he had ever uttered:
> "It was the fault of fate!"
> Rodolphe, who had directed this fate, found him very meek for a man in his situation, comic even and a little despicable.[15]

What the dying Charles Bovary in his pathetic last words takes to be fate, Rodolphe knows to be the work of human agency. Flaubert's irony recalls Napoleon's: to invoke fate is to be terminally deluded. Yet Napoleon is not saying that destiny does not exist, he is saying that it is politics. What makes Napoleon's *grand mot* so difficult is that it makes the meaning of *destiny* opaque. Napoleon challenges us to consider what *destiny* might mean in a world where the mythological meaning (the oracles, prophecies, oaths, and curses of the melodramatic Schicksalsstücke) no longer make sense. Freud's grand phrase resonates with the complexity and irony of Napoleon's original saying. A slightly tongue-in-cheek invocation of Napoleon's "politics is destiny," Freud's "anatomy is destiny" invites us to think about what *destiny* might mean in a modern, demythologized world. Just as Napoleon did not mean to say that politics belongs to a sphere unreachable by human agency, Freud probably did not mean to say that the *Diktats* of anatomy inexorably override human agency and choice.

1912: ANATOMY AND HUMAN SEXUALITY

Turning now to the contexts in which Freud's "anatomy is destiny" occurs, the first and most striking thing to be noted is that in 1912 he uses it to back up a claim about sexuality in general, whereas in 1924 the same phrase is invoked to make a point about sexual difference. Here is the phrase from 1912 quoted in its context (I apologize for quoting at such length, but if we are to grasp Freud's thought here we have to read his words carefully):

> The excremental is all too intimately and inseparably bound up with the sexual; the position of the genitals—*inter urinas et faeces*—remains the decisive and unchanging factor. *One might say here, varying a well-known saying of the great Napoleon: "Anatomy is destiny."* The genitals themselves have not taken part in the development of the human body in the direction of beauty: they have remained animal, and thus love, too, has remained in essence just as animal as it ever was. The instincts of love are hard to educate; education of them achieves now too much, now too little. What civilization aims at making out of them seems unattainable except at the price of a sensible loss of pleasure; the persistence of the impulses that could not be made use of can be detected in sexual activity in the form of non-satisfaction.
>
> Thus we may perhaps be forced to become reconciled to the idea that it is quite impossible to adjust the claims of the sexual instincts to the demands of civilization; that in consequence of its cultural development renunciation and suffering, as well as the danger of extinction in the remotest future, cannot be avoided by the human race. This gloomy prognosis rests, it is true, on the single conjecture that the non-satisfaction that goes with civilization is the necessary consequence of certain peculiarities which the sexual instinct has assumed under the pressure of culture. The very incapacity of the sexual instinct to yield complete satisfaction as soon as it submits to the first demands of civilization becomes the source, however, of the noblest cultural achievements which are brought into being by ever more extensive sublimation of its instinctual components. For what motive would men have for putting sexual instinctual forces to other uses if, by any distribution of those forces, they could obtain fully satisfying pleasure?[16]

These paragraphs are written in order to back up a claim just made in the previous paragraph. At stake here is nothing less than one of Freud's most famous and important claims about sexuality: "It is my belief that, however strange it may sound, we must reckon with the possibility that something in the nature of the sexual instinct itself is unfavourable to the realization of complete satisfaction" (188–89). This sentence, much loved by deconstructionists and other postmodern readers of Freud, is central to the psychoanalytic understanding of sexuality. Freud is here sounding a warning to all those who wish to believe that it is possible simply to "liberate" human sexuality from the shackles of repression. Sexuality is not a strong libidinous stream forced to deviate from its original, inborn, and healthy course by the repressive forces of civilization. Rather, Freud is saying, there is no such thing as pure or unthwarted human sexuality. Even in the most benign social setting, conflict and displacement will be inherent in all forms of human sexual expression. None of this means that all human beings are likely to be equally sexually conflicted, or sexually conflicted in exactly the same way, in this or in any other society.

In the part of the essay just preceding the quoted passage, Freud gives two reasons for the peculiarly self-thwarting nature of sexuality. First, he explains, there is the fact that any adult object choice is "never any longer the original object but only a surrogate for it" (189). (The original love object is the mother or the father.) This, he adds, often leads to the choice of "an endless series of substitutive objects none of which . . . brings full satisfaction" (189). Second, there is the fact that the sexual drive has had to repress a number of its original components. The most important of these is the coprophiliac aspects of the drive. A coprophiliac, we may recall, is someone who exhibits an undue interest in feces and defecation. Although we quickly learn to repress our coprophilic tendencies, they still lurk in a more or less remote corner of our psyche. This sets up a conflict: our civilized superego tells us to love what is clean, pure, and beautiful, whereas our lower instincts still take an interest in the ugly, the dark, and the dirty. This, Freud stresses, is an effect of our anatomy: "The excremental is all too intimately bound up with the sexual; the position of the genitals—*inter urinas et faeces*—remains the decisive and unchanging factor. One might say here, varying a well-known saying of the great Napoleon: 'Anatomy is destiny'" (189).

On the evidence of the quoted passages, it would seem that if anatomy is destiny, it is destiny in a peculiar way: what anatomy—the fact that the genitals are located where they are—seems to guarantee, without fail, is psychic conflict. Yet Freud is explicit that it is human civilization, the fact that every known human society socializes its children, that makes such psychic conflict inevitable. Freud always stressed that because the human baby is born prematurely (he means: born in a state of helplessness, before it can manage on its own), it is destined to interact with others.[17] Or in other words: our biology destines us to become social beings. Freud's thought here is strikingly similar to that of Maurice Merleau-Ponty, who declares, "Man is a historical idea, and not a natural species." Merleau-Ponty is not trying to deny that the body is natural; rather, his point is that it is our nature to be historical beings, just as Freud seems to be saying that it is our nature to be social creatures.[18]

This passage makes it clear that anatomy only becomes destiny in the necessary and inevitable process of bringing up children. (The word translated as "education" in the English text is *Erziehung*, which means upbringing in a wide sense, not just formal education.) It should be clear, moreover, that Freud is not suggesting that all human beings will experience sexuality in the same way or have the same sexual conflicts and problems. After all, Dora, Little Hans, and the Rat Man, three patients whose case studies were published by Freud well before 1912, had spectacularly different symptoms. The passage shows that anatomy is only one element that contributes to our psychic conflicts. Insofar as we all share the same bodily structure, however, it may be said to constitute something like the inescapable background of our choices and acts.[19]

The meaning of Freud's "anatomy is destiny" seems to be that our anatomy and our biological needs will make psychic conflict inevitable. Just as we all have to die, we will all suffer from psychic conflicts. For Freud, there is no such thing as conflict-free, unambivalent human sexuality or a homogenous, unconflicted human psyche. This is hardly a theory that denies human freedom and agency or overlooks the difference between human beings. Freud believes neither that all psychic conflicts will be of the same kind or have the same degree of severity, nor that it is impossible to free oneself from the more severe effects of psychic conflict through psychoanalytic therapy and life-changing experiences.[20] Neither the specific kind of psychic conflicts that will arise nor the meaning and importance they will acquire in any given person's life can be inferred from human anatomy.

In 1912 "anatomy is destiny" means that the fact of having a human body is bound to have conflictual consequences for the human psyche. To say this is not at all the same thing as to say that biological facts ought to ground social norms. On my reading of their works, radical antideterminists such as Beauvoir and Merleau-Ponty believe much the same thing. What Freud reveals here is not his biological determinism but rather his deep-rooted pessimism about the possibility of human happiness.

1924: THE FEMINIST DEMAND

In Freud's essay "The Dissolution of the Oedipus Complex" (1924), the phrase "anatomy is destiny" is placed in a very different context. The question is no longer about human sexuality in general but about sexual difference. Freud has just explained how little boys commonly overcome the Oedipus complex. Again I am obliged to quote at length:

> The process which has been described refers, as has been expressly said, to male children only. How does the corresponding development take place in little girls?
> At this point our material—for some imcomprehensible reason—becomes far

more obscure and full of gaps. The female sex, too, develops an Oedipus complex, a super-ego and a latency period. May we also attribute a phallic organization and a castration complex to it? The answer is in the affirmative; but these things cannot be the same as they are in boys. Here the feminist demand for equal rights for the sexes does not take us far, for the morphological distinction is bound to find expression in differences of psychical development. *"Anatomy is Destiny,"* *to vary a saying of Napoleon's.* The little girl's clitoris behaves just like a penis to begin with; but, when she makes a comparison with a playfellow of the other sex, she perceives that she has "come off badly" and she feels this as a wrong done to her and as a ground for inferiority. For a while still she consoles herself with the expectation that later on, when she grows older, she will acquire just as big an appendage as the boy's. Here the masculinity complex of women branches off. A female child, however, does not understand her lack of a penis as being a sex character; she explains it by assuming that at some earlier date she had possessed an equally large organ and had then lost it by castration. She seems not to extend this inference from herself to other, adult females, but, entirely on the lines of the phallic phase, to regard them as possessing large and complete—that is to say, male—genitals. The essential difference thus comes about that the girl accepts castration as an accomplished fact, whereas the boy fears the possibility of its occurrence.

The fear of castration being thus excluded in the little girl, a powerful motive also drops out for the setting-up of a super-ego and for the breaking-off of the infantile genital organization. In her, far more than in the boy, these changes seem to be the result of upbringing and of intimidation from outside which threatens her with a loss of love.

From a feminist perspective, this passage is packed with many of Freud's most dubious ideas. Here we find the image of woman as the dark continent, as an obscure and fragmented site where psychological exploration loses its way, and the belief that women regularly suffer from a "masculinity complex" just because they do not have a penis. Here, too, is the conviction that the founding trauma for little girls is the experience of *seeing* the penis of their little brothers or playmates and that little girls know themselves to be castrated. It is difficult to imagine a more incriminating context for Freud's (in)famous claim about anatomy.

In this short essay I cannot discuss the extremely complex subject of what Freud's theory of femininity actually is and what questions he thinks it answers. What I can show, however, is that whatever the trouble with Freud's understanding of women may be, the source of the problem does not necessarily have anything to do with the phrase "anatomy is destiny." Let me put this more clearly: even if we assume that Freud is wrong about penis envy, and about little girls' reactions to their brother's penis, this doesn't prove that Freud is wrong to assume that bodily sexual differences will produce psychological differences. He may be mistaken both about what these differences actually are and how they come about without being wrong in his underlying assumption that as a result of biological and anatomical sexual difference, *some* psychological sexual differences will arise. And none of this means that he will *have to* take a normative view of sexual difference. Even if we think that Freud does end up making normative and normalizing declarations about what a woman should be like (and I shall leave open the question of whether he does or not), this is not a compulsory consequence of the belief that in general, anatomical differences will give rise to psychological or psychosexual differences. The two questions I am going to focus on here, then, are fairly narrow: I want to ask whether this general assumption must be unacceptable to feminists and whether it makes Freud a biological determinist.

It may look as if I am dragging feminism into the argument here. Why not just subsume the question of Freud's compatibility with feminism under that of biological determinism? After all, contemporary feminists detest biological determinism, so if Freud is a biological determinist, further arguments will be moot. But here I am only following the letter of Freud's text. Let us look once more at the words that lead up to the crucial phrase: "but these things cannot be the same as they are in boys. Here the feminist demand for equal rights for the sexes does not take us far, for the morphological distinction is bound to find expression in differences of psychical development. 'Anatomy is Destiny,' to vary a saying of Napoleon's." What is it that pushes Freud to mention equal rights for the sexes in the very sentence where he sets out a theory of sexual difference? Why does he feel the need ironically to dismiss the "feminist demand" as irrelevant to his theory? And if he thinks it is irrelevant, why bring the feminist demand into this at all?

I shall consider two possible answers. Perhaps Freud chose to address the issue of feminism because he wanted to fend off accusations of social conservatism. He may have imagined that his theory of sexual difference would be unpopular with women, who would accuse him of being a reactionary antifeminist. This would have been an uneasy position for Freud, who always encouraged women to train as doctors and analysts and who was liberal and radical on many social issues, particularly those concerning sexuality and sexual practices. Against such a background, the reference to the feminists' demands may be read as Freud's attempt to stress that his theory has no relevance for feminist politics at all.

On this reading, Freud's sentence ("here the feminist demand for equal rights for the sexes does not take us far") means that the feminist demand has *no bearing* on what Freud has to say about biological and psychological sexual differences. But would the reverse also be true? Would he also gladly concede that claims about biological sexual difference have no bearing on the feminist demand for equal social rights? Feminists could then proceed with their political agitation regardless of what Freud has to say about sexual difference. Compressed and unclear as it is, Freud's reference to feminism could then be read as an attempt to *deny that biological facts ground social norms.* Such a denial is the sine qua non for effective opposition to biological determinism, and it is a position shared by the great majority of feminist theorists today.

But let us consider the alternative. What if Freud does intend to dismiss the feminist demand as impossibly unrealistic? His casual juxtaposition of the feminist demand for equal rights with his own theory of sexual difference certainly makes it look as if the misguided feminists must be denying the obvious. Does Freud think that the "feminist demand" is based on a fundamental misrecognition? That if only feminists would realize that men and women are not physically identical, they would give up their demands for equality? The major problem with this reading is that it sounds silly. Could Freud really have believed that feminists had not noticed that men have penises and women do not? Or that too much feminism would turn women into men? The term "equal rights for the sexes" clearly situates the feminist demand on the social level. The German phrase "Gleichberechtigung der Geschlechter" also makes it clear that Freud is speaking of equal *status* or *rights,* and not about bodies.[22] Most likely, Freud was simply trying to be witty. Yet, as he would be the first to acknowledge, it is often in our lame attempts at jokes that we reveal our most important unconscious investments.

Whether Freud was trying to be funny or not, his remark is extraordinarily revealing. What is at stake here, again, is the question of the relationship between a claim about social and political rights and a claim about physiological and psychological differences. As mentioned before, biological determinists believe that biology grounds social norms and that sooner or later biological differences will express themselves in the form of social differences. But as soon as we deny that there is a necessary relationship between human biology and social organization, we can cheerfully accept that there are biological differences between men and women without believing that this gives us grounds for organizing society in an unjust and unegalitarian way. This was Simone de Beauvoir's view in *The Second Sex:* "In truth a society is not a species. . . . Its ways and customs cannot be deduced from biology, for individuals are never abandoned to their nature; rather they obey that second nature which is custom, in which the desires and fears that express their ontological attitude are reflected. . . . To repeat once more: physiology cannot ground any values; rather the facts of biology take on the values that the existent bestows upon them."[23]

"Here the feminist demand for equal rights does not take us far." There is a slight but unmistakable animosity in Freud's tone here. The attempted witty aside dissolves into aggression. If we assume for a moment that my most antideterminist reading of the passage is right and that Freud is saying that our views on social justice are irrelevant to our understanding of biological sexual differences and, conversely, that biological sexual differences cannot ground our views on how to organize society, he is certainly not a biological determinist. Yet none of this would make him a feminist. Sexists may well be opposed to biological determinism: all they need to do is to claim that the gender ideology they wish to promote is the inevitable result of social construction or, alternatively, of God's plan for mankind. The animosity in his tone gives me the impression that Freud wishes to castigate the feminists of his day for underestimating the psychological importance of biological sexual differences. He may also believe that the logic of the feminists' arguments lays them open to the accusation that they do want women to be like men. Although we may disagree with such an assessment of feminism in the 1920s, we should realize that this is a critique of "equality feminism" that remains extremely common in contemporary feminist theory. Few theorists, for example, have been so frequently accused by other feminists of being "male-identified" and of wanting women to be like men as Simone de Beauvoir, always invoked as the prime example of "equality feminism."[24]

I want to explain here why I think it is conceptually confusing and politically misleading to oppose a "feminism of equality" to a "feminism of difference," first because it is possible that Freud himself bases his offhand remark about feminism on this very confusion, and because contemporary feminist responses to Freud tend to be influenced by this opposition. Usually, "equality feminism" is defined as a feminism committed to the struggle for social equality between the sexes. Very often, however, the word *social* is left out of the definition. Thus Luce Irigaray, famous for her psychoanalytically based "difference feminism," writes that her own feminism "has gone beyond simply a quest for equality between the sexes."[25] She then accuses certain unnamed equality feminists of genocide, on the grounds that they want to eradicate sexual difference. On Irigaray's account, then, if equality feminists had their way, they would be responsible for greater crimes against humanity than the Nazis:

> To demand equality as women is, it seems to me, a mistaken expression of a real objective. The demand to be equal presupposes a point of comparison. To whom or to

what do women want to be equalized? To men? To a salary? To a public office? To what standard? Why not to themselves?

. . .Women's exploitation is based upon sexual difference; its solution will come only through sexual difference. Certain modern tendencies, certain feminists of our time, make strident demands for sex to be neutralized. This neutralization, if it were possible, would mean the end of the human species. The human species is divided into *two genders* which ensure its production and reproduction. To wish to get rid of sexual difference is to call for a genocide more radical than any form of destruction there has ever been in History. What is important, on the other hand, is to define the values of belonging to a gender, valid for each of the two genders. It is vital that a culture of the sexual, as yet nonexistent, be elaborated, with each sex being respected.[26]

Irigaray's wildly exaggerated account brings out the fatal consequences of assuming that there is a real opposition between a feminism of equality and one of difference. She takes for granted that the word *equality* either must be meaningless ("equal to what?") or must mean biological and psychosexual "neutralization" of both sexes. That people using the word might want a fair and just organization of society so as to ensure that no one sex is unfairly favored over another seems to her unthinkable. That such a social organization will have to take biological facts such as female pregnancy into account is obvious. There is no equal right to education, for instance, unless it is equally possible for teenage fathers and teenage mothers to go to school. The right to maternity leave for anyone who is pregnant and gives birth (and so far, this still means women) is unproblematically accepted as part of equality feminism throughout Europe. Only on the most abstract concept of equality would it be possible to think of maternity leave as logically incompatible with the demand for social equality for women.[27]

There is some conceptual confusion here. As Rita Felski has reminded us, the opposite of difference is identity (or sameness), and the opposite of equality is inequality.[28] No concept of social equality that I know of requires the relevant parties to be identical. Yet this thought forms the basis for Luce Irigaray's unbridled polemics against equality feminism: against her own vision of a rich culture of sexual difference she posits a childless and sexless culture of identical androgynes. According to her picture one would have to be mad to wish for anything like equality between the sexes. The mythological opposition between a feminism of equality and a feminism of difference is based on an unjustified slippage between different concepts so that *equality* is taken to mean identity and *difference* is taken to be an absolute social value rather than a relational term.

Yet, someone is likely to ask, are there not real differences between the kind of feminism espoused by Simone de Beauvoir and that embraced by Luce Irigaray? How do we account for those? There are real differences between the two thinkers, but they are not well explained by positing an opposition between *equality* and *difference*. First of all, it is quite absurd to believe, as Irigaray pretends to do, that so-called equality feminists never discovered sexual difference or, that having discovered it, they then spend the rest of their lives wishing that women were men. I don't know any feminist who denies that sexual differences exist, and I doubt that Freud knew any either. Conflicts in feminist theory arise over the origin and value of current sexual differences, not over their existence. The conflict between so-called equality and difference feminists have to do with their different social visions and values, not with their understanding of biological facts. As Simone de Beauvoir teaches us: our politics is justified by our values, and our values are not given in nature. As long as we deny that biology grounds social norms, no genetic or biological discovery will prevent us from founding society on such values as freedom, equality, and solidarity, if that is what we wish to do. The difficult question of how concretely to implement such values in a way that upholds rather than undermines them cannot be solved by reference to an abstract principle, be it one of difference or equality.

The real difference between Beauvoir and Irigaray is not that one accepts psychosexual and biological sexual difference and the other does not. Beauvoir refuses to define *woman* once and for all. In so doing she refuses to engage in what Nancy Bauer has called "untethered metaphysics."[29] She is also highly critical of efforts to generalize (and thereby reify) any concept of "femininity." Since her most fundamental social and individual value is freedom, Beauvoir's feminism should rightly be referred to as a "feminism of freedom." Irigaray, by contrast, does not hesitate to define woman (as the sex which is not one, excluded from the symbolic order by the specular logic of phallogocentric patriarchy) and is quite convinced that it is necessary to found a culture permeated by sexual difference such as she herself theorizes it. For her, *difference* is a social and individual value, not simply a relational term.[30]

We now have two options: either Freud thinks that the demand for social equality between men and women conflicts with a properly psychoanalytic understanding of sexual difference, or he believes that the two have no direct bearing on each other. If the former is the case, Irigaray would be his true inheritor. If the latter is the case, he might think of bodily sexual difference as something like a situation (I elaborate briefly on this concept below), and he would have more in common with Beauvoir than with Irigaray. I am reluctant to settle this question here. Not because I think there is anything wrong with clear answers, but because only a more extensive investigation of Freud's texts about femininity and sexual difference would provide sufficient evidence to resolve the question. Resolving it would mean either coming down on one side or the other or being able to specify exactly why the question of the relations among biological sexual difference, psychological sexual difference, and social norms remain deeply ambiguous in Freud's texts.

1924: THE MORPHOLOGICAL DISTINCTION

I turn now to the second aspect of the sentence that occupies us here: "for the morphological distinction is bound to find expression in differences of psychical development. 'Anatomy is Destiny,' to vary a saying of Napoleon's," Freud writes. The different genital configuration will express itself in psychic differences, he claims. Once the question of what this has to do with equal rights is left aside, both Beauvoir and Irigaray would agree with this view, which in itself is neither particularly new nor particularly controversial in feminist theory. The question is whether Freud believes that certain psychic differences will occur with *necessity* in *all* women and men. Another question is whether he believes that the psychological differences produced by "morphology" also constitute some kind of *socially normative* femininity. The alternative would be to consider Freud's reference to "destiny" as an effort to consider the genital and other sexual differences between male and female bodies as a *situation* or a *background* on which further differences may or may not develop. This would be in keeping with his use of the word in the 1912 text.

This view would claim support from the fact that both at the end of this passage and in "Some Psychical Consequences of the Anatomical Distinction Between the Sexes" (1925), Freud stresses that it is the little girl's discovery of the Other, and the gaze of the Other on the little girl, that sets in motion the whole process of sexual differentiation that occurs in society.[31] In his case study "On the Psychogenesis of a Case of Homosexuality in a Woman" (1920), he writes that homosexuality is the outcome of the interaction of many elements:

> The mystery of homosexuality is . . . by no means so simple as it is commonly depicted in popular expositions. . . . It is instead a question of three sets of characteristics, namely—
>
> Physical sexual characters
> (physical hermaphroditism)
>
> Mental sexual characters
> (masculine or feminine attitude)
>
> Kind of object-choice

which, up to a certain point, vary independently of one another, and are met with in different individuals in manifold permutations.[32]

Here Freud sounds positively postmodern. Sex and gender (physical and mental sexual characters) may vary relatively independently of each other, and sexual object-choice may vary relatively independently of sex and gender. It is difficult to see how anyone capable of writing this passage could be a biological determinist. On this evidence, it looks, rather, as if Freud thinks of the sexually different body as constantly interacting with its environment, and particularly with other people whose reactions to us are, among other things, determined by our sex (or, to be precise, by the sex they think we are). In short, there are good reasons to believe that Freud never thought that biological sexual differences with necessity caused any specific psychosexual result. Freud may be using the word *destiny* in much the same way in 1924 and in 1912.

In the most famous passage of *The Second Sex,* Simone de Beauvoir says something similar, and she is no biological determinist:

> One is not born, but rather becomes, a woman [*femme*]. No biological, psychological, or economic destiny defines the figure that the human female [*la femelle humaine*] acquires in society; it is civilization as a whole that develops this product, intermediate between male and eunuch, which one calls feminine [*féminin*]. Only the mediation of another [*autrui*] can establish an individual as an *Other*. In so far as he exists for himself, the child would not be able to understand himself as sexually differentiated. In girls as in boys the body is first of all the radiation of a subjectivity, the instrument that accomplishes the comprehension of the world: it is through the eyes, the hands, and not through the sexual parts that children apprehend the universe.[33]

For Beauvoir, the body is our medium for having a world in the first place. We perceive the world through the body, and when the world reacts to our body in a more or less ideologically oppressive way, we react to the world. Our subjectivity is constituted through such ongoing, open-ended interaction between ourselves and the world. We constantly make something of what the world makes of us. This view considers the body—and not only the sexual different body but the sick body, the athletic body, the aging body, the black body, the white body, and so on—of fundamental importance. It is perhaps the fundamental ingredient in the makeup of our subjectivity. Yet subjectivity can never be reduced to some bodily feature or other.

Unlike Freud, Beauvoir explicitly denies that any fate (*destin*) determines what a woman is to be like. She stresses the similarities between the bodies of little girls and little boys, but she never denies that sexual differences exist or that they play a role in society. Otherwise, the newborn female (*la femelle humaine*) would simply not become a woman (*une femme*). For Beauvoir as for Freud (and Lacan, whom Beauvoir quotes in the next few pages), sexual difference is at once produced by anatomical and biological factors and by the intervention of other people (the Other), who cannot help but be the bearers of specific social values.

The major difference between Beauvoir and Freud is not to be found in their general understanding of the relationship between the body and subjectivity. They both think it is contingent—that is, not necessary, but not arbitrary either—and they both stress the fundamental role played by others, by the agents of society or "civilization." The difference is that Beauvoir is far more aware of the historically relative nature of any given set of social norms than Freud. Although sexual difference will always be with us, Beauvoir sees no reason to assume that the female sexual specificity will always be perceived as more salient, more profound, more far-reaching, more socially significant than male sexual specificity.

Freud, on the contrary, has a tendency to think of male sexuality as fairly easy to investigate and to cast female sexual difference as an unsolvable mystery, the bedrock on which both the analytic process and psychosexual research eventually founder.[34] Freud's gloomy view of femininity could not be more different from Beauvoir's political optimism, her vision of a world in which there no longer would be any social norms regulating the correct presentations of "femininity" (or "masculinity," for that matter). Toward the end of *The Second Sex,* Beauvoir writes: "Once again, in order to explain her limitations it is woman's situation that must be invoked and not a mysterious essence; thus the future remains largely open. . . . The free woman is just being born."[35] Freud could not have written this. That sexual difference was taken to be mainly a question of women's difference in Freud's time is beyond dispute. Freud failed to see the historical relativity of this perception. In 1924, as at other times, he is guilty not of biological determinism but of a failure of political vision.

Joyce McDougall writes that psychoanalysis is a form of thought that attempts to understand the psychological consequences of three universal traumas: the fact that there are Others, the fact of sexual difference, and the fact of death.[36] Freud might have said that it is our destiny to have to find a way to coexist with others, to have to take up a position in relation to sexual difference, and to face death. To say so is not evidence of biological or any other kind of determinism.

Notes

I thank Peter Brooks for inviting me to participate in the conference "Whose Freud?" This chapter is a substantially revised and expanded version of the presentation I gave there. I also thank David Paletz and Hazel Rowley for commenting on earlier drafts of this chapter.

1. Geddes and Thomson, *Evolution of Sex*, 267. I discuss biological determinism in general and the work of Geddes and Thomson and W. K. Brooks in particular in "What Is a Woman? Sex, Gender and the Body in Feminist Theory," in my book *What Is a Woman? And Other Essays*.

2. Brooks, *Law of Heredity*, 263.

3. A fuller investigation of the status of the body in Freudian theory would have to consider many more texts by Freud. Of immediate relevance are: "Some Psychical Consequences of the Anatomical Distinction Between the Sexes" (1925), the case study entitled "Case of Homosexuality in a Woman" (1920), *Three Essays on Sexuality* (1905), and the unpublished "Project for a Scientific Psychology" (1895), as well as all the texts dealing with femininity.

4. Freud, "Über die allgemeinste Erniedrigung des Liebeslebens," 209.

5. Wierzbicka, *Semantics, Culture, and Cognition*, 80, 84. Her book makes a fascinating attempt to convey the different feel of apparently similar words in different languages, but I find her analysis of the English *fate* and *destiny* less subtle than the rest. According to her, *destiny* cannot mean something bad and inevitable, and therefore the more pessimistic meanings of *Schicksal* should never be translated as *destiny* (93). She also believes that in the usage of the twentieth century, at least, the English words *destiny* and *fate* are free of metaphysical implications (93) and that they have empiricist or positivistic overtones (93–94). I thank Robert A. Paul for sending me a copy of Wierzbicka's chapter.

6. I thank Judith Butler for reminding me of this important example of Freud's use of the word *Schicksal*.

7. This is how Freud describes his findings in "Instincts and Their Vicissitudes": "We may sum up by saying that the essential feature in the vicissitudes undergone by instincts [*die Triebschicksale*] lies in *the subjection of the instinctual impulses to the influences of the three great polarities that dominate mental life*. Of these three polarities we might describe that of activity–passivity as the *biological*, that of ego–external world as the *real*, and finally that of pleasure–unpleasure as the *economic* polarity" (140, emphasis in original). Freud here sees biology, understood as activity–passivity (in itself hardly a common understanding of biology), as only one among several factors working on the drives. It is difficult to see how this could be evidence of biological determinism.

8. The debate about whether *instinct* is a good translation of *Trieb* belongs in another context. See Bruno Bettelheim's *Freud and Man's Soul*, 103–7, for a scorching critique of *instinct* and a convincing defense of *drive*. It is interesting to note that even the first English translation of the paper, done in 1925 by C. M. Baines, also used the title "Instincts and Their Vicissitudes."

9. Bettelheim, *Freud and Man's Soul*, 105.

10. Freud, "Theme of the Three Caskets," 296.

11. Beauvoir's novel *All Men Are Mortal* (*Tous les hommes sont mortels*, 1945) portrays an immortal man slowly succumbing to debilitating depression because his immortality deprives his projects of all meaning.

12. Before writing this essay I had no idea what Napoleon said, nor did any of the friends and colleagues I asked about it. My efficient and creative research assistant, Christian Thorne, found the reference for me. To my surprise he reported that it was easy: all that

was required was to look "anatomy is destiny" up in a dictionary of quotations. The dictionary provides the page reference to Goethe's text. If it is this easy to find out what Freud's reference is, why hasn't it been more widely discussed by psychoanalytic and feminist critics concerned with Freud's phrase?

13. Goethe, *Autobiographische Einzelheiten,* 546 (my translation). The destiny plays (*die Schicksalsstücke*) were Gothic melodramas, popular at the end of the eighteenth century.

14. Here it has to be acknowledged that since Goethe and Napoleon must have been speaking French together, what Napoleon in all probability actually said was "la politique est le destin." But this can have no bearing on the question of what Freud meant, since he is quoting Goethe's German text. Nothing indicates that Freud particularly wanted his readers to think of the French language in this context.

15. Flaubert, *Madame Bovary,* 104 (my translation).

16. Freud, "Debasement," 189–90 (emphasis added); hereafter cited in text.

17. Freud also thought that infantile helplessness was the psychical origin of religious idea; see *The Future of an Illusion* (1927).

18. Merleau-Ponty, *Phenomenology of Perception,* 170. Beauvoir stresses the similarity between Freud and Merleau-Ponty precisely by quoting Freud's important sentence: "'Anatomy is destiny,' said Freud and this phrase is echoed by that of Merleau-Ponty: 'The body is generality'" (*Second Sex,* 46). I discuss Merleau-Ponty's view in relation to that of Simone de Beauvoir in my essay "What Is a Woman?"

19. In *The Second Sex,* Simone de Beauvoir develops the idea of the sexed body as a background (she also, more famously, considers it a situation). See my "What Is a Woman?" for a discussion of the body as a situation, and "I Am a Woman" (in the same volume) for a discussion of the body as background.

20. Between 1911 and 1914, Freud wrote intensively on the technique of psychoanalytic therapy. Some of his best-known papers on analytic practice, including his first sustained discussions of transference, date from this period (see the section "Papers on Technique," in *S.E.* 12).

21. Freud, "Dissolution of the Oedipus Complex," 177–78.

22. "Die feministische Forderung nach Gleichberechtigung der Geschlechter trägt hier nicht weit, der morphologische Unterschied muß sich in Verschiedenheiten der psychischen Entwicklung aüssern" (*Studienausgabe* 5: 249). I note that Bettelheim's critique of the *Standard Edition*'s translation of "Unterschied" as "distinction," quoted in note 31 below, also applies here.

23. Beauvoir, *Second Sex,* 36. The translation is modified from the original; see *Le deuxième sexe,* 1: 76. Translation modified.

24. "Beauvoir's final message is that sexual difference should be eradicated and women must become like men," Tina Chanter writes in a book devoted to Luce Irigaray (*Ethics of Eros,* 76).

25. Irigaray, *Je, tu, nous,* 11.

26. Ibid., 12.

27. Such an abstract concept of equality is quite common in the United States, where the right to maternity leave is still taken by some to constitute differential treatment. One example may be found in the conservative feminist Elizabeth Fox-Genovese's book *Fem-*

inism Without Illusions, where she argues that equality feminists are guilty of a logical mistake when they demand equal rights *and* the right to maternity leave.

28. Felski, "Doxa of Difference," 15.

29. Bauer, "Recounting Women," 53.

30. The subtitle of *Je, tu, nous,* after all, is *Toward a Culture of Difference.* This book provides some revealing glimpses of Irigaray's concrete social and legal vision.

31. Bruno Bettelheim is unhappy with the English title of this essay. In German the essay is called "Einige psychische Folgen des anatomischen Geschlechtsunterschieds." Bettelheim writes: "Freud discusses the consequences of the anatomical *differences* between the sexes . . . but the translators speak instead of a *distinction. . . . Webster's* discriminates between 'difference' and 'distinction' as follows: 'different, applied to things which are not alike, implies individuality (three *different* doctors) or contrast; distinct, as applied to two or more things, stresses that each has a different identity and is unmistakably separate from the others.' If 'difference' indeed stresses contrast and individuality in what is basically likeness (as the example of three different doctors implies), then it is preferable to 'distinction' in the context of this essay and its title" (*Freud and Man's Soul,* 97).

32. Freud, "On the Psychogenesis of a Case of Homosexuality," 170.

33. Beauvoir, *Second Sex,* 267. The translation is much amended from the original; see *Le deuxième sexe,* 2: 13.

34. In his very late essay "Analysis Terminable and Interminable" (1937), Freud writes that *the repudiation of femininity* is a biological fact and the "bedrock" on which the analytic process founders: "We often have the impression that with the wish for a penis and the masculine protest we have penetrated through all the psychological strata and have reached bedrock, and that thus our activities are at an end. This is probably true, since, for the psychical field, the biological field does in fact play the part of the underlying bedrock. The repudiation of femininity can be nothing else than a biological fact, a part of the great riddle of sex" (252). This is an extremely obscure passage. In what sense is the "repudiation of femininity" a biological fact? I quote it here simply to show how difficult it is to reach a clear understanding of Freud's theory of femininity.

35. Beauvoir, *Second Sex,* 714–15.

36. In *The Many Faces of Eros,* McDougall writes: "The child's discovery of the difference between the sexes is matched in traumatic quality by the earlier discovery of otherness and the later revelation of the inevitability of death. Some individuals never resolve any of these universal traumas, and all of us deny them to some degree in the deeper recesses of our minds—where we are blessedly free to be omnipotent, bisexual, and immortal!" (xv).

Works Cited

Note: References to Freud's German text are to the *Studienausgabe,* edited by Alexander Mitscherlich, Angela Richards, and James Strachey (Frankfurt: Fischer Taschenbuch, 1982), 10 vols. plus an unnumbered supplementary volume; hereafter cited as *Studienausgabe.*

Bauer, Nancy. "Recounting Woman: Simone de Beauvoir and Feminist Philosophy." Ph.D. diss., Cambridge, Mass.: Harvard University, 1997.

Beauvoir, Simone de. *All Men Are Mortal.* Translated by Leonard M. Friedman. Cleveland, Ohio: World Publishing, 1955. [Originally published as *Tous les hommes sont mortels.* 2 vols. Paris: Gallimard, 1946.]

———. *The Second Sex.* Translated by H. M. Parshley. New York: Vintage Books, 1989. [Originally published as *Le deuxième sexe.* 2 vols. Paris: Gallimard, 1949.]

Bettelheim, Bruno. *Freud and Man's Soul.* New York: Knopf, 1983.

Brooks, W. K. *The Law of Heredity: A Study of the Cause of Variation, and the Origin of Living Organisms.* Baltimore: John Murphy, 1883.

Chanter, Tina. *Ethics of Eros: Irigaray's Re-Writing of the Philosophers.* New York: Routledge, 1995.

Felski, Rita. "The Doxa of Difference." *Signs* 23, no. 1 (1997): 1–21.

Flaubert, Gustave. *Madame Bovary.* 1857. Paris: Le Livre de Poche, 1972.

Fox-Genovese, Elizabeth. *Feminism Without Illusions: A Critique of Individualism.* Chapel Hill: University of North Carolina Press, 1991.

Freud, Sigmund. "Analysis Terminable and Interminable." 1937. *S.E.* 23: 209–53.

———. "The Dissolution of the Oedipus Complex." 1924. *S.E.* 19: 173–82. [Translation of "Der Untergang des Ödipuskomplexes." *Studienausgabe* 5: 243–51.]

———. *The Future of an Illusion.* 1927. *S.E.* 21: 1–56.

———. "Instincts and Their Vicissitudes." 1915. *S.E.* 14: 109–40. [Translation of "Triebe und Triebschicksale." *Studienausgabe* 3: 75–102.]

———. "Project for a Scientific Psychology." 1895. *S.E.* 1: 283–387.

———. "The Psychogenesis of a Case of Homosexuality in a Woman." 1920. *S.E.* 18: 147–72.

———. "Some Psychical Consequences of the Anatomical Distinction Between the Sexes." 1925. *S.E.* 19: 241–60.

———. "The Theme of the Three Caskets." 1913. *S.E.* 12: 289–303.

———. *Three Essays on Sexuality.* 1905. *S.E.* 7: 125–243.

———. "On the Universal Tendency to Debasement in the Sphere of Love." 1912. *S.E.* 11: 177–90. [Translation of "Über die allgemeinste Erniedrigung des Liebeslebens." *Studienausgabe* 5: 197–209.]

Geddes, Patrick, and J. Arthur Thomson. *The Evolution of Sex.* London: Walter Scott, 1889.

Goethe, Johann Wolfgang von. "Autobiographische Einzelheiten." In *Autobiographische Schriften,* Gesammelte Werke 10: 529–47. Hamburg: Christian Wegner Verlag, 1959.

Irigaray, Luce. *Je, tu, nous: Toward a Culture of Difference.* Translated by Alison Martin. New York: Routledge, 1993.

McDougall, Joyce. *The Many Faces of Eros.* New York: Norton, 1995.

Merleau-Ponty, Maurice. *Phenomenology of Perception.* Translated by Colin Smith. London: Routledge, 1962.

Moi, Toril. *What Is a Woman? And Other Essays.* Oxford: Oxford University Press, 1999.

Wierzbicka, Anna. *Semantics, Culture, and Cognition: Universal Human Concepts in Culture-Specific Configurations.* New York: Oxford University Press, 1992.

Bridging the Gap Between
Two Scenes

Hubert Damisch

Several years ago I participated in a colloquium on the uses of psycho-analysis and Freudian models at the Hospital of La Salpêtrière in Paris: the place where Freud attended the neurologist Jean-Martin Charcot's lessons in 1885–86.[1] I lectured on what I called "The Image in the Picture," speaking about Freud's comments in the *Studies on Hysteria* on how, during the cure, images would return to the patient's mind through the process of description and, by the same token, soon dis-appear, as if they had been talked away. An interesting problem, and a puzzling one, for the historian of art: for how are we to deal with im-ages, with works of art, if the process of describing and interpreting them, of putting them into words, may cause them to disappear as im-ages to be seen, by being cast away in the mold of discourse?

After the lecture one of the organizers, the French analyst Daniel Widlöcher, asked me, "How is it that, as an art historian, you've become so interested in Freud and his writings?" On the spur of the moment, without thinking (I rarely think of myself as an "art historian"), I ca-sually replied that practicing art history may well have been a way for me to approach Freud and get access to his thought. To my great embarrassment, I then had to comment on this assertion, which was not easy then and still isn't. What I meant was that, in order simply to be able to *read* Freud, someone like me, who had not been exposed to analysis either as an analyst or as an analysand (or both), needed a kind of expertise, a proficiency, but also some critical experience and material that would be the equivalent of clinical experience and material.

The French philosopher Gilles Deleuze has explored the multiple connections between "critique" and "clinique."[2] My own experience, as critic, art historian, and philosopher (not to mention reader of Freud!), persuaded me that "critique" is never more interesting, never more convincing, never more farsighted, than when it tends and even drifts toward "clinique." And this holds true from the outset, from the minute one starts talking or writing about works of art, which implies bridging the gap between the verbal and nonverbal domains of experience. Simply describing a painting means putting or converting it into words, processing it through language, turning it into a symbolic object that would allow and even call for interpretation, a matter of discourse. But what is there before description in a work of art, "mute" as it is, that makes us talk, with the risk of "talking it away"—as it was the case in the cure of hysteria, when the young Doctor Freud had his patients "talk away" the images, pictures, and reminiscences they were suffering from (a process one of them called "chimney sweeping")?

Freud himself paralleled the study of hysteria to digging up the vestiges of an abandoned city, the walls of which are covered with half-erased inscriptions. But when dealing with paintings, one rarely falls upon inscriptions that would make them speak, as is the case with Nicolas Poussin's famous depiction of the Arcadian shepherds discovering a tomb inscribed *Et in Arcadia Ego.* No matter how historians make pictures speak, whether by referring to their context or by citing scriptural "sources," painting as such remains what classical aesthetics meant it to be: "mute poetry."

I would not push the comparison between the give-and-take that characterizes the analytical situation and the process of describing and interpreting a work of art too far. The main difference is that, during the cure, the analyst has to remain largely silent, whereas the art historian or critic can't avoid commenting or elaborating on—even mythicizing—"silence" in painting, and in poetry and literature, too. The real issue has to do with the kind of truth we are looking for when dealing with art and aesthetics in an analytical perspective. As far as art is concerned, bridging the nonverbal and the verbal domains doesn't aim at any therapeutic effect. But there is always the risk of escaping prematurely into the discourse of interpretation or the rhetorics of hermeneutics without paying sufficient attention to what, in the work itself, seems to defy description and calls for a different approach or treatment. The common feeling that there is more in a work of art than can be put into words, the suspicion that language and interpretation can be overvalued, may well be the index of a "resistance." But, if there is resistance, where are we to locate it: in the analyst or in the interpreter? in the work itself? or in the in-between, the interface where unconscious communication takes place through more or less free association?

Gilles Deleuze stated that "clinique" starts when the free exchanges that characterize "critique" come to a dead end. But we cannot freely dispose of a work of art. What we must do is learn, from the work itself, not how to read it but how to listen to it, as Paul Claudel put it beautifully in his book on Dutch painting, *L'Oeil écoute*. We need to learn how to listen *to* the works of art, as well as to learn, *from* them, how to deal *with* them, and in what terms and along what lines, which may differ according to the nature of the works, the place where they stand, and the various ways in which they operate.

In his last essay on technique, "Constructions in Analysis," published in 1937, when he was over eighty, Freud compares the analytical work to two completely different plays, two completely different *pièces,* as we say in French (in German, *zwei ganz verschiedenen Stücken*), being played on two separate stages or scenes (*auf zwei gesonderten Schauplätzen*).[3] He then opposes *construction* to *interpretation*. According to him, interpreting aims at no more than merging the two plays into one game, the one of language. Constructing aims at bridging the gap between the two stages, the two "scenes," the silent and the talking one. To quote the historian Peter Gay, no matter how one-sided it may be, the psychoanalytical relationship is always a dialogue—a dialogue in which muteness as well as visibility plays its part. This is what I, as a layman, had to learn from works of art, from working *with* them, before I could start to approach Freud, to read him, to listen to him as I already listened to art.

Notes

1. H. D., "L'image dans le tableau," in *Actualité des modèles freudiens: Langage, image, pensée,* edited by Pierre Fedida and Daniel Widlöcher, Colloque de la Revue Internationale de Psychopathologie (Paris: Presses Universitaire de Paris, 1995), 39–54.
2. Gilles Deleuze, *Critique et clinique* (Paris: Editions de Minuit, 1993).
3. Sigmund Freud, "Konstruktionen in der Analyse," *Gesammelte Werke,* vol. 16, 43–56. I comment on this passage at some length in a small book that is both an homage to Freud and a parody, *Un souvenir d'enfance par Piero della Francesca* (Paris: Seuil, 1997), 168–81.

Psychoanalysis as a Hermeneutic Science

Peter Loewenberg

Freud pioneered modes of comprehending life and texts on several levels at once. He was a pioneer in demonstrating that the linguistic signs of which a text is composed carry complex webs of associations to the contexts from which they emerged, thus communicating multiple and hidden significations to different listeners and readers. Freud was much more than a natural scientist—he always wished to be, and was, also a humanist.[1] In his "Autobiographical Study" Freud recalled that neither in his youth, "nor indeed in my later life, did I feel any particular predilection for the career of a doctor. I was moved, rather, by a sort of curiosity, which was, however, directed more towards human concerns than towards natural objects; nor had I grasped the importance of observation as one of the best means of gratifying it. My deep engrossment in the Bible story (almost as soon as I learned the art of reading) had, as I recognized much later, an enduring effect upon the direction of my interest."[2] On New Year's Day, 1896, less than three months after sending him the "Project for a Scientific Psychology," Freud wrote to the Berlin physician Wilhelm Fliess, "I see how, via the detour of medical practice, you are reaching your first ideal of understanding human beings as a physiologist, just as I most secretly nourish the hope of arriving, via these same paths, at my initial goal of philosophy."[3] The only public award Freud won was literary—the Goethe Prize of Frankfurt—which included the delivery of an address "illustrating his own inner relation to Goethe."[4] Throughout his life he engaged such social, political, moral, and philosophical issues as religion, war and peace, marriage, criminality, public sexual policy, and death. His writing is studded with references to classic and modern artists and artifacts, writers and literature, including Leonardo da Vinci, Michelangelo, Goethe, Shakespeare, Heinrich Heine, Fyodor Dostoyevsky, Henrik Ibsen, and others.

Freud created a general psychology that is based on the humanistic method— the study of a single case in all its richness, complexity, and ambiguity. What we know of Freud's view of the interpretation of texts comes from the *Traumdeutung* (Interpretation of Dreams) and his six case histories. Freud's cases do not read like clinical texts; he writes so well that they read like the best fiction. As Steven Marcus states in his critical treatment of the "Dora" case, "Freud is a great writer and . . . one of his major case histories is a great work of literature—that is to say it is both an outstanding creative and imaginative performance and an intellectual and cognitive achievement of the highest order."[5] No one ever said this of Hermann Helmholtz or Ernst Brücke. In fact, Freud's case histories are now more taught in university literature and humanities classes rather than in departments of psychology or psychiatry. He believed in the heuristic power of the single case history, arguing, "It might teach us everything, if we were only in a position to make everything out, and if we were not compelled by the inexperience of our own perception to content ourselves with a little."[6]

In the social sciences, following Clifford Geertz, this approach is termed "thick" or "deep" description, in which a single event, artifact, or ritual, such as a Balinese cock fight, is treated as a prism by which an entire culture with its kinship ties, systems of deference and obligation, family and gender relations, generational rivalries, religious beliefs, economic power, and political authority and leadership is exposed.[7] The individual case study is also the forum of the humanist who exfoliates one poem, text, artifact, incident, or document in its overdetermined depth to interpret a historical moment or an era and its sensibility. And this, in fact, is precisely what the psychoanalyst does—working in depth with one person to interpret discrete dreams, behaviors, symptoms, and private symbols to create a complex web of associations that dilate to a full life in its familial and sociocultural context.

For Freud each human being was unique—worthy of being respected, worked with, understood, and helped when in trouble. A charming example of Freud's concerned, personal follow-up in patient care is his 1892 case of "Fräulein Elizabeth von R.," who had pains in her legs and difficulty in walking. Following the treatment Freud, who did not as a habit attend Viennese balls, wrote: "In the spring of 1894 I heard that she was going to a private ball for which I was able to get an invitation, and I did not allow the opportunity to escape me of seeing my former patient whirl past in a lively dance."[8] He invited us all to understand that neurosis was universal; it has the dignity of being a unique compromise formation of situational and life conflict. "We have seen," he wrote, "that it is not scientifically feasible to draw a line of demarcation between what is psychically normal and abnormal."[9]

Psychoanalysis is a humanistic science, a hermeneutic science of meanings, in which two people together create a secure field for the exploration of the latent and least-understood meanings of fantasies, dreams, sexuality and gender, attachments and losses, interactions (including their dialogic encounter), behaviors, and life and death. Hermeneutics grew out of the techniques of philological research of the higher biblical criticism. The purpose of early modern biblical hermeneutics was to limit rather than to enhance the meaning of the Bible and thereby undermine superstition by applying reason. Psychoanalysis both limits, or decodes, the power of the irrational meaning of dreams, fantasies, and symptoms, and at the same time expands and develops their meanings by relating them to the themes and conflicts of a life in an open-ended hermeneutic, much as a humanist does with a text.[10] The psychoanalytic hermeneutic is more than philological hermeneutics because it reaches beyond conscious intention. We understand that distortions and omissions of perception and communication have a defensive function. We are keenly interested in, and focus our inquiry on, the conscious and unconscious motives for flaws, omissions, distortions, and misunderstandings. We wish the person to know *why* he or she practices self-deception.

By *hermeneutics* I mean an exegesis of meanings of a communication, sign, or behavior. To *interpret* means to say something about something, adding understanding of multiple and equivocal meanings. By *humanism* I mean, in the case of psychoanalysis, that its primary engagement is with human beings in their own right rather than as some function of natural science, the power of the state, or the greater glory of God. Psychoanalysis pursues the causal connections between the internal conditions of the person and the distortions of presenting "texts" and behaviors. By *text* I mean all types of messages and data presented by the analysand: verbal, behavioral action or inaction, character styles, and implicit or latent myths, symbols, and fantasies. Hermeneutics in psychoanalysis was there from the beginning, and it has equal, if not greater, relevance and legitimacy as the heritage of natural science; it is essential, fully integral to the psychoanalytic discipline. I venture that most practicing analysts are hermeneuticians without knowing it.

Freud was always a hermeneutician of dreams, patterning the interpretation of dreams after the hermeneutic model: "'Interpreting a dream implies assigning a 'meaning' to it."[11] Dreams for him denoted the metaphor of the Bible: "We have treated as Holy Writ what previous writers have regarded as an arbitrary improvisation."[12] He described his method as: "the *decoding* method, since it treats dreams as a kind of cryptography in which each sign can be translated into another sign having a known meaning."[13] Psychoanalysis *is* intrinsically interpretation and translation, and the problem of translation is coextensive with the problem of meaning. As Freud put it: "The interpretations made by psycho-analysis are first and foremost translations from an alien method of expression into the one familiar to us. When we interpret a dream we are simply translating a particular thought-content (the latent dream thoughts) from the 'language of dreams' into our waking speech."[14]

Psychoanalysis is a discipline of a new kind, a twentieth-century discipline, combining both self-reflection and science but basing itself on a unique and different process of inquiry than either the natural or the cultural sciences. "The psycho-analytic mode of thought," said Freud, "acts like a new instrument of research."[15] Psychoanalysis is, as Jürgen Habermas noted, "the only tangible example of a science incorporating methodological self-reflection."[16] Psychoanalysts make themselves the instrument of knowledge not by suppressing their subjectivity but by employing it. Freud made the point explicitly in contrast to the medical model: "A doctor suffering from disease of the lung or heart is not handicapped either in diagnosing or treating internal complaints; whereas the special conditions of analytic work do actually cause the analyst's own defects to interfere with his making a correct assessment of the state of things in his patient and reacting to them in a useful way."[17]

The clinical art of interpreting the preconscious and unconscious levels of the analysand's messages and productions is analogous to the literary critic's reading of the multiple levels of a text or the historian's interpretation of new meanings and new conjunctures of theory and evidence in previously familiar facts and data. The analyst's perception of these stimuli is as central and invaluable as the critic or reader's response in the humanistic disciplines. Just as the literary critic's primary resource is a cultivated sensibility, the psychoanalyst must employ his or her self-reflective countertransferences.

In writing about "decoding," Freud used the metaphor of geographic exploration: "the repressed is foreign territory to the ego—internal foreign territory—just as reality . . . is external foreign territory."[18] Analyst and analysand share a mutual journey of discovery in this internal foreign land, exploring the complexity of the natural and human wonders of this unique new world, the rediscovered landscape of the past and the unconscious.

Psychoanalysis by its method encourages reflection, and by its interpretations it reduces the realm and power of illusions and restores the fullness of formerly hidden, and now newly discovered and rediscovered, meanings. The analysis of dreams proves that the manifest content always also refers to latent meanings. Thus every dreamer is a poet with his or her private language, private archaeology, and esoteric ciphers. Analytic work is a labor of reappropriation—recapturing meaning of previously incoherent feelings and images through interpretation applied, not only to dreams, but to symptoms, fantasies, transferences, and behaviors. Freud, in a famous line evocative of *Faust II,* invoked the image of the Dutch redeeming land from the sea: "Where id was, there ego shall be. It is a work of culture—not unlike the draining of the Zuider Zee."[19] Psychoanalysis reduces the lies, disguises, and illusions of consciousness, makes defenses conscious, presents volition and options where previously there was only compulsion, and demystifies idealizations.

Hermeneutics offers the possibilities of ambiguity, reflection that integrates several interpretations, and double meanings, of living with opposed meanings (ambivalence), both of which may be consistent with a given situation. Just as a poem or a fictional text may be understood from many points of view, a symptom, dream, behavior, or fantasy may have more than one meaning.[20] The psychoanalyst, as does the humanist, seeks meanings at multiple levels of consciousness and in cultural, intellectual, political, gender, ethnic, and familial contexts. A person lives with the more or less satisfactory integration of feelings of love and hate—indeed, inevitably does both love and hate parents, spouses, children, friends, colleagues, analyst, and analysands.

Free association makes explicit a multiplicity of meanings. Any interpretation can be reversed and certainly improved upon. There is no exegesis without contesting. Psychoanalysis presumes a series of mutual interpretations, each of which is both completed and corrected by the following ones. New sublimations promote new meanings by mobilizing and redirecting energies originally invested in archaic figures. Meaning is created through successive encounters and interpretations in which the meaning of each interpretation is dependent on the working through of previous ones. The initial meaning must be seen as provisional and is not supressed or abandoned; it is retained, supplemented, finally surpassed. "What is offered," says Paul Ricoeur, "is a three-term relation, a figure with three heads: reflection, interpretation understood as restoration of meaning, interpretation understood as reduction of illusion."[21]

The authority of hermeneutic interpretation in both humanistic and clinical work is not the Freudian canon; rather, the exegesis is directed at interpreting the analysand's signs or texts by the standard of the internal logical coherence, confluence of evidence, and validation by the production of new evidence or insight by the analysand or reader. Hermeneutics allows the analysand, upon reworking early childhood and present traumas, to make his or her own the meaning that was previously alien to him. The proof Freud seeks for the analyst's offered "construction" is a hermeneutic proof—the analysand's verification by the production of new corroborative material. The analysand's confirmation is not taken at face value. Only the context of the self-formative analytic process has confirming power: "The 'Yes' has no value unless it is followed by indirect confirmations, unless the patient, immediately after his 'Yes,' produces new memories which complete and extend the construction."[22]

Freud's distinction between the unconscious and the preconscious was language, which is a human cultural construction, and therefore on the terrain of hermeneutics. The unconscious is preverbal instinctual primary process; the preconscious is formulated in language and subject to interpretation. As he said in "The Ego and the Id":

> The real difference between a *Ucs.* and a *PCs.* idea (thought) consists in this: that the former is carried out on some material which remains unknown, whereas the latter (the *PCs.*) is in addition brought into connection with word-presentations. This is the first attempt to indicate distinguishing marks for the two systems, the *PCs.* and the *Ucs.*, other than their relation to consciousness. The question, "How does a thing become conscious?" would thus be more advantageously stated: "How does a thing become preconscious?" And the answer would be: "Through becoming connected with the word-presentations corresponding to it."[23]

Psychoanalysis, though it recognizes the importance and functions of nonverbal communication, is certainly, among other modes, a linguistic form of communication based on verbal expression. In clinical analysis we value spontaneous speech and encourage the free, open flow of language, just as we *discourage* the recitation of prepared set pieces, lists, agendas. We listen for subtle changes in tone, pitch, and inflection, as well as for errors and slips in the analysand's verbal messages. I think most psychoanalysts do not appreciate how close this actually is to the hermeneutic method. I quote Hans-Georg Gadamer's appreciation of the creative power of free associative talking. For Gadamer, language, in the form of spontaneous speech with another, is a creative path to self-reflection. In the dialogic setting, Gadamer points out, a question posed

> contains an opening for a possible answer. . . . In speaking, one word brings forth another, and hence our thinking gets promulgated. A word becomes real when it proffers itself in our speaking on its own. . . . We speak that word and it leads to consequences and ends we had not perhaps conceived of. . . . Recitation is the opposite of speaking. When we recite, we already know what is coming, and the possible advantage of a sudden inspiration is precluded. . . . In fact, language is the single word, whose virtuality opens for us the infinity of discourse, of speaking with one another, of the freedom of "expressing oneself" and "letting oneself be expressed." Language is not its elaborated conventionalism, nor the burden of pre-schematization with which it loads us, but the generative and creative power to unceasingly make this whole once again fluent.[24]

In contrast to Habermas, who has an Enlightenment faith in the power of reasoned dialogue, Gadamer has what I find to be a congenial Freudian "skepticism about the fantastic overestimation of reason by comparison to the affections that motivate the human mind."[25] Note the compatibility with ego psychology when Gadamer describes the tension between the drive for self-expression and the censorship that results in a compromise formation: "There is always a tension between the interest in expression and a censorship, which is exerted from the social field. This constantly leads to a compromise formation which the author calls an act of discovery."[26] Gadamer is intersubjective, holding that in offering an interpretation we do "not allow the interpreter to speak of an original meaning of the work without acknowledging that, in understanding it, the interpreter's own meaning enters as well."[27] There is recognition of countertransference here. These lines were written several decades ago and have yet to be fully assimilated into psychoanalysis.

There is a need to understand how psychoanalysis fits into the contemporary sociology of science and the nature of the scientific enterprise. The models of physics and chemistry are inappropriate for psychoanalysis. I recall a conversation with the late Nobel laureate in physics Emilio Segrè, who bemoaned that psychoanalysis offered no "unique explanations" (one unique cause for a single phenomenon) as is available in high energy physics. If one of the natural sciences, rather than the humanities, is to be used as a model, the appropriate candidate is biology. Science is no longer regarded as a cumulative enterprise where accretions of building blocks of discrete data construct an edifice of truth. The modern view is that each field has a scientific culture and subcultures with their own definitions of validation and "truth."

The model of science I find most congenial to psychoanalysis is that of the Polish immunologist Ludwik Fleck, who published in Basel in 1935.[28] Fleck was a practicing physician in Lvov who also became a theorist of science.[29] He defined the useful concept of the "thought collective" (*Denkkollektiv*) as "a community of persons mutually exchanging ideas or maintaining intellectual interaction." Fleck describes such a group as providing "the special 'carrier' for the historical development of any field of thought, as well as for the given stock of knowledge and level of culture."[30] Each "thought collective" has a "thought style" (*Denkstil*) that is "the entirety of intellectual preparedness or readiness for one particular way of seeing and acting and no other. . . . The thought style may also be accompanied by a technical and literary style characteristic of the given system of knowledge."[31] The thought styles and assumptions of the humanities and psychoanalysis are quite compatible. They are historical, narrative, and hermeneutical. Fleck posits that "Truth is not 'relative' and certainly not 'subjective' in the popular sense of the word. It is always, or almost always, determined within a thought style. One can never say that the same thought is true for A and false for B. If A and B belong to the same thought collective, the thought will be either true or false for both. But if they belong to different thought collectives, it will just *not* be *the same* thought!"[32]

Fleck's case example is the scientific group led by August von Wassermann that in the 1860s developed the blood serum test for syphilis. Fleck writes of the empathic understanding between Wassermann and his researchers in language reminiscent of Freud's description of the unconscious as an instrument for clinical listening. Freud asked the psychoanalyst to "turn his own unconscious like a receptive organ towards the transmitting unconscious of the patient. He must adjust himself to the patient as a telephone receiver is adjusted to the transmitting microphone."[33] Fleck describes the preverbal preconscious and nonrational empathy between Wassermann and his group in similar terms: "Wassermann heard the tune that hummed in his mind but was not audible to those not involved. He and his co-workers listened and 'tuned' their 'sets' until these became selective. The melody could then be heard even by unbiased persons who were not involved."[34] What Fleck called *Gestaltsehen*, the perception of the total context, requires learned judgment and an apprenticeship: "The ability directly to perceive meaning, form, and self-contained unity is acquired only after much experience, perhaps with preliminary training. . . . The optimum system of a science, the ultimate organization of its principles, is completely incomprehensible to the novice."[35] Fleck, as Freud often did, used the metaphors of battle and military advance and occupation for the progress of science: "The vanguard does not occupy a fixed position. It changes its quarters from day to day and even from hour to hour. The main body advances more slowly, changing its stand—often spasmodically—only after years or even decades."[36]

Using Fleck's model of science, we can *now* understand what has happened to contemporary psychoanalysis. Psychoanalysis was once a unified "thought collective" of Freud and his followers with a distinctive thought style that demanded an apprenticeship, including undergoing a personal psychoanalytic experience and supervisory learning, acquiring a body of knowledge in seminars, and viewing the world through specifically psychoanalytic lenses. This led to a certain "thought style" that we variously refer to as "being in touch with the unconscious" or "thinking analytically." In the course of time a number of psychoanalytic thought collectives and styles formed, called ego psychological, Kleinian, object relational, self psychological, intersubjective, and others, each with its own charismatic leader, cadres of apostles, sacred texts, institutions, and social group processes. Each thought collective has its special thought style, its unique *Gestaltsehen,* and its particular social group process.

In the psychotherapeutic field, as in the humanities, and in life, lack of closure is the given condition, the problem, and often the solution—where acceptance of the unknown, the tolerance of ambiguity, and the willingness to allow oneself to be surprised, is a sign of health. As Vladimir Nabakov said: "The more formal thinking becomes, the more likely it is to provide short cuts from one area of ignorance to another."[37] Hermeneutics sharpens the listening capacities of both the analyst and the analysand. John Kafka has elaborated the value of ambiguity to both analysand and analyst: "Intolerance of ambiguity . . . tends to be pathogenic. . . . A conversation, words spoken and heard, any living communication, can be placed in more than one level of abstraction. . . . All human living involves considerable paradoxical experience and struggle with paradoxical systems that represent reality (from mild déjà vu sensations to wave particle theory)."[38] He emphasizes the need for fluid nonreification in diagnoses to preserve the ever-changing human person behind any diagnostic category.[39] Most psychoanalytic work occurs in what Keats called the space of "*Negative Capability* that is when man is capable of being in uncertainties, Mysteries, doubts, without any irritable reaching after fact and reason."[40]

The gains of psychoanalysis are subjective, usually not quantifiable, reflecting the reason that the analysand entered psychoanalysis in the first place and his or her most personal view of its outcome. In concluding one of the better-known autobiographical accounts of a psychoanalysis, Lucy Freeman, a some-time *New York Times* journalist who knows and appreciates hard data, asked questions pointing to its real outcome, which could be formulated as ego integration and structural change but was experienced by her as inner grounding, peace, and contentment: "How can you prove the cause of a tear? How can you prove a spark of hatred? How can you prove the cause of love?"[41] Freeman's ironic estimation of her psychoanalytic outcome is imparted by the ingenuous observation of a friend: "You're no different today from the way you were five years ago, except you're a little calmer."[42]

A brief clinical vignette from two patients in psychoanalysis demonstrates how the shared discourse of linguistic signs and emotions may in analysis be deconstructed to the multiple associations of the personal and cultural contexts from which they emerged. I saw two patients back to back in my studio office, which lies in a terraced garden. The shared stimulus was the sprinklers that were splashing the path up the terraced hillside. The first patient, a foreign student deeply imbued with French culture, came in to my waiting area, inhaled deeply, and said, "I love coming to you here, it reminds me of the fountains of Versailles." He analyzed the positive and negative transference meanings of his associations to the palace at Versailles and to the Sun King, Louis XIV, his passive-aggressive ingratiating mockery (which is his character mode) of comparing my studio to a royal palace.

He was followed by a sardonic, fast-talking New Yorker, a Hollywood writer with whom I have a relationship marked by jocularity and "kidding." His opening gambit was: "What the hell is this, Raging Waters?" (referring to a popular entertainment park where adolescents in swimsuits ride down water slides and get doused in simulated river rapids). I answered, "No, it is the fountains of Versailles!" He replied, "Of course! I knew it all the time!" We both laughed. He analyzed his use of the "put down" as what he learned from his father's continual emotional harassment and his use of sarcastic banter as a "friendly" defense against men whom he perceives as powerful and threatening, like certain film directors who intimidate him, his father, who ridiculed, demeaned, and abandoned him, and his analyst.

The hermeneutic point is that each stimulus is not transparent, having an obvious signification. No text has one stable meaning but communicates on many levels at once and differently to each person. Each human text carries multiple associations and hidden connotations derived from the individual psychodynamic past and the cultural context of the time, setting, and person. Clinical hermeneutics is open-ended and nonhierarchical but asymmetrical. It strengthens the therapeutic alliance because it demonstrates to the analysand that the analyst cares and is trying to understand as analyst and analysand mutually co-construct meanings.

A contemporary historical case illustrates how the facts do not "speak for themselves." Data is interpreted and contextualized depending on the personal needs, psychodynamics, and the intellectual socialization and orientation of the historian. The interpretation may be in the service of denial or an emotional defense against perception, so that it appears the historian does not know what he or she has observed.[43]

Deborah Dwork and Robert Jan van Pelt are among the most authoritative of the younger generation of Holocaust historians.[44] They have written widely about Auschwitz, including an important book focusing on the architectural history of the town and its cluster of satellite labor and extermination camps, among them Birkenau. They give appropriate close attention to the prisoner barracks and the latrines. The inhumanity of the facilities is not a historical issue for them, of that Dwork and van Pelt have no doubt: "The design of the wash barracks and the privies was, in fact, lethal. . . . with the latrines submerged in excrement, with very little water to be had at very few points, and with mud everywhere, what remained was an inmate population without the means to preserve any outward sign of human dignity."[45] As architectural historians, their hermeneutic focuses on the problems of design and the putative failures of the designer, who was an S.S. architect, Fritz Ertl (1908–82). In a number of publications van Pelt interprets: "The root cause was an inadequacy of design." Of the architects, he asks: "Were they even competent?" and "Were they simply incompetent given the situation?"[46] Dwork and van Pelt interpret and compare levels of architectural competence and dedication to their task:

> In Ertl's design for Birkenau the toilets and washrooms were housed in sixteen wash barracks and eighteen latrines, or one wash barrack per 7,800 inmates and one latrine hut per 7,000 inmates. . . . Des Pres is *incorrect* that the defilement was the result of the SS's desire to exercise total power. Architects and bureaucrats are to blame: the design was inadequate, and not enough material and financial resources were allocated for the camp's construction. . . . Were the architects simply incompetent? The "privy" meant to serve 7,000 inmates was a shed with one concrete open sewer serviced by far too little water, no seats, no "shame walls" for privacy, and one long beam as a back support. . . . The attention the Auschwitz architects failed to give the latrine design was focused on the crematorium.[47]

Well they should make this comparison, because the crematoria were meticulously planned and executed, expertly designed to move masses of people in and through their undressing, gassing, and burning without gridlock or the opportunity to escape.[48]

Fritz Ertl was far from being an incompetent or inexperienced architect. Indeed, he had superior training and more than a decade of hands-on experience in design and construction. He spent four years at the Bundeslehranstalt für Hochbau (HTL), Salzburg, where among other classes, he took courses in heating and ventilation.[49] He then attended the Bauhaus, Dessau, from 1928 to 1931, passing his examinations in March, and graduating on June 9, 1931.[50] Ertl worked with his two brothers in his father's building business in Linz. After his father's death in 1935 he took over the business with his brother. Ertl was born in Linz and thus was an Austrian national. He lists his date of becoming a German citizen as March 12, 1938, the day of Austria's Anschluss to the Reich. Ertl held Nazi Party membership card number 6,318,769, issued on May 1, 1938, in Linz.[51] He entered the Waffen S.S. Krakau on November 15, 1939, as number 417,971, serving in the Death's Head unit in Auschwitz until January 25, 1943. He rose through five S.S. ranks from a simple S.S.-Sturmmann in April 1940 to S.S.-Oberscharfuhrer in August 1944.[52]

The historical hermeneutic of Dwork and van Pelt provides the case, if one need be made, for the training and sophistication of historians, humanists, and social scientists in the hermeneutics of psychoanalysis with its sensibility to multiple conscious and unconscious meanings expressed in behavior. The inherent meanings of intentionality and "competence" must be reexamined in the context of historical setting and ideology. If the Nazi intent for the prisoners of Auschwitz-Birkenau was to demean and dehumanize rather than to provide civilized accommodation, then Ertl's design did exactly what it was supposed to do—for the world of the death camps, he was supremely competent.

The sadism of the architects is demonstrable for those prepared and willing to see it. There is no need to construct the architects' unconscious meaning. They knew what they were doing in consciously designing a situation that would humiliate its users and destroy their humanity. The same architects who designed the crematoria of Birkenau with care and professional expertise *could* have designed serviceable latrines, had they wished to. If it had been S.S. latrines they designed, we may be sure there would have been enough of them, with plumbing and heating, with seating and shame walls. As the Austrian state prosecutor posited in his indictment, the architects Walter Dejaco and Ertl were responsible for the inhuman conditions of life in the camp which led to the deaths of many thousands of prisoners. Their construction activity was aimed at the short-term vegetating of the prisoners from the beginning, and it makes a mockery of the elementary principles of sound construction technique. The fact that the accused were fully aware that their tightly crowded barracks, built without windows and sufficient ventilation offered inadequate space for humans, is demonstrated by their efforts in certain barracks used by guard dogs and cows to improve the ventilation to insure a healthy environment for the animals.[53]

To treat people as feces and turn them into excrement was the task of the camp and an exercise in sadistic control. An act of architectural design is an internal object relation for the designer. It is initiated in fantasy—the architect has an idea of what he or she wishes to build, which is then molded to the demands of reality (client wishes, budget, site, aesthetics, ideology, laws and building ordinances). This is one of the challenges and inducements of architecture. The latrines of Birkenau were not a space station that had never before been built— they were for an all-too-familiar and intimate human function. In Jonathan Swift's eighteenth-century cadences: "Ye gods, what sound is this? Can Chloe, heavenly Chloe piss?"[54] "Nor, wonder how I lost my wits; Oh! Celia, Celia, Celia shits."[55] The Birkenau architects Ertl, Dejaco, and Karl Bischoff pissed and shat; they used a latrine thousands of times, they knew its elemental physical and emotional imperatives.

History is autobiography, and what matters is its unconscious function for the historian. By making the issue one of "competence" or "incompetence" of the architect and the "adequacy" or "inadequacy" of the design, these historians constructed a rational hermeneutic to protect themselves and their readers from the terrible insight that one meaning of the camps was to degrade the inmates morally and emotionally before they were destroyed physically, and that the horrendous latrines symbolized and instrumentalized that regressive criminal goal.

I wish to outline some of the strategic interpretive principles that psychoanalysis, history, and the humanities share in the space "between therapy and hermeneutics," each in their own register, for extracting, decoding, and giving meaning to a "text." Of Woodrow Wilson's Fourteen Points Georges Clemenceau said, "God himself only gave us ten!" Being neither God nor Wilson, I am not embarrassed to offer more than twenty. The following are a few guidelines derived from the hermeneutics of clinical psychoanalysis for sensing and formulating latent unconscious meanings that I have found useful in researching history, biography, and political psychology:

1. *Affect:* Listen for and follow the affect rather than the content of a communication, although the manifest text may indicate otherwise. Emotion conveys where strong commitments and conflicts reside, what is "really going on."

2. *Imagery:* The selection of words and phrases, images, metaphors, figures of speech, analogues, similes, allegories, allusions, and myths are never random but are always freighted with meaning that may be interpreted.

3. *Behavior:* A sensitivity to what is implied in observable and reported behavior, choices, management of relationships, and contingencies. The assumption is that there is some unconscious intent behind a given result.

4. *Sexuality and gender:* Sexuality and gender are important because they are conditioned early and involuntarily, and precisely because sex is the most private, secretive area of life. Object choice, intensity, institutional frame, and self-definition of gender role all tell a life story.

5. *Money:* Attitudes toward property and wealth, getting, keeping, giving, fears of impoverishment, and feelings of financial security and insecurity are not necessarily commensurate with the real situation. They convey many other meanings and postures toward the world.

6. *Character:* Consistent personal and interpersonal styles, demeanor, and activities, pervasive relationship patterns, the management of aggression and affection, ways of doing things, dress, posture, voice, and mannerisms are all expressions of unconscious states. This includes what political scientists term the "operational code" of an individual or group in handling internal and external conflict, all that we subsume under the psychoanalytical concept of "character."

7. *Repetition:* Core conflictual relationship themes and the repetition, or reversal, of specific emotions such as shame, humiliation, envy, jealousy, and rivalry. Listen for underlying thematic unity, "gestalt," structural parallels, pattern matching, identifying constantly repeated patterns, and the transferential "fit" between present conflicts and earlier events in the life of a person, a nation, or a people. The longitudinal repetition in mode or content of themes indicates a latent unconscious scenario that should be heard and interpreted.

8. *Fantasy:* If dreams are the "royal road" to the unconscious, then fantasies and associations expressed in daydreams, notes, creative writing, poetry, fiction, letters, correspondence, and memoranda are vital byways to preconscious and unconscious content.

9. *Humor:* The essence of wit is a highly condensed expression of unexpressed

and often unmentionable antagonism and hostility. The style and content—dry, sarcastic, self-deprecating, or sardonic—tells more about the humorist than about the putative target.

10. *Internal conflict:* Evidence of ambivalence—the presence of more than one feeling toward the same object (love and hate, attraction and repulsion, wanting and not-wanting, leaving and staying).

11. *Absence of material:* What is not said or even referred to often communicates where the anxieties and conflict lie. Silence speaks.

12. *Action or inhibition:* The freedom and ability to act in certain circumstances and the inhibition of action in others is visible in personal behavior and the conduct of political affairs.

13. *Frustration tolerance:* Impulse control, willingness to wait, patience, as opposed to demanding immediate gratification of needs and wishes. Recourse to action in order to relieve the tension of waiting demonstrates low frustration tolerance.

14. *Aggression and hostility:* The management of angry feelings. What are the modes of dealing with rage: direct or indirect, active or passive, expressed or stored up?

15. *Rationalization:* Constructing more or less valid "reasons" for a desired course of action in order to obviate and not recognize the real emotional reasons.

16. *Splitting:* Polarizing and dividing the world and its occupants, or individuals, into those who are wonderful, idealized "good" persons and those who are loathed, pictured as all evil, lacking redeeming features. Seek evidence of balanced, mixed feelings toward objects, gray areas, differentiation, reflecting that all people have some pleasant and some obnoxious qualities. Consider the degree to which feelings are rigid, unmodulated, and absolute.

17. *Symbolic politics and anxiety:* Politics creates and lives by symbols. This is equally true in times of stability and in times of political crisis. The symbolic codes of politics constitute transitional objects that give both meaning to life and security against anxiety in a world that feels out of control and chaotic.[56]

18. *Trauma:* Be attentive to traumas: the earlier they occur in personal development, the more vital and less conscious they are. In individuals, attend to separation, illness, surgery, hospitalization, emigration or dislocation, and incapacity or death of a parent, grandparent, or sibling. Massive trauma is a crucial bridge to history. Human history is the story of large-scale traumas of war, disease and epidemics, famine, loss and migration, economic crises, earthquakes, floods, droughts, and pestilence. Social anxiety and trauma are

the theoretical link from individual to group, cohort to leader, and population to national politics.[57]

19. *Narcissism:* The major cause of interpersonal conflict, of litigation, and of wars is perceived injury to self-esteem, reputation, "face," the symbolic undoing of real or imagined wrongs, injuries, or injustices.[58] The concept of narcissistic rage may appropriately be applied to the understanding of leadership, politics, and society.

20. *Crises:* When things are going well, the surface is smooth. Crises take us to the core of the person or institution, opening the rot to examination and exposing the covered-over fissures. Responses to crises, modes of handling conflict, stress, and decision making at crucial junctures, show us, both individually and socially, what we would not otherwise see.

21. *Life space:* The symbolism and uses of space and distance, attitudes toward time, nature, rivalry, competition, and death are all disclosures of preconscious and unconscious emplotments that may be explicated.

In each case, the psychoanalyst, historian, and humanist—using their subjective sensibility—become the decoding cryptographer, interpreter, expositor, and translator, culling and unpacking different levels of comprehension and thus transforming the analysand, the present historical experience, the reader, and the future.

Notes

This essay is dedicated to my friend and scholarly first reader, A. D. Hutter.

1. I have explored Freud's humanism explicitly in "The Pagan Freud," *Fantasy and Reality in History* (New York: Oxford University Press, 1995), 16–32.
2. Freud, "An Autobiographical Study" (1925), *S.E.,* 20: 8.
3. Freud to Fliess, Jan. 1, 1896, in *The Complete Letters of Sigmund Freud to Wilhelm Fliess, 1887–1904,* translated and edited by Jeffrey M. Masson (Cambridge: Harvard University Press, 1985), 159.
4. Editor's note, "The Goethe Prize" (1930), *S.E.,* 21: 206.
5. Steven Marcus, "Freud and Dora: Story, History, Case History," *Partisan Review* 41, no. 1 (1974): 12–108, quotation on 12.
6. Freud, "From the History of an Infantile Neurosis" (1918), *S.E.,* 17: 10.
7. Clifford Geertz, "Deep Play: Notes on the Balinese Cockfight," *Daedalus,* 101, no. 1 (1972): 1–37.
8. Josef Breuer and Freud, "Studies on Hysteria" (1893–95), *S.E.,* 2: 160.
9. Freud, "An Outline of Psycho-Analysis" (1940), *S.E.,* 23: 195.
10. I am indebted to my colleague Steven Frankel for this suggestion.
11. Freud, "The Interpretation of Dreams" (1900), *S.E.,* 4: 96.
12. Ibid., 5: 514.

13. Ibid., 4: 97.

14. Freud, "The Claims of Psycho-Analysis to Scientific Interest" (1913), *S.E.*, 13: 176.

15. Ibid., 185.

16. Jürgen Habermas, *Erkenntnis und Interesse* (Frankfurt: Suhrkamp Verlag, 1968), translated by Jeremy J. Shapiro as *Knowledge and Human Interests* (Boston: Beacon Press, 1971), 214.

17. Freud, "Analysis Terminable and Interminable" (1937), *S.E.*, 23: 248.

18. Freud, "New Introductory Lectures on Psycho-Analysis," (1933), *S.E.*, 22: 57.

19. Ibid., 80.

20. Robert Waelder, "The Principle of Multiple Function," *Psychoanalytic Quarterly* 5 (1936): 45–62.

21. *Freud and Philosophy: An Essay on Interpretation*, translated by Denis Savage (New Haven: Yale University Press, 1970), 56. Ricoeur relies on and interprets Freud's text as though it were the ultimate authority against which explanations must be tested, a use which I venture Freud would not have approved. Ego psychologist David Rapaport also treated Freud's text as the ultimate authority against which all interpretations are to be measured. See Rapaport's exegetic notes in *Organization and Pathology of Thought* (New York: Columbia University Press, 1951). Charles Hanly terms Ricoeur "naive and unsatisfactory" on the point of the authority of Freud's system. "Such a dictum makes nonsense of the clinical testing of his ideas, which Freud advocated." *The Problem of Truth in Applied Psychoanalysis* (New York: Guilford Press, 1992), 8, 105. By 1932 Freud is writing, "The theory of the instincts is so to say our mythology. Instincts are mythical entities, magnificent in their indefiniteness." "New Introductory Lectures," 95.

22. Freud, "Constructions in Analysis" (1937), *S.E.*, 23: 262.

23. Freud, "The Ego and the Id" (1923), *S.E.*, 19: 20.

24. Hans-Georg Gadamer, *Truth and Method*, 2d ed., translated by Joel Weinsheimer and Donald G. Marshall (New York: Continuum, 1993), 548–49 passim.

25. Ibid., 567 passim.

26. Hans-Georg Gadamer, "Heidegger und die Soziologie: Bourdieu und Habermas" (1979/85), *Gesammelte Werke*, vol. 10 (Tübingen: JCB Mohr, 1995), 47.

27. Gadamer, *Truth and Method*, 576.

28. Ludwik Fleck, *Genesis and Development of a Scientific Fact* (Chicago: University of Chicago Press, 1979), translated by Fred Bradley and Thaddeus J. Trenn, from *Entstehung und Entwicklung einer wissenschaftlichen Tatsache: Einführung in die Lehre vom Denkstil und Denkkollektiv* (Basel: Benno Schwabe, 1935).

29. See Robert S. Cohen and Thomas Schnelle, eds., *Cognition and Fact: Materials on Ludwik Fleck* (Dordrecht: D. Reidel, 1986), particularly Cohen and Schnelle's "Introduction," ix–xxxi, and Schnelle's biographical essay, "Microbiology and Philosophy of Science, Lwów and the German Holocaust: Stations of a Life—Ludwik Fleck, 1896–1961," 3–36.

30. Fleck, *Genesis and Development*, 39.

31. Ibid., 64, 99.

32. Ibid., 100.

33. Freud, "Recommendations to Physicians Practicing Psychoanalysis" (1912), *S.E.*, 12: 115–16.

34. Fleck, *Genesis and Development*, 86.

35. Ibid., 92, 104.

36. Ibid., 124.

37. Personal communication.

38. John S. Kafka, *Multiple Realities in Clinical Practice* (New Haven: Yale University Press, 1989), 10, 41, 48.

39. "Psychoanalysis is not a brief encounter, and in an enduring therapeutic encounter the limitations, perhaps falsifications, inherent in some diagnostic classifications become apparent. Over an extended period, each patient seems to have many different 'disorders.' . . . The tolerance of . . . fluidity is at the center of this kind of diagnostic thinking, and is matched by the extent to which tolerance of fluidity can be modified and increased in treatment; perhaps better, flexible diagnostic thinking centers on the degree to which obstacles to the creative expansion of the patient's tolerance of ambiguity can be removed by appropriate treatment" (ibid., 162). "For the analyst, the work is always 'in progress.' Conceptualization of the patient's problems must always be unfinished as meanings and realities come and go, as connections move from haphazard to persuasive and vice versa. When the analyst finds that he is able to take a position, he recognizes at the same time that it is a contextual position and that it is in response to a change in the patient's contextual position, both temporally and spatially" (182).

40. John Keats to George and Tom Keats, 21, 27(?) December 1817, Robert Gittings, ed., *Letters of John Keats* (London: Oxford University Press, 1970), 43. I thank Stuart Ende for directing me to this quotation.

41. Lucy Freeman, *Fight Against Fears* (New York: Crown, 1951), 317.

42. Ibid., 292.

43. This point was made courageously by Joel Williamson with reference to his own changing perceptions and misperceptions of lynching in the American South in "Wounds Not Scars: Lynching, the National Conscience, and the American Historian," *Journal of American History* 83, no. 4 (1997): 1217–53. In an unprecedented departure from editorial policy, the unedited referees' reports follow, 1254–72. See also the subsequent correspondence in *Journal of American History* 84, no. 2 (1997): 748–65.

44. I participated in a two-day tour of Auschwitz-Birkenau conducted by Dwork and van Pelt sponsored by the International Society of Political Psychology in conjunction with its July 1997 meetings at Jagiellonien University, Kraków. I was familiar with their published interpretations and now heard them present their hermeneutic in the barracks and latrines. Dwork objected vociferously to any question of her interpretations of German motives in latrine construction. Of course, we were all traumatized at what we saw and none of us was at our best scholarly form.

45. Deborah Dwork and Robert Jan van Pelt, *Auschwitz: 1270 to the Present* (New York: Norton, 1996), 268. They quote a survivor of Birkenau: "There was one latrine for thirty to thirty-two thousand women and we were permitted to use it only at certain hours of the day. We stood in line to get in to this tiny building, knee-deep in human excrement. As

we all suffered from dysentery, we could rarely wait until our turn came, and soiled our ragged clothes, which never came off our bodies, thus adding to the horror of our existence by the terrible smell which surrounded us like a cloud. . . . The latrine consisted of a deep ditch with planks thrown across it at certain intervals. We squatted on these planks like birds perched on a telegraph wire, so close together that we could not help soiling one another." Gisella Perl, *I Was a Doctor in Auschwitz* (New York: International Universities Press, 1948), 33.

46. Robert Jan van Pelt, "Auschwitz: From Architect's Promise to Inmate's Perdition," *M: Modernism/modernity* 1, no. 1 (1994): 80–120, quotation on 106. See also "A Site in Search of a Mission," in Y. Gutman and M. Berenbaum, eds., *The Anatomy of the Auschwitz Death Camp* (Bloomington: Indiana University Press, 1994), 93–156, quotations on 130–31.

47. Dwork and van Pelt, *Auschwitz,* 267–69. Terrence Des Pres argued that the "excremental assault" on the inmates was designed to destroy the prisoner's self-worth: "Spiritual destruction became an end in itself, quite apart from the requirements of mass murder." *The Survivor: An Anatomy of Life in the Death Camps* (New York: Oxford University Press, 1976), 60.

48. *Entwurf für das krematorium: Grundriss vom Untergeschoss,* signed by Dejaco and Bischoff, Jan. 18, 1942; *Deckblatt zum Grundriss vom Untergeschoss,* signed by Dejaco and Bischoff, May 13, 1942. Trial of Dejaco and Ertl, 15 St 12.081/64, Landesgericht, Vienna. I am obliged to Irene Etzersdorfer for her aid in obtaining these documents.

49. Testimony of Fritz Ertl, Jan. 21, 1972, Fourth Day of Trial, *Landesgericht für Straafsachen Wien,* 20 Vr 3806/64 Hv 35/71, 101 (hereafter cited as *Ertl Trial*).

50. *Fritz Ertl File,* folder 18, Bauhaus-Archiv, Berlin. See also *Ertl Trial,* where he emphasized that the Bauhaus "brought him together with enemies of the NS regime" (129) and that "the school was hostilely oriented toward the SS" (142). Ertl and Walter Dejaco (born 1909 in Innsbruck, Austria) were tried in 1972 in Vienna as architects of the Auschwitz-Birkenau Concentration Camp. Ertl was acquitted by the jury.

51. Nazi Party membership card, *Fritz Ertl File,* Bundesarchiv, Berlin (formerly Berlin Document Center). An example of the purifying rewriting of history is a memorandum written shortly after Ertl's death by Hubert Hoffmann (b. 1904), a fellow *Bauhäusler* and friend, which asserts that he was told that Ertl demonstrated "in several buildings [that] he was an excellent and wide ranging architect. Above all, he showed a capacity to think constructively from the total structure to the details." He describes Ertl's wife, Genia, as being from a Polish feudal family who were "famous fighters in the opposition against Hitler" and as the daughter of a Polish resistance fighter murdered by the Nazis. Hoffmann's text, which is replete with anti-Semitic innuendos about "Jews and Communists" at the Bauhaus and "the rich Blumenthals, the Mendelsohns and Wertheims who supported it," declares that Ertl was "a true democrat. In the Bauhaus he had three half-Jews as friends. . . . If Ertl had refused to deliver the barracks for Auschwitz, he would have immediately been shot. . . . He was not a party member." Hubert Hoffmann, "Memoir" (1983), typescript, *Fritz Ertl File,* folder 18, Bauhaus-Archiv, Berlin, 2–4 passim.

52. Fritz Ertl, "Lebenslauf" [Autobiography] in his own hand, Sept. 11, 1944, in *Fritz Ertl File*, Bundesarchiv, Berlin (formerly Berlin Document Center).

53. Indictment of Walter Dejaco and Fritz Ertl, State Prosecutor, Landesgericht, Vienna, 15 St. 12.081/64, 53.

54. Jonathan Swift, "Strephon and Chloe," in *The Complete Poems*, edited by Pat Rogers (London: Penguin, 1983), 459, ll. 178–79.

55. "Cassinus and Peter: A Tragical Elegy," 466, ll. 117–18, and "The Lady's Dressing Room," 451, l. 118, both in Swift, *Complete Poems*.

56. D. W. Winnicott defined the transitional object as the symbol of the mother's presence and security for the infant and small child and the space between mother and child as the arena of first symbolization and creativity. See "Transitional Objects and Transitional Phenomena," "Playing: A Theoretical Statement," "Playing: Creative Activity and the Search for the Self," "Creativity and Its Origins," and "The Location of Cultural Experience," all in *Playing and Reality* (London: Tavistock, 1971).

57. Peter Loewenberg, "The Psychohistorical Origins of the Nazi Youth Cohort," in *Decoding the Past: The Psychohistorical Approach* (1983; reprint ed., New Brunswick, N.J.: Transaction Publishers, 1996), 240–83. See also "Germany, The Home Front (I): The Physical and Psychological Consequences of Home Front Hardship," in Hugh Cecil and Peter Liddle, eds., *Facing Armageddon: The First World War Experienced* (London: Leo Cooper, 1996), 554–62.

58. Heinz Kohut defined narcissistic rage as arising from a deficit of early parental empathy. The specific distinction of narcissistic rage is "the need for revenge, for righting a wrong, for undoing a hurt by whatever means, and a deeply anchored, unrelenting compulsion in the pursuit of these aims, which gives no rest to those who have suffered a narcissistic injury." "Thoughts on Narcissism and Narcissistic Rage," in Paul H. Ornstein, ed., *The Search for the Self: Selected Writings, 1950–1978*, 4 vols. (New York: International Universities Press, 1978), 2: 637–38.

The Pain in the Patient's Knee

Mary Jacobus

BETWEEN THERAPY AND HERMENEUTICS

What is the place of a psychoanalysis that exists "between" therapy (considered both as a theory and a practice, but also as a theory *of* practice) and hermeneutics, or the theory of interpretation and understanding? How do we understand "understanding" itself, considered as a mental process involving both analyst and analysand? I want to approach these questions by way of the writing of the British post-Kleinian psychoanalyst Wilfred Bion (1897–1979). Bion is best known outside psychoanalytic circles as a proponent of the leaderless group and as a theorist of group process.[1] But his collected theoretical and clinical oeuvre represents—especially in its "epistemological" period during the 1960s—the most sustained, original, and philosophical revision of psychoanalytic theory since Melanie Klein's development of Freudian ideas during the middle decades of the twentieth century.[2] Bion's influence pervades and in some cases underpins post-Kleinian rethinking of theory and practice.[3] In particular, it gives contemporary Kleinian analysis its distinctive focus on (not) learning, (non)-meaning, and (un-)knowing; in other words, it brings to the fore difficulties associated especially with interpretation and under-standing.

Noted for its stylistic obscurity, its paradoxical combination of difficulty and directness, not to mention its abstraction on one hand and its rigorous clinical focus on the other, Bion's writing is read wherever the evolution of British ob-ject relations psychoanalysis is seriously taught and studied in its post-Kleinian form.[4] But it remains surprisingly unknown within the academy, and especially to American academics, even to literary critics and theorists with an interest in psychoanalysis (who are often, by contrast, steeped in Lacan and well versed in Continental psychoanalytic writing more generally). Yet his work is particularly relevant to issues involving the relation between therapy and hermeneutics. In "Making the Best of a Bad Job," a seminar delivered in 1979 at the end of his long working career, Bion serendipitously anticipates what we know today (thanks to Frederick Crews) as "the Freud wars." His brusque pronounce-ments—couched in terse yet circumlocutionary telegraphese—are characteris-tic of many of his psychoanalytic communications: "Will psycho-analysts study the living mind? Or is the authority of Freud to be used as a deterrent, a barrier to studying people? The revolutionary becomes respectable—a barrier against revolution. The invasion of the animal by a germ or 'anticipation' of a means of accurate thinking, is resented by the feelings already in possession. That war has not ceased yet."[5] Bion typically sees the psychoanalytic encounter as a site of turbulence and struggle, "a mental space" for ideas yet to be developed. This site is constantly subject to renegotiation, as existing feelings and ideas war with new, uncomfortable ideas—the "anticipation" of accurate thought—that are bound to be resented or rejected. For Bion, anticipatory thoughts constitute a revolu-tion or an upheaval in themselves. We may prefer the old revolution, the one we know, to the thought-revolution we don't know, let alone want to think about. In what follows, I address the kind of communication made by Bion himself (which is subject to its own interpretive difficulties and obscurities) while try-ing to say something about both therapy and hermeneutics as they are prob-lematized and rethought in his work.

By invoking Bion's thinking I hope also to draw attention to an alternative to the psychoanalytic and literary discourse more usually associated with "Freud" and Freudianism (whether the term implies authority, theory, or a particular psychoanalytic school). That is, I want to introduce a different, but no less geopolitically distinct perspective on the Freud wars. At the same time, I want to point to the internal dynamic at work when we ask the question "Whose Freud?" (yours or mine? and which aspects of Freud's contribution are we talking about anyway?). The "between" of therapy and hermeneutics is a space equally expressive of the oscillation between two poles and, importantly, of avoidance. We can imagine ourselves as steering anxiously between the Scylla of "therapy" on one hand and the Charybdis of "hermeneutics" on the other. What is going on in this imaginary in-between (a space that Bion suggests we might see as a site of explosive energies and violent currents of resistance, rather than, say, as a Winnicottian potential space of play, creativity, and culture)?[6] In Bion's epistemology, thinking is more like having a breakdown than a breakthrough. For him, there is something inherently catastrophic about change (hence the lengths we go to avoid it and the anxiety it produces in us). The very notion of "changing one's mind" starts to look different when one thinks of the mind as actively resenting change, with all the additional conservatism and destructiveness that attends Kleinian understandings of the death drive. This may help to explain why, whether we happen to be theorists or therapists, we affiliate so tenaciously to one version of Freud rather than another and why we hate each other's psychoanalytic paradigms so much; why what is, or has been, or may be again revolutionary in Freudian psychoanalysis can indeed become a barrier to "accurate (that is, disinterestedly "scientific") thinking." In addition, the question "Whose Freud?" bears directly on the ways psychoanalysis has evolved dynamically over time and the radical breaks that have occurred within it, as well as the contemporary struggle over the ownership of Freud's ideas—not to mention the passion that inevitably accompanies attempts to legitimate or delegitimate them.

Bion's essay "Making the Best of a Bad Job" provides an interesting example of the ambiguous cultural and public functioning of what one might call psychoanalytic effects. It points to the way in which, even as we argue over psychoanalysis, we are bound to undergo or experience in ourselves, collectively or individually, what we might describe as psychoanalytic processes (whether we like it or not, and most often we don't)—processes we can better understand with the help of psychoanalysis. Here is Bion again: "Perhaps the problem can be approached more easily by projection. Let us consider it not in each one of us individually, but by regarding it as a problem of the body politic. Can we then locate in the community the origin, the source, the emotional storm centre? In my experience it is always caused, or associated with, or centered on a thinking and feeling person who can make his Self infectious or contagious."[7] Bion's example of the contagious cultural shaker-up is thoroughly canonical (Shakespeare); but he might have said Freud—or even himself, bearing in mind that Bion elsewhere defines the personality as a multivocal and argumentative group

capable of making a thorough-going nuisance of itself (see, for instance, his autobiographical trilogy, *A Memoir of the Future* [1975–79], in which "Bion" is one
among a cast of characters that includes both "Psycho-Analyst" and "Myself").[8]
All of us have probably had the experience of being in a group, say at a conference, where the projection of overwhelming or unwanted parts of the self into
others, or the contagiousness of one person's feelings, passions, and ideas, has
generated turbulence of some sort or another. Often such turbulence emerges
as contretemps, but it may also take the form of attempts at conversion. No
doubt there will be moments or manifestations of such psychic "projection"
(what Kleinians call "projective identification") during even the best-behaved
gathering.[9] Someone will lose their temper or something unexpected or unto-
ward may occur; words and intentions will be symptomatically mistaken or mis-
heard in the heat and dust of the encounter. These will be anxious moments, I
suggest, when the impulse to resistance or destructiveness or sheer anomie (or
even sleep) can best be understood in terms that derive from the therapeutic development of originally Freudian concepts. Arguing over different versions of
Freud may well be less significant, psychoanalytically speaking, than the fact that
an argument of some sort is occurring, whether we want to hear it or not.
"Whose Freud?"—mine or yours?—is partly a question of understanding, but
it is also, inevitably, a matter of intense ressentiment; a resentment that Bion
would link with difficulties involving the link between pain and change.

"YOU'LL PROBABLY SAY IT WAS THE GIRL"

What we call *therapy* (a practice of psychoanalysis that is also a theory) has its
own hermeneutics, often simply called *interpretation*. This is the form of action
we recognize as peculiar to psychoanalysis, whether in its clinical or theoretical
mode. The making of meaning in the context of psychoanalytic practice is inevitably subject to many of the same conditions and difficulties that come into
play when we read a text, hence the relevance of psychoanalytic theory to literary and textual theories of interpretation. For instance, as is well known, we habitually make sense of the part in terms of a prior theoretical preconception of
the whole, rather than making deductions from empirical data. Yet that theoretical preconception—at once speculative and based on past experience—can
only be known via its presenting parts or clinical impressions (the well-trodden
hermeneutical circle). A clinical example from Bion's *Transformations* demonstrates the point. Bion offers a clinical vignette that is, by his own account, radically overdetermined by certain theoretical preconceptions. Ostensibly, the

fragment of case-material illuminates a necessarily preexisting understanding of the Freudian theory of "transference" (specifically, the transfer of oedipal feelings to the analytic relationship)—in dynamic conjunction, however, with a theory of projective identification derived from the work of Melanie Klein. Such ideas allow Bion (and his readers) to make sense of an obscure yet crucial exchange between him and his patient. But, far from accounting for everything, Bion says, these theoretical concepts gesture toward a considerable area of unstated thinking about what is actually going on. I shall take the liberty of an extratextual excursion in the interests of trying to go beyond the ellipses and seeming impersonality of the psychoanalytic process.

Here, first, is Bion's short verbatim record of the opening of a session with his patient:

> The patient came in, but, though he had been attending for years, seemed uncertain what to do. "Good morning, good morning, good morning. It must mean afternoon really. I don't expect anything can be expected today: this morning, I mean. This afternoon. It must be a joke of some kind. This girl left about her knickers. Well, what do you say to that? it's probably quite wrong, of course, but, well, I mean, what do *you* think?" He walked to the couch and lay down, bumping his shoulders down hard on the couch. "I'm slightly anxious . . . I think. The pain has come back in my knee. You'll probably say it was the girl. After all."[10]

Bion observes of this extraordinarily obscure, disconnected, and altogether Beckettian communication (with its "changes of tone expressing depression, fear, anxiety, confidentiality, and others"), that "the general impression . . . was itself intended to give a general impression."[11] He assumes from the start that the patient's communication conveys a meaning that is not fully available to the patient himself, yet is at the same time fully intended by him (intended, that is, "to give a general impression," as opposed to conveying a particular piece of information). The analyst's job is to make sense of what the patient is saying rather than lose his or her own mind. Accordingly, Bion submits the initial communication to a sustained metareading or meditation in which, he says, "a high proportion of speculation . . . depends on [his own] theoretical pre-conceptions."[12] He calls this second mode of representing the patient's communication an analytic "transformation" (that is, a psychoanalytic "representation," rather than an attempt to describe what took place in the session's opening moments). Importantly, this transformation is not in itself an interpretation, although it might preface or give rise to one at an appropriate moment later on in the session.

Bion starts by noting, at once in great detail and with considerable abstraction, the relation between closeness and distance, precision and imprecision as they emerge from the minutiae of the patient's behavior and speech. His account makes the reader intensely aware of the analyst's interpreting presence as well as the patient's subtle and indirect attempts at communicative obfuscation. The effect is not joking, exactly, but neither does it have (unlike the patient's communication) "no tincture of humour about it." The patient, Bion tells us, in a way that immediately implies that we, too, will be able to "gather" something from his account,

> whispered his good mornings as if he were pre-occupied with an object he had lost but expected to find close at hand. He corrected himself in a tone that might imply a mental aberration that had led him to think it a "good morning." The speaker of the words "good morning," I gathered, was not really the patient, but someone whose manner he caricatured. Then came the comment that nothing could be expected. That was clear enough, but who was making the comment, or of whom nothing could be expected, was obscure. It might have been myself; I did not think it was he. Then he spoke of the joke. The way this term was used implied that the joke had no tincture of humour about it. . . . When he spoke of "this" girl it was evident that I was supposed to know her; in fact I did not nor did I know whether she had left her knickers lying about or given notice on account of some episode connected to her knickers. "What do you say to that?" meant that in either case I would know as well as he did what her behaviour signified, though, as his next sentence showed, the significance (unmentioned) attached to her behaviour by both of us was probably mistaken, girls being what they are.[13]

Who is the girl about whose essential nature—"girls being what they are"—the patient (and by implication, the analyst) can be imagined as being in such collusive, knowing, and mistaken agreement? In reading this passage I was reminded of a painfully personal episode from Bion's bleak, posthumously published autobiography of the interwar years, *All My Sins Remembered*. Bion—who had not been lucky in his early relations with women—describes how, on a solitary walking holiday, he unexpectedly encountered his ex-fiancée ("an extremely beautiful young woman"), apparently weekending in the company of another man. The meeting, he says, aroused a storm of feeling in him, and he cut the weekend short. He behaved with apparently civilized composure to the couple, but a very different scenario plays out in his imagination. Imperceptibly, Bion's narrative assumes the form of a police inquiry: what really happened? While walking along the river after meeting this maddeningly happy and conventional couple, Bion imagines, vividly and murderously, the following crime of passion:

> I was haunted by that walk along the reedy path of the river. If I had had my service revolver with me I would have shot him. Then I would have shot her through the knee in such a way that the joint could not be repaired and she would have had a permanently rigid leg to explain to her future lovers. I would not give myself up because that would not be enough of a mystery to occupy the newspapers. But when in the course of ordinary routine inquiries they closed in on me I would make my report.[14]

"A sordid little murder," comments Bion's imaginary interlocutor (his older self). Certainly, as far as his rival goes. But in this lurid phantasy involving two men and a girl, Bion also projects into his ex-fiancée's knee a crippling pain that operates in a peculiarly omnipotent and concrete fashion. He then reproaches himself for his failure to negotiate the oedipal scene as regards both sexual and generational difference; that is, for not having known, when he became engaged to the "girl," the crucial difference "between a boy and a girl, and wife and a girl, a husband and a boy, a wife and a mother, or a husband and a father."[15] Bion's imaginary interlocutor dismisses the dismal litany of his exploits in love and war (for the record, Bion was a traumatized war hero of World War I, in which he served as a tank commander) as an *"extremely uninteresting and commonplace story."*[16] But the other Bion replies, "It was very painful to me." So perhaps the question is not who is this girl (this internal object) over whom two men are presumed to be struggling, but rather to whom does the pain in the knee belong and what does it mean? Does it, perhaps, circulate in phantasy, like the part-object it is, among all the split-up parties in this transferential and countertransferential oedipal triangle?[17] Significantly, Bion writes elsewhere in *Transformations* of the psychotic personality's "probing, incessantly active, designed to tap sources of counter-transference. The patient's associations are directed to obtaining evidence of meaning and emotion"[18]—typically, meanings involving love and hate (rather than knowledge, the quest in which both he and the analyst should be engaged). Such meanings are ultimately reassuring antidotes to the problem rather than representing any approach to solving it. The patient's and analyst's (mistakenly) assumed familiarity with the typical behavior of girls ("girls being what they are") masks the probing of an old wound, a countertransferential pain. Both men are supposedly at a loss about a girl, viewed here as an internal object—"an object [the patient] had lost but expected to find close at hand," presumably in the analyst's possession: "but, well, I mean, what do *you*

think?"[19] In any event, lying down on the couch seems to mean trying to get a rise out of the analyst.

THE THEORY OF INTERNAL OBJECTS

Returning from this oedipal expedition to Bion's extended metacommentary on his patient's opening communication, we find that envy, aggressivity, and violence are still at issue in the micromovements of the anxious analytic encounter:

> When he lay on the couch he did so as if trying to express surreptitiously his wish to damage my property. I thought his next comment compatible with this surmise in that it might mean that, being confused with me and yet detached from both of us, he hazarded a guess that I was anxious at his violence, that I supposed him to be anxious and not aggressive, that he thought the feelings he experienced were what I would call anxiety. His reference to the pain in his knee was typical of certain very rare statements in that it meant "The pain in my knee, which I now experience, is what you as analyst think is really the girl inside me." Such a statement meant that despite evidence to the contrary he had knowledge of my analytic theories and that he was now having an experience which I would explain by that particular theory. It might mean that he wished me to know what experience he was having and that the correct interpretation could be arrived at through the theory of internal objects.[20]

What's going on in Bion's interpretation of the patient's manner of lying down on the couch, and what relation does it have to what follows? I think Bion is showing us how the patient caricatures—with hostile and aggressive intent—the very psychoanalytic theory ("the theory of internal objects") by which the analyst tries to understand and alleviate his pain. The concept of the internal object—introduced by Klein in the 1920s and 1930s—is generally regarded as among the two most complex, crucial, but also most mysterious of her theoretical innovations (the other controversial concept being that of unconscious phantasy).[21] At one extreme, the internal object can be imagined as a troublesome physical object literally located inside the body, while at the other, it implies the introjected objects that are assimilated into the ego and constitute our very identities.[22] If we turn back to Bion's patient, we can see how, in his wish to damage the analyst's property (his couch, but also his intellectual property, not to mention his mind, his life, or his knee), the question to whom this property belongs is already moot. The patient has become so confused with the analyst in his mind ("Good morning, good morning, good morning") that he attacks his own mental functioning when he attacks the analyst's. Bion comments,

"His 'after all' is typical; it is meaningless, but can act as a stimulus to speculation"—which might be equivalent to saying that patient's entire communication is about his need to reduce Bion's theory of internal objects to meaninglessness (a meaninglessness, however, worth speculating about).[23] Indeed, the
patient's efforts seem devoted to ensuring that his communication will be regarded not just as obscure but as "bad," and therefore forcefully evacuated to a
great distance by the analyst, frustrating all attempts at understanding.[24] The
patient's personality is in fragments, and the bits are meant to be contagious and
to get under the skin of the analyst in order to prevent him from thinking (or
else to make him think of his own difficulties instead of the patient's—scatter-
ing his thoughts and perhaps even taking him on a different journey).

Bion's lengthy metacommentary (of which mine is a highly abbreviated version, inevitably placed at yet another speculative remove) has mentioned his dependence on both "classical analytical [that is, Freudian] theory" and "Kleinian
theories of splitting and projective identification." He expects, he says, to find
that the confusion between analyst and patient in the patient's mind "would be
illuminated by applying the theory of projective identification to the patient's
inability to distinguish between himself and myself."[25] But even this primitive
level of relating represents the building blocks of thought; some form of communication is taking place. Bion then asks a characteristically difficult question
involving two utterly opposed answers: whether the obscurity of the patient's
communication is "due to the difficulty of the matter of the problem for which
he seeks help or is it due to his need to conceal," and concludes, categorically,
that "the analyst's task is to distinguish one from the other."[26] This is not a matter, then, of radical *un*decidability, in the aporetic mode familiar from the era of
deconstructive reading, where indeterminacy dominated the question of meaning. Rather, Bion advances a model that might be called that of radical *de*cid-
ability. Two distinct and opposed meanings masquerade as a single confusion in
the analytic encounter (the same confused and confusing pain, rather than a differentiated and differentiating pain). For Bion, anything does *not* go, depending how you look at it or where you stand. Psychoanalysis is not, for him, a rel-
ativistic science. There's all the difference in the world between the pain in the
patient's knee and a cruel joke, between a surreptitious attack and the actual difficulty of the patient's problem—not to mention between the patient's pain, the
analyst's, and the injury done to his ex-fiancée, from whom, Bion says, he had
withdrawn to a great distance after their chance encounter. In *All My Sins Remembered,* Bion's imaginary interlocutor remarks apropos of his angry emo-

tional self-distancing: "*that must have been a terrible loss to her.*"[27] In *Transfor-mations,* Bion refers to "the sense of being at a loss" apparent to the reader in his account of his psychotic patient—a loss or failure of understanding (an angry emotional distancing) that replicates a version of the missing understanding which the patient, too, seems to have lost, "but expected to find close at hand" when he arrives at his analytic session.[28]

The barriers erected against change and communication by the patient him-self ("After all"—a moment of insistent stasis in his stalled, repetitive, and baf-fling monologue) underscore how events involving psychoanalytic understand-ing between persons may provoke covert or open hostility, aggressivity, and even (as we've seen) murderous violence. But, Bion seems to say, better an obscure communication than none at all. At least there's a pain in the patient somewhere, even if it masquerades as a girl or a part-object, or travesties Bion's theory of in-ternal objects—or takes the form of an uncannily accurate probing and resen-sitizing of the analyst's stalled history of pain, loneliness, and premeditated mur-derousness. On one level, then, the oedipal pain in the patient's knee is the part that stands for an entire body of internalized theoretical knowledge belonging to the analyst. The patient "knows" the analyst's theoretical stance and envies it and seeks to destroy it. There's "understanding" psychoanalysis, Bion seems to say, and then there's the "psychoanalysis" of understanding, which can involve a surprising degree of destructiveness. Reversible perspective (a term also used by Bion to describe a peculiarly intractable and destructive form of psychoana-lytic impasse) might also be used to conceptualize the "between" of therapy and hermeneutics, redefined as a difficult terrain that bears on the avoidance or ex-periencing of pain.[29] Bion writes elsewhere that "reversible perspective is evi-dence of pain; the patient reverses perspective so as to make a dynamic situation static."[30] The relation between therapy and hermeneutics simultaneously poses itself as conjunctive and disjunctive—as the place not only where things and thoughts might come together but where the links between things and thoughts constantly risk being broken or mis-taken, so that the psychoanalytic process halts. But in that break, pain speaks. Sometimes it speaks with the voice of the patient. Sometimes, as here, it speaks indirectly, via the psychotic patient's abil-ity to tap into the analyst's countertransference (not to mention my own "psy-chotic" excursion into the analyst's autobiographical associations between love, hate, and knee injuries).

In a final return to *Transformations,* I wish to invoke what Bion has to say about meaning as it bears on the hermeneutics of psychoanalysis. Bion writes about how the pressure on the analyst to give interpretations can disguise an anxiety about meaninglessness (ultimately, annihilation—whether of the object or the self). The patient's intolerance of meaninglessness, he says, leads him to "pour out a flood of words so that he can evolve a response indicating that meaning exists either in his own behaviour or in that of the analyst."[31] Think of the patient's repeated "Good morning, good morning, good morning" (and its farcically assumed bonhomie). The effect of such intolerance, writes Bion, is to stifle curiosity about the possibility of no-meaning as well as meaning. Without the possibility of a no-thing (absence), the temptation, he suggests, is to substitute a thing. For instance, "The actual murder is to be sought instead of the thought represented by the word 'murder.'"[32] The complex or dangerous elaborations of acting out would replace thinking, just as Oedipus misunderstood Tiresias's words to him by understanding them in a literal way. Such processes, Bion reminds us, produce states of stupor, hallucination, or megalomania (or the fear of such states), but they also lead to the abolition of boundaries. For the psychotic, no division exists between inside and outside, analyst or analysand (no "dividing membrane"). The effect is to deny the difference between the patient's knee, the analyst's pain, and the girl whom neither of them actually possessed or assaulted—eliding differences not only between persons but between meanings (including the crucial distinction between inside and outside) while paradoxically ensuring that things are kept apart. Pain circulates without being acknowledged or understood, concealed in the purposive hostility of the patient's obscure communication.

Bion insists elsewhere that pain is an "element" of psychoanalysis: "An analysis must be painful . . . because an analysis in which pain is not observed and discussed cannot be regarded as dealing with one of the central reasons for the patient's presence."[33] In *Transformations,* he observes that "the need to manipulate the session to evoke evidence of the existence of meaning extends to a need to evoke evidence of the existence of love and hate" in the analyst.[34] To the extent that the patient evokes evidence of such feelings, the analysis fails; the tables have been turned and stasis results. Bionic hermeneutics makes change possible by introducing a third term, *knowledge.* Psychic change is indissociable from the experiencing and relocating of pain in the patient's mind—in the analysis—as opposed to locating it in his knee or projecting it into the analyst (as the analyst had imagined vengefully shooting a girl in the knee). The patient's elliptical "You'll probably say it was the girl" and Bion's insistent "It was very painful to me" converge to create the strange form of knowledge that links them in the analytic encounter, equally probing and probed. Yet who is to say to whom this psychoanalytic knowledge belongs, if not to the analysis itself? That is, the "between" that links therapy and hermeneutics.

Notes

1. See W. R. Bion, *Experiences in Groups, and Other Papers* (1959; reprint ed., London: Tavistock, 1961). For an informative study of Bion's life, thought, and writing, see Gérard Bléandonu, *Wilfred Bion: His Life and Works*, 1897–1979, translated by Claire Pajaczkowa (London: Free Association Books, 1994). See also León Grinberg, Darío Sor, and Elizabeth Tabak de Bianchedi, *New Introduction to the Work of Bion*, rev. ed. (Northdale, N.J.: Jason Aronson, 1993).

2. See, e.g., W. R. Bion, *Learning from Experience* (London: William Heinemann Medical Books, 1962), *The Elements of Psycho-analysis* (London: Heinemann, 1963), *Transformations: Change from Learning to Growth* (1965; reprint ed., London: Karnac Books, 1984), *Second Thoughts: Selected Papers on Psychoanalysis* (London: Heinemann, 1967), and *Attention and Interpretation: A Scientific Approach to Insight in Psycho-Analysis and Groups* (London: Heinemann, 1970).

3. For collections of essays relating to Bion's contribution to post-Kleinian psychoanalytic theory and practice, see *Do I Dare Disturb the Universe? A Memorial to W. R. Bion,* edited by James S. Grotstein (London: Karnac Books, 1983); *Clinical Lectures on Klein and Bion,* edited by Robin Anderson (London: Tavistock, 1992); and *Melanie Klein Today: Developments in Theory and Practice,* edited by Elizabeth Bott Spillius, 2 vols. (London: Routledge, 1988).

4. In practice, this means psychoanalytic institutes in Britain, South America, and the west coast of the United States. On the Continent, André Green provides a rare instance of a psychoanalytic writer whose orientation toward British object relations includes Bion; see Green, *On Private Madness* (Madison, Conn.: International Universities Press, 1986).

5. W. R. Bion, *Clinical Seminars and Other Works* (London: Karnac Books, 1994), 331.

6. See D. W. Winnicott, *Playing and Reality* (1971; reprint ed., London: Routledge, 1991), especially the essays "Transitional Objects and Transitional Phenomena," "Playing: Creative Activity and the Search for the Self," and "The Location of Cultural Experience." See also Adam Phillips, *Winnicott* (Cambridge: Harvard University Press, 1988), especially chap. 6, "The Play of Interpretation," for a relevant discussion of interpretive processes in Winnicott's work.

7. Bion, *Clinical Seminars*, 330.

8. See W. R. Bion, *A Memoir of the Future* (London: Karnac Books, 1991); Bion's unconventional autobiographical trilogy was first published as *The Dream* (1975), *The Past Presented* (1977), and *The Dawn of Oblivion* (1979).

9. For an overview of the contemporary vicissitudes of this expansive term, see R. D. Hinschelwood, *A Dictionary of Kleinian Thought* (London: Free Association Books, 1991), 179–208; Bion's use of the term takes on a distinctive inflection in his epistemology, since for him projective identification represents the primitive basis of all thought.

10. W. R. Bion, *Transformations,* 19–20. For a discussion of *Transformations* in the larger context of Bion's "epistemological" period, see Bléandonu, *Wilfred Bion,* 193–214.

11. Ibid., 20.

12. Ibid., 21.

13. Ibid.

14. W. R. Bion, *All My Sins Remembered: Another Part of My Life* (1985; reprint ed., London: Karnac Books, 1991), 29–30.

15. Ibid., 30.

16. Ibid., 32.

17. See Hinschelwood, *Dictionary of Kleinian Thought*, 57–67, for the Bionic twist given to Klein's revision of the Oedipus complex.

18. Bion, *Transformations*, 81–82.

19. Ibid., 21.

20. Ibid. For a survey of the various theoretical permutations and understandings of the mental or "internal" object in psychoanalytic theory, see Meir Perlow, *Understanding Mental Objects* (London: Routledge, 1995). For a literary elaboration of Klein's understanding of the "internal object," see Joan Riviere's classic essay, "The Unconscious Phantasy of an Inner World Reflected in Examples from Literature" (1952), in Athol Hughes, ed., *The Inner World and Joan Riviere: Collected Papers, 1920–1958* (London: Karnac Books, 1991), 301–30.

21. For the divisive war of ideas that took place over Klein's innovative concepts between Freudians and Kleinians in the British Psycho-Analytic Society, see Pearl King and Riccardo Steiner, eds., *The Freud-Klein Controversies, 1941–45* (London: Routledge, 1991).

22. See Hinschelwood, *Dictionary of Kleinian Thought*, 68–83.

23. Bion, *Transformations*, 21.

24. "Subsequent remarks meant that what had been taking place in the session was a pictorial representation, an externalization of a visual image, not likely to be regarded by me as good and therefore evacuated by me with such force that this fragment of his personality would be projected as far away from me as Durham is from London" (ibid., 21). Bion is elaborating on a puzzling reference by the patient that concludes his original communication: "'This picture is probably not very good as I told him but I should not have said anything about it. Mrs. X. . . . thought I ought to go to Durham to see about, but then' and so on" (20).

25. Ibid., 21.

26. Ibid., 22.

27. Bion, *All My Sins Remembered*, 29.

28. Bion, *Transformations*, 22, 21.

29. For reversible perspective, a favorite and powerfully deployed concept in Bion's writing, see Bléandonu, *Wilfred Bion*, 180–82: "Bion shows how reversible perspective facilitates the avoidance of the mental pain that is essential to all growth. . . . Here the conflict is between the analyst's point of view and the patient's. . . . The inverted perspective enables the patient to avoid the discomfort of acknowledging the existence of the parental couple, and of being in overt conflict with his analyst" (180, 182). The classic instance of reversible perspective would be Oedipus's misunderstanding of Tiresias.

30. See W. R. Bion, *Elements of Psychoanalysis* (1963; reprint ed., London: Karnac Books, 1989), 60.

31. Bion, *Transformations,* 81.
32. Ibid.
33. Bion, *Elements of Psychoanalysis,* 61–62.
34. Bion, *Transformations,* 81.

Discussion

Esther de Costa Meyer, Moderator: Professor Loewenberg, you were talking about Robert Jan van Pelt, who was the first architectural historian to work on Auschwitz seriously. It struck me that the first man to publish the fact that Bauhaus architects were involved in the actual building of the concentration camps was in fact a negationist. It was Jean-Claude Pressac: a man who went to Auschwitz for other purposes, and there discovered all these boxes of documents, and in this about-face—which in itself calls out for psychoanalytic interpretation—then turns around, has this conversion, and begins to publish all this material. Would this also fall into your category? What resistance do you see there? How would one explain this fact, and is this an isolated incident?

Peter Loewenberg: It's correct that Jean-Claude Pressac first did the research and went as a so-called revisionist and became convinced of the Holocaust. This is an example, not of psychoanalytical method, but of good historical method. It follows the method of Marc Bloch, a great French medievalist, who said you don't study medieval France from the documents—that's the mistake that Fustel de Coulanges made, when he said there was no open field system in France. Bloch said get out and look at the villages, look at how the peasants lived, and you will see grazing on the arable.[1] So that the open field system exists but you have to use all of yourself, go out and look in situ. And that is what Pressac did. He went and saw. It's a case of immersion, of a very particular kind that the analyst would not generally do.

Mary Jacobus: Toril [Moi] said that Joyce McDougall had drawn attention to three inescapable facts of the human condition: the existence of others, sexual difference, and death. And I agreed very much with her test case, the question of death. Who can challenge that question as a destiny? I'd like to add another. The question of the excremental, which Toril brought up, brings to mind an excremental issue connected with the latrines in Auschwitz, which comes up in a book by Binjamin Wilkomirski called *Fragments.*[2] The narrator, who is a child camp survivor, has an excruciating form of survivor guilt. He is asleep lying with the other children in their barracks. And there's a new boy who doesn't know the rules: that when the pail in the middle of the room is full, you just have to live with it. And you are not allowed to get out of your bunk. And when this new kid cries out—he had dysentery, as they all had—the narrator finally says, "I just couldn't keep quiet any more." He was frightened that there would be anger from the guards and reprisals. And his voice says, "Do it where you are." Of course in the morning there's excrement on the straw, and then all the kids are called out, and finally that child is killed. He's simply struck down for his unsanitary behavior.

Now, if you ask what could make possible what you've described in terms of latrines, or the killing of that child for soiling the straw, you have to add another fact, another inescapable fact about the human psyche, to the three that Toril mentioned. You could call it Auschwitz, or you could call it destructiveness; you could call it the death drive.

Hubert Damisch: What I've been told about the excremental issue reminds me of a moment in the trial of [Maurice] Papon which is taking place right now in France. And people are asking: "What did he know about the fate of the people he would send to Germany?" At a certain moment the prosecutor produced receipts signed "Papon," for the buying of three hundred pails which were to be put in the wagons where the Jewish people would get imprisoned for two days. So what did he mean by doing this? He knew that the people would be kept enclosed in these wagons for two days, one hundred people at least in one wagon, with one pail. This would be enough to condemn him, you know. But the thing was totally dismissed. Nobody paid attention to it. A very curious moment in the trial.

Toril Moi: I suppose if I have a general comment, it's that the panel seems to be very united in its coprophiliac interests. Apart from that, I think the other thing that unites us is precisely the question of interpretation. My paper didn't talk about interpretation, but it did practice interpretation, on a psychoanalytic text. Both for a psychoanalytically minded critic and for a literary critic *tout court,* nothing is more appalling than quick readings out of context. We have to have the patience to listen to the text for good and for bad, what Professor Damisch has called "the listening eye." And if psychoanalysis teaches us to listen to the text, so that psychoanalytic listening is crucial to literary criticism, in the same way we have to bring that critical attention to bear on Freud's own texts.

Robert Jay Lifton: With this discussion of architecture of Nazi Germany I thought I could convey an experience I had that seems directly relevant to our preoccupations. While studying and interviewing Nazi doctors I had the chance to interview Albert Speer, who was Hitler's architect and for a while his second-in-command and also in charge of the whole industrial project toward the latter part of the war. Speer told me a couple of things that seem directly relevant to our discussion. One was that Hitler came to his university when everybody was down and out and in great despair, and gave his relatively intellectual speech as opposed to his thuggish speech in the streets. It wasn't so much anti-Semitism; it was, "Follow me and you'll have hope, Germany will be strong again, and you'll be strong again." And Speer, as a young academic with absolutely no hope, was thrilled by this and the next day joined the Nazi Party, walking wildly through the Berlin woods the night before.

Speer asked me whether I would do therapy with him, so that he could understand how he got so fascinated and drawn into the life and project of such a simple and unworthy man. I politely declined to do that therapy, but I did indeed investigate those things with him. And there's nothing more conducive to a sense of immortality than the architectural opportunity to create the whole future, which was meant to be eternal, of the thousand-year reich. I mean it's an absolute immortalization in physical concrete. And that enormous attraction to the revitalization of Germany can't be left out of the Nazi equation, in combination with the sadistic and controlling side. The immortalization that various people high up in the Nazi regime could feel, and particularly the architects, seems to me of great importance.

Peter Brooks: I was interested by Peter Loewenberg's remark that psycho-analysis bridges medical science and the humanities. And I agree that that's the ideal and that it creates a dynamic and a tension which has produced a great deal of insight and creative work. But what worries me is this: what if psychoanalysis loses its base in medicine, in therapy, if medicine completely abandons psychoanalysis in favor of psychopharmacology or whatever? And then psychoanalysis comes to find its home exclusively within the humanities, exclusively within the interpretive disciplines. Don't we as a result lose something which came precisely from the tension that was in that bridge, that was in that effort to move from elaborating the dynamics of the mind to elaborating the dynamics of text or culture? So what I fear, and, in fact, one of the questions that I would want to ask linking the first panel to this one, is: is there a danger that in the next century psychoanalysis will become exclusively the province of the humanities and in that process lose a great deal of its driving force?

Peter Loewenberg: The first part of your question, Peter, is already fact. You heard Robert Michels this morning about the states of departments of psychiatry. And there was irony in his happy look to the future, to the day when the Western New England Institute will be part of Yale University, and so on. Because twenty years ago the Yale Child Study Center and that whole wonderful galaxy of people in the Child Study Center were Western New England psychoanalysts, and were very much a part of the university.

Now, about the second part of your presumption that psychoanalysis will not be used in therapy any more. Today all the varieties of psychotherapy—I don't know about the four hundred plus of Fred Crews, and I'll make my value judgment—all the *good* kinds of therapy are reflective and self-reflective. They all use the transference as ubiquitous. In fact we live in fields of transferences whether we're in therapy or not and the psychotherapies interpret it. So the kinds of therapies that are now part of the culture, outside of medical schools and departments of psychiatry, certainly will be here in the twenty-first century and can play with the humanities.

Hubert Damisch: Professor Crews didn't refer to the collapse of psychoanalysis as a therapy, he referred to the collapse of psychoanalysis as an alleged, as a so-called, science. Let's imagine that we will stop using psychoanalysis as a therapeutic device. Then there would be a chance for psychoanalysis to turn into some sort of a science. This is not at all what I see happening, but this could be the case. Psychoanalysis could then be used in the humanities as a tool, as a scientific tool. It's the same with Marxism, you know. There was a time in America, twenty years ago, when Marxism collapsed as a political force, and the art historians took charge of it. I remember that because I was part of it. There were big fights, really playing the game as a party: why did Comrade Clement Greenberg do that or this, you know. There were famous moments in American art history which were very important. So what about Marxism in the next century? You could ask exactly the same question.

What I mean is that psychoanalysis didn't only change our approach to art or to the humanities in general, it changed the very idea of art. Walter Benjamin said that photography obliged us to think about art in different ways. But what about psychoanalysis? Much more, you know. The same with beauty. The very idea of beauty has totally changed. Freud claimed that he had nothing to say about beauty—in fact what he had to say took only three lines, but it was decisive: that beauty has to do with displacement from the genitals to secondary sexual things.

I think that we have to face the fact that due to psychoanalysis we are working with the work of art differently. Speaking for myself now, I am no longer interested in working *on* the work of art. I am no longer interested in applying any tool *upon* or to the work of art. I am interested in working *with* the work of art, in exactly the same way that an analyst works with an analysand. This is what I tried to introduce in my short speech. How can we compare the analytical situation or relationship with the relation between the analyst and the work of art—you know, these two scenes, each playing its own *pièce,* its own Stück, its own play? How are we to understand that? Even if psychoanalysis will lose ground in the therapeutic field, there will be something kept of the therapeutic approach to the humanities.

What is the equivalent of the therapeutic bent in psychoanalysis when we deal with art? We are not only looking for an objective truth as the positivists would do—you know, who painted this painting, what date, and so on, the facts—we are interested in something else, something that has to do with a different type of truth, something that has to do with the right of the subject as such. Lacan refers to a work of art as dispositive, in the face of which the subject has to find its bearings, its marks. I think this is it. And *this* would be the equivalent of therapy, in a way.

And that's why I would oppose the idea of hermeneutics—because hermeneutics means not only meaning, it's not only dealing with meaning, it's dealing with meaning as *text.* Hermeneutics has to do with the text, and it means that everything reduces to a text. I'm interested in dealing with a work of art because there are *no* texts.

Angela Dalle Vacche: I just wanted to return to Peter Brooks's comment about psychoanalysis emigrating into the humanities and basically leaving medicine altogether, and pharmacology proliferating in medicine. One week ago I called the National Institutes of Health because I was doing some research for a friend of mine who has breast cancer, and I requested information about alternative medicine, since my friend has already gone through all the cycles of possible, imaginable chemotherapy. And I got these papers of recent research, and it's all about positive imaging and stuff like that. So, I would think that in the next millennium, the case is precisely opposite to the one proposed by Peter. Without necessarily throwing psychopharmacology out of the window, which is useful and handy to have around, I think psychoanalysis will be even more vibrant and exciting in the area of medicine. Especially because now, even in cancer therapy, people are thinking about positive imaging, which, I would say, has some kind of isomorphic relationship to the talking cure.

And, one more observation. Professor Damisch's comment was very interesting because his use of the preposition "with" takes us back to the idea of interpenetration proposed by Judith Butler vis-à-vis story as top layer.

Mary Jacobus: This doesn't relate directly to what she said, but I think it has a bearing on it and it takes us back to Bob Michels this morning, to the question of scientific verifiability or the medical framing of psychoanalysis. I'm thinking about Peter Loewenberg's remark that psychoanalysis is the only discipline that reflects on itself, where it's almost constitutive that it has that self-reflexive, self-reflecting dimension. And his own account of the journey into the consulting room, as seen by the patient, switched so dramatically to the journey *he* took. That is, to what he gestured toward, the countertransferential aspect of his own work as an analyst. And I'm wondering how one could possibly subject such a process to research or testing? What are you testing there? Our sense that psychoanalysis might lose purchase if it loses touch with medicine should be balanced with Freud's own insistence that you do not have to be a medically trained doctor to do psychoanalysis. It was a very important dimension to psychoanalysis, from the outset.

Peter Loewenberg: I want to comment on Damisch's reference to works of art not being texts. I do not see why we cannot dilate the concept of text to include symbols, fantasies, myths, images, works of art.

Hubert Damisch: I studied with [Maurice] Merleau-Ponty, and maybe it is due to Merleau-Ponty that I oppose the idea of the text. Of course there are texts and first Freud's text. That's what we're dealing with. But what I am more interested in dealing with is art—and that's why as a philosopher I moved to the study of art. I am interested in the pre-text, the foretext. In Merleau-Ponty's dealing with Cézanne, you know, what Cézanne was interested in was painting the world *before* it takes symbolic form, before it takes the form of language, before it can be described. You cannot *describe* a painting by Cézanne in the same way as you describe a painting by Poussin.

And this leads us back to the very interesting moment in this morning's panel about the story. And I really learned a lot from the other panelists. Shall we get rid of the story or not? This is exactly what's going on in the arts right now. For centuries "history," the *historia* in Italian, has been considered the main goal of painting. Painting had to build up the stage for the story to take place on it. What happened at the same time is that this stage was destroyed and painters were no longer interested in telling stories.

What I am interested in is: What makes us talk about art? Why can't we deal with it as nonverbal, and not talk about it? Why do we have to talk about it? Why do we have to inscribe art in the linguistic domain, in the verbal domain?

Question: I want to agree with Peter Brooks's remark about the need to relate hermeneutics and science, and I also want to agree with Professor Jacobus's caution not to reduce the science to medicine. We heard the idea of a medicine that didn't have a theory or a conception of the mind, and I think that what we're losing sight of is, really, the power and unity of the original conception. The best example I could give is *The Interpretation of Dreams*. Freud interpreted the Irma dream in 1895, and he wrote out the book in the next year. But he didn't publish it, didn't finish it, for another three years. And the reason was because he didn't have a conception of the mind. He hadn't finished the last chapter, Chapter 7, which considers the ideas of primary process, secondary process, the unconscious, and so forth. This is a very powerful conception, and it's a conception that was formulated in line with the science of his day, especially Lamarckian evolution, neurophysiology, and so forth. He didn't remain content with it, we can't remain content with it. But it is not a conception that can be reduced just to therapy—and it would be a terrible loss if we forgot about it.

I also wanted to make one brief comment on Toril Moi's point. I think Freud here, in the 1924 remark, is really pretty simple. This was the period when the women's movement had won the suffrage throughout the Western world, right after World War I, and the debate was similarity versus difference. And Freud is saying here very simply, it seems to me, do women develop an Oedipus complex, a castration complex, etc.? And he says, yes they *do*, but not the same as boys. Here the feminist demand for equal rights doesn't take us very far. Maybe he has a bit of humor here, a bit of sideshow, but he's saying basically: men and women are not just the same, there *are* differences. And that's why Freud was so attractive to so many women in the 1920s, because they were interested in the question: given equal rights, what are the differences?

Toril Moi: I am aware of the historical period in which Freud wrote the 1924 paper. Actually there's a kind of logical mistake in the comment, which is very frequently repeated in lots of feminist theory. You said that the question was similarity or difference. By similarity you probably also mean identity. It's true that the opposite of identity is usually difference, or vice-versa, but what Freud is talking about is equality. And the opposite of equality is inequality. It's as though there's a kind of short circuit in a lot of feminist theory these days, where we get this identity-difference debate, and it sort of shades into a debate about equality. But that's collapsing together two distinctions. Equality is something you may be in favor of because you're against *in*equality in the law and other places. That doesn't commit you to any specific position on psychological difference or identity between men and women. You may, of course, have views on both things, but they are actually distinct. It would be very illuminating if we stopped confusing identity and equality. We might get somewhere.

I otherwise agree. On the basic view on whether bodily, anatomical distinction gives rise to differences, Freud says yes. I don't disagree with the second half of his sentence. I'm just struck by this gratuitous remark about equality, which is not at all what he's discussing in the rest of the paper. So that was my point. I don't disagree with the idea that bodily structures *give rise to, feed into* an endless social process that produces us as men or women, who are happy or unhappy with the fact, who want to change sex, who want to be feminine or not feminine, or whatever. All that happens because we are perceived as having different bodies. But that's not exactly the same thing as the traditional interpretation of destiny.

Notes

1. See Marc Bloch, *French Rural History: An Essay on Its Basic Characteristics,* translated by Janet Sonheimer (Berkeley: University of California Press, 1966), xxvii–xxviii. See also Bloch, *The Historian's Craft,* translated by Peter Putnam (New York: Vintage Books, 1964).
2. Binjamin Wilkomirski, *Fragments: Memories of a Wartime Childhood,* translated by Carol Brown Janeway (New York: Schocken Books, 1996).

Part Three **Psychoanalysis and Sexual Identity**

Introduction

This section considers the role of psychoanalysis in posing the question of sexual identity: a question crucial to psychoanalysis, but also one in which Freud's own views have been most open to attack. Paul Robinson, an intellectual historian, begins by showing how an ambivalent or vacillating perspective toward homosexuality—within Freud's own work—generates various perspectives on sexual desire and social norms in twentieth-century psychoanalytic thought. On one hand, as Robinson claims, "no one has done more to destabilize the notion of heterosexuality than Freud." For Freud, the "homosexual object choice" is present in *all* individuals' psychic development; it is a "universalized" rather than "minoritized" aspect of desire. One legacy of Freud, then, is thinkers like Herbert Marcuse and Norman O. Brown, who invoke him as an early theorist for a liberated sexuality. On the other hand, the universality of homosexual desire is often stigmatized by Freud "as regressive, . . . as an atavism in which the child gets stuck—fixated—at some more primitive stage of psychic evolution." Freud's normative *evaluation* of that homosexual desire that he finds everywhere helps generate an entirely different strand of psychoanalytic thought: the insistence that homosexuality is a psychic illness that needs to be cured. This legacy of American psychoanalytic therapy, Robinson forcefully notes, belongs "less to the history of ideas than to the history of prejudice."

If Freud is father to both the liberatory and normative evaluation of sexual identity, to both ideas and prejudices, this speaks to the complexity of his modeling of sexual desire. The point of inquiry should not ultimately be to discover *which* Freud is the real one but rather to use his complicated, contradictory, and often prescient maneuvers around this question as models for contemporary concerns about identity, sexuality, and difference. In this sense, Freud provides different models of sexual identity in much the same way as he can provide models for cognitive science without *accurately* mapping the structure of the human mind (see Part V). In regards to neuroscience, Freud was himself aware that as scientific knowledge advanced, his specific theories about the brain might be supplanted while his conceptual models could remain vital to the field. Similarly, as understanding of sexual identity has progressed—on both political and theoretical planes—Freud's own contradictory thinking is not authoritative but can still be potentially useful and inspiring, and not least useful for the disagreement that it catalyzes.

The second and third panelists, Kaja Silverman and Leo Bersani, thus approach the question of psychoanalysis and sexual identity not from a historical but from a contemporary theoretical perspective. Both writers imagine—from a shared position of liberatory sexual critique—two distinct models that draw on psychoanalytic insights, returning, in quite interesting ways, to that central question of the "norm" within Freudian identity theory. Their debate, which dominates the discussion of this chapter, hinges on the relationship of the Oedipus complex to social normativity. Both agree that the Oedipus complex contains the *potential* to lead to a rigid, normative model of sexual identity. In the face of such norms—and their cultural strength in contemporary society— Silverman tries to think alternative sexual identities *through* the Oedipus complex, whereas Bersani tries to think such possibilities *against* the Oedipus complex.

The two approaches to the Oedipus complex revolve around the question of psychic mobility and the possibility of leaving "home," or the initial configuration of infantile desire. Silverman stresses how oedipal desire is always, and only, repeated in a displaced form: "we can only stay in the same place here," she notes, "by moving." Bersani argues that psychoanalysis always presents "the world entirely reformulated as the self"—so that its very stress on the psychic mediation of external reality prevents a more radical encounter with the world. Bersani insists that moving away from our own psychic economies into an exterior world is impossible in Freud: "we move by forgetting—and no human faculty is more alien to psychoanalysis than forgetting."

The radically divergent readings of the Oedipus complex Silverman and Bersani present can only send us back to Freud, back to the original and contradictory texts. In the discussion that ensues, Judith Butler notes how the tropes of "betrayal, fidelity, and promiscuity" have informed the language of the debate. Paul Robinson extends this figural motif by talking about the "seductive" quality of Freud's prose, a seduction that only becomes stronger upon rereading.

Freud and Homosexuality

Paul Robinson

My topic here is, to state it in a necessarily crude and abbreviated fashion, the question, "Has Freud been good or bad for homosexuals?" The question is worth asking because a number of scholarly writings in the 1990s represented Freud as among the foremost inventors of modern homophobia—just as, a quarter of a century earlier, Kate Millett represented him as the forefather of modern misogyny. I am thinking of books like Jonathan Ned Katz's *Invention of Heterosexuality* (1995) or Daniel Boyarin's *Unheroic Conduct* (1997), in which Freud appears as a chief architect of the modern medical category of the homosexual (as well as that of the heterosexual). These categories—so the argument goes—created the tendentious notion that humanity is divided between those (presumably a small minority) devoted exclusively to sexual relations with their own sex and those (the vast majority) no less exclusively devoted to relations with the opposite sex.

I think this conception is fundamentally wrong. But it contains an element of truth, especially if we broaden our view to include not just Freud himself but the psychoanalytic tradition as a whole, especially its American variant in the middle years of the twentieth century. I don't wish to get into the broader argument about whether in fact "the homosexual" was invented—or merely codified—by turn-of-the-century sexologists (an argument that has pitted what are called "essentialists" against "social constructionists"). The kernel of truth that links Freud to what can legitimately be considered a homophobic discourse is his famous developmental conception of identity formation, according to which heterosexual object choice is seen as the ideal, or at least the "normal," outcome of the child's psychic evolution. As Katz points out, Freud repeatedly, almost compulsively, refers to heterosexuality as the "normal" result, and he uses "normal" not just in a statistical sense but evaluatively, equating it with psychic maturity. By way of contrast, homosexuality in this scheme is always construed as regressive: Freud invariably speaks of it as an atavism, in which the child gets stuck—fixated—at some more primitive stage of psychic evolution, whether it be narcissistic, oral, or anal. Freud's language, in other words, is "normalizing," although one needs to point out that Freud's feelings about "normality," like his feelings about "civilization," were ambivalent. One strain in his thought protested against the libidinal sacrifice that "normal" adult genitality entailed, and, as thinkers like Herbert Marcuse and Norman Brown argued years ago, one can read Freud as, at least in part, a critic of normalization and a prophet of a liberated, "polymorphously perverse" sexuality. In *Civilization and Its Discontents*, for example, Freud gives a distinctly critical account of the sacrifices that so-called psychic maturity entails: "As regards the sexually mature individual," he writes, "the choice of object is restricted to the opposite sex, and most extra-genital satisfactions are forbidden as perversions. The requirement, demonstrated in these prohibitions, that there shall be a single kind of sexual life for everyone, disregards the dissimilarities, whether innate or acquired, in the sexual constitution of human beings; it cuts off a fair number of them from sexual enjoyment, and so becomes the source of serious injustice."[1]

Although Freud's treatment of homosexuality was "normalizing," it was not "pathologizing." The distinction is important, because later on American psychoanalysts would argue, unambiguously, that homosexuality was a sickness. But Freud insisted that it was not a sickness. He did so most famously in his 1935 letter to the mother of an American homosexual. In fact, one can argue that Freud conceived of homosexuality as the opposite of sickness. As he said, more than once, the neuroses were, in his view, the "negative" of the perversions, by which he meant that homosexual urges become pathogenic only when repressed. The person who acted on his or her homosexual impulses was in theory immune to neurosis, whereas those impulses became dangerous precisely when they were driven into the unconscious. Perhaps the best-known instance of the phenomenon is Freud's theory of paranoia, worked out in the Schreber case, where paranoia is said to be caused by repressed homosexual desire.

Even more fundamentally, however, the notion that Freud participated in the radical conceptual separating of homosexuals from heterosexuals gets the story exactly backwards. On the contrary, he opposed any notion that homosexuality can be so isolated, or that homosexuals constitute an essentially separate class of persons and that heterosexuals are thus safe from homosexual contamination. Freud expressly opposed the version of this idea advanced by a number of homophile theorists, such as Karl Heinrich Ulrichs and Magnus Hirschfeld, even though he supported the political goal that the conception was meant to advance—namely, the decriminalization of homosexuality—because, he contended, it ignored the evidence, turned up by psychoanalysis, that homosexuality is universally present in psychic development. As he says in the *Three Essays,* "All human beings are capable of making a homosexual object-choice and have in fact made one in their unconscious."[2] To use the language invented by Eve Sedgwick, Freud's conception of homosexuality is unambiguously "universalizing," as opposed to the "minoritizing" ideas advanced not only by homosexuals like Ulrichs and Hirschfeld but by such influential straight thinkers of the period as Richard von Krafft-Ebing and Havelock Ellis. In Freud's psychic universe, homosexuality is everywhere, insinuating itself into the psychic lives of the most impeccably "normal" and presentable individuals. Indeed, no one has done more to destabilize the notion of heterosexuality than Freud. In Freud's universe there simply are no heterosexuals, at least not psychologically. Similarly, he insists that manifest heterosexuality, far from being a fact of nature, is a precarious psychic achievement, and one that needs to be accounted for. As he writes, again in the *Three Essays,* "The exclusive sexual interest felt by men for women is also a problem that needs elucidating and is not a self-evident fact based upon an attraction that is ultimately of a chemical nature."[3] Nor did Freud exempt himself from this universalizing conception: he frequently diagnosed his own relationship with Wilhelm Fliess as the manifestation of a passive homosexual attachment on his own part, most famously at the time of his fainting spell in Munich in 1912 when, speaking of his long connection with Fliess, he remarked in a letter to Ernest Jones, "There is some piece of unruly homosexual feeling at the root of the matter."[4]

This universalizing conception is most spectacularly on display in the famous case histories. The only one who appears to be innocent of homosexual desire is the Rat Man, and here we almost feel that Freud missed the obvious homosexual implications of the Rat Man's rat fantasy. With the exception of Leonardo, all the male protagonists of the case histories (I'll come to the women in a moment) were manifest heterosexuals. Yet homosexual urges are found in each of their psychic lives, most emphatically of course in the case of the Wolf-man and Schreber, where the repression of their desire to be sodomized by the father, Freud argues, is the fundamental source of their illness. I would also suggest that Freud's attitude toward these men ranges from admiration (in the case of Leonardo, with whom, in fact Freud profoundly identified) to at the very least dispassionate interest and sympathy, although one can argue that he is most enthusiastic about a homosexual like Leonardo who has sublimated his desires (and thereby become a culture bearer—rather like the Jews in *Moses and Monotheism*). He is made more nervous by passive anal sex (which, as Leo Bersani has complained, he illegitimately equates with castration, and thus with feminization) than he is by fellatio, which, as he notes in the Leonardo case, is "loathsome" in the eyes of "respectable society" but, he goes on to say, "may be traced to an origin of the most innocent kind," namely, the child's sucking at its mother's breast.[5] I would point out that, from a historian's point of view, one of the most remarkable things about Freud's discussions of homosexuality is their astonishing rhetorical evenhandedness, which contrasts not only with the habitual prejudice of his society but also with the more judgmental tone of even such relatively enlightened figures as Krafft-Ebing and Ellis. As he says when introducing the sexual aberrations in the *Introductory Lectures,* "What we have here is a field of phenomena like any other."[6]

The story is very different, of course, when it comes to the two most famous lesbian case histories, Dora and the anonymous woman of 1920. These cases, as Mary Jacobus has shown, are remarkably alike: both involve prepossessing young women in their late teens who react to Freud with marked hostility and whom he treats with a corresponding contempt, which of course invites the suspicion that the real problem is Freud's, not his patients'. Put another way, I see in Freud's failure to extend to lesbians the same dispassion he lavishes on his male homosexuals a reflection of his larger problem with women. Indeed, I think it is hard to separate lesbianism from femininity in Freud's conceptual universe, because both are analyzed by him in terms of women's psychic problems with the penis and their disappointment in men. It's also interesting that although Freud insists that in men there is no necessary connection between homosexual object choice and "character inversion" (that is, effeminacy), he makes just the opposite assertion about lesbians: in his view they are nearly always mannish. In other words, I don't think Freud's hostile treatment of lesbianism—which contrasts both substantively and above all rhetorically with his treatment of male homosexuality—can be separated from his misogyny.

More important, finally, than any of the issues I've addressed so far—all of which might be said to belong to the "sticks and stones" category—is the question of therapy: the question of whether homosexuality can be treated or, more radically, cured. Although Freud often said that (manifest) homosexuality was probably grounded in some constitutional predisposition, the general thrust of his thinking was to insist that homosexuals are made rather than born, which seems to leave him open to the possibility that they might be "unmade," that is, turned into heterosexuals. But in fact Freud took just the opposite position. Although his pronouncements aren't absolutely categorical, he comes very close to saying that homosexuality is entirely beyond the range of not only analytic therapy but any therapy whatsoever. His statement in the lesbian case of 1920 is representative: "In general," he writes, "to undertake to convert a fully developed homosexual into a heterosexual does not offer much more prospect of success than the reverse."[7]

Freud's humane therapeutic pessimism must be contrasted with the profoundly homophobic and insanely utopian therapeutic optimism of his American acolytes, above all the evil trio of Edmund Bergler (a European transplant), Irving Bieber, and Charles Socarides—who, alas, is still among the quick and still issuing the same mad pronouncements. Not only do they call all homosexuals pathological, as well as manipulative liars, but they also insist that the homosexual's only hope lies in converting to heterosexuality. Bergler went so far as to claim that such "cures" could be effected "in 99.9 percent of all cases of homosexuality."[8] Here we are no longer dealing with sticks and stones but with a brutally oppressive therapeutic practice that profoundly damaged a generation of American gay men in the middle decades of the twentieth century. If you want to take the measure of that damage in an individual life, I recommend the autobiography of Martin Duberman, entitled *Cures,* which documents the horrific treatment that Duberman received at the hands of three American Freudians in the 1950s and 1960s. In other words, American psychoanalysts exactly reversed Freud's ideas as well as his therapeutic practice. They transformed homosexuality into a disease, and a curable one at that, and they categorically separated it from "normal" heterosexuality by expressly rejecting Freud's universalizing notion of constitutional bisexuality. They even reversed Freud's prejudices on the subject, because in the midcentury American literature lesbianism is ignored, whereas male homosexuality, toward which Freud had a distinct softness, is thoroughly demonized. As the historian of this unhappy story, Kenneth

Lewes, has said, in America the Freudian theory of homosexuality ceased to be a matter of the history of ideas and became instead a matter of the history of prejudice. And as Lewes further suggests, the transformation had much more to do with the Cold War and McCarthyism—and with the eagerness of foreign-born analysts to ingratiate themselves with their American hosts—than with anything that Freud ever wrote on the subject.

There is a sweet Freudian footnote to this lamentable history: Robert Socarides, the son of the last and arguably the most vulgar of the American psychoanalytic homophobes, Charles Socarides, is not only a gay man himself but an activist in the cause and Bill Clinton's principal liaison to the gay community. I like to think of it as the return of the repressed.

Notes

1. Freud, *Civilization and Its Discontents, S.E.,* 21: 104.
2. Freud, *Three Essays on the Theory of Sexuality, S.E.,* 7: 145n.
3. Ibid., 146n.
4. Ernest Jones, *The Life and Work of Sigmund Freud,* vol. 1 (New York: Basic Books, 1953), 317.
5. Freud, *Leonardo Da Vinci and a Memory of His Childhood, S.E.,* 11: 86–87.
6. Freud, *Introductory Lectures on Psycho-Analysis, S.E.,* 16: 307.
7. Freud, "The Psychogenesis of a Case of Homosexuality in a Woman," *S.E.,* 18: 151.
8. Cited in Kenneth Lewes, *The Psychoanalytic Theory of Male Homosexuality* (New York: Simon and Schuster, 1988), 112.

The Language of Care

Kaja Silverman

It is often assumed that the primary function of the Oedipus complex is social normalization. I am no longer as certain as I once was that this is an adequate account of the Oedipus complex. It now seems to me that the primary function of this complex is to satisfy an irreducible *structural* imperative, albeit in a variable form. This imperative is not so much, as Claude Lévi-Strauss has argued, to facilitate exchange between families; it is to induct the subject into the speaking of his or her language of desire. It is an imperative because without it there can be no world.

Affect is not the strictly private affair we generally assume it to be. As Freud makes clear in his Schreber case history, it is in our own "bosom" that we build or destroy the world. This does not mean that other creatures and things do not exist in reality unless they exist for us subjectively. We do not have the capacity to confer or withdraw being. Our power is both greater and less: we determine whether other creatures and things will continue to languish in the darkness of concealment or whether they can enter the light of Being. The names for this space are many. Freud, as we have seen, calls it "breast" in his Schreber case history. Martin Heidegger prefers "clearing," and Jacques Lacan "manque-à-être."

In eroticizing a particular familial axis or set of axes, the Oedipus complex awakens in us something that none of us can do without but that would otherwise be foreclosed to us: the capacity to be concerned with someone other than ourselves. And in obliging us to surrender the one we love for a series of substitute love objects, it makes room in our psyche for other people and things. Only if we pay this exorbitant price early in our lives can things and other people "matter" to us. Indeed, the case could be stated even more starkly: only insofar as we are thrown into a kinship structure, for the effectuation of which the Oedipus complex is one possible vehicle, can there *be* a world.

It might seem a contradiction in terms to attribute the effect of an opening up rather than a closing down to the Oedipus complex. Have we not learned from psychoanalysis that those who love and lose their fathers choose men who resemble them as replacements, just as those who love and lose their mothers choose women who resemble their mother? I would like to suggest that it is only through substantializing the terms *mother* and *father* that we can impute either predictability or determinant meaning to such libidinal substitutions. As phenomenology helps us to understand, *mother* and *father* do not in fact designate encompassable entities. Nor do they represent fixed symbolic constructs that largely transcend the actuality of the persons so designated. Rather, *mother* and *father* constitute complex discursive events that can take very different forms from one subject to another, and even from one moment to another.

As Freud's analysis of dreams, jokes, and parapraxes makes clear, the displacements at the heart of psychic life are not at the simple disposition of the conscious individual. However, they are even less at the absolute behest of the larger culture, although the surrounding environment always leaves its imprint there. Because of the unstable and heterogeneous nature of every love object, desire can extend itself in entirely unpredictable directions. Perhaps what permits an early love object to replace the mother, for instance, is not the smell of breast-milk, but the name *Persephone,* which seems to the infant subject akin to the mother's name, *Penelope,* and which leads, through many detours and circumlocutions, to an adult passion for classical literature. And for another subject, the word *mother* might signify a mole at the corner of a shapely mouth, which he many years later rediscovers on the face of an eighteen-year-old boy.

Our object choices are also always made from within specific geographical, social, economic, and historical circumstances. These circumstances can profoundly inflect our unconscious signifying network and so further particularize it. We might think, in this respect, of the role played by the servant girl in Freud's case history of the Wolfman, whose posture while washing the floor establishes the erotic disposition of a middle-class man. Equally germane to the present discussion is the geographical displacement implicit in the slippage from the English *glance* to the German *Glanz* in Freud's essay on fetishism; here the movement from one language and culture to another determines a shine on the nose as the compensatory supplement. Although most of us make an initial libidinal investment in either our mother or our father, there is potentially nothing more individual and multifaceted, though less within conscious control, than the constellation of signifiers through which we signify those personages.

Two dangers nevertheless attend the speaking of our language of desire. The first is that with it we will say again only what has been said before; that far from expanding the world through an innovative series of displacements, we will signify the categories of "mother" and "father" in purely "functional" ways. The second danger is that we will fail to speak intelligibly: that we will forget that it is the defining attribute of all speech acts, whether verbal or libidinal, to be in dialogue with the Other.

A culture's kinship structure represents the equivalent, at the level of desire, of an abstract language system. It provides the *langue* according to which the libido can signify. As Lacan puts it in the Rome discourse, "The marriage tie is governed by an order of preferences whose law concerning the kinship names is, like language, imperative for the group in its forms, but unconscious in its structure. In this structure . . . the startled theoretician finds the whole of the logic of combinations." But a language without speakers is soon a dead language. A verbal or libidinal langue can sustain itself only so long as it is spoken, and inherent in speech is the capacity to work in a transformative way upon the categories that it deploys. When we use our culture's kinship structure in this manner, we individuate it; we make out of it our own language of desire. We also make room in the world for new creatures and things.

In arguing for the importance of the particularization of desire, I am not saying anything new. Many people today aspire not to desire as others have desired before them but rather to break free of their culture's kinship structure. This is in my view neither possible nor desirable. Were we to succeed in desiring a-oedipally, we would stop speaking altogether, in the libidinal sense of that word. Speech is by definition dialogical, and a dialogue can only take place where there is a common frame of reference. The loss of speech would be too high a price to pay for absolute libidinal freedom, even assuming there were such a thing. Not only are passions that we cannot communicate hardly worthy of the name; it is through sharing our passions with others that we make our world a common world, rather than an infinity of private worlds. It is also only through speech that we can actively assume our particular language of desire, in the Lacanian sense of that word. Only when our linguistic and libidinal words return to use from the site of the Other can we really "hear" them.

Finally, to refuse to speak our desire in the language of our culture's kinship structure would be to deny what is by no means the least significant of our little freedoms as subjects: our capacity to articulate its categories in a new way. To say, "My desire has nothing to do with the Oedipus complex," would be to essentialize and detemporalize what is finally nothing but a structural imperative. It would be to make something closed out of the very thing whose function is to open us up to the multiplicity and multifariousness of the world.

Speaking Psychoanalysis

Leo Bersani

What exactly is psychoanalytic thought, and how might answering this question help us to define what might be called the psychoanalytically constituted subject? One of the most curious aspects of *Civilization and Its Discontents* is Freud's reiterated self-reproach to the effect that he is not speaking psychoanalytically. The work was written in 1929, late in Freud's career, so it's not as if he hadn't had time to develop a distinctively psychoanalytic language. You would think that by now Freud would be "speaking psychoanalysis" fluently. But the complaints start in Chapter 3, where he laments that "so far we have discovered nothing that is not universally known," nothing, that is, that might not have been said without the help of psychoanalysis. Given the repetition of this complaint three more times in the work, we should be alert to anything that breaks the self-critical trend, to any moment when Freud might be saying: "This is it! Now I'm being profound, saying things that people didn't know before I said them! Now I'm speaking the language of psychoanalysis!" And indeed there is just such a moment. In the middle of Chapter 7, Freud announces an idea worthy of the founder of a new science, a new way of thinking, about the human mind. "And here at last an idea comes in which belongs entirely to psycho-analy-sis and which is foreign to people's ordinary way of thinking."[1]

What is that idea? It tells us, Freud continues, that although "conscience is indeed the cause of instinctual renunciation to begin with, . . . later the rela-tionship is reversed. Every renunciation of instinct now becomes a dynamic source of conscience and every fresh renunciation increases the latter's severity and intolerance." And Freud declares himself "tempted to defend the paradox-ical statement that conscience is the result [rather than the cause] of instinctual renunciation."[2] It would seem, then, that paradox is central to psychoanalytic thinking. There is, however, something troubling in the fact that *Civilization and Its Discontents* has been dealing in paradoxes long before Freud announced the arrival of an idea worthy of psychoanalysis. We have learned, for example, that the more virtuous a man is the more severe is his superego and that he blames himself for misfortunes for which he is clearly not responsible. Such paradoxes may be puzzling at first, but they are resolvable. To renounce instinctual satis-faction is not to renounce instinctual desire; the frustration of desire increases its intensity, and so saints, Freud remarks, "are not so wrong" to call themselves sinners: frustrated temptations are inescapable temptations.[3]

Freud moves on, however, to say something quite different: renunciation it-self *produces* conscience. The more familiar view, Freud reminds us, is that "the original aggressiveness of conscience is a continuance of the severity of the ex-ternal authority and therefore has nothing to do with renunciation."[4] But in-ternalization turns out to have two very different aspects. On one hand, the au-thority becomes an internal watchdog and is thereby able to continue to exercise its prohibitive functions. On the other hand, Freud tells us, it is internalized *in order to be attacked.* The authority's imagined aggression toward the desiring sub-ject is taken over by the subject not only to discipline desire but in order to at-tack the authority itself. It is *as if* the subject-ego were still being punished for its guilty desires, but the punishing energy is taken from the subject's fury at the agent of punishments, who in fact also becomes its object. The child is show-ing the father what a good punishing father he or she, the child, would be, but because it is aggression toward the father that allows for this instructive demon-stration, the object of it is bound to be the father, "degraded," as Freud says, to sitting in for or as the child in the punished ego. This ferociously severe con-science enacts the phenomenology of the renounced instinctual drives. We no longer have the paradox of virtue intensifying the reproaches of conscience, a paradox explained, and dissolved, by the role of secret desires compensating for the renounced behavior. Now we are speaking not of degrees of guilt or of moral severity but rather of an aggressiveness that accompanies renounced desires. The external authority's severe demands on the subject are, as it were, fused with the subject's revengeful anger at those demands, both of which constitute the subject's renunciation: the consequence, and the content, of renunciation is a doubly reinforced conscience.

This idea may be called distinctively psychoanalytic in that it describes a process in which the world has been sacrificed but *nothing has been lost.* The external authority now exists only as a function of the subject's fantasies: both as the reappropriated angry father originally projected onto the real father and as a carrier of the subject's revengeful aggressiveness toward the father. Psychoanalysis does not deny the world's existence, but it does document the procedures by which the mind dephenomenalizes the world, freezes it in a history of fantasmatic representations, or persistently resists the world with its fantasy of lost *jouissance.* To complain, for example, as critics have done, that Freud turned away from the real world and studied the seduction of children only as fantasy is like complaining about astronomers turning their analytic attention to the stars. Psychoanalysts are no more and no less capable than anyone else of recognizing such phenomena as real child abuse, but that recognition is irrelevant to what is "psychoanalytic" in psychoanalysis. In fact psychoanalysis is hyperbolically aware of the world as different from the self—which is why it can so brilliantly describe all our techniques for erasing that difference and why it is of so little help in constructing an epistemology and an ethics grounded in perceptions of sameness, an epistemology and an ethics that might allow us to build a nonviolent relation to the real.

In psychoanalysis, nothing is ever forgotten, given up, left behind. In Chapter I of *Civilization and Its Discontents,* Freud claims that "in mental life nothing which has once been formed can perish," and, soon after this "everything past is preserved."[5] Everything persists; psychoanalysis classifies the modalities of persistence and return: conscious memory, slips-of-the-tongue, repression, symptomatic behavior, acting out, sublimation. *Civilization and Its Discontents* textually confirms this law. It wanders, and Freud appears to have trouble finding his subjects (the function of religion, the conditions of happiness, the nature of civilization, erotic and nonerotic drives, the etiology of conscience). And yet aggressiveness comes to include everything: it is accompanied by an intense erotic pleasure; like the oceanic feeling discussed in Chapter I, it breaks down the boundaries between the self and the world; it gives expression both to instinctual needs and, in the form of conscience, to the inhibiting energy of civilization. With the analysis of aggressiveness, the boundaries separating concepts are broken down; manifesting a kind of oceanic textuality, ideas flood together in a dense psychoanalytic mix that obliterates such cherished distinctions as those between Eros and nonerotic aggression, even between the individual and civilization (both are at once objects and sources of aggression).

Distinctions between ideas are perhaps ontologically grounded in assumptions of a difference of being between the self and the world. In demonstrating the mind's resources for erasing that distinction, psychoanalysis understandably has difficulty articulating its concepts, keeping some space between them. For Freud, this meant holding on, for dear intellectual life, to dualisms he himself recognized as fragile. Their terms may constantly be collapsing into one another—sadism into masochism, the nonerotic into the erotic, even, as Jean Laplanche has demonstrated, the death drive into sexuality—and yet Freud continued to insist, to insist all the more tenaciously, on the validity of his dualisms. "Our views," he writes in *Beyond the Pleasure Principle,* "have from the very first been *dualistic,* and today they are even more definitely dualistic than before."[6] The logical incoherence that results from the breakdown of conceptual distinctions accurately represents the overdetermined mind described by psychoanalysis. For overdetermination, far from being merely a characteristic of primary process thinking, defines the psychoanalytic mind—that is, the mind that has renounced none of its interpretations of the real.

This also is an oceanic phenomenon—not exactly, however, the "limitless narcissism" of the self everywhere present in the world but rather that of the world entirely reformulated as the self. The distinction, which may appear tenuous, is actually of the greatest importance, for what I take to be psychoanalysis's most serious limitation is precisely the difficulty it has imagining that we can find ourselves *already* in the world—there not as a result of our projections but as a sign of the natural extensibility of all being. This is the presence to which art—not psychoanalysis—alerts us. I have recently been interested in tracing the communication of forms in art as the affirmation of a certain solidarity in the universe, a solidarity we must perhaps first of all see as one not of identities but rather of positionings and configurations in space. The narcissistic pleasure of reaching toward our own "form" *elsewhere* has little to do with the flood of an oceanic, limitless narcissism intent on eliminating the world's difference. Rather, it pleasurably confirms that we are inaccurately replicated everywhere, a perception that may help us, ultimately, to see difference not as a trauma to be overcome but as the nonthreatening supplement to sameness. Psychoanalysis profoundly describes our aptitude for preserving the world as subjectivity; only art gives us the world *as world,* one we "know" as aesthetic subjects thrown outward, "defined" by relations that at once dissolve, disperse, and repeat us.

We move by forgetting—and no human faculty is more alien to psychoanalysis than that of forgetting. Freud initiated the systematic study of all the ways in which we remain faithful, the strategies by which we manage to go on loving and fearing our first fantasmatic objects. Psychoanalysis, with its obsessive concern with the difference between the self and the world, necessarily sees the world as the repository of everything hostile to the self. It is a place to which, at best, we adapt and from which we retreat and regress to the imagined familial securities nourished by such privileged institutions as monogamy and marriage. The family is the psychoanalytic haven to which we regress, a regression that might be unnecessary if we had ever left it in the first place. If psychoanalysis, in its account of the extraordinary mobility of childhood and, more specifically, even oedipal desires, has itself described for us the original inconceivability of a monogamous fixity of desire, and therefore of a stable sexual identity, monogamy nonetheless is the relational figure most congenial to what we might call the psychoanalytic fidelity of the self *to* the self, its indifference to signs of self that are not signs of interpretation, and, finally, its profoundly immoral rejection of our promiscuous humanity.

Notes

1. Freud, *Civilization and Its Discontents,* trans. James Strachey (1930; New York: W. W. Norton, 1961), 50, 90.
2. Ibid., 90.
3. Ibid., 87.
4. Ibid., 91.
5. Ibid., 16, 19.
6. Freud, *Beyond the Pleasure Principle,* trans. James Strachey (1920; New York: W. W. Norton, 1961), 63.

Discussion

Paul Robinson: I have a question for Kaja Silverman. I was struck, unless I misunderstood, by the fact that she and Judith Butler [see Part I] were saying very similar things about what I would call "denaturalizing" the family. They both suggest that "mother" and "father" are culturally contingent categories and that we should be open to other ways of thinking beside the traditional, biological one that we have in the West, which I find a very attractive idea. I'm wondering whether Professor Silverman thinks Freud himself is open to this kind of culturally relative or culturally contingent way of thinking about the family. It brings to my mind, in a slightly different context, the critique that Malinowski made of Freud's psychic universalism half a century ago now. And I didn't hear in her talk, nor did I in Judy Butler's talk this morning, whether they thought that the way they were encouraging us to think about "mother" and "father," think about "the family," think about kinship, was one that was authorized by Freud's own thinking.

Kaja Silverman: It's very strange that we have always assumed that in the process of displacements that leads away from the parental object, meaning starts there punctually at the beginning, rather than understanding that it's through a series of displacements that we signify that original term. The original term is a nonsensical term, as Lacan insists in his Seventh Seminar, in his reading of *Project for a Scientific Psychology*, of *that* particular Freud. And its meaning is constituted through the displacements away from it. Freud himself, in *Project for a Scientific Psychology*, has the very rich idea that the value of a term is determined by the largeness of the semantic field that surrounds it. So how does *mother* come to be valuable? By the terms that are collected around it, through which it is signified. And the larger the field of saturation, libidinal saturation, the greater that term. Then we arrive at the very extraordinary notion that we are faithful to mother or father by moving away from her or him. We are faithful because we are increasing the value of that original term with every subsequent displacement. It's a peculiar notion of fidelity, not what we usually think of as fidelity, which is staying in the same place. But we can, in a sense, only stay in the same place here by moving.

That's the model that I'm working with at the moment, and my current feeling is that the stakes are very, very high for this notion. It's not just about opening up our libidinal options. We're dealing here with the category of the world, which I see Leo, who's always somehow thinking alongside me, is also concerning himself with. I'm not really thinking about cultural variability here. I'm thinking about the variability of *each* subject, about the particularity of each subject's language of desire.

Leo Bersani: I wanted to ask Paul Robinson something about the discussion of Freud's relation to homosexuality. I'm wondering whether in addition to his expressions of sympathy, and the distinction between that and the homophobic analyst that he draws, there's anything significant in the remarks Freud made a few times about the relation between homosexuality and *social* feeling? That homosexuals have a particular aptitude toward social feelings . . .?

Paul Robinson: Oh yes, I know what you mean. He says it in the Wolfman case and he says it in the Leonardo case—that they have a particular capacity for humanitarianism, just as they have a particular capacity for culture. The only thing one might say by way of regretting those remarks is that they have a certain feel of "pedestalism" about them. It's sort of homosexuals on the pedestal, and they are almost always, of course, sublimating homosexuals. It is the Wolfman as he *gets better*, that's where this passage occurs in the *Wolfman*. It's in the moment of recuperation that Freud goes into this little speech, how it's remarkable that as the Wolfman gets better he becomes devoted to humanitarian causes. Because what is the Wolfman doing but sublimating those desires in what Freud thinks is, not necessarily an appropriate, but the best way? Just as Leonardo is so admirable because *all* of his homosexual desire goes not into having sex with his handsome apprentices, which is what Freud says he really wants; it all goes into the creation of art, into the creation of science, and so forth. So I think that's consistent with what I would call his homophile ideology.

Leo Bersani: I wonder whether there's a correlative of some kind of developmental *in*aptitude for sociality among nonsublimated heterosexuals.

Kaja Silverman: I've always loved very much Leo's notion of the communication of forms. And today it occurred to me that he is also worrying not only about the world but about communication. And I wanted to ask him: how do forms communicate?

Leo Bersani: Well, they can communicate obviously only through our perception of them. But there are two orders of formal communications that I've been interested in. One is an order between nonhuman objects. And that is something that Ulysse Dutoit and I have been interested in, in studying examples of visual art. Assyrian sculpture, the paintings of Rothko. These are not figurative, and the kinds of forms that we noted were not *communication* in any human sense of the word but, rather, certain formal similarities and therefore what one might call certain correspondences of form, in the Baudelarian sense of correspondences.

The thing that interests me right now is how that might be transposed to a perception of sameness among human beings. And the kinds of communication that might be made possible, if, for example, we were trained not to think of others as different, but first of all to recognize that which replicates the subject in the other. Rather than that which is different from the self, in the other. I think the communication that might be built on the basis of *that* perception is quite different from the communication that is built on what is at first a *differentially* based sense of the world.

Kaja Silverman: Let me ask one follow-up question. You began with the issue of aggression, and it's a strange feature of most subjectivities that the largest amount of aggression is directed against those who are most similar. The narcissism of small differences. And so can you elaborate a little bit more on how we could avoid the narcissism of small differences?

Leo Bersani: I don't feel secure about answering that question, which is an extremely important one. But I suspect that that hostility towards small differences is something like a *subset* within a differential perception of the world to begin with and that it explains the greater hostility there, a hostility in which the perception of sameness has already been stigmatized in a way. That stigmatization, I suspect, results from the original valorization of difference as primary.

I'm interested in the way in which we describe our projects. And with all the similarities of what we're interested in, I was very struck by the way in which you said: we can remain *faithful* to the early object in ways that seem very *different* from being faithful. And it's the persistence of that category, of remaining faithful, where there's something different going on in what we're pursuing right now. In other words, I don't care if we remain faithful, and I'm interested in what the modalities of a socially productive *betrayal* might be, rather than one of fidelity. Why do we always have to keep the term—to prove that somehow however different we are, or rather however far we go from the original interpretation or the original object, we're still remaining faithful to it? Do you see that as a fundamental difference?

Kaja Silverman: Well, but what constitutes being faithful to the original term is defined entirely through the subsequent terms. So it's not fidelity in any strict sense of the word.

Leo Bersani: No, I know it's not. And that's very interesting to me, that it is a kind of redefinition of fidelity. But it seems to me that the language of affective ties to objects has to be reinvented along with what we're trying to do, rather than proving that what we're trying to do still fits the old language.

Katherine Kearns, Moderator: Let's open the floor up for questions.

Question: This question is addressed primarily to the debate between Kaja Silverman and Leo Bersani. And the wider framing for my question is the importance that psychoanalysis has had recently for questions that are historical and ethical. I take as an example the discussion in [Part II] about Auschwitz. Now, listening to what Leo Bersani was saying on the subject of forgetting, I'm wondering whether he shouldn't have had his place on the panel on "Psychoanalysis and Its Discontents." If I understand you well, you suggest that there should be a place for forgetting and that psychoanalysis does not enable that by the very way in which it works. There seems to be a desire to leave behind, in order to be able to enjoy what Mallarmé would have called a "vierge et vivace aujourd'hui." So I'd be interested in hearing more about forgetting and ethics.

Leo Bersani: Well, I think that's exactly what I'm trying to see whether we can construct. What would an ethics in which forgetting would play an important part be like? I don't know really. This is by no means a kind of final statement. And by forgetting I don't mean *literally* that we're incapable of remembering anything. But by forgetting I mean that possibility of recognizing the self in the world, of recognizing a certain familiarity in the world that is not based on being faithful to our interpretations of the world. And that's why the communication of forms in art interests me very much. Because they're very often recognitions of purely formal, external, superficial correspondences that have nothing to do with interpretation but that really are simply certain shapes that happen to go in the same direction. Similarities of volume. I think that that's a very good place from which to begin thinking of ways of moving on from certain sets of objects to other sets of objects through forgetting. And what you're forgetting *is* that which is being left out. And which I think it might be *ethically* interesting to try leaving out—which are the masses of interpretations, which is really that to which we remain faithful.

Question, continued: But then to look at a painting by Rothko is to look at a painting that has no history and that does not remember anything, if I understand you. You took him as an example.

Leo Bersani: Well no, in fact, the painting, like all art, is full of memories in a certain sense, in the sense that it implicitly remembers other art. But it implicitly remembers its formal correspondences with other art, which is a very interesting way to think of a relation to the past in which memory would of course not be eliminated, but which would involve a certain kind of forgetting when it comes to the human mind, which unlike a painting includes a history of faithful interpretations. Whereas the memory that Rothko—or that Caravaggio, or that any of the work we've been talking about—has of art before it is a memory that's translated entirely in the volumes and shapes and forms, which are themselves a kind of interpretation, obviously, but which remain interpretations on the surface.

Kaja Silverman: I guess there is a fundamental disagreement between Leo and me on this issue. It has to do with the fidelity topic, again. I'm interested in that moment in visual perception which functions in the mode of care, in the mode of what Heidegger would call care towards the world. And I believe that can only happen in the meeting of the perceptual object with memory. I think those are the only conditions under which that can happen. So I guess I would say that there can be no ethics of forgetting. But, of course, that formulation is subject again to the notion that what *was* is reincarnated in a new form in the perceptual event. That what was becomes something other in the process of making itself seen.

Peter Loewenberg: On the issue of homosexuality, as early as 1905 in the *Three Essays on the Theory of Sexuality,* Freud said, "The pathological approach to the study of inversion has been displaced by the anthropological."[1] Thus he moves from biology to culture, from pathology to anthropology. That is an absolutely critical move in the early twentieth century. And you could collapse your Leonardo examples with Michelangelo, whom Freud also thought to be a homosexual—the broken nose and so on.

Paul Robinson: I think the issue of Freud and the biological and cultural understanding of homosexuality is very complicated. And it's politically complicated, as well as conceptually. There's a long tradition of homosexual thinking, you might say, which has seen the biologizing or the medicalizing of the category of the homosexual as fundamentally a progressive political event, a progressive intellectual event. Because what medicalization did—and this is the viewpoint, for example, of John Addington Symons in the late nineteenth century—was to rescue homosexuality from the moralists. It ceased to be a vice as it became an illness, or something like an illness. And many gay men, and I presume women as well, have seen in the part of Freud that is biologizing something desirable. Something good for the cause, good for their situation. It's only very recently that what we might loosely call queer theorists or social constructionists have consistently argued that the biological dimension in any kind of conception of homosexuality, including Freud's, is regressive or at least regrettable, and have insisted that the really progressive position is a radically cultural one. That we're not fated to this sexual destiny, it is in some sense within the realm of—I don't want to say choice because that makes it too simple, but it is not in the biological realm.

Kaja Silverman and others have identified three or four different etiologies, psychological etiologies, causes of homosexuality, in Freud' writings. And so much of his time is spent talking about psychological causes, psychological etiologies, that one senses that the biological stuff, constitutional predisposition and so forth, falls into the background. And you can argue—I don't know if Leo Bersani claims this himself, but this is attributed to him—that Freud is the first queer theorist, because he has an essentially constructionist notion of homosexuality.

Leo Bersani: I just wanted to add one thing to that; since you just mentioned me it gives me a pretext to add this. I think that everything that Paul said is true, but I continue to be extremely bothered by a discrepancy between the theoretical radicality of psychoanalysis about homosexuality and its therapeutic conservatism. And I'd love to be wrong about this, so if people have other evidence than what I'm going to suggest I'd like to hear about it. I don't know of one example of a Freudian or post-Freudian analyst who has come out and said that for a preferential outcome in treatment it makes absolutely no difference whether the patient is heterosexual or homosexual. You're going to give me an example of someone who did?

Question: I'm not going to name names, because they're legion. I just want to mention that the American Psychoanalytic Association, at its last meeting, voted to support the LAMBDA society on the issue of homosexual marriage. So I think there has been a radical shift in the therapeutic stance of American analysts. And I guess the news hasn't filtered down.

Leo Bersani: That's very interesting to me because I've been following recently in France the attempt to have the rights of domestic partners for gay and lesbian couples passed in something that's called the Contract of Social Union. And it's been extremely difficult, if not impossible, for the people gathering signatures for this to get any of the famous French psychoanalysts to sign that petition—analysts whom we think of as being the most radical thinkers about human sexuality.

Judith Butler: These are my colleagues from Berkeley and Stanford. It's kind of funny that we all traveled across the country to talk to one another (although we actually do talk to one another). I wanted to pose a question for Kaja, but also more generally for the panel to think about, since Paul's the one who raised the question of the cultural variability of kinship and I think Kaja was not precisely interested in that formulation. And I'm going to try to figure out why there's been a little bit of a misfire there.

If I'm right, Kaja, and correct me if I'm wrong, you refer to a certain structural imperative of kinship. And you talked in your remarks about kinship in our culture. I wondered whether this kinship in our culture is in some way a set and static structure. And I realize that you have a distinction operating between a structure and the various possible modes of its realization or expression. But I still want to know whether the structure is set and static, even though its possible modes of realization are potentially infinite. For instance, can the structure take into account dynamic change? Is there dynamic change within kinship? What happens when the intelligible, which as you claim is secured by kinship, gives rise to the unintelligible, or indeed unintelligible kinship, which then in turn breaks into the established modes of intelligibility and reestablishes intelligibility in a different direction? Can we talk about epistemic breaks in the structure of kinship? Are the culturally emergent forms of kinship that we have now—I think we are seeing all kinds of forms of kinship emerging that are in some ways socially unprecedented—are they expressions of an already established structure, simply new realizations of a structural possibility that is always already there? Or do they rather constitute something like a break in structure or the inauguration of new structure?

And this is related to the problem of betrayal, promiscuity, and fidelity that came up, since one of the things that Kaja Silverman's saying is that kinship has to work by way of betrayal. Right? You must leave your first love in order to love. And yet, paradoxically, by loving your second love you remain true to your first. But is there a betrayal that is not already built into the structure of kinship? That is to say a betrayal *of* the structure, one that's not anticipated and contained by the structure itself.

Kaja Silverman: Yes, I guess I'm a Lévi-Straussian in this one respect, since I think there has to be a prohibited object. That's the only structural imperative that I see. The point here simply is to open the psyche and to teach it the beginnings of the relationship that we might call love, with respect to other things. That's all that I'm talking about as a structural imperative. So clearly that can take endlessly variable forms. But we can't just start all by ourselves speaking it differently. It's something that happens at a cultural level. Perhaps you're right, there was a kind of misunderstanding here. I thought Paul was asking me about different cultures, and what you're suggesting is the need to think his question within our own culture.

Question: Lacan has a very fascinating use of a theatrical metaphor in "The Rome Discourse" when he compares the one who assumes his or her desire to an actor speaking lines to an audience. And in this formulation there's a chorus but they're also spectators. And it's a very strange kind of instance that we're being asked to think about. The person speaks the lines as if they had quotes around them, so there's this sense of assuming one's history as already somewhat detached from one.

But the fascinating thing about the formulation is that he says, "in a language intelligible to this person's contemporaries." And the word *contemporaries* there is a very crucial one, because it immediately temporalizes this langue that we're talking about, it immediately suggests that to speak my kinship structure in an intelligible way today and next year are not necessarily the same thing, that kinship is in a constant process of mutation. Not through my punctual speech acts, but through our speaking together we are changing what is there. And I think it is a terrible mistake to not realize that the imperative to communicate can actually work for us, and to see it only as a kind of binding or entrapment. Because by staying within those terms we can completely remake what they are, as we are exchanging them with each other, whereas to defiantly break with the langue altogether is in effect to leave it intact and untouched.

Leo Bersani: Could I just answer one thing in that? There are interesting precedents for taking an anticommunication stance. I'm thinking of two figures whom I find as impressive as Lacan, and they're Blanchot and Mallarmé, both of whom thought deeply about the possibility of addressing the other in a way that defied communication, and who therefore left open the possibility of redefining what might happen when an address is made. Whereas this insistence on speaking the language which is immediately recognized by the community makes it impossible to move beyond certain parameters of what is going to be communicated, I think.

Mary Jacobus: I'm not quite sure how to ask this question, but I'll address it to Leo Bersani. I was very interested in what you said, and have been pondering it since you said it, that the most psychoanalytic aspect of psychoanalytic thought was the paradox of the superego—that conscience is the *cause* of instinctual dissatisfaction rather than the other way around; that every renunciation of instinct increases the severity and intolerance of the superego. It's an elegant formulation and a satisfying way of reading psychoanalysis. But then I think about the way in which, say, in *The Ego and the Id,* the terribly archaic cruelty of the superego is diagrammed as connecting right back to the primitive id, and about that moment in around 1930 when people like James Strachey say the great task of psychoanalysis is to extend the boundaries of the ego and diminish the hideous cruelty of the superego. That's a therapeutic question that depends on a certain hermeneutic, if I can use that word. It depends also on the notion of the death drive. And of course for Melanie Klein the superego is above all the manifestation of the death drive.

I'm wondering how one would put together what you see as inherently, by definition, psychoanalytic with the somewhat different understanding of psychoanalysis that comes from saying that the superego is the manifestation par excellence of the death drive. They're two different registers. Both positions agree that there's a major problem for human living and for civilization in that cruelty. But they have somewhat different political implications, and also therapeutic implications. Of course, it isn't a question that I expect you to be able to immediately sort out. But an assumption that there's only one way to think about psychoanalysis, whether Lacanian or some other way, diminishes the multivalence and multiple political possibilities of psychoanalysis.

Leo Bersani: There's a lot there, and as you say I can't possibly address it all. But I would like to say one thing about it. Of course there's more than one way of thinking about psychoanalysis. In spite of all that I guess has happened to me in recent years—and my sort of turning against something that I've been interested in for many years, which is psychoanalysis—there's one extraordinary thing that still interests me very much. I wrote about *Civilization and Its Discontents* twenty years ago and then just reread it recently for a course I was teaching. Nothing I've said is meant to suggest that Freud is less impressive or great, I mean whatever conventional terms we want to use, because he obviously is all of that.

But the thing that struck me as so extraordinary about this work, and about every work when I read Freud, is the way in which it enacts psychoanalysis textually. I don't really know any other psychoanalytic writer that I read who does that. That seems to me, more than the mass of concepts, to be the extraordinary thing about it. An example in *Civilization and Its Discontents* is that the first chapter brings up that thing which everyone knows in psychoanalysis: that in the mind everything persists, nothing is lost. And the book, in an extraordinary way, demonstrates this is not only by coming back to that strange concept of the oceanic feeling later on, but when he finally gets to that idea that is psychoanalytic, it is about the way in which everything in relation to the external authority in the oedipal complex persists and is not lost. So there's a way in which that remark in the first chapter has almost the function of a symptom which is then worked out through a concept in Chapter 7. That to me is the extraordinary thing of psychoanalysis. That as *text* it enacts a peculiar relation of the mind to its own interpretations. And Freud enacts that more "genuiusly" than anyone else has ever done.

Paul Robinson: I guess I just want to endorse that opposition at a humbler level. I haven't been working on Freud for some time. So the last month or so, in preparation for today, I started reading, or rereading, the case histories, rereading the *Three Essays,* rereading a number of things. This is going to be bad news for Fred Crews, at least in terms of his campaign. It's like falling in love all over again. This guy is incredibly powerful. He's not going to go away. He always surprises you. There's a quality about these texts which is incredibly seductive. I come back to it after a number of years and I can't endorse the particular proposition that you're making, although it certainly sounds true to me, but the power and the seductiveness of this writing it seems to me are undeniable.

John Forrester: It's a general question, but it's specifically in response to Leo Bersani asking about a psychoanalyst talking about homosexuality. It made me think of a famous, or rather infamous, case by Masud Khan in a book called *When Spring Comes* which I think has a different title in the United States.[2] The book led to his excommunication from the British Psychoanalytic Society. He describes his initial encounter with a homosexual, a fifty-year-old American homosexual who was coming to him to say, "I'm committing suicide," but the lover is financing the analysis even though it's hopeless. And he presents himself as telling this man: "Why don't you—you're a filthy Yid queer—go off and do some Yid analysis, instead of coming to me who's a handsome, beautiful Pakistani prince, with nothing to do with Yid psychoanalysis." The dénouement of the paper is that the man didn't commit suicide, that Masud Khan basically managed the death of the man's lover and the falling in love of this man with another man, and supervised their effective homosexual marriage.

Now the interventionism of Masud Khan is scandalous to most psychoanalysts, and it was very interesting that the airing of a prejudice, of these banned words as they were used in the consulting room, also led to a scandal when they were published, a scandal as words reported in a text. Now that's alongside the fact that the British Psychoanalytic Society, like some other psychoanalytic societies, has a view that homosexuals have great difficulty in becoming analysts. Because if they don't confront the primal scene in a certain "correct" way—and it's not clear which are the "incorrect" ways and which are the "correct" ways—they cannot work their Oedipus complex through as psychoanalysis requires one to. Now what do you think of that kind of a case history? And what issues does it raise, about the scandal of homosexuality in relation to the Oedipus complex? A relation which I don't feel has been sufficiently thought out in what Kaja Silverman said in her comments praising the structural necessity of the Oedipus complex.

Kaja Silverman: I was not simply praising the Oedipus complex. And even if I were I think I've gone on record as opening it up in all kinds of ways. It's double, it admits of all kinds of permutations and hybrids, etc. In fact, the main point of my project was to show that the terms *mother* and *father* are themselves meaningless. And far from determining in advance where we can go after that, they are themselves only given meaning by where we do go. Now, Leo, you're on.

Leo Bersani: I'll stick to the Oedipus complex. It is a little strange when the Oedipus example is used as a primary example of structuration. I mean there's that famous thing in Chapter 2 and 3 of *The Ego and the Id* where Freud talks about the so-called positive Oedipus complex. The importance or primacy given to it is a way of schematizing something which—the terminology is extraordinary—as a practical convenience is all right but not much more than as a practical convenience. Now what does *that* mean? It means that there are numerous ways of thinking about the Oedipus complex. When I presented that to a class recently we discovered that the oedipal triangle, and please don't ask me to give all the figures in it, really has *eighteen* partners in it, when you take both the positive, the negative, and the bisexuality. Now put that together with two famous statements. First, that "every time we find we are always refinding," and second, Freud's statement in an early letter to Fliess: "I am now getting accustomed to every relation between two people as a relation between four people." Well when you take into account oedipal situation of both of those partners it comes to close to twenty partners. So how you can talk about that as a model of structuration seems to me very strange, unless you keep to the original sort of canonic, triangular interpretation of it.

Hubert Damisch: I was interested in Leo Bersani's referring to Blanchot as defying communication. With one restriction. You're referring to Blanchot and Mallarmé at the same time. Blanchot didn't criticize Mallarmé, but he insisted on the fact that Mallarmé was part of the superstition of silence. And he did it on a piece on Jean Paulhan, the French writer Jean Paulhan, who wrote beautifully on cubism. When you said that defying communication means going *beyond* communication, this is the old difference between cubism and Rothko, you know. Cubism is the space before reason and Rothko is *beyond* reason. And this is what I tried to introduce with an antihermeneutic approach to art. Going *beyond* language, not regressing to a preverbal state of thoughts.

Leo Bersani: I didn't say preverbal state. I take three different figures, two of them more alike, that is Mallarmé, Blanchot, and Beckett. Three artists who seem to be doing something that it's hard to take seriously as long as they continue doing what they're doing. Being against the communication that they're obviously participating in.

It's not silence. The easy way to talk about Mallarmé is to talk about it as silence, as *la page blanche*. But in fact Mallarmé had an extraordinary versatility in writing. I mean he did just about everything, poetry, essays, fashions, theatrical . . . so that there was this constant sort of speaking. As in Beckett, who also tried practically every form of literature imaginable, never stopped. But it's very interesting, this discourse—which I'm sort of engaging in myself now—that never stops talking without communicating very much.

Notes

1. Freud, *Three Essays on the Theory of Sexuality, S.E.,* 7: 139n2.
2. Masud Khan, *When Spring Comes: Awakenings in Clinical Psychoanalysis* (London: Chatto and Windus, 1988); published in the United States as *The Long Wait and Other Psychoanalytic Narratives* (New York: Summit Books, 1989).

Part Four **Psychoanalysis and the**

Historiography of Modern Culture

Introduction

Near the beginning of his essay Robert Jay Lifton argues: "Without psychoanalysis, we don't have a psychology worthy of address to history and society or culture. But at the same time, if we employ psychoanalysis in its most pristine state, its most traditional form, we run the risk of eliminating history in the name of studying it." The eclectic essays in this part all point to both the "worth" and the "risk" of a psychoanalytically inflected historiography. Such an enterprise can move toward one of two extremes. On one hand, "psychohistory" has sometimes devolved into the simplified analysis of historically significant individuals through received Freudian models. As Dominick La-Capra describes this cookie-cutter approach, one "tak[es] the conceptual repertory of psychoanalysis and appl[ies] it to figures or groups in the past, so that you have an analysis of Max Weber in terms of his Oedipus complex." On the other hand, the psychoanalysis of culture often applies Freudian models derived from individuals to the social body as a whole: analyzing an entire society or culture as though it were one large psyche.

These two approaches both founder on, and thus call attention to,

the complex relation between historical change and individuals. Eric L. Santner's suggestive essay shows how psychoanalysis might productively focus on the
relationship *between* individuals and their sociohistoric roles, or on the psychodynamic processes that govern an individual's insertion into history. Santner examines this space between individual desire and social role by analyzing Schreber's psychosis (in Freud's case history) as it sheds light on the way that
individuals take on, or fail to take on, social and historical identities. He begins
by highlighting "symbolic investiture," a process that mediates between psychoanalysis and history: "By symbolic investiture I mean those social acts, often
involving a ritualized transferal of a title and mandate, whereby an individual is
endowed with a new social status and role within a shared linguistic universe.
It's how one comes into being as, comes to enjoy the predicate of, husband, professor, judge, psychoanalyst, and so on." Although we often assume such roles
unconsciously, the unfortunate Schreber, according to Santner, constantly experiences and reenacts the liminal point where an individual cathects onto a social role: "the rites of investiture become a repetition compulsion that never stabilizes into the status of a second nature." We might notice that in Santner's list
of roles we find both "professor" and "psychoanalyst." And, indeed, Schreber
here is almost a metaphor for the psychoanalytic historian, who must remain
acutely aware of that space between the individual and the social roles that this
individual assumes.

Like Santner, Meredith Skura addresses fundamental questions about the
project of psychoanalytic history through a case study. Her essay, a meditation
on Richard Norwood's seventeenth-century diary, begins with the risks of applying a twentieth-century cultural discourse back onto seventeenth-century
subjects. Citing recent scholarship on early modern culture that seeks to historicize the very notions of "experience" and "personhood," Skura concedes that
"we do not know enough to take anything for granted about early modern subjectivity." But she goes on to show how psychoanalysis does not need simply to
provide a culturally specific explanation of Norwood's psyche; it can also bring
out "new patterns" that reside within the textual material and "new questions"
that emerge from Norwood's specific historical situation. Rather than simply
seeing the diaries as evidence—or as a site that can yield psychoanalytic *interpretation*—Skura discovers the psychoanalytic process itself at work in the diary. Her interpretation comes to focus on overlooked formal aspects of the diary itself (what she calls "latent patterns in the narrative") rather than simply on
the psyche that lies beneath the diary. Norwood's language cannot be read, in
other words, simply as an object to be scrutinized but rather as his own compli-

cated process of self-exploration and self-construction. As Skura states, "I am less interested in analyzing a historical subject like Norwood than in historicizing analysis by seeing how useful it turns out to be in looking at early modern diaries more or less in their own terms."

While Santner and Skura both focus on a case history, Robert Jay Lifton takes a historical approach to psychohistory, spinning a narrative about the development of his intellectual work as it has moved through Chinese thought reform, Hiroshima survivors, Vietnam veterans, Nazi doctors, and the Aum Shinrikyo cult in Japan. While Skura laments her inability to *talk to* her historical subjects (in the early modern period), Lifton highlights the importance of the interview within psychohistory. Psychoanalysis—with its attention to transference and countertransference—can bring out the dialogic potential of the interview, so that it becomes, as Lifton writes, a "beautiful method, still much underused within psychiatry, psychology, and humanistic studies." Interviewing is a skill that needs endless cultivation; the interviewer must strive to pay constant attention to his or her own role, to the full impact of the interviewee's specific words, and to the evolving relationship between these two. The interview, when it can achieve this flexibility, might become the methodologic equivalent to the "protean self" that Lifton has studied in relation to twentieth-century historical traumas, just as Lifton notes that the "totalism" that he has critiqued for decades in its sociopolitical forms can find its own version in more rigid kinds of psychoanalytic training.

Dominick LaCapra tries to strike a similar balance between psychoanalysis and historiography in yet another way—in the guise of an urgent intervention into current theories of trauma that begins with a warning: "I shall at times make assertions that should be taken as contestable." This tour de force insists on the possibility of writing *contemporary* history: of seizing the disparate voices that constitute the current intellectual debate about trauma and loss and organizing them into a coherent structure. LaCapra ranges widely, discussing among others Jacques Lacan, Samuel Beckett, Martin Heidegger, Judith Butler, Lawrence Langer, and Slavoj Žižek. Invoking the Freudian contrast between mourning and melancholia, LaCapra calls for a distinction between historical loss and metaphysical absence. Too often, LaCapra insists, contemporary thinking about trauma turns loss into absence, absolutizing a historic process and thus eliminating the possibility for change and recovery. Reconceptualizing historical trauma as loss will create more opportunities for "working through" rather than "acting out" the past.

Reflections on Trauma, Absence, and Loss

Dominick LaCapra

In this essay, I shall touch upon what I consider to be some of the most difficult and controversial problems at the intersection of history and theory. In the interest of opening up certain questions to further analysis and discussion, I shall at times make assertions that should be taken as contestable. My metahistorical and philosophical—at times even speculative—objective is to raise and explore certain crucial problems in tentative terms that may stimulate inquiry into insufficiently investigated relations.

To begin, problematic distinctions are not binaries and should be understood as having varying degrees of strength or weakness. Yet the distinction between absence and loss is significant and is related to a distinction between structural trauma and historical trauma. The difference (or nonidentity) between absence and loss is often elided, and the two are conflated with confusing and dubious results. This conflation tends to take place so rapidly that it escapes notice and seems natural or necessary. Yet it threatens to convert subsequent accounts into displacements of the story of original sin wherein a prelapsarian state of unity or identity—whether real or fictive—is understood as giving way through a fall to difference and conflict. It also typically involves the tendency to avoid addressing historical problems, including losses, in sufficiently specific terms or to envelop and etherealize them in a rashly generalized discourse of absence. Still, the distinction between absence and loss cannot be construed as a simple binary because the two interact in complex ways in any concrete situation, and the temptation is indeed great to conflate one with the other, particularly in post-traumatic situations or periods experienced in terms of crisis.

In an obvious and restricted sense, losses may entail absences, but the converse need not be the case. Moreover, the type of absence to which I refer is situated on a transhistorical level, whereas loss exists on a historical level. Absence in this sense is not an event and does not imply tenses (past, present, or future). By contrast, the historical past is the scene of losses that may be narrated as well as of specific possibilities that may conceivably be reactivated in the present or future. The past is misperceived in terms of sheer absence or utter annihilation. Something of the past always remains, if only as a haunting presence or revenant. Moreover, losses are specific and involve particular events, such as the death of loved ones on a personal level or, on a broader scale, the Holocaust in its effects on Jews and other victims of the Nazi genocide, including both the lives and the cultures of affected groups. I think it is misguided to situate loss on an ontological or transhistorical level, something that happens when it is conflated with absence and conceived as constitutive of existence.

When absence itself is placed in a narrative, it is perhaps necessarily identified with loss and even figured as an event or derived from one (as in the fall, the primal crime, or the oedipal scenario). Here there is a sense in which such narrative—at least in conventional forms—must be reductive, based on misrecognition, and even close to myth. But one also has a reason why nonconventional narratives addressing the problem of absence, for example, those of Samuel Beckett or Maurice Blanchot, tend not to include "events" in any significant way and seem to be abstract, evacuated, or disembodied.[1]

Absence appears in all societies or cultures, yet is likely to be confronted differently and differently articulated (or possibly conflated) with loss. In the light of absence, one may recognize that one cannot lose what one never had. Absence (not loss) applies to ultimate foundations in general, notably to divinity and to metaphysical grounds that tend to be substituted for it.[2] In this sense, absence is the absence of an absolute that should not itself be absolutized and fetishized such that it absorbs or downgrades the significance of particular historical losses. The conversion of absence into loss gives rise to both Christian and oedipal stories (the fall and the primal scene)—stories that are very similar in structure and import. Divinity when understood as lost becomes hidden or dead—lost because of some sin or fault that could be compensated for in order for redemption or salvation to occur and to return one to unity with the godhead. Paradise lost could be regained, at least at the end of time. One may, moreover, ask whether the conversion of absence into loss is essential to all fundamentalisms or foundational philosophies. In any case, the critique of absolute foundations is best understood as related to an affirmation of absence, not a postulation of loss.[3]

Within the Oedipus complex, the penis in woman is fantasized as lacking or even as having been once present in a "totalized," fully integral or intact phallic mother; it would have been lost through some mishap that may also occur to men if they do not overcome castration anxiety in the "proper" way by finding a substitute for the mother. A golden age fulfills a similar function to the divinity or the phallic mother in that—either as a putative reality or a fiction—it is situated at a point of origin that could be recuperated or regained in an ideal future. The fully unified community, or *Volksgemeinschaft*, in which there is no conflict or difference is another avatar of the essential foundation, and anti-Semitism or comparable forms of prejudice against "polluters" of the city are projective modes of displacing anxiety away from the self. The oceanic feeling, correlated with the presymbolic, pre-oedipal imaginary unity (or community) with the mother, would also be "lost" by separation from the (m)other with the intervention of the (name of) the father and the institution of the symbolic under the sway of the phallus. (This is of course the story Freud tells in *Civilization and Its Discontents* and that Jacques Lacan repeats in his own register.) When they are interpreted in a certain way, a similar conflation of absence and loss occurs with respect to the passage from nature to culture, the entry into language, the traumatic encounter with the "real," the alienation from species-being, the anxiety-ridden thrownness and fallenness of *Dasein*, the inevitable generation of the aporia, or the constitutive nature of melancholic loss in relation to the genesis of subjectivity.

Eliding the difference between absence and loss is also crucial to conventional narrative structure, dialectical sublation (or *Aufhebung*), and sacrifice. In a conventional narrative, a putatively "naive" or pure beginning—something construed as a variant of full presence or intactness—is lost through the ins and outs, trials and tribulations, of the middle only to be recovered, at least on the level of higher insight, at the end. In speculative dialectics, an original identity is lost as it is dismembered or torn apart through contradiction and conflict to

be recovered on a higher level through Aufhebung—the movement of negation, preservation, and lifting to a higher level. In sacrifice an innocent or purified victim (typically a substitute or surrogate) is violently torn apart in order
that communicants may be regenerated or redeemed and attain a higher unity
or proximity to the godhead. Regeneration through violence may of course itself be displaced or find a substitute in secular scenarios that disguise—or even
involve denial of—their relation to sacrifice.

Loss is often correlated with lack, for as loss is to the past, so lack is to the present and future. A lost object is one that may be felt to be lacking, although a
lack need not necessarily involve a loss. Lack nonetheless indicates a felt need or
a deficiency; it refers to something that ought to be there but is missing. Just as
loss need not be conflated with absence, for example, by not construing historical losses as constitutive of existence or as implying an original full presence,
identity, or intactness, so lack may be postulated without the implication that
whatever would fill or compensate for it was once there. But this inference is
commonly drawn, and lack is frequently understood as implying a loss, especially in conventionally narrative, dialectical, and sacrificial scenarios. Moreover, absence may be converted into a lack, a loss, or both.

Here an example may be useful. Martha Nussbaum writes, "Saul Bellow's
rhetorical question—where would we find 'the Tolstoy of the Zulus, the Proust
of the Papuans'—has been widely repeated as a normative statement critical of
the cultural achievements of these societies. The person who repeats it in this
spirit is to a degree observing accurately; many non-Western cultures do lack a
form comparable to the novel."[4] Nussbaum goes on to criticize the attempt to
privilege the novel and is ostensibly trying to counter forms of ethnocentrism
and chauvinism. But her formulation threatens to incorporate what she is opposing or to be implicated in a transferential repetition. It would clearly be more
accurate to say that forms comparable to the novel are absent rather than lacking in other cultures (if indeed they are in fact absent). Such a formulation might
be best for all crosscultural comparisons unless one is willing to argue that the
absence represents a lack. How to make this argument concerning lack in
nonethnocentric terms, which do not simply privilege something presumably
distinctive of, or unique to, one's own culture, poses a difficult problem in normative thinking. Of course, on an empirical level, an absence may be experienced as a lack if members of the culture in question come to hold that position, for example, as a result of their contact with another culture and perhaps
through the need to express, more or less ambiguously, resistance to the domi-
nation of that culture by making critical use of its forms (such as the novel).

In *Cultivating Humanity,* Nussbaum's own understanding of narrative tends to remain rather conventional. (Her primary guides are figures such as Wayne Booth, Lionel Trilling, and F. R. Leavis.) One may, however, argue that there are forms of narrative that do not unproblematically instantiate the conventional beginning-middle-end plot, which seeks resonant closure or uplift and tends to conflate absence with loss or lack. In fact there are forms that both contest it and suggest other modes of narration that raise in probing and problematic ways the nature of the losses and absences, anxieties and traumas, that called them into existence. Indeed most significant novelists from Gustave Flaubert through James Joyce, Robert Musil, Virginia Woolf, and Samuel Beckett to the present experimentally explore alternative narrative modalities that do not simply rely on a variant of a conventional plot structure, and their novels have earlier analogues, especially in the picaresque and carnivalesque traditions (novels such as *Don Quixote* and *Tristram Shandy,* for example). (One may suggest that narratives in other cultures that differ from the conventional narrative may show more striking resemblances to experimental, open-ended novels than to the stereotypical "conventional" novel.) In a somewhat comparable fashion, one may point to an open dialectic that does not reach closure but instead enacts an unfinished, unfinalizable interplay of forces involving a series of substitutions without origin or ultimate referent—an interplay that may enable more desirable configurations that cannot be equated with salvation or redemption.[5] With respect to sacrifice, which typically combines oblation and victimization, one may distinguish the element of gift-giving from victimization and attempt to valorize the former while situating it in possible modes of interaction and subject-positioning that do not entail victimization or the construction of the victim as the gift to a deity or godlike being.[6]

One may argue that the affirmation of absence as absence rather than as loss or lack opens different possibilities in general and requires different modes of coming to terms with problems. It allows for a better determination of historical losses or lacks that do not entail the obliteration of the past (often a past seen as subsequent to a "fall") or hyperbolically construed as sheer absence or as utterly "meaningless."[7] Historical losses or lacks can be dealt with in ways that may significantly improve conditions—indeed effect basic structural transformation—without promising secular salvation. Paradise absent is different from paradise lost: it may not be seen as annihilated only to be regained in some hoped-for, apocalyptic future or sublimely blank utopia that, through a kind of creation ex nihilo, brings total renewal, salvation, or redemption. It is not there, and one must therefore turn to other, nonredemptive options in personal, social, and political life—options other than an evacuated past and a vacuous or blank yet somehow redemptive future.[8]

For Freud anxiety had the quality of indefiniteness and absence or indeterminacy of an object; for Søren Kierkegaard and Martin Heidegger, it was the "fear" of something that is nothing. In these conceptions, the idea that there is nothing to fear has two senses. There is no particular or specific thing to fear. And anxiety—the elusive "experience" or affect related to absence—is a "fear" that has no thing (nothing) as its object. A crucial way of attempting to allay anxiety is to locate a particular or specific thing that could be feared and thus enable one to find ways of eliminating or mastering that fear. The conversion of absence into loss gives anxiety an identifiable object—the lost object—and generates the hope that anxiety may be eliminated or overcome. By contrast, the anxiety attendant upon absence may never be entirely eliminated or overcome but must be lived with in various ways. It would allow for only limited control that is never absolutely assured. Any "cure" would be deceptive, and avoidance of this anxiety is one basis for the typical projection of blame for a putative loss onto identifiable others, thereby inviting the generation of scapegoating or sacrificial scenarios. In converting absence into loss, one assumes that there was (or at least could be) some original unity, wholeness, security, or identity that others have ruined, polluted, or contaminated and thus made "us" lose. To regain it, therefore, one must somehow get rid of or eliminate those others—or perhaps that sinful other in oneself.

Acknowledging and affirming—or working through—absence as absence requires the recognition of both the dubious nature of ultimate solutions and the necessary anxiety that cannot be eliminated from the self or projected onto others. It also opens up empowering possibilities in the necessarily limited, nontotalizing, and nonredemptive elaboration of institutions and practices in the creation of a more desirable, perhaps significantly different—but not perfect or totally unified—life in the here and now. Absence is in this sense inherently ambivalent—both anxiety-producing and possibly empowering or even ecstatic. It is also ambivalent in its relation to presence, which is never full or lost in its plenitude but in a complex, mutually marking interplay with absence.[9]

Desire has a different impetus and configuration with respect to absence and loss or lack. In terms of loss or lack, the object of desire is specified: to recover the lost or lacking object or some substitute for it. If the lost object is divine or Edenic, the goal may be a new god or heavenly city, possibly a secular hero and/or a utopia that will save the people and legitimate the self as well as confirm the identity of the follower. Especially with respect to elusive or phantasmatic objects, desire may be limitless and open to an infinite series of displacements in quest of a surrogate for what has presumably been lost. Moreover, desire may give way to melancholic nostalgia in the *recherche du temps perdu*. By contrast, the object or direction of desire is not specified in relation to absence. The problem and the challenge become how to orient and perhaps limit desire that is inherently indeterminate and possibly limitless. Desire may again become infinite (as the desire of or for desire). But the foregrounding of the question of desire and the problematization of its objects may also enable a distinction between desire and desirability (or the normative articulation of desire) as well as the attempt to generate a viable interplay between desirable limits to desire and the role of excess, ecstatic transgression, or transcendence of those limits. It would also require the specification of historical losses or lacks and the differential ways they may be addressed, for example, through structural change in the polity, economy, and society.

Here one might suggest that in Lacan desire is related to absence, although the oedipal scenario and the status of the phallus as the ultimate, elusive object of desire may induce a slippage of desire in the direction of loss or lack (the absence or gap in being [*béance*] deceptively being misrecognized as a constitutive lack [*manque à être*]). Desire would more definitely be related to loss or lack as well as to future possibilities when it is specified in terms of demand (which Lacan distinguishes from desire). In Emile Durkheim the key problem is the generation and establishment of legitimate limits to desire that are themselves normatively desirable and able to turn desire back upon or against itself in the interest of collective morality and the mutual articulation of rights and duties. Desirable normative limits would define legitimate demands but be open to "anomic" excess or transgressive challenge, ideally in terms that both tested and reinvigorated or renewed limits. (Mikhail Bakhtin's notion of the functioning of the carnivalesque in a relatively stable and legitimated society might be argued to have similar assumptions but with a different stress than Durkheim's more "serious" and ethically motivated conception of desirable social life.)

One may further argue that the absence of absolute or essential foundations does not eliminate the possibility of good grounds for an argument. But these grounds are contestable and have to be developed in and through discussion and argument involving dialogic relations both to others and within the self. Dialogic relations are nonauthoritarian in that an argument is always subject to a response; it may be answered or criticized on an ongoing give-and-take (in contrast to an authoritarian command or to what may be termed a hit-and-run riposte that evasively flees dialogic engagement with the other).[10] Criticism may of course even reinvigorate or validate an argument that can withstand it. Given the force of narcissism and the limits of insight into the self, concrete others are crucial in discussing the bases of certain judgments, policies, and practices, and—at least on certain issues (such as the undersirability of victimization)— one should (in my judgment) seek as wide agreement as possible without confounding agreement with a uniform way of life, an avoidance of strenuous argument, or the exclusion or elimination of all significant differences. Indeed a particularly contestable object of discussion and argument is precisely the kinds of difference one judges desirable (or possibly preferred or at least permitted) and those one judges undesirable in a collectivity or a life. Such debate might go on within the self as well as between selves, and one might not be able to reach agreement or a unified position on all important issues. But incommensurability in the sense of nonnegotiable difference (what Jean-François Lyotard terms a *différend*) need not be prematurely generalized as characteristic of all group relations. It might rather be seen as the limiting case of incommensurability in another sense: that of the ability to translate from perspective to perspective and perhaps to reach agreement or a decision on certain issues without having some superordinate master language, absolute foundation, or a final arbiter (God, the sovereign, the community, reason, or what have you). Hence relativism need not be inevitable on a normative level.

Nor should relativism be seen as inevitable on a cognitive level. The idea that there are no pure facts and that all facts have narrative or interpretive dimensions does not entail the homogeneity of narrative or interpretation. In other words, one might agree that there is in some sense interpretation "all the way down" but argue that interpretation is not homogeneous all the way down. Indeed some dimension of fact may be so basic that one might argue that any plausible or even any conceivable interpretation would have to accommodate it, hence that it would make little sense even to refer to this level as interpretive. Generally this is the level of simple declarative statements involving observations ("There is water in this glass") or well validated assertions ("I was born in 1939"). These statements are banal and depend on conventions that may in certain contexts be questioned (for example, the role of a calendar oriented around the birth of Christ), but they are nonetheless important and indispensable in discourse and life. (For example, it is not plausible to justify being late for an appointment on the grounds that one objects to the hegemony of a certain calendar, although different conceptions of time may indeed be crucial in cross-cultural misunderstandings.)

Moreover, there are narratives and narratives. As I noted earlier, not all narratives are conventional, and the history of significant modern literature is in good part that of largely nonconventional narratives. It is curious that theorists who know much better nonetheless seem to assume the most conventional form of narrative (particularly nineteenth-century realism read in a rather limited manner) when they generalize about the nature of narrative, often to criticize its conventionalizing or ideological nature.[11] Moreover, not all discourse is narrative, and a crucial problem is the relation of narrative to other modes of discourse. Indeed, nonconventional narratives often explore in critical ways their relation to myth as well as to nonnarrative genres or modes such as the lyric, image, conceptual analysis, argument, or essay. (Here it would be useful to return to, and try to develop further, the reflections on the essay found in George Lukács, Theodor Adorno, and Robert Musil.) In my judgment, it is dubious to assert with Fredric Jameson or Paul Ricoeur (who themselves paradoxically often write in an essayistic form) that narrative is *the* basic instance of the human mind or that all discourse (at least all historical discourse) is ultimately narrative in nature. Such assertions usually rely on a very attenuated or overly expansive notion of narrative and are interesting as hyperbole only when they enable a far-ranging inquiry into the different possibilities and modalities of narrative (as they do in the work of Jameson and Ricoeur).

By contrast to absence, loss is situated on a historical level and is the consequence of particular events. The nature of losses varies with the nature of events and responses to them. Some losses may be traumatic while others are not, and there are variations in the intensity or devastating impact of trauma. There are of course also particular losses in all societies and cultures, indeed in all lives, but the ways in which they might be confronted differ from the responses more suited to absence. When absence and loss are conflated, melancholic paralysis or manic agitation may set in, and the significance or force of particular losses (for example, those of the Shoah) may be obfuscated or rashly generalized. As a consequence, one encounters the dubious ideas that everyone (including perpetrators or collaborators) is a victim, that all history is trauma, or that we all share a pathological public sphere or a "wound culture."[12] (As a recent advertisement would have it: "Violence makes victims of us all.")[13] Furthermore, the conflation of absence and loss would facilitate the appropriation of particular traumas by those who did not experience them, typically in a movement of identity formation that makes invidious and ideological use of traumatic series of events in foundational ways or as symbolic capital.

Unlike absence, particular losses are not inevitable. Hence one's own death, which is inevitable, could be seen as a necessary absence; it would become a loss only in the eyes of others. In this sense, one would oneself experience loss only with respect to the death of others—not to one's own death. One day one will indeed be absent, but without further specification (for example, with respect to things left undone), death is not a loss to the self. (The belief in heaven or the resurrection of bodies can be seen as implying that one's own death is a loss that can be recuperated or redeemed, but it is unclear whether this belief refers to a loss to the self.) The view I am exploring is of course not incompatible with a concern for an "afterlife" in the form of a legacy or memory kept active by others—a concern that might well influence one's behavior in the present. Nor would it lessen—indeed, it might accentuate—the importance of ritual practices (such as mourning) even if one were to question a certain idea of divinity. On the level of belief and practice, the line of thought I am suggesting might even lead to a seemingly paradoxical, nonfanatical religious atheism that is not the simple negation, opposite, or reversal of established religions (as most atheisms tend to be). Instead it would indicate the value of elements of religion (for example, certain rituals) and might even seek to honor the name of God in God's absence. An important tendency in both religious and secular thought might be seen as going in this direction, for example, in Heidegger, Emmanuel Levinas, and Jacques Derrida.

Additional losses besides the deaths of others occur in any life or society, but it is still important not to specify them prematurely or conflate them with absences. Historical losses can conceivably be avoided or, when they occur, at least in part compensated for, worked through, and even to some extent overcome. Absence along with the anxiety it brings could be worked through only in the sense that one may learn better to live with it and not convert it into a loss or lack that one believes could be made good, notably through the elimination or victimization of those to whom blame is imputed. Conversely, it is important not to hypostatize particular historical losses or lacks and present them as mere instantiations of some inevitable absence or constitutive feature of existence. Indeed, specific phantoms or ghosts that possess the self or the community can be laid to rest through mourning only when they are specified and named as historically lost others. And particular forms of prejudice (such as anti-Semitism or homophobia) can be engaged ethically and politically only when they are specified in terms of their precise, historically differentiated incidence (including the different ways in which they may involve the conversion of absence into loss with the identity-building localization of anxiety that is projected onto abjected or putatively guilty others).

I would also suggest that the unconscious and the drives might be apprehended as active or generative absences that are ambivalent. They may not be recovered as if they were losses or lacks and made fully present to consciousness. Rather they are destructive and enabling absences—potentiating and nihilating forces—that are recurrently displaced. They create gaps or vortexes in existence that both threaten to consume the self or others and may be sources of activity, even sublimity or elation and *jouissance*. (The status of one's own death and of the unconscious as absences may be a reason why Freud believed one could never accept one's own death on an unconscious level. Such an acceptance might not make any sense since nothing—no "ego"—could do the accepting.)

Here one must be extremely tentative, but perhaps one should "see" the sacred in terms of absence. Hence it would be misguided to situate the sacred on the level of particular losses (such as the death of God) and the attempt to compensate for them. This attempt at compensation for a putative loss might induce a misguided quest for the sacred as a correlate of unheard-of worldly transgression (especially in the form of a crazed sacrificialism involving ritual anxiety and the desire to get rid of putative impure or polluting forces) along with an effort to transcend all limits and limitations. (I think such a quest on the part of committed Nazis was one component of the tangled complex making up the Holocaust.) By contrast, "immanent" features of the world could be seen as problematic indexes of the sacred that itself would be inaccessible or, in Lyotard's term, un(re)presentable—in Lacanian terms barred or foreclosed with respect to any direct experience (or, in the terms I am suggesting, absent). In more traditional religious terms, radical transcendence would point to an absence rather than a loss or lack. A similar argument could be made with respect to the sublime as a displaced secular sacred or mode of radical transcendence.

The analysis I am suggesting need not eliminate all forms of the immanent sacred or sublime, but it might lead one to defend certain "sublimated" modes of approaching them—not the violent killing of humans or animals but symbolic activities such as the Mass or comparable rituals and feasts. To the extent that one might defend more dangerous ventures that are close to the near-death experience and involve the actual risk of death, one might confine them to agonistic relations among relatively equal contenders where the outcome is unpredictable or to individuals and groups that voluntarily place themselves at risk, for example, in hazardous forms of mountain-climbing or auto-racing—more generally, activities that do not involve victimizing others, exploiting the helpless or weak, or putting (as in certain forms of terrorism) unwilling or nonconsenting others (such as noncombatant civilian populations) at risk. Hence one might conclude that duels limited to relative equals or peers are more justifiable than an activity such as bullfighting that pits a human against a generally less able and certainly nonconsenting animal. Events such as dog- or cock-fighting that take place between animals trained by humans are even less acceptable; they would be indicative of anxieties and weaknesses in the self that one denies or refuses to confront. Sadomasochistic relations might pose problems from this point of view, and insofar as they are legitimated through the appeal to mutually agreed-upon limits among consenting adults, the question is whether and to what extent notions of contract and consent mask underlying sacrificial scenarios. The periodic inversion of the roles of victim and victimizer would not necessarily create ethically desirable mutuality in that the periodic inversion of victimization would not change the nature of victimization as a practice, just as the periodic reversal of absolutist or authoritarian relations would not create a democracy.

I would also distinguish in nonbinary terms between two additional interacting processes—acting-out and working-through, which are interrelated modes of responding to loss or historical trauma. As I have intimated, if the concepts of acting-out and working-through are to be applied to absence, it would have to be in a special sense. I have argued elsewhere that mourning might be seen as a form of working-through and melancholia, a form of acting-out.[14] Freud compared and contrasted melancholia with mourning. He saw melancholia as characteristic of an arrested process in which the depressed, self-berating, and traumatized self, locked in compulsive repetition, is possessed by the past, faces a future of impasses, and remains narcissistically identified with the lost object. Mourning brings the possibility of engaging trauma and achieving a reinvestment in, or "recathexis" of, life that allows one to begin again. In line with Freud's concepts, one might further suggest that mourning be seen not simply as individual or quasi-transcendental grieving but as a homeopathic socialization or ritualization of the repetition-compulsion that attempts to turn it against the "death drive" and counteract compulsiveness by re-petitioning in ways that allow for a measure of critical distance, change, resumption of social life, ethical responsibility, and renewal. Through memory-work, especially the socially engaged memory-work involved in working-through, one is able to distinguish between past and present and to recognize something as having happened to one (or one's people) back then that is related to, but not identical with, "here and now." Moreover, through mourning and the at least symbolic provision of a proper burial, one attempts to assist in restoring to victims the dignity denied them by their victimizers. In any case, I am suggesting that the broader concepts that include, without being restricted to, melancholia and mourning are acting-out and working-through—concepts whose applicability must of course be further specified in different contexts and with respect to different subject-positions.[15]

Mourning, moreover, is not the only modality of working-through, although it is a very important one. Among a variety of possible modalities, one may mention certain forms of nontotalizing narrative and critical as well as self-critical thought and practice. For example, Beckett may be read as a novelist and dramatist of absence and not simply loss, indeed a writer whose works deploy ways of both acting out and working through absence. One might perhaps say that his world is one of paradise absent, not paradise lost. He is the non-Milton, not simply the anti-Milton, of narrative. In Beckett, any intimation of a lost or a future utopia becomes evanescent and insubstantial. Seen in a certain light, deconstruction is itself a way of working through and playing (at times acting) out absence in its complex, mutually implicated relations to non-full presence. (In this respect it may be similar to Zen Buddhism.) The distinction between absence and loss would permit the rereading of many figures and movements in order to understand their relations to these concepts and related processes.[16]

Deconstruction is in one sense misunderstood when it is applied to historical losses. Historical losses call for mourning—possibly for critique and transformative sociopolitical practice. When absence, approximated to loss, becomes the object of mourning, the mourning may (perhaps must) become impossible and turn continually back into endless melancholy. The approximation or even conflation of absence and loss induces a melancholic or impossibly mournful response to the closure of metaphysics, a generalized "hauntology," and even a dubious assimilation (or at least an insufficiently differentiated treatment) of other problems (notably a limit-event such as the Holocaust and its effects on victims) with respect to a metaphysical or meta-metaphysical frame of reference. On the other hand, deconstruction in another of its registers may also be understood as a form of immanent critique that may be applicable to historical phenomena and practices, including losses. It is especially significant politically in the undoing of pure binary oppositions that subtend a scapegoat mechanism involving the constitution as well as victimization of the other as a totally external, impure contaminant or pollutant; it also enables one to pose more precisely the problem of distinctions that are not pure binary opposites. In this sense it does not entail the blurring of all distinctions (including that between absence and loss) but instead the recognition that the problem of distinctions becomes more—not less—pressing in light of the unavailability or dubiousness of binary oppositions. Moreover, deconstruction may be extended in the direction of modes of social and political practice that address losses, lacks, and possibilities that are neither conflated with absence nor imply a redemptive full presence in the past or future. If it is so understood, the mourning deconstruction enables need not merge with quasi-transcendental, endless grieving that becomes altogether impossible. Even in terms of absence, deconstruction may open other possibilities of response, including more affirmative, carnivalesque, and generally complex ones (for example, in terms of a displaced wake in which the carnivalesque has a role in mourning itself). In any case, losses would have to be specified or named for mourning as a social process to be possible. (This point may provide some insight into the desire of intimates to locate the bodies and determine the names of victims so that they may be given a proper burial.) When mourning turns to absence and absence is conflated with loss, then mourning becomes impossible, endless, quasi-transcendental grieving and scarcely distinguishable (if at all) from interminable melancholy. If mourning applies to absence in a manner that resists conflation with loss, it would have to be in some unheard-of, radically unfamiliar sense that does not simply fold back into interminable (even originary or constitutive) melancholy or quasi-transcendental grieving. In any case, the relation of deconstruction to problems of absence and loss should be posed and explored as an explicit object of inquiry.

In acting-out, the past is performatively regenerated or relived as if it were fully present rather than represented in memory and inscription, and it hauntingly returns as the repressed. Mourning involves a different inflection of performativity: a relation to the past that involves recognizing its difference from the present—simultaneously remembering and taking leave of, or actively forgetting, it, thereby allowing for critical judgment and a reinvestment in life, notably social and civic life with its demands, responsibilities, and norms requiring respectful recognition and consideration for others. By contrast, to the extent that someone is possessed by the past and acting out a repetition compulsion, he or she may be incapable of ethically responsible behavior. Still, with respect to traumatic losses, acting-out may be a necessary condition of working-through, at least for victims—or, in certain ways, for all those directly involved in events. Even the secondary witness (including the historian in one of his or her roles) who resists full identification and the dubious appropriation of the status of victim through surrogate victimage may nonetheless undergo what might perhaps be termed empathic unsettlement or even muted trauma. Indeed, the muting or mitigation of trauma that is nonetheless recognized and, to some extent, acted out may be a requirement or precondition of working through problems. Acting-out and working-through are in general intimately linked but analytically distinguishable processes, and it may be argued that a basis of desirable practice is to create conditions in which working-through, while never fully transcending, may nonetheless counteract the force of acting-out and the repetition-compulsion in order to generate different possibilities—a different force field—in thought and life, notably empathic relations of trust not based on quasi-sacrificial processes of victimization and self-victimization.

There is at times a tendency in certain contemporary theories to eliminate or obscure the role of problematic intermediary or transitional processes (including the very interaction between limits and excess) and to restrict possibilities to two extremes between which one may be suspended: the justifiably rejected or criticized phantasm of total mastery, full ego-identity, definitive closure, "totalitarian" social integration, redemption, and radically positive transcendence (whether poetic or political), on one hand, and acting out repetition compulsions with endless fragmentation, melancholia, aporias, and double-binds, on the other. I find this all-or-nothing tendency in different ways in the works of Paul de Man, Lawrence Langer, and Slavoj Žižek among others.[17] Even Judith Butler in her important and thought-provoking book *Bodies That Matter: On the Discursive Limits of "Sex"* at one point restricts theoretical possibilities to phantasmatic total mastery and the disruptive repetition-compulsion when she stresses the "difference between a repetition in the service of the fantasy of mastery (i.e., a repetition of acts which build the subject, and which are said to be the constructive or constituting acts of a subject) and a notion of repetition-compulsion, taken from Freud, which breaks apart that fantasy of mastery and sets its limits."[18] The implication here seems to be that only the repetition-compulsion sets limits to the fantasy of total mastery, thereby foreclosing the possibility of forms of working-through that check, or generate counterforces to, compulsive repetition but are not tantamount to total mastery or definitive closure. On my reading of Butler's formulation at least at this point in her analysis, one tends to be confined to two extremes—total mastery and the endless repetition-compulsion—extremes that attest to the predominance of an all-or-nothing logic. One also threatens to confine critical theory and conceptions of performativity to impossible mourning and modalities of melancholic or manic acting-out of post-traumatic conditions.

Butler's reprise of problems, however, gets more complicated in *The Psychic Life of Power: Theories in Subjection*. If it is taken as a "stark and hyperbolic construction" (as she puts it in passing), I find persuasive her account of the formation of (rigid) heterosexual identity on the basis of a "melancholic" repudiation of homosexual desire that involves an inability to mourn abjected losses (such as victims of AIDS). But I find less convincing her tendency, especially in her final chapter, to generalize her account of the formation of subjectivity on the basis of a constitutive or originary melancholy. In the latter respect, her strategy is one of reversal in the form of metaleptic performativity: melancholy, which would seem to be the effect of the superego insofar as melancholia (as analytically distinguished from mourning) involves self-criticism and even self-berating, is the "cause" of the superego—indeed a terroristic superego as a vehicle of the death drive—in its distinction from the ego. Moreover, for Butler melancholia itself is the disguised precipitate of social power:

> By withdrawing its own presence, power becomes an object lost—"a loss of a more ideal kind." . . . The subject is produced, paradoxically, through this withdrawal of power, its dissimulation and fabulation of the psyche as a speaking topos. Social power vanishes, becoming the object lost, or social power makes vanish, effecting a mandatory set of losses. Thus, it effects a melancholia that reproduces power as the psychic voice of judgment, addressed to (turned upon) oneself, thus modeling reflexivity on subjection.[19]

Although one may certainly recognize the importance of (always already) internalized (and often occulted or encrypted) social power in the generation of subjectivity and subjection, Butler's analysis is, I think, insufficiently specific in its one-sided if not demonized idea of the superego, its rather unmediated derivation of the psyche from occulted social power, its inadequate account of critical judgment (seemingly a "residue" with respect to internalized social power), and its limited conception of the interaction between self and other in the constitution of a superego (notably in the family as the conduit for social norms and values). One may even have here one of the latest avatars of the long story of conflating absence with loss that becomes constitutive instead of historical: the notion of loss related to melancholia as originary or constitutive of the subject and of the socialization of the psyche.[20] Social power, in its omnipresence, omnipotence, and ability to occult its "real" presence, itself tends to become a hidden god-term, and how precisely it is transformed or translated into the superego, judgment, and the "voice" of conscience (which cannot be reduced to mere symptoms of internalized and occulted social power) remains rather mysterious. In any case, the broader problem in Butler's formulation in her final chapter is the unproblematic postulation of an originary or constitutive loss or lack—a postulation that would seem to remain within an oedipal scenario (which she elsewhere criticizes) and to be in some sense yet another secular displacement of the fall or original sin. An absence, gap, or structural trauma (related to anxiety and perhaps to radical ambivalence) is converted into, or equated with, a constitutive or originary loss (of social power and homosexual desire) as an unexamined presupposition for the postulation of melancholy as the origin or source of subjectivity. As Butler at points seems to intimate, absence not conflated with loss would not entail the postulation of melancholy as the source of subjectivity; by contrast, it would allow for various modes of subjectivity (of course including melancholy, which may indeed be especially pronounced in modernity).[21] In any event, if a special status were to be claimed for melancholy as a mode of subjectivity, this claim would be sociocultural and would have to be investigated and substantiated in differentiated historical terms.[22]

Sometimes evident as well in recent thought is a perspective fixated on failed transcendence or irremediable, even inconsolable and constitutive loss or lack in which any mode of reconstruction or renewal is seen as objectionably totalizing, recuperative, optimistic, or naive.[23] What is not theorized in this frame of reference is the possibility of working-through in which totalization (as well as redemption or radical transcendence—whether putatively successful or failed) is actively resisted and the repetition-compulsion counteracted, especially through social practices and rituals generating normative limits that are not conflated with normalization—limits that are affirmed as legitimate yet subject to disruption, challenge, change, and even radical disorientation.[24] Without this notion of working-through, mourning may be treated only as endless grieving and not as a social process involving not simply alterity in the abstract but others—possibly empathic, trustworthy others. I have noted that mourning, if linked to an originary or constitutive loss, would necessarily seem to merge with endless, quasi-transcendental grieving that may be indistinguishable from interminable melancholy.[25] The possibility of even limited working-through may seem foreclosed in modern societies precisely because of the relative dearth of effective rites of passage, including rituals or, more generally, effective social processes such as mourning. But this historical deficit should not be absolutized and conflated with absence, as occurs in the universalistic notion of a necessary constitutive loss or lack or an indiscriminate conflation of all history with trauma.[26]

A related point bears on the problematic but important distinction between structural trauma and historical trauma—a distinction that enables one to pose the problem of relations between the two in other than binary terms. One may argue that structural trauma is related to transhistorical absence (absence of–at the origin) and appears in different ways in all societies and all lives. As I indicated earlier, it may be evoked or addressed in various fashions—in terms of the separation from the (m)other, the passage from nature to culture, the eruption of the pre-oedipal or presymbolic in the symbolic, the entry into language, the encounter with the "real," alienation from species-being, the anxiety-ridden thrownness of Dasein, the inevitable generation of the aporia, the constitutive nature of originary melancholic loss in relation to subjectivity, and so forth. I would reiterate that one difficulty in these scenarios is the frequent conversion of absence into loss or lack, notably through the notion of a fall. One can nonetheless postulate, hypothesize, or affirm absence as absence and recognize the role of something like untranscendable structural trauma without rashly hyperbolizing its role or immediately equating it with loss or lack. By not conflating absence and loss, one would historicize and problematize certain forms of desire, such as the desire for redemption or totality or, in Jean-Paul Sartre's words, the desire to be in-itself-for-itself or God.[27] One would also help prevent the indiscriminate generalization of historical trauma into the idea of a "wound culture" or the notion that everyone is somehow a victim.

Historical trauma is specific, and not everyone is subject to it or entitled to the subject-position associated with it. It is dubious to identify with the victim to the point of making oneself a surrogate victim who has the right to the victim's voice or subject-position.[28] The role of empathy and empathic unsettlement in the attentive secondary witness does not entail the conflation of victim and secondary witness. But opening oneself to empathic unsettlement is, I think, a desirable affective dimension of inquiry that complements and supplements empirical research and analysis. Empathy is important in attempting to understand traumatic events and victims, and it may (I think, should) have stylistic effects in the way one discusses or addresses certain problems. It places in jeopardy fetishized and totalizing narratives that harmonize events and often recuperate the past in terms of uplifting messages or optimistic, self-serving scenarios. (To some extent the film *Schindler's List* relies on such a fetishistic narrative.) Empathic unsettlement also raises in pointed form the problem of how to address traumatic events involving victimization, including the problem of composing narratives that neither confuse one's own voice or position with the victim's nor seek facile uplift, harmonization, or closure but allow the unsettlement that they address to affect the narrative's own movement both in terms of acting-out and working-through. Without discounting all forms of critical distance (even numbing "objectivity") that may be necessary for research, judgment, and self-preservation, one may also appeal to the role of empathy in raising doubts about positivistic or formalistic accounts that both deny one's transferential implication in the problems one treats and attempt to create maximal distance from them—and those involved in them—through extreme objectification.[29] But empathy that resists full identification with, and appropriation of, the experience of the other would depend both on one's own potential for traumatization (related to absence and structural trauma) and on one's recognition that another's loss is not identical with one's own loss.[30]

One basis for the conflation of structural and historical trauma is the elusiveness of the traumatic experience in both cases. In historical trauma, it is possible (at least theoretically) to locate traumatizing events. But it may not be possible to locate or localize the experience of trauma that is not dated or "punctual."[31] The belated temporality of trauma makes of it an elusive experience related to repetition involving a period of latency. At least in Freud's widely shared view, the trauma as experience is "in" the repetition of an early event in a later event—an early event for which one was not prepared to feel anxiety and a later event that somehow "recalls" the early one and triggers a traumatic response. The belated temporality of trauma and the elusive nature of the shattering "experience" related to it render the distinction between structural and historical trauma problematic but do not make it irrelevant. The traumatizing events in historical trauma can be determined (for example, the events of the Shoah), whereas structural trauma (like absence) is not an event but an anxiety-producing condition of possibility related to the potential for historical traumatization. When structural trauma is reduced to, or figured as, an event, one has the genesis of myth wherein trauma is enacted in a story or narrative from which later traumas seem to derive (as in the case of original sin attendant upon the fall).

Everyone is subject to structural trauma. But with respect to historical trauma and its "representation," the distinction among victims, perpetrators, and bystanders is crucial. "Victim" is not a psychological category. It is, in variable ways, a social, political, and ethical category. Victims of certain events will in all likelihood be traumatized by them, and not being traumatized would itself call for explanation. But not everyone traumatized by events is a victim. There is the possibility of perpetrator trauma, which must itself be acknowledged and in some sense worked through if perpetrators are to distance themselves from an earlier implication in deadly ideologies and practices. Such trauma does not, however, entail the equation or identification of the perpetrator and the victim. The fact that Heinrich Himmler suffered from chronic stomach cramps or that Erich von dem Bach-Zelewski experienced nocturnal fits of screaming does not make them victims of the Holocaust. There may of course be ambiguous cases in what Primo Levi called the gray zone, yet these cases were often caused by the

Nazi policy of trying to make accomplices of victims, for example, with respect
to the Jewish councils or kapos in the camps. But the gray zone does not imply
the blurring or collapse of all distinctions, including that between perpetrator
and victim. The more general point is that historical trauma has a differentiated
specificity that poses a barrier to its amalgamation with structural trauma and
that poses particular questions for historical understanding and ethicopolitical
judgment.

Structural trauma is often figured as deeply ambivalent—as both shattering
or painful and the occasion for jouissance, ecstatic elation, or the sublime. Although one may contend that structural trauma is in some problematic sense its
precondition, I would reiterate the basic point that historical trauma is related
to particular events that do indeed involve losses, such as the Shoah or the drop-
ping of the atom bomb on Japanese cities. The strong temptation with respect
to such limit-events is to collapse the distinction and to arrive at a conception
of the event's absolute uniqueness or even sublime, indeed sacral quality. Perhaps this is the tangled region of thought and affect where one should situate
the founding trauma—the trauma that becomes the basis for collective and/or
personal identity. The Holocaust or slavery—even suffering the effects of the
atom bomb in Hiroshima or Nagasaki—can become a founding trauma, and
such a trauma is typical of myths of origin and may perhaps be located in the
more or less mythologized history of every people. But one may question the
founding trauma that typically plays a tendentious ideological role, for example, in terms of the concept of a chosen people or a belief in one's privileged status as victim. As historical events that are indeed crucial in the history of peo-
ples, traumas might instead be seen as posing the problematic question of
identity and as calling for more critical ways of coming to terms with both their
legacy and such problems as absence and loss.

One may well argue that the Holocaust represents losses of such magnitude
that, though not absolutely unique, it may serve to raise the question of absence,
for example, with respect to divinity. Still, despite the extremely strong temptation, it is misleading to reduce, or confusingly transfer the qualities of, one dimension of trauma to the other—to generalize structural trauma so that it absorbs or subordinates the significance of historical trauma, thereby rendering all
references to the latter merely illustrative, homogeneous, allusive, and perhaps
equivocal, or, on the contrary, to "explain" all post-traumatic, extreme, uncanny
phenomena and responses as exclusively caused by particular events or contexts.
The latter move—what one might term reductive contextualism—is typical of
historians and sociologists who attempt to explain, without significant residue,

all anxiety or unsettlement—as well as attendant forms of creativity—through specific contexts or events, for example, deriving anxiety in Heidegger's thought exclusively from conditions in interwar Germany or explaining structuralism and the turn to the history of the *longue durée* in France solely in terms of the postwar avoidance of Vichy and the loss of national prestige and power.[32] The former tendency—deriving historical from structural trauma—is a great temptation for theoretically inclined analysts who tend to see history simply as illustrating or instantiating more basic processes. It should go without saying that the critique of reductive contextualism and theoreticism does not obviate the importance of specific contexts or of theory that addresses them and both informs and raises questions for research.

In *Telling the Truth About History,* the noted historians Joyce Appleby, Lynn Hunt, and Margaret Jacob write: "Once there was a single narrative of national history that most Americans accepted as part of their heritage. Now there is an increasing emphasis on the diversity of ethnic, racial, and gender experience and a deep skepticism about whether the narrative of America's achievements comprises anything more than a self-congratulatory masking of the power of elites. History has been shaken down to its scientific and cultural foundations at the very time that those foundations themselves are being contested."[33] In this passage, one is close to reductive contextualism involving a variant of a golden age mythology, a variant in which the proverbial "past-we-have-lost" becomes the metanarrative we have lost. The purpose of the authors' own narrative is to explain current forms of multiculturalism and skepticism, and the contrast between past and present serves to frame or even validate that explanation. Yet we are never told precisely when "there was a single narrative of national history that most Americans accepted as part of their heritage." Nor are we told from what perspective that putative narrative was recounted. How, one might well ask, could one ever have fully reconciled narratives from the perspectives of Plymouth Rock, Sante Fe, and the Alamo? What about the perspective of American Indians in relation to the "open frontier" and "manifest destiny"? Where does one place the Civil War and the narratives related to it? I think one might argue that there never was a single narrative and that most Americans never accepted only one story about the past. The rhetorical attempt both to get one's own narrative off the ground and to account for current conflicts or discontents by means of a questionable opposition between the lost, unified past and the skeptical, conflictual present runs the risk of inviting underspecified if not distorted views of the past and oversimplified interpretations of the present.

Specificity is also in jeopardy when the important theorist Slavoj Žižek, who tends to be preoccupied if not obsessed with structural trauma and constitutive loss or lack, complements his convincing indictment of reductive contextualism with the dubious and comparable reductive assertion: "All the different attempts to attach this phenomenon [concentration camps] to a concrete image ('Holocaust,' 'Gulag' . . .), to reduce it to a product of a concrete social order (Fascism, Stalinism . . .)—what are they if not so many attempts to elude the fact that we are dealing here [with respect to concentration camps] with the 'real' of our civilization which returns as the same traumatic kernel in all social systems?"[34] Here, in an extreme and extremely dubious theoreticist gesture, concentration camps are brought alongside castration anxiety as mere manifestations or instantiations of the Lacanian "real" or "traumatic kernel."

One way to formulate the problem of specificity in analysis and criticism is in terms of the need to explore the problematic relations between absence and loss (or lack) as well as between structural and historical trauma without simply collapsing the two or reducing one to the other. One may well argue that structural trauma related to absence or a gap in existence—with the anxiety, ambivalence, and elation it evokes—may not be cured but only lived with in various ways. One may even argue that it is ethically and politically dubious to believe that one can overcome or transcend structural trauma or constitutive absence to achieve full intactness, wholeness, or communal identity and that attempts at transcendence or salvation may lead to the demonization and scapegoating of those on whom unavoidable anxiety is projected. But historical traumas and losses may conceivably be avoided and their legacies to some viable extent worked through both in order to allow a less self-deceptive confrontation with transhistorical, structural trauma and in order to further historical, social, and political specificity, including the elaboration of more desirable social and political institutions and practices.

Notes

1. One difficulty with Blanchot's *Writing of Disaster* (1980), translated by Ann Smock (Lincoln: University of Nebraska Press, 1986), is that, under the heading of "disaster," it tends to treat absences and losses (such as those of the Shoah) in insufficiently differentiated terms. This is to some extent in contrast with the more complex treatment of absence in Blanchot's *L'Entretien infini* (Paris: Gallimard, 1969) or in narratives such as *Death Sentence* (1948), translated by Lydia Davis) Tarrytown, N.Y.: Station Hill Press, 1978). Moreover, the tendency to envelop loss and the historical in general in a discourse of absence and structural trauma is prevalent in theoretical (or theoreticist) discourses that threaten to be all-consuming. I later touch on such tendencies in the recent work of Shoshana Felman and Cathy Caruth or, in another register, that of Slavoj Žižek.

2. Absence in contrast with loss or lack would also apply to the penis in woman within the context of the Oedipus complex and to the phallus as a transcendental signifier. It is debatable whether separation from the mother after the rupture or dissolution of putative pre-oedipal unity of mother and child—as it is played out, for example, in the *fort–da* ("gone" or "away"–"there") game—should be seen as an absence or a loss. Freud observed this much-discussed "game" in the behavior of his one-and-a-half-year-old grandson. In it the child compensates for the uncontrolled comings and goings of the mother by "playing" with a bobbin attached to a string that it throws over the side of its crib while uttering the sound "ooo" and retrieving it with the sound "aaa." Sometimes the first gesture (throwing) takes place without the second. Freud interprets the sounds as meaning "fort" and "da" and speculates that the child is substituting the bobbin (what might be seen as a transitional object in the phrase of D. W. Winnicott) for the mother. One might speculate that the "game" would seem to combine a compulsive repetition that is acted out as well as an attempt to achieve some control over events and, to some extent, work through them. It would thus seem suspended between melancholia and mourning with respect to an absent object that is easily experienced or interpreted as lost. (Insofar as the pre-oedipal symbiosis or bond is a fictive projection from a post-oedipal position, one may argue that, in the separation from the mother, one is dealing with an absence that is readily misperceived or experienced as a loss that can somehow be recuperated or made good.) When the first part of the "game" is autonomized, one would seem caught up in a melancholic loop that comes close to endless grieving. If these speculations are cogent, the "game" is a crucial instance of what Clifford Geertz refers to as "deep play"—play that is quite serious and even a matter of life and death.

3. One may note that, in contrast to the famous assertion "God is dead" (whose relation to Friedrich Nietzsche's voice is complex), one may argue that one finds an affirmation of absence as absence in the final passage of Nietzsche's "How the 'True World' Finally Became a Fable," in *The Twilight of Idols*, from *The Portable Nietzsche*, selected and translated by Walter Kaufmann (New York: Viking, 1954): "The true world—we have abolished. What has remained? The apparent one perhaps? But no! *With the true world we have also abolished the apparent one.* (Noon; moment of the briefest shadow; end of the longest error; high point of humanity; INCIPIT ZARATHUSTRA" (486). One would have to read closely the entire section that concludes with this passage, including the interplay of principal text and parentheses in which what is included as seemingly marginal in the parentheses becomes increasingly insistent and important. The implications of the passage are explored, as Nietzsche intimates, in *Thus Spake Zarathustra*.

4. Martha Nussbaum, *Cultivating Humanity: A Classical Defense of Reform in Liberal Education* (Cambridge: Harvard University Press, 1997), 132.

5. This type of "open" dialectic was sought by Maurice Merleau-Ponty and, in more insistently "negative" terms allowing for an impossibly utopian or redemptive hope against hope, by Theodor Adorno. It may also be found in an important dimension of Marx's work. On Marx in this respect, see my *Soundings in Critical Theory* (Ithaca, N.Y.: Cornell University Press, 1989), chap. 6.

6. The work of Jacques Derrida is crucially concerned with the problem of absence. But in his important *Gift of Death* (1992), translated by David Wells (Chicago: University of

Chicago Press, 1995), Derrida's analysis of sacrifice is limited by the fact that he focuses on the gift without thematizing the question of its relation to victimization. (For example, he has nothing significant to say about Isaac as victim and his relation to his father.) The result is a vision of relations in terms of superogatory virtues (perhaps even a secular analogue of grace) in which generosity beyond all calculation is extended to every other figured as totally other (on the model of a radically transcendent divinity). (In the repeated phrase Derrida employs, "tout autre est tout autre"—every other is totally other.) The difficulty here is that, from this perspective, one seems unable to pose the problem of the tense relation between ethics (based on justice, normative limits, and reciprocity) and what "generously" exceeds ethics—with the possibility that excess relates to a society of saints or an elect group who may not have limiting norms that interact with and, to some extent, check excess, including the excess of violence and the "gift" of death.

7. This entailment may at times be found in Hayden White's more hyperbolic moments, for example, in "The Politics of Interpretation," in *The Content of the Form* (Baltimore: Johns Hopkins University Press, 1987), 72–73.

8. One finds blank utopian longing, at times conjoined with nihilating destruction, in the early Walter Benjamin as well as in recent figures such as Fredric Jameson. See Jameson's *The Political Unconscious: Narrative as a Socially Symbolic Act* (Ithaca, N.Y.: Cornell University Press, 1981), 11.

9. This relationship of mutual marking that places in question notions of pure identity and binary opposition is crucial to Derrida's *différance*.

10. The nondialogic riposte has become typical of such genres as the talk show, the letter to the editor, and the book review.

11. The view of narrative as conventionalizing is crucial to Sande Cohen's argument in *Historical Culture: On the Recoding of an Academic Discipline* (Berkeley: University of California Press, 1986). One might, however, contend *both* that historiography has stricter theoretical limits than the novel in experimenting with narrative (for example, with respect to inventing events as well as on more structural levels, such as the use of free indirect style) *and* that it probably has not been as experimental as it could be. On these issues, see Dominick LaCapra, *History and Criticism* (Ithaca, N.Y.: Cornell University Press, 1985); Hayden White, *The Content of the Form: Narrative Discourse and Historical Representation* (Baltimore: Johns Hopkins University Press, 1987); Philippe Carrard, *Poetics of the New History: French Historical Discourse from Braudel to Chartier* (Baltimore: Johns Hopkins University Press, 1992); and Robert J. Berkhofer, *Beyond the Great Story: History as Text and Discourse* (Cambridge: Harvard University Press, 1995).

12. For a critical investigation of the latter concepts, see Mark Seltzer, *Serial Killers: Death and Life in America's Wound Culture* (New York: Routledge, 1998).

13. I thank Richard Schaefer for this example.

14. See *Representing the Holocaust: History, Theory, Trauma* (Ithaca, N.Y.: Cornell University Press, 1994) and *History and Memory After Auschwitz* (Ithaca, N.Y.: Cornell University Press, 1998).

15. See "Remembering, Repeating and Working Through" (1914), *S.E.*, 12: 145–46, and "Mourning and Melancholia" (1917), *S.E.*, 14: 237–60. I would agree with Judith But-

ler that "in *The Ego and the Id* [Freud] makes room for the notion that melancholic identification may be a *prerequisite* for letting the object go." *The Psychic Life of Power: Theories in Subjection* (Stanford, Calif.: Stanford University Press, 1997), 134. But I think this
is already implied by the analysis of the complex, ambivalent relation of melancholia
and mourning in "Mourning and Melancholia." Moreover, I think that acting-out in
general may be a prerequisite of working-through, at least with respect to traumatic
events, although, as I argue later, I do not think that melancholia should be given an
originary position as constitutive of the socialized psyche.

16. Such a rereading might include Judaism, especially in the post-Holocaust context
wherein the felt or affirmed absence of God might be paradoxically combined with an
attempt to honor his name and engage in ritual practices and other traditional forms
such as prayer.

17. The all-or-nothing tendency (including the somewhat histrionic idea that one should
"never say never") also appears in the assumption that any critique of excess must even-
tuate in an indiscriminate affirmation of a *juste milieu* or a blandly general belief that
one must never exaggerate, be hyperbolic, or go too far. On the contrary, one may recognize that, in certain contexts (notably post-traumatic ones), one must undergo at least
the temptation of excess and even engage in forms of hyperbole but still attempt to signal the importance of, and help bring about, a viable interaction between excess and legitimate normative limits.

18. Butler, *Psychic Life of Power,* 244n. For a fuller discussion of this problem, see my *Representing the Holocaust: History, Theory, Trauma* and *History and Memory After Auschwitz.*

19. Ibid., 197–98.

20. In the penultimate chapter, by contrast, melancholia is more dynamically related to arrested mourning without being given an originary or constitutive status. Adam Phillips's
critique, which was addressed to a version of the penultimate chapter and, in the book,
separates the two last chapters, may have prompted a change in Butler's argument—a
questionable change in my judgment. Phillips, in tune with much contemporary
thought, tends almost to foreclose working-through—a tendency abetted by a rather
pollyanna if not redemptive and dubious construction of it—and simultaneously to see
melancholia as the more "radical" option.

21. As Butler puts it in her penultimate chapter, "I would argue that phenomenologically
there are many ways of experiencing gender and sexuality that do not reduce to this equation [of melancholic gender identity derived from the repudiation of homosexual desire
and its incorporation as a lost identity], that do not presume that gender is stabilized
through the installation of a firm heterosexuality, but for the moment I want to invoke
this stark and hyperbolic construction of the relation between gender and sexuality in
order to think through the question of ungrieved and ungrievable loss in the formation
of what we might call the gendered character of the ego" (136). The difficulty is that the
"stark and hyperbolic construction" tends to govern the entire analysis and forecloses the
attempt to "think through" other possibilities that may, to a greater or lesser extent, even
constitute countervailing forces in existing society. Among these possible modes of subjectivity is trust or a trusting attitude, which of course applies differently with respect to
a subject's relations with different others and groups of others. Along with working-

through, trust is a category that may not hold a sufficiently prominent place in recent critical theory. To avoid certain inferences, I would note that trust is not purely "positive" or related to a pollyanna view of existence. The attitude of trust, which is, I think, common in people and especially evident in children, opens one to manipulation and abuse. The prevalence of the confidence man (or, more generally, the trickster figure) as a social type in both history and literature is one sign of the openness of trust to abuse. Yet trust also has other possibilities in child care and in social relations more generally. Indeed, one might suggest that the intensity and prevalence (not the mere existence) of melancholia may be related to the abuse or impairment of trust, and melancholia is often pronounced in those who have experienced some injury to trust.

22. On these problems see, e.g., Juliana Schiesari, *The Gendering of Melancholic Feminism: Psychoanalysis and the Symbolism of Loss in Renaissance Literature* (Ithaca, N.Y.: Cornell University Press, 1992); Winfried Schleiner, *Melancholy, Genius, and Utopia in the Renaissance* (Wiesbaden: O. Harrassowitz, 1991); Mitchell Robert Breitwieser, *American Puritanism and the Defense of Mourning: Religion, Grief, and Ethnology in Mary White Rowlandson's Captivity Narrative* (Madison: University of Wisconsin Press, 1990); and especially Wolf Lepenies, *Melancholy and Society* (1969), translated by Jeremy Gaines and Doris Jones, foreword by Judith Shklar (Cambridge: Harvard University Press, 1992).

23. On this problem, see my "Temporality of Rhetoric," in *Soundings in Critical Theory,* 90–124.

24. Normalization involves the postulation of the statistical average (or perhaps the dominant) as normative. This postulation is certainly open to criticism, but its critique does not imply the avoidance or delegitimation of all normativity, including alternative normativities. Indeed a crucial problem with respect to homophobia would be the development of a normativity that did not "abjectify" homosexual desire and practice—a normativity that engaged the problems of commitment and trust without simply taking the conventional family as its model.

25. Walter Benjamin's *Origin of German Tragic Drama* (1963), translated by John Osborne, introduction by George Steiner (London: Verso, 1977)—*Trauerspiel* would be better translated as "mourning play" and understood in terms of an impossible mourning in closest proximity to interminably melancholic grieving—may have provided an important paradigm for what has become a prevalent move in recent theory. In my judgment, Benjamin's thought is not restricted to this framework, but it does play an important role especially in his early work. Benjamin might be reread "against the grain" to elicit forms of mourning and "working-through" intricately related to melancholy as well as for indications of absence not conflated with loss and blank messianic hope. Indeed a distinctive appreciation of his turn to Marxism would be significant in this rereading.

26. This conflation tends to occur in Shoshana Felman's contributions to the work she cowrote with Dori Laub, *Testimony: Crises of Witnessing in Literature, Psychoanalysis, and History* (New York: Routledge, 1992).

27. At least in one movement of his argument, Sartre did historicize this desire. See *Being and Nothingness* (1943), translated by Hazel E. Barnes (New York: Washington Square Press, 1953).

28. I find this tendency toward surrogate victim status in Claude Lanzmann as interviewer in his film *Shoah*. See my discussion in *History and Memory After Auschwitz*, chap. 4.

29. Compare the formulation in Saul Friedländer, *Memory, History, and the Extermination of the Jews of Europe* (Bloomington: Indiana University Press, 1993), 130–34.

30. The type of empathy I am defending is discussed by Kaja Silverman in terms of heteropathic identification. See *The Threshold of the Visible World* (New York: Routledge, 1996).

31. Bessel A. van der Kolk makes the questionable attempt to localize in a portion of the brain the trace or imprint of the experience of trauma. See his "The Intrusive Past: The Flexibility of Memory and the Engraving of Trauma," cowritten with Onno van Hart, in *Trauma: Explorations in Memory*, edited by Cathy Caruth (Baltimore: Johns Hopkins University Press, 1995), 158–82. Curiously, Caruth, despite her stress on the elusiveness and belated temporality of the experience of trauma, accepts van der Kolk's literalizing view. Along with her contributions to *Trauma: Explorations in Memory*, see her *Unclaimed Experience: Trauma, Narrative, and History* (Baltimore: Johns Hopkins University Press, 1996).

32. The important and influential work of Pierre Bourdieu is often prone to contextual reductionism or at least to a very limited understanding of differential responses to contextual (or "field") forces. See, e.g., *L'Ontologie politique de Martin Heidegger* (Paris: Editions de Minuit, 1988), and *The Rules of Art: Genesis and Structure of the Literary Field* (1992), translated by Susan Emmanuel (Stanford, Calif.: Stanford University Press, 1995).

33. *Telling the Truth About History* (New York: W. W. Norton, 1994), 1.

34. *The Sublime Object of Ideology* (London: Verso, 1989), 50.

States of Emergency: Toward a Freudian Historiography of Modernity

Eric L. Santner

In my most recent book, which focused on the case of Daniel Paul Schreber, made famous by Freud's 1911 study of Judge Schreber's *Memoirs,* I argued that one area where psychoanalytic thought can deepen our understanding of modernity concerns the processes and procedures of symbolic investiture.[1] By symbolic investiture I mean those social acts, often involving a ritualized transferal of a title and mandate, whereby an individual is endowed with a new social status and role within a shared linguistic universe. It's how one comes into being as, comes to enjoy the predicate of, husband, professor, judge, psychoanalyst, and so on. Within social reality—that is, a universe of symbolic relations—one never simply "has" a predicate; whether one likes it or not, whether it is a source of pleasure or not, one's bond to a predicate has a libidinal component and the rites of symbolic investiture are among the means at a society's disposal for the cultivation and regulation of this "predicative enjoyment."

Whatever new status these rites establish, they do so by combining the two basic meanings of this word *establish*. On a first level, the utterance issued by the minister of justice conferring on Schreber the ti-

tle Senatspräsident of the Saxon Court of Appeals merely established, in an of-
ficial way, Schreber's qualifications for the position; it publicly ascertained that
Schreber was, as it were, "in himself" already presiding judge. But a symbolic investiture necessarily includes a second level of linguistic effectivity, a more properly performative notion of "establishing," whereby the "in itself" is converted
into a "for itself." Pierre Bourdieu has called this conversion "the principle behind the performative magic of all acts of institution."[2] My reading of Schreber
proposed that his experience of what he referred to as "soul murder" and the cos-
mic disaster associated with it—that is, Schreber's sense that the world had been
destroyed—was grounded in a fundamental impasse in his capacity to metabolize this performative magic, to be inducted into the normative space opened by
it (Schreber's psychotic break followed quickly upon his nomination as Senatspräsident). As Slavoj Žižek has put it, this means that "the subject is confronted
with an 'inert' signifying chain, one that does not seize him performatively, affecting his subjective position of enunciation: towards this chain the subject
maintains a 'relation of exteriority.'"[3] As Žižek has further noted, this inertness
can—and in Schreber's case no doubt did—assume the malevolent aspect of a
persecutory superego bombarding the subject with seemingly nonsensical injunctions. The *capacity to enjoy* the predicate posited by the investiture is con-
sumed by such injunctions. This is how I understand the Lacanian lesson Žižek
draws from such a crisis: "At this precise point, as the subject confronts the
'agency of the letter' in its original and radical *exteriority,* the signifier's nonsense
at its purest, he encounters the superego command 'Enjoy!' which addresses the
most *intimate* kernel of his being."[4] Another way of put-ting it would be to say
that the space of possibilities opened by the investiture, this capacity, or, in Martin Heidegger's terms, this *Seinkönnen,* has become stuck in its "enjoyment," thus
blocking the normal functioning of symbolic identification. As Schreber's experience testifies—and his *Memoirs* are best understood as an effort to disseminate
this testimony—when the space of possibilities has been, as it were, fully ab-
sorbed by this dysfunction, it is fair to say that the world no longer exists.

Now at first glance, Freud's reading of the case material (recall that Freud chose
not to research the biographical particulars of the case and limited himself to a
reading of Schreber's *Memoirs*) would seem to have a rather different focus. According to Freud, Schreber's delusion of world destruction was precipitated by a
homosexual panic leading Schreber to withdraw his libido not only from the immediate cause of the panic—his psychiatrist, Paul Flechsig—but from all things,
from beings in their totality. The paranoid symptoms elaborated in the *Memoirs*
in such extravagant detail, above all the torturous *jouissance* of sexual transfor-

mation experienced under the influence of God's penetrating rays, are understood by Freud as efforts on Schreber's part to return his libidinal attachments to people and things, to bind himself, once more, to the normative space of symbolic titles, mandates, and obligations. We might say, then, that Freud's reading comes down to the thesis that Schreber experienced, indeed found himself unable not to experience, the drive dimension of this normative space, the erotic and aggressive kernel of its bindingness, or *Verbindlichkeit*. Put somewhat differently, the claim would be this: to metabolize acts of institution and the performative magic they depend on means, in some sense, to reenact the potentially traumatic opening and passionate assumption of one's being-in-the-world. I think it's safe to say that such reenactments normally constitute a good part of the mental activity that Freud circumscribed by the term *unconscious;* in the case of a psychotic like Schreber, this activity fills waking life in its entirety. He is caught in what I'd like to call the *state of emergency of normativity,* a disaster of perpetual and failed emergence. At this extreme point, every aspect of linguistic life—life with norms—is affected, thus the sense that the world has been destroyed. The world collapses, in other words, because it is constantly in *statu nascendi,* because the rites of investiture become a repetition compulsion that never stabilizes into the status of a second nature. And once again, Schreber's testimony has something crucial to teach us. When the world as a space of possibilities of concerned, normative engagement sustained by fundamental acts of symbolic investiture collapses, one is left not with nothing—a pure void—but rather with a kind of "proto-cosmos" or what Wolfram Hogrebe, in a commentary on Schelling's *Weltalter*-fragments, has referred to as the *Triebschicksale des Seins,* the drive vicissitudes of Being.[5] We are in the "proto-cosmos" when predicative enjoyment no longer stays in the background, as it were, serving to support the *Verbindlichkeit* of each predication, but rather comes to light as such, emerges into a kind of independent existence. Schreber himself characterized these conditions as "circumstances contrary to the Order of the World."[6] Given the sexual nature of so much of Schreber's suffering, we might say that this coming to light of predicative enjoyment is, literally and figuratively, "out of this world."[7]

A somewhat different way of approaching these "circumstances" would be to recall Ludwig Wittgenstein's remarks apropos of the feeling of being guided in one's normative activities, for example, when one adds a set of numbers or draws a line parallel to another one after having been initiated into such activities: "When I look back on the experience I have the feeling that what is essential about it is an 'experience of being influenced' . . . but at the same time I should not be willing to call any experienced phenomenon the 'experience of being influenced.' . . . I should like to say that I had experienced the 'because,' and yet I do not want to call any phenomenon the 'experience of the because.'"[8] The psychotic, however, is plagued by such "experiences of the because"; Schreber was flooded by them.[9] It was these "impossible" experiences of a *direct* influence by norms, of what we might call the *specters* or *spirits* (rather than the *spirit*) of normativity—and this is how I understand the Lacanian notion of the *agency of the letter*—that Schreber registered as a sexual intensification and feminization of his body.[10] The well-known tendency toward literalization in psychotic states suggests that the subject is unable to be animated by the *spirit* of normativity because he is haunted by its *spirits,* because he or she is stuck in the protocosmos of predicative enjoyment and thus unable to sustain a symbolic identification. The process of *healing,* then, is closely related to the messianic conception of the "Last Days." Healing in this secular sense also involves a kind of resurrection, a coming back to the world and thus to life, only here the reanimation of the "dead" might perhaps be better understood as a *deanimation of the undead* and so a kind of *mourning.*

Let me try to make this a bit more concrete by recalling a crucial episode from Schreber's *Memoirs.* He describes a night when he encountered, with an exceptional force and immediacy, the voices that had been tormenting him (he addresses them with the names of the Zoroastrian deities). It is another scene of investiture and interpellation, one, however, that is closer to a variety of hate speech. My hunch is that in this scene Schreber is describing the breakdown products of his investiture crisis:

> I believe I may say that at that time and at that time *only,* I saw God's omnipotence in its complete purity. During the night . . . the lower God (Ariman) appeared. The radiant picture of his rays became visible to my inner eye . . . that is to say he was reflected on my inner nervous system. Simultaneously I heard his voice; but it was not a soft whisper—as the talk of the voices always was before and after that time—it resounded in a mighty bass as if directly in front of my bedroom window. The impression was intense, so that anybody not hardened to terrifying miraculous impressions as I was, would have been shaken to the core. Also *what* was spoken did not sound friendly by any means: everything seemed calculated to instill fright and terror into me and the word "wretch" [*Luder*] was frequently heard—an expression quite common in the basic language to denote a human being destined to be destroyed by God and to feel God's power and wrath. [124]

The appellation favored by the deity—*Luder*—has especially rich connotations in the context of Schreber's torments. It can mean wretch, in the sense of a lost and pathetic figure, but it can also signify: a cunning swindler or scoundrel; a whore, tart, or slut; and, finally, the dead, rotting flesh of an animal, especially in the sense of carrion used as bait in hunting. The last two significations capture Schreber's fear of being turned over to others for the purposes of sexual exploitation as well as his anxieties, which would seem to flow from such abuse, about putrefaction. We might add to this list of connotations—and here I am indebted to Jerry Flieger's suggestion—the notion of the *ludic,* and thus of Schreber as a kind of *Homo ludens.* What Schreber condenses in this *homoludic* epiphany are, I am suggesting, the effects of coming too close to a spectral materiality that, at least under certain circumstances, appears to be secreted within and by the procedures of investiture, procedures that profoundly inform our relation to possibility. It seems to me that one of the tasks of a genuinely psychoanalytic historiography of modern culture would be to specify, on the basis of a prior ontology of the specter, just what these circumstances might be. Finally, given the ludic aspect of life with the undead, it would make sense, in our efforts to understand the process of healing as one of mourning, to emphasize that process as one of *Trauer-Spiel* and not simply as one of *Trauer-Arbeit.* For it may be that the dream of a total deanimation of the undead—of a final solution to the specters of normativity—is also the greatest threat to human life and to what inspires ethical bonds between subjects.

Notes

1. See *My Own Private Germany: Daniel Paul Schreber's Secret History of Modernity* (Princeton, N.J.: Princeton University Press, 1996). Schreber's *Denkwurdigkeiten eines Nervenkranken* is available in English as *Memoirs of My Nervous Illness,* translated by Ida Macalpine and Richard A. Hunter (Cambridge: Harvard University Press, 1988).
2. Cited in Santner, *My Own Private Germany,* 12. I think that anyone who has gone through the tenure process understands something about this magic.
3. Slavoj Žižek, *The Metastases of Enjoyment: Six Essays on Woman and Causality* (Verso: London, 1994), 12.
4. Ibid., 20.
5. See Wolfram Hogrebe, *Pradikation and Genesis: Metaphysik als Fundamentalheuristik im Ausgang von Schellings "Die Weltalter"* (Frankfurt: Suhrkamp, 1989).
6. Schreber, *Memoirs,* 47.
7. When we speak of Schreber's *testimony,* it is important to remember that he lived this testimony as a bodily transformation and, indeed, as a retraction of his *testicles* as part of a more general process of feminization. This retraction of phallic attributes—of what testifies to masculinity—which he experienced as a kind of martyrdom accompanied by intense sexual excitation of a feminine kind (he speaks of *weibliche Wollust*) was initiated by God in order to make possible Schreber's calling as mother-to-be of a new race of human beings who would repopulate the world after its demise. In a word, Schreber's privileged testimony of a crisis in the order–ordering of predicative enjoy-

ment was registered as an exciting disordering of predications in the domain of sexuality and gender.

8. Ludwig Wittgenstein, *Philosophical Investigations,* translated by G. E. M. Anscombe (Oxford: Blackwell, 1997), paragraph 176.

9. For a detailed reading of the Schreber case in light of Wittgenstein's thought, see Louis A. Sass, *The Paradoxes of Delusion: Wittgenstein, Schreber, and the Schizophrenic Mind* (Ithaca, N.Y.: Cornell University Press, 1994).

10. Michel Foucault has, of course, analyzed such "experiences of the because" of direct influence by norms, under the heading of *disciplinary power* and *bio-power.* In each case, Foucault notes that the result of contact with these forms is an intensification of the body. For a discussion of Foucault's relevance to the Schreber case, see *My Own Private Germany,* chap. 2.

Early Modern Subjectivity
and the Place of Psychoanalysis
in Cultural Analysis: The Case
of Richard Norwood

Meredith Skura

For more than three hundred years Richard Norwood (1590–1670) was known to historians primarily through his public roles as navigator, inventor of the diving bell, and surveyor of Bermuda. The publication of his journal in 1945, however, promised scholars a rare opportunity for learning about the relation between public roles and private life in the seventeenth century. The trouble is that Norwood's journal is different from the confessional memoirs familiar from today's bestseller lists. It concerns itself primarily with external events and spiritual development, and like other early autobiographical texts, it remains stubbornly reticent about feelings and fantasies—so much so that many literary and historical scholars have argued that sixteenth- and seventeenth-century writers like Norwood *had* little "private" life, or none that we can learn about.

Psychoanalysis, which is designed to tease out the implications of reticent speech, provides a way into such texts and the larger questions they bear on. There are problems, of course, with applying analysis to seventeenth-century writing—hence the question, Can psychoanalysis be used in analysis of past cultures? Objections to historical psychoanalysis formerly depended on its lack of evidence to answer questions about past experience: we have almost no data about the most elusive aspects of the past, thoughts and feelings; even if we did, interpretation is problematic unless the subject is there to free associate and take part in a transference relationship with the analyst. These objections have been contested by Erik Erikson and others, and they needn't be addressed here. A newer post-Foucauldian objection, however, deserves mention because it signals a new view of analysis as a historically determined practice. Rather than objecting that we have no data about experience, it dismisses the basic psychoanalytic assumption that experience is what matters in the first place. According to this view, early modern subjects lived in so different a world and were so unlike us that psychoanalysis is anachronistic; indeed, the very notion of personhood may be irrelevant to them. The questions analysts ask about individual experience are now thought to be problematic in themselves because "experience" is the product of more fundamental discursive or material pressures. Norwood's diary, for example, gives no insight into his private inner life; rather, as Tom Webster argues, it "testifies to a socially determined technology of the self, fulfilling the demands of a particular religious institution" rather than the dictates of a particular "person."[1]

This argument provides an essential reminder that we still do not know enough to take anything for granted about early modern subjectivity. But psychoanalysis is no worse an offender on this count than any other approach. Every reading must make *some* unproved assumptions about Norwood's psychology—including Webster's reading, which assumes that Norwood was a completely blank slate before being interpellated into Puritan patriarchal culture. The best readers can do is to make their assumptions clear and to use them as hypotheses to be tested, not explanations to be defended. I propose to do just that, analyzing Norwood's journal as I would had he come to consult an analyst and presented his life story as background. How much can I learn this way? What new patterns appear as a result? What details are newly explained? What new questions emerge to investigate?

I begin with three assumptions, none of them, I trust, as "scandalous" as Frederick Crews might expect. First, human beings like Norwood are not wholly reducible to cultural (or to biological) origins, though they are inseparable from both. In addition to understanding whatever biological and cultural constraints were operating in Norwood's world, we also need to take account of psychological ones. That is, unlike rocks or plants, people are conscious of and respond to their own production—thus affecting its outcome. Even babies have a particular way of seeing and reacting to their world: fussy ones prompt different treatment from their caretakers than do easygoing babies, and the difference affects the way they behave as toddlers, which further affects the way they are treated as older children, and so on. Continual interaction between "character" and environment over a lifetime makes any explanation of causality extraordinarily elusive.

Second, characteristic responses begin in earliest childhood, when "ways of seeing" the world are irrational, narcissistic, emotionally fraught, rigid, and often antisocial. These older ways of seeing and feeling linger on, influencing and being influenced by new ones. This doesn't mean, as Crews might parody it, that Norwood's personality was determined by his toilet training experience; but it does imply that a three-year-old's way of seeing things may very well play some part in adulthood, along with all the other ways of seeing that developed later. Nor does it imply pathology on Norwood's part; only a cumulative history.

In any case, questions about the origin of current subjectivity cannot be addressed without close investigation of Norwood's current way of seeing things, his adult psychic reality. This is the primary material of psychoanalysis, the only real evidence and the final court of appeal for hypotheses. This doesn't mean, as Crews implies, that external or communal reality is irrelevant. Nor does it mean that cultural forces like ideology are irrelevant. It simply marks an interest in individual variation on communal norms. Norwood's journal cannot be understood apart from its Puritan context, but our understanding of what "Puritan" means should also note that Norwood, perhaps uniquely, saw Puritans as kind women with sickly daughters.

In addition, a psychoanalytic reading must approach psychic reality through a subject's report of it, ideally by free association in a clinical situation but, lacking that, through any first-person account. A psychoanalytic reader must suspend all preconceptions (an impossible goal, of course, but the reader must try and must keep track of failures) and read not only for literal but also for other meanings, as if the text were the product of free association as well as rational planning. Look for slips, trivial connections, and the kind of detail emphasized in Rorschach and Thematic Apperception Tests: How does Norwood represent other people? animals? How much movement and color are there in his imagery?

More than anything else, a psychoanalytic reader must treat the journal as the occasion for an exchange between two people. In addition to listening to what Norwood says, I must pay attention to what he is doing by saying it. Who is he talking to? (Not to me, obviously; but to someone, and I must read from the position of that someone.) Why? Why now? What effect is he trying to have on his listener?

Last, the most psychoanalytic part of psychoanalysis. I, too, am part of the exchange, and I must keep track of my own reactions even more than Norwood's. They are the most immediately reliable evidence I have; they are my primary "analytic instrument."

Earlier readings of Norwood's journal confine themselves to its content, and I'll start with these so that I can go on to suggest the differences between them and a contemporary psychoanalytic reading of both content and performative aspects. The content of journals like Norwood's can be analyzed in many ways. Owen Watkins, for example, who devoted a chapter to Norwood in his book on *The Puritan Experience* (1972), was interested primarily in intellectual history and Puritan belief, and he based his optimistic interpretation of the journal on a passage describing Norwood's lifelong quest to find an Edenic summum bonum, first conceived as a literal garden:

> For in my youth and childhood [Norwood says] I had many childish conceits and fancies: as how far it might be from earth to heaven? Whether there might not be some means devised to go up thither? Whether the heavens did not touch the earth in some places, as at the horizon?—and this I was much persuaded it did, . . . And there I conceived were sundry rarities and excellent things to be seen. Besides I thought, why might not. . . . Garden of Paradise be found. . . . might haply find. . . . way to get in, although the Angels. . . . the gate of it . . . might prevail with him by entreaties to let him in. . . . When I saw rivers they seemed to be as it were some infinite thing, the waters always running and yet remaining full. I wondered whence they came, and thought, when I should be my own man, I would search from whence and whither they were, supposing to find there many rare things.[2]

Norwood explains that he outgrew this literal view of paradise, and Watkins takes Norwood at his word, stressing the narrative's manifest content. Reading analytically, however, I would look also for possible references to physical, emotional, and unique personal experience in the same words and for possible signs of conflict in Norwood's dismissal. Norwood juxtaposes without further explanation his "conceit" about Paradise and his conceit about rivers. The association has multiple determinants in seventeenth-century theology (for example, the rivers of Eden). But it also has determinants in his inner world, which Norwood, like other early autobiographers, does not describe more directly. The river seems bound up with what I think Norwood saw as the power—sometimes wonderful, sometimes terrible—of his own physical being, his own flowing, running body. Seen this way, the river makes an important counterpoint to the many other strikingly kinesthetic images of falling, running, leaning, hanging, pinching, and tossing that appear throughout Norwood's memories.

In his life, as opposed to his fantasies, Norwood is a man who restrains his

flows. Rather than letting his narrative run on, for example, he controls it, carefully separating his description of internal and external experiences and always
keeping track of what he has just said. His flow of speech was always kept in
check, too, insofar as Norwood suffered since childhood from stuttering or
"draggling in my speech." "To this day," he writes, "it is something laborious to
me to speak" (9). Other flows cause problems, too. Much of Norwood's energy
is spent trying to control the flow of actual liquids out of his body. Semen "pol-
lutes" him when he periodically succumbs to his master sin, masturbation. Tears
betray him when he "is no longer able to contain [him]self" and weeps in the
standing corn (21), or when he leaves school, and "qualms of grief and dismay
began to seize on my heart. . . . [and] my heart was ready to break and my eyes
to gush abundantly with tears" (6). Less tangible emotions are also experienced
as liquids. He tells us that he cannot make his way to God because "such a violent stream of affections carri[ed] me another way to evil that it seemed to be altogether in vain to strive against them" (45). Like Othello figuring himself in the
Pontic Sea, Norwood makes us aware of the *motion* in emotion, the almost physical sense in which the "affections" were taken to be "the feet of the will." Such
internal forces can be terrifying, but Norwood constructs his own paradise in
which the streams are beneficent. His is not only a land of milk and honey to be
taken in but of semen and "corrupt affections" and tears that can gush freely out.
If these implications are at work, then Norwood's repudiation of paradise takes
on individual meaning along with the traditional one Watkins explores.

Two other readers, Paul Delany (*British Autobiography in the Seventeenth
Century;* 1969) and John Stachniewsky (*The Persecutory Imagination: English
Puritanism and the Literature of Religious Despair;* 1991), who are more interested
in forces outside Norwood's statable beliefs, have emphasized a quite different
part of the journal, a passage describing Norwood's recurring nightmare after
he ran away from home and nearly converted to Catholicism: "Oft-times I ver-
ily thought I descended into Hell and there felt the pains of the damned. . . .
Usually in my dreams methought I saw my father always grievously angry with
me. . . . And sometimes I seemed to see a thing upon my breast or belly like a
hare or cat, etc.; whereupon I have sometimes taken a naked knife in my hand
when I went to sleep, thinking therewith to strike at it, and it was God's mercy
that I had not by this means slain myself" (26). And sometimes, "Methought as
I looked back I saw myself far entered within the gates of hell and now if the
percullis should be let fall I should be kept in and could no more return, and I
. . . endeavored to recover myself . . . secretly and as it were to steal away, that if
it were possible Satan might not perceive it" (95). Rather than invoking Nor-

wood's beliefs to illuminate his journal, these two readers point elsewhere. The early Freudian Delany sees in Norwood's hellish visions "a textbook case of neurosis" (59) induced by strict guilt-instilling parents and fueled by unconscious castration anxiety.[3] The new historicist Stachniewsky finds a more fundamental hegemonic ideology at work, unconsciously instilling in Norwood the masochistic self-image that encouraged him, along with other dutiful Puritans, to subject himself to the will of a clerical elite.

All three of these interpretations call attention to important features of Norwood's journal, but each moves so quickly to the question of genesis (was it the parents or the Puritans who gave him nightmares?) that it cuts analysis short. I would stay closer to the experience itself, exploring, for example, the dynamics that take Norwood from Edenic desires to nightmarish fears and back again, shunting between opposite yet curiously similar versions of the desire to get past the forbidden gates of paradise and the fear of what he might find there. I would explore still larger dynamic patterns in the narrative that, for example, present the Edenic dream as a response to Norwood's childhood "fall" from being the master's favorite in an expensive school into being an impoverished exile. Here I'll focus on only one additional part of the pattern, Norwood's earliest memory, a feature of life stories that often plays an important role in psychoanalysis. A subject's earliest memories matter in analysis not because they report accurately about childhood, although they might; but because as "screen memories" they can provide evidence of the way in which the adult Norwood sees his childhood, and thus of the way his mind works. Significantly, Norwood's version of his life story begins with a literal fall: "whilest I was . . . going to school with my sister about a mile from home (the very day I left off my long coats to wear breeches) I was in danger to have been drowned by swinging on a stake by a ditch of water, which broke, and I fell into the ditch, my head forwards, but by God's providence I was drawn out by one that came with a cart" (5). Breeching marks the transition between the ungendered nursery and the male world beyond it. But no sooner does young Norwood put on his breeches and exercise a boy's freedom to swing dangerously on stakes—the sister stays behind on the ground—than he falls headfirst into the water and nearly drowns. Did this really happen? It might have; Norwood's Stevenage was chalk country, riddled with pits where chalk workers had been digging. But the literal fall here from activity to passivity, from upright to upside-down, from swinging above his sister to drowning below her, inscribes a more figurative experience of the world. And the associated details point to recurrent themes in the journal: the strenuous muscular activity ("swinging"), the connection between gender and danger, the importance of water.

With this as a first memory, Norwood's quest for paradise can be seen as a fighting response to such a disturbing psychic birth. It is significant, for example, that the man whose first memory is falling headfirst into a ditch went on to invent a diving bell that allowed him to descend safely—and feet first—into deep water to harvest pearls and that much of his life was spent studying navigation or successfully navigating across oceans. Such patterns suggest a life with its unique internal coherence, as well as one shaped by common external constraints.

Finally a psychoanalytic reading is concerned to identify not only latent patterns in the narrative but patterns in the narrator's behavior and in his expectations about the reader. Analysis of what he says is complemented by an exploration of Norwood's motives for saying it, of what an actor would call Norwood's "spine," or "through line," spanning the drama of his presentation. My exploration here is limited to the first and last acts of this drama. I cannot begin this exploration as a seventeenth-century analyst might have, by asking Norwood directly, "What brings you here?" But the journal itself, together with the historical record, provides evidence of an interesting conflict. On one hand, both Norwood's title, *Confessions,* and his preface point to a self-conscious focus on conventional religious categories and practices: "In the 49th year of my age, a day which I had set apart to give unto the Lord by fasting and praying privately, some occasion (then) requiring it. Amongst other things that day I endeavored to call to mind the whole course of my life past, and how the Lord had dealt with me. [But] some things began to grow out of memory, which I thought I should scarce ever have forgotten; and considering that as age came on forgetfulness would increase upon me, I determined to set them down in writing" (3).

Writing, Norwood implies, is the product solely of his relationship to God. This is not surprising; the conventional terms for dealing with and understanding emotional disturbance were religious. Norwood makes an account of his sins in order to explain his unease; God's forgiveness, he hopes, will resolve it. But although he doesn't mention them, circumstances suggest that Norwood's vulnerability in 1639 was exacerbated by political and psychological forces—by things he leaves out or slurs over, for example, the turmoil that was to produce England's civil war and Norwood's recent flight from it. "The times were dangerous" for a nonconformist teacher in England, as he would write two years later, "by reason of many innovations in Religion."[4] Fearing ruin, Norwood sought out and won a post back in Bermuda in 1638. But he could not thereby escape a second, more psychological upheaval. In 1639–40, Richard

Norwood was a married man with several children whose navigational exploits were past and who was beginning to feel that "the evening of my life and age approacheth" (110). It was time to take stock, and when he realizes that he is starting to forget parts of his past, he decides to set everything down in writing. In other words, despite his overt reliance on religion, Norwood copes not only by praying and fasting but also by taking stock, organizing, surveying, getting control—and writing things down. He confronts a crisis in his life now by surveying his whole life in the past.

The same coping style is evident throughout the journal, with its cautious disclaimers ("as I saw it" and "to my sight at that time," and so on), its carefully structured separation of the chronological account of external events (pages 1–59) from a more descriptive account of his inner spiritual development (pages 59–80), its dutifully marked digressions from this outline ("but to return" and "to proceed"), its marginal notes, its inked-out passages, and finally its preface—written after Norwood finished the journal—which is a survey of his survey, yet one more level of control over the chaotic material of his life.

Other texts confirm this as Norwood's habitual style. Norwood's prior survey of Bermuda explains proudly that in his map the islands, which were "before as it were an unsettled and confused Chaos . . . receive[d] a convenient disposition, forme, and order."[5] Similarly, his earlier books had constituted efforts to bring order to intractable materials and were for the most part orderly collations of other men's discoveries and translations from other languages. Again and again Norwood is drawn to the excitement of unknown territory, across the ocean or beneath it, in books, or in himself, but only if he can survey it, encompass it, translate it into a familiar language.

Norwood's style characterizes not only his attitude toward his material but also his exchange with the reader. As the preface makes clear, Norwood begins by speaking to, and indirectly invoking mercy from, God. Yet the exchange also bears some resemblance to that in a confession booth in the old religion to which Norwood had for so long been so attracted, or perhaps to the exchange in a psychoanalytic interview, which encourages transference and countertransference reactions. In any case, I think that many analysts would single out the transference-like exchange implied by the journal's last section as one of the most interesting, although no other biographer has spent time with it.

Just before this last section, the journal culminates in an account of Norwood's religious conversion in Bermuda and a prayer that ends halfway down the page. He left the rest of the page and its verso blank. It looks and sounds like "the end." But then, almost as an afterthought, the narrative continues on the following recto (which is unfortunately torn out) and goes on for an additional seventy pages. In the added section Norwood describes his return to England after the Bermuda conversion—his backsliding, his renewed nightmares, and Satan's renewed attacks—and he sounds like a different man. He seems now at times to be talking to himself or to be addressing—even at one point lecturing to—a human equal rather than God. And his material seems to have escaped his careful control, so much so that the journal's editor dismisses this section as of "more interest to the psychologist than the historian." It's more emotional; the neat division between internal and external narratives dissolves; and both chronology and causality are disrupted—so that, for example, Norwood blames his temptation not only on too much sin but also on too much piety (overzealous prayer and fasting make him delirious), and also on his landlady: "I was something doubtful of some sorcery by the woman of the house for sundry carriages which I have observed" (104). Even more surprising, Norwood goes on to ask why "the Lord should lead me into these temptations," and he scripts a debate about whether they are good for him. He describes a minister who misled him and doctors who bled him almost to death, so that he was so permanently enfeebled that he would "never be his own man again" (105)—a poetically unjust reversal of his quest "when I should be my own man" to find the magical origins of those rivers "always running and yet remaining full." This last section, which purports to reach final acceptance of God's will, comes closer than anything in the earlier and more superficially rebellious sections to being a protest. It was not unusual for seventeenth-century spiritual diarists to describe backsliding like Norwood's after conversion, but usually they do it in order to boast about overcoming trials and passing God's tests. Norwood instead seems to be putting God on trial.

The journal concludes, of course, that the suffering has all been for the best: it was necessary to humble his pride; it could have been worse; and it has left him a better human being. Yet in spite of the reaffirmation, everything else leaves a modern reader—this modern reader—with questions. It is as if Norwood recognized, at some level, that the only paradise God offered at the end of the quest required Norwood to give up his lifelong dream, a dream that extends backwards to the affective and kinesthetic core of his selfhood. I have no doubt that many, perhaps most, early modern readers—or even a contemporary religious reader—would agree with Norwood that his sacrifices were worthwhile. But to the atheist in me, that last section told another story as well.

I conclude by turning from transference to countertransference, to my own quite subjective responses to Norwood and the role they play in my psychoanalytic interpretation. I was ambivalent at first about studying Norwood. On one hand, he had those wonderful dreams straight out of Freud. How could anyone deny the historical continuity of the unconscious in the face of such dreams? On the other hand, at first reading I found the journal more tedious than I would have liked it to be, and I wasn't sure how to approach it. My interest quickened, however, when on rereading the journal I reached the epilogue where Norwood started sounding very different, when he loosened up and began to challenge God—when, in other words, he began to sound more like me. My reaction tells me little about the inherent interest of that last section of the journal; nor does it tell me anything about what might have interested a seventeenth-century reader. But it does alert me to changes in Norwood's style and attitude, changes that fit neither the specific image of Norwood gleaned from the earlier passages nor the general commonplaces about Puritan piety. What exactly was it about Norwood at the end that got me? What was he doing before? Why did he change? How were his two attitudes related?

What is going on? I think that the process of writing the journal changed Norwood, and that my own subjective twentieth-century responses made me sensitive to those changes. Norwood's journal allows us to glimpse one of the functions that writing a journal might have served for the people who kept them. Recalling his troubled past—surveying it, recording it, writing it down in a book that he could reread and rewrite—enabled Norwood to do something about a current internal disturbance, just as making maps had allowed him to do something with external chaos. The first section allowed Norwood for the first time to reach a point where he could reveal (or remember?) his childish longing for a paradise and his joy at conversion. He writes that he had never told anyone about these experiences "many years agone whilst they were fresher in memory" because he had been afraid (87). Recalling his past—surveying it—and telling it to God while also recording it on paper that he could own, reread, and rewrite allowed him to reclaim the past as his own. Once he has reclaimed his dream, Norwood could then go on in that strange last section to reclaim his anger at not being allowed to realize that dream. Not only does he tell a different story at the end about his relation to God; he talks differently to God—and not only to God. His voice has changed in a way that was easier for me to hear.

In an actual clinical case report, after describing the case material in this way, an analyst would now suggest a developmental account of Norwood's current state and would apply some specifically psychoanalytic categories and terminology that would be strange to Norwood. Here, however, I am less interested in analyzing a historical subject like Norwood than in historicizing analysis by seeing how useful it turns out to be in looking at early modern diaries on more or less their own terms. Any theory about early modern psychology is precarious, and the usefulness of the one offered here cannot be decided on the basis of Norwood's evidence alone. But a reading of additional journals can be tremendously useful in testing our more general theories about early modern subjectivity—and its causes, too. If we read enough diaries as closely as Norwood's we can ask: Which experiences were common to the writers (or to all men or all women or all Puritans or all sailors), and which belong to Norwood? What in his world and his past made him different? Did many other seventeenth-century scientists have such muscular memories? Did any other Puritans identify with sick women? If so, what else did they have in common? What "conceits" of paradise did other navigators have? Merchants? Ministers and politicians?

The voices preserved in seventeenth-century autobiographies and the stories they tell are not to be mistaken for ours today. But they provide the best evidence for testing our theories about how and why people tell—or told—the stories they do.

Notes

1. Tom Webster, "Writing to Redundancy: Approaches to Spiritual Journals and Early Modern Spirituality," *Historical Journal* 1 (1996): 33–56.
2. Richard Norwood, *The Journal of Richard Norwood, Surveyor of Bermuda*, with introductions by Wesley Frank Craven and Walter B. Hayward (New York: Published for the Bermuda Historical Monuments Trust by Scholars' Facsimiles and Reprints, 1945), 3–39. All subsequent quotations are taken from this edition and page numbers are cited in the text.
3. Paul Delany, *British Autobiography in the Seventeenth Century* (New York: Columbia University Press, 1969), 59.
4. Letter to the Bermuda Company, 28 February 1641–42. Cited in the Introduction, "Norwood and Bermuda," *Journal,* xlvi.
5. "The Description of the Sommer Ilands, Once Called the Bermudas" (1622), reprinted in *Journal,* lxxvi.

Whose Psychohistory?

Robert Jay Lifton

In this essay I wish to discuss my work not as applied psychoanalysis—
that term still has some of the aura of early psychoanalytic imperialism, Freud's talk about "conquering" various spheres of thought—but
rather in connection with psychoanalysis as its source. My work in psychohistorical areas begins with psychoanalytic influence, and never
loses that influence, but it does evolve in its own way in certain additional directions. There is a real paradox here, important to keep in
mind particularly in historical and cultural studies: without psychoanalysis, we don't have a psychology worthy of address to history and
society or culture. But at the same time, if we employ psychoanalysis
in its most pristine state, its most traditional form, we run the risk of
eliminating history in the name of studying it. That is so because the
two classical psychoanalytic approaches to history (however modified
more recently) are the *Totem and Taboo* and the individual-psychopathological models. In *Totem and Taboo*, the narrative is that of the
rebellion of the sons against the father, the killing of the father, and
then the consuming of the father. It's essentially a mythic, prehistoric
model, one that is interesting and has value, but not as a means of

looking at actual history. And the individual-psychopathological model, perhaps exemplified in the worst fashion in the Freud-Bullitt study of Woodrow Wilson (written mostly by Bullitt, no doubt, but applying Freud's model), in which most of history is eliminated in the name of individual psychopathology.

Erik Erikson is a key figure in what might be called a new wave of psychohistory, and I had the invaluable experience of about three decades of friendship and dialogue with him. What Erikson managed to do was to hold to psychoanalytic depth while immersing himself in the historical era being studied and then relating those currents to that figure. This sounds quite obvious now, but it was not being done by psychoanalysts until Erickson did it. The model then becomes that of the great man or the great person in history. The breakthrough came with Erickson's study of Martin Luther, perhaps his finest book. The operative word is *in:* not only the great man being studied but psychoanalysis itself in studying the great man is *in* history. So with the word *in* began this new moment in psychohistory. Erikson tells us that "you cannot take the case history out of history," and that Luther tried "to solve for all what he could not solve for himself alone." That is the interaction Erikson is talking about.

Incidentally, there is also a bit of history behind the word *psychohistory.* It is a dubious noun, and there may always be a problem in changing an adjective to a noun. In this case it was transforming *psychohistorical,* a word that Erikson used for his approach, into *psychohistory*—and that transformation took place at Yale University. During the late 1960s, a young undergraduate named Daniel Yergin, who has since gone on to justified fame, wrote a profile of me and my work on Hiroshima for the *New Journal,* Yale's answer to the *New York Review of Books.* He said that what I was doing was "psychohistory," and when I read the piece and asked him where he got the word, he answered, "I don't know. I just thought that's what you were doing." We puzzled over where the word had come from, and I finally discovered that it was used in Isaac Asimov's science fiction classic *Foundation Trilogy.* I could say a lot more about this sequence, but I will leave it here with the observation that words and images can, and usually do, have strange origins.

Instead of the great man or great person in history, my own approach has been that of *shared themes,* of studying individuals and groups who have had a strong impact on, or from, history—and of course, it is usually a combination of both. To put it briefly, the model I follow seeks an empirical center via interviews, then moves outward into comparisons and finally to speculation. The interviews are crucial, and I would emphasize that the interview method is a beautiful one, still much underused within psychiatry, psychology, and humanistic studies. But I have found that the interview has to be modified for work in psychohistorical areas, modified in the direction of dialogue with more of one's own self on the line. After all, these aren't patients who ask to see you out of their need but rather people you seek out because they have some experience, some knowledge, that you want to know more about. The dimension of their experience is pivotal: they offer their words, and whatever hermeneutic process one wants to apply begins with those words.

Let me illustrate how I have used this method in a few studies I have done. My first study, which goes back to the mid-1950s, was of Chinese thought reform—so-called brainwashing—which led me to develop a set of concepts about what I called *ideological totalism*. The word *totalism* came from Erikson's work, and ideological totalism had to do with the collective energies and structural elements that create this thought reform project. Interestingly, I found that the Chinese *over*-reformed. That is, the Maoists emerged as heroes in the late 1940s and 1950s: they had been heroic in achieving their revolutionary goals and at that time seemed incorruptible. But they could not stop reforming and re-reforming, because they were, in effect, both a religious and a political movement. And that overreforming was detrimental to their goals. In connection with this work, I tried to think more generally about ideological totalism as manifested in other despotic political regimes and in our own McCarthyite era. And in a much more modest but still important sense, I looked at the totalism of certain training procedures, where you must come out with a certain cast of mind in order to be considered properly trained. This included some psychoanalytic training, where one was simultaneously patient, student, and candidate. The combination is unhealthy because it veers toward totalism, as many observers have said since.

In 1962 I lived in Hiroshima for six months interviewing Hiroshima survivors. It was, to say the least, an extraordinarily powerful experience, because one had to immerse oneself in their stories, which meant immersing oneself in massive death. And when one does a study of that kind, one is likely to see much of the world subsequently through the prism of that experience. Then I compared my observations on Hiroshima survivors to those made by others of Holocaust survivors, and through that comparison I developed, at the end of the study, a phenomenology of the survivor. In general, I prefer the term *survivor* to *post-traumatic syndrome*. Of course there are times when you have to use the word *post-traumatic,* but the term *survivor* implies an encounter with death and more readily suggests a nonpathological perspective. This work on the survivor has since been useful to people studying various kinds of trauma, including different forms of abuse.

But after coming back from Hiroshima, I found that there was relatively little in the psychoanalytic or psychiatric literature on death and the conceptualization of death-related issues. So after writing about Hiroshima, I struggled with these larger physiological considerations and came to write a book I called *The Broken Connection*. The subtitle of that book, *On Death and the Continuity of Life,* is really about evolving a new paradigm (also the oldest of all paradigms) on the symbolization of life and death—that is, on death and the continuity of life. The main focus is life-continuity, but the requirement here is giving death its due, which is giving it a lot. That work was much influenced by the symbolizing philosophy of Ernst Cassirer and Suzanne Langer, and also importantly by the work of Otto Rank. Among the early Freudians, only Rank took the issue of death seriously and developed concepts about immortality systems that remain valuable.

During the early 1970s, I studied Vietnam veterans, most of whom were against the war, and participated with them in "rap groups," largely in New York but also in New Haven. I conducted intensive individual interviews as well. I learned a lot from that work, including how, under certain conditions involving a personal confrontation with death, people can undergo rapid changes, taking place not over years but over months or even weeks. This didn't mean that everything in them changed but, rather, significant aspects of them, including attitudes toward country and authority, and toward maleness and toward women (these were all men), and of course attitudes and feelings toward war and death. In some the changes could include much greater capacity to function in everyday life. In exploring with them the terrors and ambiguities of combat in Vietnam, I arrived at the principle of what I call an *atrocity-producing situation.* By that I mean an environment so structured and psychologically determined that ordinary people entering it are quite capable of committing atrocities.

In the late 1970s I did work on Nazi doctors, which was for me the most difficult of all my studies. I approached these doctors and their German and Nazi context with two dimensions in mind. One was the broad psychohistorical dimension in which they connected with Nazi ideology to create what I call a *biomedical vision.* This means viewing the whole Nazi project as (in the words of a doctor I interviewed) "applied biology." The genocide was a project of therapy for the "Nordic race," once strong and glorious but recently undermined by a Jewish "infection," which had in some way to be removed. But there was also the nitty-gritty question of how Nazi doctors could do what they did. Here I developed the concept of *doubling,* the formation of a functional second self that can engage in evil. This concept draws on the work of Otto Rank. Nazi doctors formed an *Auschwitz self,* which permitted them to be deeply involved in killing—in fact in Auschwitz supervising the entire killing project—yet going home to Germany on weekends or on leave and once more becoming ordinary fathers and husbands. The doubling was hardly foolproof psychologically, but unfortunately it was functional. Of course, both "selves" were part of the same overall self, but the kind of inner division that took place endowed each subself with a holistic quality, so that it was more than mere splitting. To me this was a troubling insight, because it suggests that such dissociation is part of the human repertoire for adaptation, in this case to evil. It gives one pause about the human genius for adaptation, which, I would now claim, is inseparable from our capacity for mass killing and genocide. That is so because, although genocidal projects have an ideological hard core, ordinary people readily adapt to them in ways that enable these projects to be carried out. In this and in other studies I have become interested in the role of professionals, in the ways professionals enter into projects of mass killing. Indeed, professionals are indispensable for genocide.

My most recent study has been of the Aum Shinrikyō cult in Japan: the zealous group of people who released sarin gas in Japanese subways in 1995. They had the modest ambition of destroying the world in the name of salvation and renewal.

What makes them notable and dangerous is the combination of megalomania and ultimate weapons. The megalomania began with the guru (and there has never been more extravagant guruism), but came to include his followers, too. The ultimate weapons were not only chemical but biological (lethal anthrax and botulinus preparations) and, by intention, nuclear (inquiries about obtaining nuclear bombs). Nor can we assume that the combination of megalomania and ultimate weapons in a group determined to "force the end" (*bring about* rather than wait for Armageddon) has to be limited to Aum Shinrikyō. From that standpoint I have also been trying to bring this work home by looking at American apocalyptic violence: the Charles Manson family, Heaven's Gate, the People's Temple, and the violent far right.

In all of this there are important questions of method, about how one makes one's imaginative psychological immersion into historical events. "Methodology" is an idol, but we do need to be concerned about questions of method, and, where possible, we do best to make interviews an important component of that method.

I close by speaking of a more hopeful direction. When people ask me what my work is about, I answer in three words: holocaust and transformation. Some may then reply, "That's fine. I see lots of holocaust, but where's the transformation?" I understand those questions, and I have two answers. One is that I believe there to be an important aspect of transformation in the actual studies of highly destructive events. Confronting those events contributes, or can contribute, to deepening our quest for alternatives. And my second answer lies in the evolution, over a number of decades, of the concept of the "protean self" as capable of change and transformation.

What I have in mind is the tendency of the contemporary self toward multiplicity and shifts. The protean self encompasses several dimensions. One is constant change—shifts in involvement with people, in ideas, and in actions, shifts that may have minimal psychological cost. A second dimension is simultaneous multiplicity, having in our head many different images that we act upon, some of them antithetical to others. Third is a kind of social proteanism. For instance, those attending a conference may all come from very different backgrounds and have very different kinds of self-presentations, but they converge on a certain set of interests. All these dimensions may sound obvious today, but historically they are quite new. Protean tendencies emerge at times of major historical shifts, such as the Renaissance or Enlightenment in the West or the Meiji Restoration in Japan. But in these past historical appearances, the expression of protean behavior has been largely limited to an elite. Now it is so pervasive, that, in one way or another, and to different degrees, it is in us all.

There are thus historical reasons for protean developments. I locate three large contemporary historical forces but am sure one could find others. The first is what I call *psychohistorical dislocation*. It is very similar to what Norman Cohn wrote about in terms of the dislocation that gives rise to millenarian movements. Psychohistorical dislocation concerns the breakdown of symbol systems associated with authority, religion, education, family, and the life cycle—that is, all the major areas of life. Second is *imagery of extinction,* whether specifically associated with nuclear weapons or other weapons of mass destruction, or with environmental destruction. Nuclear weapons have become the symbol of this imagery, of our new capacity to extinguish ourselves as a species, with our own technology, by our own hand, and to no purpose. The third historical force concerns the mass media and information revolutions. That these are occurring is obvious enough, but we have difficulty grasping just how they are affecting us.

In spite of these forces, or in relation to them, most of us manage to function. We do so, I believe, by means of the protean self, which I consider not pathological but a modus vivendi for our time. The protean self also offers us the dignity of a term for our experience of feeling scattered but nonetheless surviving and sometimes even flourishing. Although one's social and economic standing has a lot to do with successful proteanism, I would claim that the pattern exists for everyone in American society and, for that matter, throughout the world, though in ways that differ in specific cultures. There are, of course, problems with the protean self, including the need to combine mutability with an ethical core and the very real danger of diffusion. But I would hold that it is difficult to function anywhere in our present world without calling forth such protean tendencies.

Because psychoanalytic theorizing and practice take place within culture, they must be affected by elements of proteanism. And many therapists do find that their patients tend to be more diffuse and less specific in connection with their problems. This does not mean that, say, hysteria has totally disappeared, but it does suggest that hysteria or any other neurotic tendency is likely itself to be more amorphous and ambiguous. Certainly patients, like the rest of us, have all of the classical emotions, though they may be less clear about where these emotions come from or what their target may be. And beyond analysts and patients, proteanism affects the holding of ideas and is in keeping with the broad contemporary mistrust of large idea systems. In that sense proteanism connects with certain expressions of postmodernism. One reviewer of my recent book on the protean self said something nice about it in describing it as "affirmative postmodernism." I like that description because I am critical of the direction in postmodernism that seeks to eliminate self and author. In that sense, the protean self is a kind of rescue operation, both for the function of the self and for our way of conceptualizing the self.

People can be uneasy with the ambiguity of proteanism, and they can be vulnerable to plunges into totalism—into various forms of apocalypticism of the kind I have suggested in connection with Aum Shinrikyō and related American cultic environments. Yet proteanism, where functional, includes a capacity for nuance, paradox, and contradiction. It can allow us to avoid dead ends and to find expressions of resilience and therefore of hope.

I close by quoting two wise writers. First, Polish poet Czeslaw Milosz: "Who will free me / From everything that my age will bequeath? / From infinity plus. From infinity minus. / From a void lifting itself up to the stars?" And finally, Gershom Sholem, the great student of Jewish mysticism: "The story is not ended, it has not yet become history, and the secret life it holds can break out tomorrow in you or in me."

Discussion

Eric Santner: I'd like to ask Dominick LaCapra a couple of questions, really for clarification. I'm very taken by this effort to distinguish structural trauma from historical trauma or episodic, contingent trauma, and to distinguish absence or gap from loss. I was wondering if you think that this comes down to the problem of establishing what the object of anxiety is? That is, anxiety at some level is that something has gone missing. Well, what's gone missing? Well, nothing has gone missing. We don't know. Yet there's something objectlike which seems to have gone missing. And part of what might at times bring together structural trauma and historical trauma is anxiety, and the problem of the peculiar object of anxiety.

Dominick LaCapra: I think that's right. And an important project at the present time is attempting to decide what distinctions one wants to blur radically, in the aftermath of a deconstruction of binaries, and what distinctions one might try to elaborate, by attributing varying degrees of weakness and strength. Now this is made difficult by two mutually reinforcing tendencies, both of which I see as questionable. One is the attempt to totalize or to take analytic categories and project them upon life and to try to make life conform to analytic categories in their purity. This is one aspect, for example, of the notion of racial purity. You arrive at a concept of racial purity and then try to make life fit that concept. And in one way or another this attempt to make reality live up to concepts, to use the Hegelian formulation, is very important in history and very dangerous in history. Because it leads to an intolerance of all forms of hybridization or confusion, which I think is disastrous.

But the mutually reinforcing tendency is to believe that the necessary critique of binaries, in their purity, entails the obliteration or radical blurring of all distinctions. So you continually remain at the stage of blurring distinctions, or contesting a dominant normativity which tends to be elided with normativity in general, rather than at least confronting the problem, which one might not be able to address adequately, of conceivable alternative normativities which have a somewhat different shape and configuration.

Now, this is a preface to answering your question. The attempt to elaborate problematic distinctions that are not binaries is a way to, in a sense, generate *Angstbereitschaft,* which may enable you to better confront anxiety—both necessary anxiety and more particular anxieties that are generated by historical phenomena. This is the one way I would justify the history of the limit case. The limit case, at its best, helps to generate a preparedness to feel anxiety, which is very, very important. But, again, there is a tendency for what I'm calling structural trauma and historical trauma to merge in the case of limit events, or for loss to be perceived as the necessary analogue of absence in certain extreme or limit events.

Now this bears on real questions that have agitated people, such as the uniqueness of the Holocaust. The Holocaust is unique in a nonnumerical sense. In the Holocaust a certain limit was transgressed. And there's a sense in which, whenever a certain limit is transgressed, something unique happens in history. But people then go from that to the point of trying to argue in a numerical sense that this is something unique in contrast to all other things, with some undesirable consequences, such as a kind of competition for first place in victimhood, a lowering of the significance of other events, which one wants to avoid.

Robert Jay Lifton: I have comments for each of my colleagues on our panel. First, Dominick LaCapra: In addition to what you said about melancholia and its activity, so to speak, I think one can look at Freud's view of narcissism, which is so prominent in melancholia. He used the term *narcissism* in some of the most severe conditions—melancholia, schizophrenia, and severe traumatic war neuroses—because underneath that use of narcissism is a fear of falling apart. One reason why I don't like the term *narcissism* much in psychoanalytic or psychological discourse is that there's a confusion. It usually is taken to refer to an instinctual idea of libido as almost a physical force directed into the self. But it also describes how a person becomes more self-absorbed because of the fear of falling apart.

I'd also mention someone whose work I'm sure you're familiar with: Alexander and Margarete Mitscherlich in their book *The Inability to Mourn,* about Nazi Germany and post-Nazi Germany.[1] Their thesis was that because Germans had embraced evil and were unable to confront the evil which they had embraced, neither could they confront how much they loved their Führer, and they couldn't mourn his loss and death and the loss of the Nazi movement. And this inability to mourn interfered with what might be called social vitality in the German postwar era.

And then, finally, a thought about your discussion of mourning as a recovery process and a renewal process, which is very important and I think has important applications in history. I mentioned doubling in Nazi doctors in my presentation. You can also get doubling in historical victims. For instance, Auschwitz survivors will sometimes say to you (I interviewed quite a number of them), "I was a different person in Auschwitz," and want you to take that seriously, because you had to be a different kind of a person. One had to develop an Auschwitz self as a survivor for the sake of surviving, in dealing with very brutal kinds of matters.

Listening to Meredith Skura's paper, I felt very comfortable with her approach. Psychoanalysis *as* an approach. And I would suggest that you're probably more interested in theory than you acknowledge. I think theory is still very important, but maybe what you were calling for is theory derived directly from experience, as opposed to the imposing of theory on experience. Of course, as Judith Butler and others said yesterday, we always impose theory on experience; we can't approach experience without some conceptual predisposition. But you can hold back on theory and really focus on experience, and I think that's always very important.

Finally, just a couple of comments for Eric Santner and the Schreber case, which is infinitely useful in a lot of directions. Paranoia has been called a disease of power, and I think it is. It's a loss of life power and a sense of falling apart which one then compensates for with forays into the world, sometimes violent ones, and with a sense of the world imposing upon one or attacking one. There is a relationship between gurus in extremist cults that I've been concerned about, or even someone like Hitler, the most demonic of gurus, and someone like Schreber. In this recent book called *Feet of Clay*, Anthony Storr talks about how the guru needs disciples.[2] I would go further and say the guru is always struggling with disintegration, and he or she can hold off that disintegration by being confirmed by disciples. The difference between Asahara in Japan, whom I've been studying, and Schreber was that Schreber didn't have disciples, he was alone. But, incidentally, he *did* believe he would be the only survivor and in that sense resembles what Elias Canetti has written (and Canetti leaned heavily on the Schreber case) in his book *Crowds and Power* on the danger of the only survivor.[3] All this, of course, is a plea for a broad death-and-the-continuity-of-life perspective in looking at these issues. Really, I don't see how one can look at historical process in general without some such model.

Dominick LaCapra: I'll be very brief. One interesting distinction between melancholia and mourning—which I don't think really happen apart—is that mourning, to have any effect in people's lives, has to be in some sense a *social* process and has to involve the naming of for whom one mourns. There has to be a specification of the objects of mourning. Otherwise the mourning is indeed an impossible mourning that continually loops back into endless melancholia. In postwar Germany, I would agree, Germans had a problem naming the victims for whom they had, at best, arrested mourning. It was unclear whether people felt bad because of the loss of Hitler and the glories of the *Hitlerzeit* or because of the Jews. The two things were often confused in people's minds. But one of the distinctions that I would want to be a relatively strong distinction is between experiencing trauma and being a victim. There are people who can be traumatized by events who are not victims in the relative sense. And often perpetrators are indeed traumatized, may have identical symptoms as victims, but should not be conflated with victims for that reason, because the status of victims is a social, ethical, political category. It's not a psychological category.

Robert Jay Lifton: To say just a word more about the Mitscherlich issues. The thought occurred to me as we were talking that he was struggling with the problem of mourning, what had happened to the Germany he had been part of. And he was a heroic figure. He had been an anti-Nazi student; had put up a sign the Nazis didn't like in his bookstore, showing lemmings going over a cliff, which was his version of following the Nazis, following each other; and then, during World War II—he had already been in prison several times for underground activities—he was allowed to go to medical school but had to report to the Gestapo every single day. And after that he was picked up by the occupation as an anti-Nazi and had a place in the occupation hierarchy. And then he was asked to go to Nuremberg, to the Doctors' Trial, by the German Medical Society. He went there, and they wanted a whitewash from him—to say that, you know, there are just a few bad apples. Instead he told the truth and said that everybody was involved, as the medical profession was virtually turned over to the Nazis. Of course they never gave him a medical professorship after that. But he became a psychoanalyst, reintroduced Freudian psychoanalysis into Germany in the late 1960s and 1970s, and it was vital and lively because it had the subject of the Nazis. That's a problem for psychoanalysis: what kind of subject does it have for it to remain vital, not just its own methods. And he was one of our few psychoanalytic heroes, because he was a real heroic intellectual figure in postwar Germany.

Meredith Skura: I wanted to bring up again that question of individual versus group. For example, in mourning, what is the difference between talking about mourning and melancholia as an individual experience and identifying a group process of mourning? I think that's one of psychoanalysis's weakest areas. It cannot really yet talk about groups except as a collection of individuals who are acting similarly. Whether it ultimately will be able to or not I don't know, but that's an area to look into. However, using the individual model, I'm struck—though we all use different terms—by the way that so many of us are interested in the same things and are making roughly similar kinds of points. I'm rejecting theory, Dominick LaCapra's rejecting structural trauma,

Dominick LaCapra: No, I'm not rejecting it—

Meredith Skura: No, no, no. I'm not rejecting it either. You're rejecting using structural trauma as the only explanatory mechanism. I don't reject theory at all, obviously, I didn't mean to imply that. Robert Jay Lifton is rejecting the *Totem and Taboo* model as a structural trauma of its own kind. And, it seemed to me, that when Eric Santner was asking to specify what those circumstances might be, he, too, was calling for an effort to integrate the levels between a group process, a group structure, and the individual specifics.

And I wonder if we can talk more about what the relationship is between these two levels and the normal psychoanalytic distinction between the conscious and the unconscious? Are we saying that you can't just go to the unconscious meaning of a trauma, you have to look at the conscious? Are we saying we can't talk about id, just ego? Is there any relationship between traditional psychoanalytic terms and these?

Eric L. Santner: A kind of a footnote: this is actually not about your remarks about my paper, although I'd like to say something about that, too. I did some work on the Mitscherlichs in my last project and was extremely enthusiastic about their approach. Indeed, I thought I was in some ways continuing their work into the second and third generation. Then I started hearing, and was very unnerved by, voices in Germany, partly from the psychoanalytic community— I'm thinking of Tilmann Moser and some others—who had tremendous rage toward the Mitscherlichs for what they perceived as a moralization of the grieving process. This led, according to Moser, to a reification of the very defenses the Mitscherlichs set out to dismantle. The continual shifting between voices and modes of address—from therapist to cultural historian to national pedagogue to moral philosopher—along with excessively utopian expectations about the social and political efficacy of psychoanalytic thinking in general, were bound, in Moser's view, to limit the effects of the Mitscherlichs' intervention on individual behavior and the larger political culture.

The fundamental question raised by the Mitscherlichs was how to understand the mourning process on the part of defeated perpetrators, who mourned first and foremost for their own losses, their own shattered universe. The Mitscherlichs argued that such mourning was the necessary first step toward the possibility of experiencing the enormity of their own responsibility for their crimes. But the criticisms of the Mitscherlichs I have noted suggest that their approach may in some ways have actually hindered this very process by soliciting it in a way that would be experienced as persecutory. And this then allows somebody like a Hans-Jürgen Syberberg, in his last book from 1990, to make what I would call an *Antigonal* gesture of saying that the Germans still have to bury their Polynices—that is, to grieve, to name their dead. The madness of Syberberg's book was, of course, that he blamed the enormous difficulties of the mourning process on the Jews, on the Jewish presence in the Frankfurt School, which, to stay with the model of *Antigone,* he clearly associates with Creon.

I think at some level I disagree with Canetti, and with Canetti's reading of Schreber (and I guess to some extent with yours), that the only thing that made Schreber different was that he didn't have a disciple. I think there is a line, maybe a fine line, between Schreber's system, his epiphany, and his elaboration of the epiphany into a system, and, let's say, *Mein Kampf.* And the distinction is that Schreber refused to engage in projective identification. Schreber didn't project, he incorporated, drew in the rot, into himself, and in a certain sense announced it, disseminated it as knowledge about something amiss in the culture. And he didn't say it comes from out there; he says, "It's in here." And at some level he's saying, "I am Jew," "I am woman," "I am homosexual." Not literally, but I think his symptoms are announcing something like that, rather than trying to eject something. I think that is an important difference.

Robert Jay Lifton: I think it's a difference. And it's a difference in emphasis. To me, Freud's rendition of the Schreber case is invaluable, but his theory of it being a product of repressed homosexuality is inadequate. And again: why was Schreber incorporating these dimensions of culture? He was struggling to survive, so to speak, amidst his psychosis. In any case I would accept pretty much what you said.

I'm more interested in the first comment about the Mitscherlichs. I don't know the German psychoanalytic situation that closely. And inevitably, the Mitscherlichs held sway so long, there's got to be a critique of their work. And I also agree very much with the problems of the German and the Japanese dead. Because they were the aggressive people in World War II, one doesn't realize what they lost. And I feel this very strongly in doing a lot of work in Japan very recently. But nonetheless, in terms of the moralizing of psychoanalysis, this may come from an assumption that psychoanalytic work isn't moral. But certainly the work of mourning—if one can see it collectively, as one did in Germany as the Mitscherlichs described it—was a very moral process. And I found, in working on the Nazi doctors and in other studies, one wants to be careful about how one brings in the moral dimension, but one can't do without it either and it's part of that engagement.

Dominick LaCapra: I thought about that quite a bit as well, and have a couple of comments. One, I think it's important to distinguish between moralizing and ethics. Often in psychoanalysis I tend to avoid entirely the language of normality and pathology, because I think it really is a language of encrypted normativity. And I think norms should be made explicit, so that they can be seen more clearly. Including in all their problematic dimensions, and what it is you're valorizing and what it is you're not valorizing. Certainly mourning is a process that is related to ethical considerations.

Two, I think it is indeed the case that the people who were perpetrators or collaborators or bystanders may have legitimate losses that they're entitled to mourn. That's true of Germans on the Eastern Front. The invasion of the Russians did cause some very severe damage to the German population. The problem in Germany has been a tendency always to present German losses as a kind of balancing of the books with the Holocaust. So that the typical move is to say: "If you're going to talk about the Holocaust, talk about the Eastern Front." And this is Heidegger, this is Hilberg. And I think what has to happen is for the losses of the perpetrators to be extricated. Because the only way perpetrators can in any sense work through a past is if their own losses are also given justifiable representation, and they have the opportunity to come to terms with them.

Kevis Goodman, Moderator: Perhaps we can open it up to the audience.

Mary Jacobus: I have a question for Dominick. This comes not just from hearing you talk about these issues before but from considering, as you spoke, your focus on what you might call a translation into social forms of interpsychic processes. So one could think of, as it were, a *program* for mourning in our society and the need for greater attention to varieties of forms of mourning, social and communal forms of mourning. And my question would be: what about the other term, acting out? One could also conceive of acting out as a profoundly disruptive social process, with terrible consequences, into which one might want to intervene in some way—not only as a psychohistorian thinking about it and analyzing it, and perhaps not only in some therapeutic way, say to enable a group to cease to act out, but also in political terms. And it seems to me that the problem of acting out is much harder to think about. One can think about a program for mourning. How does one think about both the social forms of acting out and how one might intervene, so that the intervention would not be subsumed into a continuance of the acting out?

Dominick LaCapra: A great question. And by the way these are problems which don't fall under any single discipline. They're often problems that historians don't think about or sociologists don't think about because it's not *their* problem. And I think that's absolutely wrong. These problems, in fact, cut across disciplines and have to be addressed in all disciplines.

Equally difficult problems are raised when we think about mourning and when we think about acting out or melancholia. Most interesting contemporary theory has really been focused on melancholia and acting out, in relation to performativity, and not on working through and mourning. And I would like to see more of an attempt to relate the two. Acting out on a collective level is very important and in certain ways quite justified. For example, people in oppressed positions have a right to express anger and rage, and to act out anger and rage, as an aspect of their response to difficulties. One of the problems is to try to develop *relatively* safe havens for acting out. The analytic session, as Freud said, is one relatively safe haven for acting out problems. And he thought that one should discourage the acting out of problems in other dimensions of life, that in some sense it should be confined to the safe haven of the analytic session.

I think there are other safe havens. One interesting and nonreductive way to see art is as a relatively safe haven for enacting the relationship *between* acting out and potentials for working-through. Often some of the most powerful art is precisely art that is engaged in processes of acting out which somehow envelop us: Dostoevsky, for example, even Beckett. I think Beckett is very interesting, because he is someone who is thinking absence rather than loss very often. Or Heidgger you could also see as in many interesting ways addressing the problem of absence, which is not immediately converted into loss. And when it *is* converted into loss in Heidegger, in *Being and Time,* those are the most dubious dimensions of the text, for example, in terms of seeking your hero in history, as a way to combat the problem of the anxiety of *Dasein.*

Then I think there are other forms. Support groups are also a media for acting out problems in relatively safe havens. Support groups, for instance, can develop new modalities of the interviewing process. You've heard me say before that I think one of the problems of the interviewing process, including in the Yale testimonials, is that people tend to be interviewed only as individuals or at best as couples, at least in the things I've seen. And that brings out the most depressed and melancholic sides of people, which are certainly real. But if people were interviewed in their groups, to the extent that they would make themselves accessible to an interviewing process, you might see other dimensions of people, including jokes, humor, laughter.

Meredith Skura: I keep wanting to get back and ask where's the psychoanalysis in what we're doing and how is this history related to psychoanalysis? And how are we thinking psychohistorically, as opposed to just historically about these problems? Acting out, for example. When one acts out, or when one has a safe place to act out, *what* is one acting out? If you're acting out a rage that you feel quite consciously about something very real that has just happened to you, that's one situation. But if you're acting out a rage that's totally inappropriate, that you are carrying from a past incident you may or may not have forgotten, which happened long ago and is not part of the present, that's another situation. And it's the second, I think, where the psychoanalyst has something to add, rather than the first.

Robert Jay Lifton: I wanted to follow up on that. We're agreeing that the real conceptual problem of method has to do with how collectively a group or a country or a people responds to loss and a mourning process. And it's quite difficult, because if there's a large historical event every individual person has his or her immediate concerns in family and in everyday life and the event hits them tangentially very often. Yet it's important. And I want to throw into this discussion the American experience with mourning or not mourning about Vietnam and about Hiroshima. Situations where we can be seen as the perpetrator. In terms of Hiroshima we were fighting against a real evil, but it ended up with a certain act that is hard for Americans to accept. And I think that there's a profound resistance to the mourning process in *particular* when one is a perpetrator. Because one is unable psychologically, and especially in terms of political collectivity, to take it in.

Elise Snyder: I was very interested in what Meredith Skura had to say, both as regards the papers that we've heard today and a number of the papers that we heard yesterday. So I have a question for the other panelists. If you would take seriously Meridith's notions of the psychoanalytic attitude, what would you say in your papers differently than you have said?

Robert Jay Lifton: I don't think I'd say anything differently. Because I think I share that psychoanalytic attitude, which emphasizes the search for motivations and an effort to grasp behavior that doesn't necessarily identify itself—that is, looking for patterns or forces that are outside of awareness. What I would consider a desirable use of the psychoanalytic attitude is to move into spheres that free oneself, at times when it's quite necessary, from psychoanalytic dogma.

Eric L. Santner: I'm also not sure if I would change anything. I would just maybe emphasize that—to go to something that Professor Lifton said, about the phrase "in history." I think that the psychoanalytic contribution is about what it means to get a foothold in history and to lose that foothold in history and then regain it again. In a way, psychoanalysis is about the difficulties of assuming a place in a historical space. And how easy it is to lose the foothold in the historical space, through, for example, traumatic events. Or through *stuckness* in something, one knows not what. Psychoanalysis is about inflexibility, about stuckness, about this obnoxious stuckness that inhibits our movement through the space of reasons. And psychoanalysis is honing in on that stuckness, a kind of inertness that's also sometimes a kind of mechanical automatism. And I think that what that stuckness is about is some impasse in assuming a place in the historical field.

Meredith Skura: Can I come in here even though I wasn't asked a question? I think the kinds of things that I would be looking for, and that Elise might be looking for, and that other people are perhaps not interested in because they're primarily interested in historical process rather than the psychoanalytic process, are things like: a difference in the way I would conduct interviews with people who are survivors, whether we'd call them victims or perpetrators. I would think about how I felt about somebody I was interviewing, what my reactions were, especially what my emotional reactions were, and whether that could tell me something about this person which the person himself or herself could not tell me or chose not to tell me. Second, I would think about how that person is treating me, the transference as well as the countertransference. Can I see anything in the way that person treats me which tells me something about how that person feels and what that person has been through? Although he or she may not be able to articulate that in words and convey it to me in narrative form, he or she will act it out. Then, can I use that understanding in order to understand the experience that person has gone through, and maybe change my theories about it? To understand the *kind* of stuckness, for example, or the details, the specificity of the stuckness of this person rather than some other person.

Leslie Brisman: I wanted to ask Meredith Skura to say something about what she didn't get to say about transference. Is this a concept that is relevant any time there is a transcription or does it degenerate into a commonplace? Do you need certain conditions in order to bring in the concept of transference?

Meredith Skura: I think transference is always present. Another way of talking about it is character—that is, the behavioral dispositions, conscious and unconscious, of any given person, which are repeated in every situation. That said, I would add that there are some situations which bring out *more* aspects of the transference that the psychoanalyst is interested in than other situations—the couch, for example, free association. These bring out the emotional fantasy level of experience, which normally we tend to inhibit. It's always there, it's just easier to detect in certain situations, in things like spiritual autobiographies, where the person is essentially talking to God most of the time or to a god figure, the transference elements are very strong. You can say: Who is this person? How does he image God now? How does his image of God change? How is he changing what he's saying in order to make an impression on God?

Robert Jay Lifton: On that score, there's transference in the interviews, as was just said, but there are also examples—as for instance in Chinese thought reform or any systematic effort to coerce and get a hold over people's minds—where there is a demand for permanent transference, as opposed to what one would like to see as an always conscious effort to dissolve the transference in responsible psychoanalytic work. But one has to be aware of that demand for permanent transference in a lot of historical experiences.

Peter Brooks: Bob Lifton said that only psychoanalysis is worthy of the address to history. And I entirely agree with that, but it seemed to me that there was a prior question that never got addressed by this panel and that is: why *need* psychoanalysis be addressed to history? Because after all history continues to be produced by the bushel, without any reference to anything other than a sort of commonsense, everyday psychology. And I know that you all four are profoundly committed to the notion that history cannot be addressed without reference to psychoanalysis, but that's the question that somehow didn't quite get articulated here.

Robert Jay Lifton: Well, I wouldn't say that history cannot be addressed without psychoanalysis. There's lots of other ways to do history, and they can be very valuable. But if you're approaching history psychologically, I doubt whether there's another psychology that gives one an adequate perspective or point of view. It also has to be said that, for instance, Erikson, who has been such a great figure in the developments that we've been describing, was enormously influenced by William James, and also to some extent by Camus. There are very important voices who contribute to the psychological approach to history.

Another comment, about another dimension of Peter's question: there is an impulse on the part of psychology and history to ignore each other or to destroy each other. Psychology or certain forms of psychoanalysis can negate history in the name of studying it, as I said. But also history can negate psychology or, as you said, Peter, make interpretations of certain events with a kind of commonsense psychology that can be profoundly misleading. But there's also a kind of useful tension that one can maintain. It's a very difficult enterprise, and we do it very imperfectly, because the further something is from the laboratory, the less certain you can be of your conclusions. And therefore the more experiential one can be in the work, I think, the better address one makes to it. But I think we should always see our approaches as limited in what they can achieve.

Dominick LaCapra: I'd like to chip in something there. The interest of psychoanalysis is that it may help us to rethink the disciplines. Ordinary forms of psychology tend to reinforce common sense and really don't do anything to encourage people to rethink problems. I think that one of the more traditional ways of using psychoanalysis in psychobiography is also very limited, which is taking the conceptual repertory of psychoanalysis and applying it to figures or groups in the past, so that you have an analysis of Max Weber in terms of his Oedipus complex. What is more challenging for historians is the attempt to rethink historiography, and the nature of historical inquiry, in relationship to psychoanalytic problems; to ask, what is the implication if you take psychoanalysis seriously for your activity as a historian? And that means one's relationship to the past. One way I would define positivism, which still has a strong afterlife in historiography, is as the denial of transference in one's relationship to the object, the attempt to fully objectify the object and to disimplicate oneself and one's relationship to the past from historiography. So that you address that relationship only in a footnote or in a preface; it's contained in the text rather than made to inform the argument.

Eric L. Santner: Can I add something to that, just apropos of the footnote? On the plane, I noticed a review of Tony Grafton's new book about the footnote.[4] And the title of the review was "The Ego and the Ibid." I think that there's actually something profound about that title. In my book about Schreber I write a lot about Freud's footnotes in the case study, because that's where he both acknowledges and also disavows a lot of debts. We can read, through the footnotes, his relationship to legacies, his own nonoriginality, the way he has been invested with symbolic authority and has difficulties acknowledging that—in a way, his placement into history and the difficulties of assuming that historical place as a debt. So thinking of the id as connected to the ibid. is important.

Notes

1. Alexander and Margarete Mitscherlich, *The Inability to Mourn: Principles of Collective Behavior,* translated by Beverley R. Placzek (New York: Grove, 1995).
2. Anthony Storr, *Feet of Clay: A Study of Gurus* (London: HarperCollins, 1996).
3. Elias Canetti, *Crowds and Power,* translated by Carol Stewart (New York: Viking, 1962).
4. Anthony Grafton, *The Footnote: A Curious History* (Cambridge: Harvard University Press, 1997).

Part Five **Psychoanalysis and**

Theories of Mind

Introduction

This section continues to emphasize the fruitfulness of psychoanalysis's methodological *dis*placement, its position betwixt and between other disciplines. All four contributors—coming from a spectrum of different medical and scientific backgrounds—are interested in the potential interaction, *across differences,* between psychoanalysis and cognitive science. Morton Reiser thus carefully distinguishes between conflating these two disciplines and finding productive parallels, or isomorphisms, between the two.

Reiser gives the first example of such an isomorphism, focusing "on aspects of dreaming for which cogent data from both psychoanalysis and neuroscience are available." His essay succinctly shows how the idea of nodal association in dreams travels from Freudian dream theory to recent work on neural memory networks. Whereas earlier work in neuroscience presumed that "dream imagery was randomly generated" by excitatory (PGO) waves, Freudian analysis insists on the overdetermination of dream content. Reiser demonstrates an interplay between randomness and meaning: memory traces, linked to specific conflictual affects, make certain images "more sensitive to the stimu-

lation by PGO waves during sleep." As he concludes, "The concept of instigation of REM by chemical changes . . . and the concept of the instigation of the
dream by a wish are not the same—but they can be considered functionally parallel and compatible."

Dovetailing with Reiser's example, David Forrest presents a similar interaction between cognitive science and psychoanalytic theory, and between brain
and mind. As he puts it: "The human brain adds its flavor of organism to mind.
Our minds are not the only logically possible minds; they are the highly particular minds that evolved in the wetware of our brains." This kind of synthesis,
Forrest reminds us, is crucial on a therapeutic as well as an intellectual level.
Besides advancing research, the dialogue between psychoanalysis and neurobiology can help a patient who otherwise faces the familiar divide between "biotherapy, which lacks understanding of mental interrelations, and purely psychological psychotherapy, which lacks an appreciation of the embeddedness of
mental processes in brain function." Forrest focuses on a fascinating example:
the isomorphism between Freud's theory of the transference and propagnosia,
a brain disorder in which faces are misrecognized. Once again, this misrecognition is biologically triggered but does not take random form: "misidentification,
a neurological condition, also partakes of the psychodynamics of interpersonal
object relations." Halfway between mind and brain, certain types of the disorder follow lines of association that come to light through psychoanalytic theory.
As Forrest modestly puts it, "A neurological substrate for excessive transference
is of interest."

Forrest goes on to consider a different aspect of the mind-brain problem: how
local points of activity can be fit into a dynamic structural model. This question
is the focus of Robert Shulman, whose work in magnetic resonance imaging
has been crucial to research advances in local brain activity. Shulman, far from
resting on his accomplishments in the field of brain imaging, rigorously considers the problem of how to *read* the new data his innovations have helped bring
to light. Shulman (whose revised essay is cowritten with Douglas L. Rothman)
suggests that psychoanalysts both need to pay attention to advances in the observation of brain activity and have a unique opportunity to present models for
interpreting this activity. Shulman links a host of disparate approaches to consciousness—from psychoanalysis to John Searle's philosophy of mind to G. M.
Edelman's work in cognitive science—that together form an alternative to today's dominant paradigm for analyzing brain activity, where "the brain is modeled as consisting of separate functional modules, each performing a discrete
mental process." As Shulman describes his association of psychoanalysis with

Searle and Edelman: "There are significant differences in these several schools of thought about the nature of mind and particularly about the nature of subjective, conscious and unconscious activity. They are grouped here because of their shared view of the holistic and comprehensive relation between brain activity and mind. Each opposes the cognitive psychology position that mental activity can be considered as a series of computational processes that are separable from the subjective, personal activities of mind." The discussion that concludes this section revolves around Shulman's contribution—both his sense that psychoanalysis can help move beyond this contemporary version of phrenology and his admonition to psychoanalysts to "formulate your hypotheses and put them to work in experiment."

The kind of dialogue that Shulman advocates, and that Reiser and Forrest demonstrate, has become possible only because of developments within psychoanalysis. Using a spatial metaphor that Freud would have appreciated, Reiser argues that "psychoanalysis as a discipline has had to abandon the position that the other disciplines should orbit around it in an attempt to justify and confirm Freud's models." Arnold Cooper focuses on the historical development of psychoanalysis, its shift away from such an "orbital" disciplinary model to a pluralistic approach more suitable to dialogue with the sciences: "We have moved very far from the reasonably clear and rather dogmatic model that has usually been referred to as the 'orthodox' or 'classical' psychoanalysis toward a *multiplicity of competing models* that tend to be more open-ended and blurry" (emphasis added). It is precisely these models that are played with in the other three essays. Crucially, Cooper links such conceptual variety with other important changes in psychoanalysis: a widened definition of both the unconscious and the drives; a shift from a genetic, etiologic framework toward heightened attention to current experience; and an increasingly interpersonal, self-reflexive hermeneutics. The increasing availability of psychoanalysis to cognitive science, then, might be analogous to a broader dialogic tendency of recent psychotherapy, which, as Cooper argues, "has abandoned a one-person psychology (the analyst examining his patient) for a two-person psychology of intermeshed minds."

Can Psychoanalysis and Cognitive-Emotional Neuroscience Collaborate in Remodeling Our Concept of Mind-Brain?

Morton F. Reiser, M.D.

If, as many of us believe, mental life is dependent upon and most likely originates in the biological functions of brain-body, it should *in principle* be possible to reconcile psychologically derived information about mental function with biologically derived information about brain function. Freud understood and believed this. Yet he wisely abandoned his early attempts (1895) to relate his psychoanalytic psychologically based model of mental function to the limited understanding of brain function available in his time. Instead he constructed his hypothetical model of mind *without taking into account* what was then known about the brain and its function. He based it exclusively upon his understanding of mental function as he was able to observe it using his psychological method of inquiry into the mental life of his patients and of himself.

We now know much more about the brain and how it functions than was the case in 1895. It should now be possible to achieve a better reconciliation than was possible in Freud's time. But there are conceptual and procedural problems to be solved. The question I wish to pose is this: Can psychoanalysis and neuroscience collaborate in finding a better resolution—not only than was possible a century ago but also than could be achieved now by the disciplines working separately? I believe that such a collaborative effort is indicated and that it would constitute an important role for psychoanalysis in contemporary culture.

We have before us for consideration two very different generic models of mind, different in that they that derive from different kinds of empirical data. First, there are the subjectively based psychoanalytic models of mind and mental function that are derived from data produced by the process of free association in clinical psychoanalysis. Second, there are the objectively based neurobiologic models that are derived from data generated by biologic study of the brain, including cognitive neuroscience and computer modeling of mental operations. The data belong to two different domains. The first set of data comes from the domain of mind that deals primarily with meanings and motives that are immaterial in nature. The second set is material in nature—it comes from the domain of brain that deals with physico-chemical phenomena (matter and energy). Units are not interchangeable between domains, and covariant data cannot be interpreted as signifying cause-effect sequences. It should be noted, however, that emotion occupies both domains. Experimental studies on the psychophysiology of cortico-limbic circuits and mechanisms that link cognitive with the somatic components of emotion (cognitive-emotional neuroscience) are providing new links for deepening our understanding of the connection between mind and body (LeDoux 1996). And Bucci (1997) has extended the scope of this field into the clinical psychoanalytic area.

Yet none of the models thus far derived from either domain alone is entirely satisfactory or complete. Are the psychoanalytic and neurobiologic models incompatible and mutually exclusive? Should we keep one and throw out the other, as some think? Or will they turn out in principle to be mutually reducible or translatable one to the other? This was Freud's belief. Current efforts to effect a global mapping of mind onto brain reflect this position (Levin 1991; Schore 1997).

There is another way. Rather than choose between one of these two alternatives, psychoanalysis and neuroscience could collaborate by engaging in a virtual dialogue, comparing their respective findings regarding specified functions that are of interest to both. It should then be possible—since both sets of data pertain to the same function—to modify each of the separately derived models to conform to the data from both disciplines. A process such as this could be carried out in stages, retaining features from each of the two domains that are isomorphic with each other, modifying others to conform, and adding new features to replace outmoded ones as new information accumulates. The goal would be to construct a new (composite) functional model that would be acceptable to both disciplines. The composite model would be identical with neither of the previous ones but would possess key features of both. An illustrative "dialogue" focused on dream imagery, a function both domains have addressed, follows.

FROM THE MENTAL DOMAIN

The mental functions that engaged Freud's interest from the start included perception, imagery, memory, language, emotion, consciousness, the unconscious, and dreams. And he was concerned with understanding the functional interrelationships among them, formulating the concepts of repression, the dynamic unconscious, primary and secondary process, transference, mental defense mechanisms, and his theory of dreaming. He understood his first patients to be hysterics who were suffering from symptoms that he thought of as expressive of repressed reminiscences and strangulated affects. These affects and memories he thought could be released by converting their "thing presentations" in the repressed unconscious to word labels ("word presentations"). This would undo repression, release the affects, and admit the repressed contents into consciousness, thus rendering the symptoms unnecessary—"the talking cure." Sound quaint? We no longer accept this as an adequate explanation of the therapeutic dimension of psychoanalytic process. But maybe it, like other of the early prescient ideas, such as those related to dreams, will also turn out to be not so quaint when considered in relation to important (including newly-to-be-discovered) principles of brain function. The role of language and identification of the cortico-limbic circuitry involved in verbalization of memories during emotional arousal remain to be demonstrated and clarified, but now these brain mechanisms are potentially within the reach of modern noninvasive imaging techniques. The findings could be entered into a dialogue with clinical psychoanalytic information.

From the broad list of mental functions that interested Freud, I have focused here on aspects of dreaming for which cogent data from both psychoanalysis and neuroscience are available. The first model of the mind that emerged from Freud's studies was the "picket fence" topographic model (1900), which he formulated to account for his observations on dreams and dreaming. Freud hypothesized a mental instrument containing three zones: conscious, preconscious, and unconscious for processing, discharging, and/or storing stimuli that impinged upon it from the outside or from within the body. He proposed further that the mental apparatus would be stimulated to dream from within by a "wish," which he regarded as the mental representation of a bodily need, such as hunger, thirst, or sex. Eventually he thought of the "wish" in a special way— that is, as the derivative of an instinct that is manifested in the mental realm as "a demand made upon the mind for work in consequence of its connection to the body" (1915: 122).

In his analysis of his "Dream of the Botanical Monograph," Freud observed that the ideas, images, and memories represented in that dream were arranged in nodal networks. "Botanical" and "Monograph" could be regarded as nodal concepts. All of the ideas that arose in associating to the dream connected to one or the other of them. Since then, clinical psychoanalytic studies have led to the development of a central core psychoanalytic concept of enduring nodal memory networks and the principle of affective organization of memory. This concept and the associated functional principle can be summarized as follows (Reiser 1990): Each of us carries within our mind-brain an enduring network of stored memories encoded by images that are associationally linked by a shared potential to evoke identical or highly similar complexes of emotion. Such networks are organized around a core of memories of early events that, as children, we experienced as highly stressful, even cataclysmic. As development proceeds, the networks branch out as later events evoke similar conflicts and emotional states. Encoded images that connect strongly and closely with several others in the network (and through them with still others) can be thought of as nodal points in the enduring memory networks of mind-brain (for example, the dried plant "as if from an herbarium," in Freud's "Dream of the Botanical Monograph," 1900: 169).

FROM THE COGNITIVE-EMOTIONAL NEUROSCIENCE REALM

Beginning in the 1970s, cognitive neuroscientists, including Mishkin (1987) and Squire (1987) and their colleagues, demonstrated that percepts encoding memories are inextricably linked by circuitry in cortico-limbic neural networks to the affects that accompanied their registration during a meaningful life experience. This clearly establishes a principle of neural memory networks that parallels, and is isomorphic with, the psychoanalytically derived concept of nodal memory networks and the related principle of the affective organization of memory.

Psychophysiologic studies of REM (dreaming) sleep indicate that mnemonic perceptual images stored in the association cortex are activated in dreaming sleep by ascending excitatory (PGO) waves originating in the brain stem (pons) (Hobson 1988). This activation is considered to be responsible for their appearance in the dream. The REM state itself is initiated by neurochemical changes in the pons. Dream researchers Hobson and McCarley (1987) had previously assumed that dream imagery was randomly generated by the PGO waves and only secondarily organized into narrative sequences (similar to Freud's concept of secondary revision): "the activation-synthesis hypothesis."

Meanwhile, on the basis of clinical psychoanalytic studies, I had concluded that emotions connected to current life conflicts and conscious worries about them during the day would activate historically relevant memory traces that are linked to the same conflictual affects. This would render them more sensitive to the stimulation by PGO waves during sleep (Reiser 1990), indicating that dream imagery is meaningful rather than randomly generated. Furthermore, Hobson and McCarley's activation-synthesis hypothesis could not account for repetitive dreams in which the repetitive images are invariant. This can hardly be explained by random stimulation. Positron emission tomography (PET) imaging studies by Braun and colleagues (1998) in human subjects have demonstrated that the emotional and memory systems of the brain are active during REM sleep. This is consistent with the clinical anatomical studies (Solms 1997) of dreaming in patients with neurological lesions. For reasons derived from both domains, the activation-synthesis hypothesis could be modified to account for the meaningful significance of dreams, bringing us closer to an understanding of the relationship between the domains.

But Freud's hypothesis that the dream is instigated by a wish seems no longer tenable as originally proposed, since psychophysiolgic studies have indicated that REM is instigated by neurochemical changes in the pons. Is it then entirely untenable? Perhaps not, if the issue of different domains with their different terminologies is taken into account. REM is a brain state. The subjective experience of a dream is a mental phenomenon. An "immaterial wish" as defined by Freud belongs primarily in the mental domain. It cannot instigate REM, which is a (material) brain state. On the other hand, neurochemical changes in pons (biological domain) cannot instigate the subjective mental experience of dreaming. I have elsewhere proposed the idea that the mind can exploit the special physiologic conditions that are extant in the brain during REM sleep (Reiser 1990). What I am referring to is the fact that during REM sleep connections between the limbic system and prestriate cortex are active and could provide the backward neural reentrant pathways that were implicitly postulated by Freud's concept of the "wish." The wish, he proposed, would instigate a regressive backward current in the mental apparatus in order to achieve the perceptual experience (in dream consciousness) of the wish satisfied. An example would be the common "dreams of convenience," for example, a dream of drinking water that satisfies a thirsty dreamer. The concept of instigation of REM by chemical changes in the pons and the concept of the instigation of the dream by a wish are not the same—but they can be considered functionally parallel and compatible. Such considerations, taken along with psychophysiologic evidence of the evolutionarily developed memory organizing function of dreaming sleep (Winson 1985), make it possible to construct a modified psychobiological definition of the dream process: "Dreaming in man can be defined as the subjective experience of vital memory and problem-solving cognitive functions made possible by the special psychophysiological conditions that obtain in mind/brain-body during REM sleep" (Reiser 1990: 200). This contemporary psychobiologic definition of the dream process conforms to both psychoanalytic and neuroscientific findings. Each separate theory had to be modified to achieve this new composite conceptualization, and each contributed unique material. *It couldn't have been constructed from either side alone.*

Although this overview is sketchy, it illustrates how thoughtful dialogue between clinical psychoanalytic and cognitive neuroscience data can be reciprocally enriching and lead to modifications of concepts derived from the disciplines separately, and to formulation of a contemporary psychobiologic formulation acceptable to both. But studies such as these will not take us all the way. Some think that a satisfactory reconciliation will never be possible—that perhaps the best we can do is learn to translate between very different disciplines that use different languages, techniques, and concepts formulated at different levels of abstraction. The definition of dreaming offered above is certainly not complete, nor does it answer all questions about dreams and dreaming; for example, is there a dream censor, and if so, how might it be understood to function in neurobiological terms? But it does extend our understanding of important aspects of dreaming and does represent progress. Will such an approach take us far enough to help clarify the status of psychoanalysis as a discipline in contemporary culture? I think so. Psychoanalysis as a discipline has had to abandon the position that the other disciplines should orbit around it in an attempt to justify and confirm Freud's models. Rather, it seems to me that scholars should take from each field of study observations and facts that are cogent to the others and hence conducive to interdisciplinary collaboration and concept construction. Because psychoanalysis provides access to critically important levels and kinds of mental functions that are not addressed by other disciplines, I conclude that it is in a unique position to contribute in this way to contemporary culture.

References

Braun, A. R., et al. 1988. "Dissociated Pattern of Activity in Visual Cortices and Their Projections During Human Rapid/Eye Movement Sleep." *Science* 279: 91–95.

Bucci, W. 1997. *Psychoanalysis and Cognitive Neuroscience: A Multiple Code Theory.* York: Guilford Press.

Freud, S. 1895. *Project for a Scientific Psychology. S.E.,* 1: 295–341.

———. 1900. *The Interpretation of Dreams. S.E.,* 4, 5: 1–626.

———. 1915. *Instincts and Their Vicissitudes. S.E.,* 14: 109–17.

Hobson, J. A. 1988. *The Dreaming Brain.* New York: Basic Books.

Hobson, J. A., and R. W. McCarley. 1977. "The Brain as a Dream State Generator." *American Journal of Psychiatry* 134: 1335–48.

LeDoux, J. 1996. *The Emotional Brain: The Mysterious Underpinnings of Emotional Life.* New York: Simon and Schuster.

Levin, F. M. 1991. *Mapping the Mind:* Hillsdale, N.J.: Analytic Press.

Mishkin, M., and T. Appenzeller. 1987. "The Anatomy of Memory." *Scientific American* 256: 80–86.

Reiser, M. 1990. *Memory in Mind and Brain: What Dream Imagery Reveals.* New York: Basic Books; reprint ed., New Haven: Yale University Press, 1994.

Schore, A. M. 1997. "A Century After Freud's Project Is a Rapprochement Between Psychoanalysis and Neurobiology at Hand?" *Journal of the American Psychoanalytic Association* 45: 807–40.

Solms, M. 1997. *The Neuropsychology of Dreams: A Clinical Anatomical Study.* Institute for Research in Behavioral Neuroscience Monograph 7. Mahwah, N.J.: Erlbaum.

Squire, L. R. 1987. *Memory and Brain.* New York: Oxford University Press.

Winson, J. 1985. *Brain and Psyche: The Biology of the Unconscious.* New York: Doubleday-Anchor.

Freud's Neuromental Model:
Analytic Structures
and Local Habitations

David V. Forrest, M.D.

Subjecting psychoanalysis to scientific scrutiny in its current rococo era of development reminds me of Gary Larson's *Far Side* cartoon depicting scientists suspending a rhinoceros upside down before "testing whether or not rhinos land on their feet." But it also reminds me of the heft of psychoanalysis, its resilient hide, and the memorable horns of its dilemmas.

Perhaps psychoanalysis is already a complete science of human description, like gross anatomy, in which new discoveries are made only by going to the electron microscopic level or by adding functional tagging by antibodies or radioisotopes. Abram Kardiner said that Freud contributed *the anatomy of the integrative process.* Anatomy can be used by a physician to localize an ill and remedy it, or by an artist to create works of beauty and sometimes artistic license, or by an archaeologist or paleontologist or evolutionist to establish the history of our species. Psychoanalysis also becomes largely what it is applied to and by whom, its relatively simple elements providing systematic logical structures for argumentation or instantiation.

MIND, BRAIN SYNTHESES

A natural goal of contemporary psychiatry is a synthesis of our two great intellectual traditions, psychoanalysis and neurobiology, in order to avoid splitting
the care of the patient into the partial domains of biotherapy, which lacks understanding of mental interrelations, and purely psychological psychotherapy,
which lacks an appreciation of the embeddedness of mental processes in brain
function. George Vaillant noted that the most stable and reliable constructions
in personality are the defenses. We can observe similarly configured defensive
patterns along continua from the normal or neurotic mental mechanisms of defense, through neuropsychic defenses that are influenced by the neurological
state, to more direct neurological cortical mechanisms (Forrest 1996). These
continua are the way the human brain adds its flavor of organism to mind. Our
minds are not the only logically possible minds; they are the highly particular
minds that evolved in the wetware of our brains. Analysts who are not familiar
with clinical neurology may assume the brain is like the boring back of a televi-
sion set, uninvolved with higher-level program content beyond some atomistic
level. In fact, the stamp of the brain is pervasive. We are not immediately aware
of it because we are too immersed in it. A short list of brain traits of mind follows. The brain-mind is: redundant/displacing; analogical/transferring; recog-
nitive/projective; statistical/approximate; computational/summative; erro-
neous/reliable; spatial/sensory/motoric; affectively indexed/state dependent;
connective/self-instructing; condensing/crystallizing; staged/layered; architec-
tonic/logically gated.

MISIDENTIFICATION SYNDROMES
AND TRANSFERENCE

One neuromental domain involving recognition includes prosopagnosia, a
brain disorder in which one cannot recognize faces; misidentification syndromes; and transference. Stephen Signer described seven variant forms that
share a delusion of substitution:[1] in Capgras delusions, the "Body Snatchers"
type, people are being replaced by identical doubles; in subjective doubles, the
Capgras type, unseen doubles, phantom boarders, or deceased persons are felt
to be present; in the Frégoli type (fig. 1), named for the great Italian actor who
was a master of disguised identities, a familiar person has assumed a bodily form;
in intermetamorphosis, both minds and bodies of people are interchanging; in
subjective doubles, the autoscopic type, a person's own double is projected onto

FIGURE I. Frégoli delusions

another person in the positive form, and in the negative form the person cannot see himself or herself, even in a mirror; in reverse autoscopic doubles, the person feels either like an imposter or as if he or she is in the process of being replaced; and in the reverse Frégoli type, the person feels other people are misidentifying him or her as if *they* have Frégoli delusions of misidentification.

The Frégoli type, in my opinion, is closest to the normal mechanisms of transference and transference neurosis. It is often associated with pathologically reduced frontal brain function. Although transference is universal, perhaps the patients who experience it most intensely are functionally less frontally cerebrotonic in some way. Transformations are also a normal product of brain function; they are common in dreams[2] and in folk tales and myths. But in any case, a neurological substrate for excessive transference is of interest.

The misidentification syndromes appear to parse and dissect Freudian object relations. Their relation to brain disorders and lesions is clear. Often, but not always, anatomical localization is possible. A retired professor in his seventies I am treating for delusional effects of medicines he takes for Parkinson's disease had an episode of misidentification after his wife returned from a weeklong professional trip, an absence that upset him. He imagined that her return meant he was being visited by an old male friend and colleague who, like his wife, had gray hair—although she lacked a beard. As we worked on this delusion, he remembered that the friend had been undependable during the student riots of 1972. Thus the misidentification, a neurological condition, also partakes of the psychodynamics of interpersonal object relations. In fact, Sandamu Kimura notes that the misidentified are often important to the misidentifier, married persons most frequently choosing to misidentify their spouses.[3]

IMAGING FREE ASSOCIATION

Another example of higher-order storming of the higher-order sphere of psychoanalysis is the attempt at Positron Emission Tomography (PET) scan imaging of free association by Nancy Andreasen (1995), for which the American College of Psychoanalysts gave her its Laughlin-Freud award in 1996. Using PET scanning, she localized the brain areas activated while the patients were asked to do three memory tasks: recalling a personal event from the past, or focused episodic memory; recalling words that start with C, or semantic memory; and her model of free association, which was lying quietly in a PET scanner (with eyes closed and no specific instructions about mental activity—this is the "resting baseline" for PET studies). To avoid objections of analysts, she did not call this free association; she called it Random Episodic Silent Thinking, or REST. REST activates the association cortex, the most human and complex parts of the brain. Responding as a psychoanalytic consultant before publication, I still have problems with REST, because one thing humans are incapable of is randomness (the Internal Revenue Service uses this to catch cheaters) and many things other than episodic recalling may occur during free association, such as directed thinking, like Andrew Wiles proving Fermat's Last Theorem (Kolata 1993), or mental rehearsals of implicit skills, as downhill racers and ballet dancers do. But most important, Andreasen didn't have an analyst listening behind the PET machine. Her work shows that the imaging community is beginning to reach toward psychoanalysis for meaningful things to study and demonstrates the need for collaboration with psychoanalysts. She has also suggested that she has localized ego functions, if I may provide a target for Robert Shulman. But my point is not to emphasize the coarseness of these first approximations. Rather, it is to recognize that the ball is now in the court of us psychoanalysts to refine our concepts operationally. How exactly would we wish to characterize free association, in addition to the REST state?

Karl Pribram and Merton Gill, in discussing Freud's Project (1895), differed on the importance of the Project for psychoanalysis. Pribram, the neurosurgeon and neurophysiologist, proposer of a holographic metaphor of memory, wished to advance Freud's original idea of welcoming psychoanalysis back into the natural sciences; and Gill echoed the caution of many psychoanalysts of that time that such a brain theory and model can have no bearing upon the data from the subjective experience of the psychoanalytic situation, and that psychoanalysis should be purged of its natural science metapsychology.[4]

Does work such as that of Andreasen and her colleagues realize the ambitions of Freud's Project? It is certainly a step. In the May 1995 editorial of the *Journal of the American Psychiatric Association,* Bruce Cohen and colleagues start with the Project and argue that magnetic resonance spectroscopy "is capable of determining changes in brain chemistry that may be directly related to the processes by which the brain reacts to stimuli and accomplishes its conscious and unconscious tasks." But the new imaging is not without its critics. Jonathan Brodie (1995) has argued that images are "vivid pictorographic representations that can be manipulated to emphasize or distort anything," that it overemphasizes static points in dynamic neuronal systems of linked neurotransmitter chemistry in continuous readjustment, when it is a local loss of elasticity and variance in a system that is pathological.

What is new is the direct observation of the physiological process of thought, sensation, cognition, emotion, and consciousness.

FREUD'S ECONOMIC THEORY OF QUANTITY
AND THE MATHEMATIZING OF ANALYSIS

The whole of our empirical experience of the world is moving toward mathematics. Physics, then chemistry, then biology, and eventually psychoanalysis will be quantified. We see it already in computer models of neuromental processes. As George Steiner, complaining about lowered expectations in the humanities, has said, "You can't graduate as a literate being without knowing something about what Galileo meant when he said, 'Nature speaks algebra and geometry.'"[5]

I predict with confidence that Freud's whole system of quantity—his economic theory of libidinal investment, which the psychoanalytic world has largely abandoned—will again seem to presage the very edge of brain science. Freud's system alone will not comprise our new system: his work from a century ago in the Project is far too simple to mathematize into a description of what we know about the brain; but he will, once again, have shown us the way and provided the guiding principle.

The advantage of neurocomputations as a way of thinking about the brain and an arena of theory production is that every theory comes premathematized and is computationally enactable. One can run one's theories and measure how they work.

SCRUTIN DE LISTE AND NEURAL NETWORKS

As one example of Freud's prescience, or should I say provision for the future, I would suggest his theory of the means of election of materials into dreams.[6] All computation involves the gating of input in some way so that the number of outputs differs from the number of inputs, and Freud explicitly portrayed this in the mental process, comparing condensation in dreams to the French political procedure known as *scrutin de liste,* or scrutiny of the list. Freud's description has uncanny similarities both to attractor neural net architecture and to feature discovery by competitive learning, as in the self-organizing Kohonen feature map networks: associative paths lead from one element of the dream to several dream-thoughts, and from one dream-thought to several elements of the dream. Thus a dream is constructed not by each individual dream-thought, or group of dream-thoughts, finding (in abbreviated form) separate representation in the content of the dream—in the kind of way in which an electorate chooses a parliamentary representative. A dream is constructed, rather, by the whole mass of dream-thoughts being submitted to a sort of manipulative process in which those elements that have the most numerous and strongest supports acquire the right of entry into the dream-content—in a manner analogous to election by scrutin de liste.

Freud here is describing condensation and overdetermination in dreams, and the similarity to the competitive and dynamic nature of neural networks is only less remarkable when one reflects that Freud, thinking as a neurologist and neuropsychiatrist, also based his theoretical structures at first on a neural model, just as neural net modelers do.

Now it is probably foolish to say that Freud anticipated neural networks, far before the computer or even Karel Čapek's *term* for robots. That honor goes to another psychiatrist, Warren McCulloch (1943, 1951, 1988), who together with Walter H. Pitts developed the theory of partial knowledge, after the question arose of how he could still think while drinking with his friends, who included Norbert Wiener. Yet as he so often does elsewhere, Freud anticipated the logical system requirements for a machine to do logic at the same time as he was describing a brain's need to crunch data and make output differ from input, in order to compute. Thus when we see feedforward networks, so successful in speech recognition, or recurrent networks, capable of self-organizing into maps of sensory experience, we are able, for the first time, to glimpse how it all actually might work in the brain, with its billions of dendritic connections—how the theory of order emerges in neuronal processing.

BRAIN-IMITATING NEURAL NETWORKS
IN A NUTSHELL

Neural networks are networks of extremely simple electronic processors or *neurodes* that are densely interconnected, hence the term *connectionism.* The processors do not contain memory; their connections with one another do, hence the term *distributed.* They do not follow an algorithm or program, and like the brain they are fundamentally analog. The neurode consists of inputs (X), which are added up, a linear summation function designated by the capital Greek letter sigma, and an S-shaped or sigmoid threshold function for firing (fig. 2). One can visualize many interconnected neurodes containing paired sigmas and sigmoids. The varying synaptic weights (W) are in the interconnections. They are ganged together in the nets and are often put in input, middle, and output layers in the backpropagation error feedback networks that have been so successful in speech recognition. The Freudian point about all this is that to make sense of a morass of cognitive data, the designers have found themselves constructing a *dynamic* system in which the data are massaged as a whole and compete for election into the result. This competitive learning is very like scrutin de liste and condensation. The Parallel Distributed Processing folks at Carnegie Mellon and the University of California at San Diego have some delightful examples identifying whether a given teenager is one of the Jets or the Sharks gangs in *West Side Story.* The highly interconnected self-organizing Kohonen networks are especially illustrative of this competitive learning. The fact that they automati-

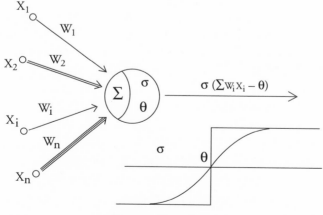

FIGURE 2. Neurodes

Equation for matrix $W_{ij} = \sum_{K} v_i^K v_j^K$

To retrieve smile, only one bit (here two) need be entered (sweep downward).

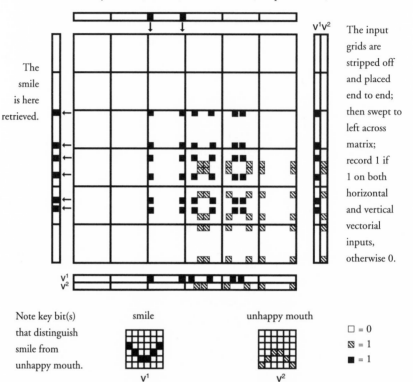

v^1v^2

The smile is here retrieved.

The input grids are stripped off and placed end to end; then swept to left across matrix; record 1 if 1 on both horizontal and vertical vectorial inputs, otherwise 0.

v^1
v^2

Note key bit(s) that distinguish smile from unhappy mouth.

smile

unhappy mouth

v^1

v^2

$\square = 0$
$\boxtimes = 1$
$\blacksquare = 1$

FIGURE 3. Retrieving a smile from a single bit. This is adapted from Yechiam Yemini's neural network computing course given at Columbia University in spring 1990. Smile (V1) versus unhappy mouth (V2) are stripped off small input grids, placed end to end, and entered as two dimensions (activations, or orientation, and weights) of the large vector space. Where bits coincide, a pattern is entered. Only 15 percent of the space can be used without overload. A fragment entered (above) retrieves memory at left, illustrating partial knowledge (McCullogh), holographic memory (Pribram), and condensation (Freud).

cally read and organize data shows and models the way mind qualities may emerge from neuronal connection without the need to postulate a homunculus.

In a neural network, information is stored in a logical matrix that illustrates partial knowledge and Freudian condensation. Yechiam Yemini of Columbia University's computer science department has presented a simplified grid that memorizes a smiling or frowning mouth and retrieves either by a single bit of information. To illustrate the principle of partial knowledge in memory retrieval I have adapted Yemini's graphic representation (fig. 3) of a neural network vector matrix of zero-or-one bits to measure facial affects. At the bottom of the figure are two grids, one of an upcurving smile (solid bits) and one of a downturning unhappy mouth (gray bits), which are stripped off row by row and placed end to end as vector inputs V1 and V2 at both the bottom and the right side of the matrix. Then they are registered as memories wherever they coincide when swept respectively up and to the left across the matrix. To retrieve the smile, only two bits (top) from the corners of the mouth (differentiating smile from unhappy mouth) need to be swept down from above. Where the bits encounter another solid (1 rather than 0) bit, they retrieve the entire V1 grid, as shown at the left. The potential for overloading the network with interfering information can readily be deduced, as can a model for Freudian condensation. These informational dimensions of brain function are less easily translated into brain chemistry and visualization. Mathematical models are not so much metaphors as they are abstract structures of a necessary underlying logic.

THE RELIABILITY OF CONSCIOUS SUBJECTIVITY

Some of the mystification about consciousness that was recently expressed in an email psychoanalytic chat room (JAPA__NETCAST@psychoanalysis.net) is a stimulus to thinking about epistemology. This is worth doing to avoid what Mark Solms has called the radical unknowability of inner and outer reality, an often alleged notion of the isolation of subjectivity from the empirical behind which psychoanalysts who do not like neuroscience or objectivity of any kind take refuge.

The epistemological reliability of conscious subjectivity would seem to me to be establishable *mathematically* by (1) the detailed and statistically improbable conformity between self-reported internalized models of the world by different observers; (2) the synesthetic conformity of various sensory modalities in the same observer; and (3) the mathematical impossibility of our minds, considered as computational machines, creating all the informational bits of the world of our experience. (Other arguments in the same direction have been made by Ilise Lombardo along the lines that we do not have to know that we know something in order to know something.)[7] As Steven Pinker puts it in *How the Mind Works,* the crowning accomplishment of our brain is the real world of our experience, an adaptive interpretation of the really real world of physics.[8]

If I construct a miniature model of an electric locomotive and it runs, I have not only a visual corroboration via my own hands of the accuracy of my visual perception but also an operational, tactile one, a synesthetic corroboration. If we construct a working model of a brain (or a retina, a part of the brain, which has already been done), we have a consensual, synesthetic corroboration of the truth of our experience of our brains.

Although it is true that single glimpses of scenes are often unreliable and differ among witnesses, it is also true that prolonged and repeated checking can ascertain the reliability and accuracy of our mental representation of the outer world. The analogy is an upgraded echoplanar magnetic resonance imaging machine, with which, for three million dollars and a lot of computational power, one can reduce the noise and distill the signal until it is highly accurate.

The world is far too banally detailed to be the theoretical projection of our minds (or of a demon trickster's creating it for us, as the philosophers state). Our minds lack the computational power, the K, to project the changing scenes we see. It is a matter of mathematical fact, as Pinker and others have asserted, that the real world must be impinging upon and registered by our retinas and our visual cortexes, not created by our brains.

We do make compromises in visual quality at the fringes of our vision, in rapid vision, and certainly in dreams, where we condense and conflate the visual memory of objects, but we do not make up what we see out of whole cloth. Rather, we statistically sample, but repeatedly, for high operational accuracy. In fact, all our vision, even twenty-twenty foveal vision, is a statistical sample and relatively gross. We don't see all the mites living on our lover's eyelids—unless we magnify.

But there is a certainty of astronomical numerical power in our accumulated statistical samplings of the visual world. Just as a sequence of grainy images can be upgraded into clarity, our continued and *shared* experience of the outside world coheres effectively to certainty about it. Those who believe that no knowledge of another's subjectivity is possible should consult a good interior decorator, art teacher, optometrist, or ensemble dancer who does this every day of his or her life. There is no way that the ambient visual and tactile and auditory experience of a company dancer on stage could be invented by a mind: there are too many photons, waves, and angles. And all our evolution has tuned our minds to one another's. As Emily Dickinson put it,

> The Brain is just the weight of God—
> For—Heft them—pound for pound—
> And if they differ—if they do—
> As Syllable from Sound—

Our minds are cut from the same cloth; they are designed to work together, and they do. In real ways we are dedicated terminals for one another (for example, in facial recognition) and for the physical world in which we evolved. Computational models of the mind are not only computationally Freudian, but they have the additional advantage that they are able easily to leap the interpersonal gap, as our interpersonal theory recognizes.

Some in the JAPA_NETCAST chat room have also said that there are no sense organs for inner reality. This is incorrect. Such organs include enteroreceptors of all sort, for pressure, chemistry, temperature, and so on. We are also able to observe our brains working in many natural and pathological states, including migraine, vertigo, strokes, and misidentification syndromes, among others.

The *Eagle* has once again landed, this time on the brain. Clark Kerr at the University of California was quoted in the *Economist* as saying that the only thing holding the modern university together is a common grievance over parking.[9] For his part, Edward O. Wilson has suggested that *consilience,* or the unification of thought, will come from sociobiology.[10] Freud himself may not unify the disciplines, but our common interest in the things he was interested in has a chance.

Notes

1. S. F. Signer, "Capgras Syndrome: The Delusion of Substitution," *Journal of Clinical Psychiatry* 48 (1987): 147–50.
2. D. Forrest, "Dreams of the Rarebit Fiend: Neuromedical Synthesis of Unconscious Meaning," *American Academy of Psychoanalysis* 15 (1987): 331–63.
3. S. Kimura, "Review of 106 Cases with the Syndrome of Capgras," in *The Delusional Misidentification Syndromes,* edited by G. N. Christodoulou (Karger: Basel, 1986).
4. K. H. Pribram and M. M. Gill, *Freud's Project Re-Assessed: Preface to Contemporary Cognitive Theory and Neuropsychology* (New York: Basic Books, 1976).
5. Peter Applebome, "A Humanist and an Elitist? Perhaps," *New York Times,* Apr. 18, 1998, B9.
6. Freud, *The Dream Work A: The Work of Condensation, S.E.,* 4: 284.
7. Ilise Lombardo, "Reliabilism and Theories of Justification" (M.A. thesis, Cambridge University, 1991).
8. S. Pinker, *How the Mind Works* (New York: Norton, 1997).
9. Clark Kerr, "Universities Survey: Inside the Knowledge Factory," *Economist,* Oct. 4, 1997.
10. Edward O. Wilson, *Consilience: The Unity of Knowledge* (New York: Knopf, 1998).

Further References

Anderson, J. A., and E. Rosenfeld. *Neurocomputing: Foundations of Research.* Cambridge, Mass.: MIT Press, 1988.

Andreasen, N. C., et al. "Remembering the Past: Two Facets of Episodic Memory Explored with Positron Emission Tomography." *American Journal of Psychiatry* 152 (1995): 1576–85.

Brodie, J. "Imaging the Brain: Is the Brain Really Like the Liver?" Presentation at Grand Rounds, New York State Psychiatric Institute, July 28, 1995.

Cohen, B. M., P. F. Renshaw, and D. Yurgelin-Todd. "Imaging the Mind: Magnetic Resonance Spectroscopy and Functional Brain Imaging." *American Journal of Psychiatry* 152 (1995): 655–58.

Forrest, D. V. "Psychotherapy of Patients with Neuropsychiatric Disorders." In *The American Psychiatric Press Textbook of Neuropsychiatry,* 3d ed. Edited by S. C. Yudofsky and R. E. Hales. Washington, D.C.: American Psychiatric Press, 1996.

Freud, S. "Project for a Scientific Psychology." *S.E.,* 1: 295–397.

Kolata, G. "Math Whiz Who Battled 350-Year-Old Problem." *New York Times,* June 29, 1993.

McCulloch, W. S. *Embodiments of Mind.* Cambridge, Mass.: MIT Press, 1988.

———. "Why the Mind Is in the Head." In *Cerebral Mechanisms in Behavior: The Hixon Symposium,* edited by L. A. Jeffress. New York: Wiley, 1951.

McCulloch, W. S., and W. H. Pitts. "A Logical Calculus of the Ideas Immanent in Nervous Activity." *Bulletin of Mathematical Biophysics* 5 (1943): 115–33. Reprinted in McCulloch, *Embodiments of Mind,* 19–39.

Minsky, M., and S. Papert. *Perceptrons.* Cambridge, Mass.: MIT Press, 1969, 1–20. Reprinted in Anderson and Rosenfeld, *Neurocomputing,* 161–69.

Morgan, A. E., J. D. Brodie, and S. L. Dewey. "What Are We Measuring with PET?" *Quarterly Journal of Nuclear Medicine* 42 (1998): 151–57.

Freud's Theory of the Mind and Modern Functional Imaging Experiments

Robert G. Shulman and Douglas L. Rothman

What relations are there between Freud's theories of the mind and modern functional brain imaging experiments? To anchor this question, we present two statements from Mark Solms's recent article about the nature of consciousness.[1] First, Solms emphasized Freud's definition that "mental processes are in themselves unconscious," arguing the relevance of this definition to modern controversies about brain-mind-consciousness. We are willing to accept a moderate form of this position, in which the unconscious is acknowledged to contribute significantly to mental processes. The second quotation is less familiar: "psychoanalysis and PET scanning study one and the same underlying object: the mental apparatus and its functions." We do not plan to discuss Solms's use of this identity in pursuit of consciousness. This statement is evocative and needful of comment, however, particularly in a period of intense research in the neurosciences when functional magnetic resonance imaging (fMRI) and positron emission tomography (PET) methods have been experimentally localizing brain activities. These functional imaging methodologies map neurophysiological responses to cognitive, emotional, or sensory stimulations.[2] The experiments are noninvasive and may be done repeatedly. The rapid progress made using these methods has encouraged widespread optimism about our ability to understand activities of the mind.

In applying modern functional imaging methods to understanding the mind, it is assumed that the imaging signal directly measures mental processes. That is, in fact, not true. The signals come from changes in blood flow and brain energy parameters. To interpret these energy signals in terms of mental processes, one must proceed cautiously, since, as we shall show, inferences about the mental derived from functional imaging experiments have depended upon assumptions about mental activity. Hence, before functional imaging methods may study "the mental apparatus and its functions," these assumptions must be examined. The psychological assumptions in the field today are so pervasive that their acceptance is usually unquestioned. The paradigm in the field is cognitive psychology, in which mental processes handle information by computational modules. Subjectivity is usually not acknowledged, but when it is tested for, it, too, becomes a module of, for example, attention or working memory. However, since the basic premise of the field differs from Freud's view that mental processes have strong unconscious elements, psychologists and psychiatrists must be particularly precise about their assumptions when proposing and interpreting functional imaging experiments.

Functional imaging experiments are generally set up to measure directly or indirectly differences seen in the brain image between two behavioral tasks.[3] One task is usually the subject at rest, with minimum stimulation. Images collected during rest are subtracted from those during a task, and the difference images are evaluated statistically to establish the probability that they are not random. Difference images, as shown in many publications, are plots of regions in which the differences between images during the task and at rest are statistically significant. This presentation does not mean that imaging signals elsewhere are nonexistent, merely that they don't show on the difference image because their magnitudes do not change significantly between task and control.

To understand the meaning of these experiments we need to know the connection between the magnitude of these functional imaging signals and neuronal activity in the brain, in other words the biological foundations of the signals. Functional imaging signals are caused by changes in neuronal activity and are detected via changes in blood physiological parameters by changes in cerebral metabolic rate of glucose (CMRglc), cerebral metabolic rate of oxygen (CMRO$_2$), and the correlative changes in cerebral blood flow (CBF). Until recently, the relation between functional imaging signals (S) and neuronal activity (N) (which hithertofore has been interpreted as changes in physiological parameters) was not known. However, results of our recent experiments have established a quantitative relation between the *signal* S measured in functional imaging experiments and N, the neuronal activity, which consists of neurotransmitter activity.[4] In these experiments, neurotransmitter activity, N, was shown to consist almost entirely of glutamate to glutamine neurotransmitter cycling, so that the energy measured in a functional imaging experiment, S, provided a measure of N. This recent calibration of the relation between S and N has been achieved in rats and humans by new methods that enable the neurotransmitter activity to be measured directly while energy consumption is simultaneously measured. This is shown in figure 1 as a solid line.

Although the ability to measure cortical neurotransmitter flux (N) is important for mechanisms of brain activity in neuroscience, for the moment we direct attention to its role in mental activity (M). The dotted line between N and M is the unanswered "hard problem," the relation between neuronal activity and mind that is the paradigm of neuroscience Francis Crick has summarized so well: "The scientific belief is that our minds—the behavior of our brains—can be explained by the interaction of nerve cells (and other cells) and the molecules associated with them."[5]

At this point we return to the functional imaging experiments that seem to represent the cutting edge of scientific studies of brain activity. If functional imaging experiments had followed the neuroscience path of figure 1, they would have sought a measure of N. Having done so, we would be facing the hard problem of neuroscience. How does N interact with M? But functional imaging has

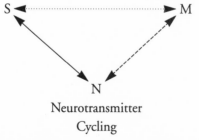

Neurotransmitter
Cycling

FIGURE 1. Schematic for relating the functional imaging signal S to mental activity M. In psychology this connection is made directly by interpreting S obtained during stimulation. In neuroscience, a biological interpretation shows that S arises from changes in the neuronal energy consumption determined by N. This shows up as changes in glucose or oxygen consumption, which may be accompanied by changes in blood flow. In this interpretation, N still has to be related to M.

not proceeded this way. Generally, functional imaging bypasses biology in favor of a top-down cognitive psychology approach. In this approach, based upon psychology, not on neuroscience, the brain is modeled as consisting of separate functional modules, each performing a discrete mental process. Because these processes are assumed to be functionally separable, any change in S is directly assigned to a mental process (M), reflected by the dashed line in figure 1. The signals are being used to measure M directly with interpretations derived from a psychological methodology proposed by cognitive psychology.

To see how functional imaging bypasses neuroscience, consider how the mental operations are localized and measured in a typical experiment. The approaches of cognitive psychology were pioneered in PET studies by Posner, Raichle, and their colleagues.[6] In Raichle and Posner's view (generally described above), the computational module of brain activity is to be found in a PET differencing experiment where images from two tasks are subtracted: one task presumed to stimulate the computational module, the other designed not to. Each difference scan is considered to have localized these postulated mental functions by measuring the magnitude and location of the computational module of mental activity required for the task. It is assumed that the difference signal between the two images represents all the brain activity needed to produce the mental activity. As pointed out previously, it is further assumed that the difference in the task has been uniquely identified.[7] This is problematic and in fact circular, since it ends up locating in the brain modules of activities whose existence are merely postulated.

A generalized description of the signals during a typical functional imaging experiment is shown in figure 2. From the recent metabolic studies,[8] it is now known that the height, S, represents the energy needed for neuronal activity N.

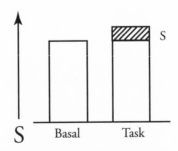

FIGURE 2. Schematic of the small changes in neuronal activity during a task showing how the differencing subtracts two large numbers.

A large body of information has shown that the incremental activity ΔS is typically less than 10 percent of rest values during a cognitive task. In the cognitive psychology paradigm, ΔS is assumed to measure the modular brain activity needed to do the computation required by the task. The baseline value of N is ignored since the mental module is assumed to be inactive at rest. Put simply, this interpretation assumes that $\Delta S = \Delta N = M$. The mental activity needed for the task, in this interpretation, is measured by the incremental signal ΔS which is assumed to measure incremental neuronal activity ΔN. But this interpretation, that the mental activity M depends only on ΔN, is based upon the concept that the internal processes represented in the baseline neuronal activity (N) are separable from and not needed for the mental activity of the "module." Although this assumption is consistent with the computational model of the brain, and also justifies the subtraction of a baseline signal, it is *not* supported by the ^{13}C NMR results, which have shown that the resting N is much greater than ΔN.

How would other theories of mind, which consider subjective, conscious, or unconscious neuronal activities to be essential for mental activities, interpret these data? One of the early criticisms of cognitive psychology, from a biochemical viewpoint, comes from Jean Pierre Changeux, who introduced the hypothesis that the mental processes internally induced by the subject (such as thoughts and mental images) are the same as those induced by external stimuli,[9] a view that differs from the modular theories of mind,[10] which neglect internal processes. Changeux's view that the totality of mind activity is required for mental processes is shared with several major philosophical and psychological theories of mind. These theories (certainly including Freud's) accept the existence of subjective activities, claiming for them an important role in mental processes and contributing to any computational activities of the type considered in cognitive psychology.

John Searle has sharply delineated these differences in his monumental critique *The Rediscovery of the Mind*. He writes, "In the philosophy of mind, obvious facts about the mental, such as that we all really do have subjective, conscious mental states, are routinely denied by many, perhaps most, of the advanced thinkers in the subject."[11] Searle thus shares to some extent the view that mental processes include unconscious elements, although he does have a *very* different view of the unconscious. Similar criticisms of the computational basis of cognitive psychology have been made deftly by Gerald Edelman, who, while presenting his own comprehensive view of the mind, critically dismisses the claims of cognitive psychology because "they are disregarding a large body of evidence that undermines the view that the brain is a kind of computer."[12]

There are significant differences in these several schools of thought about the nature of mind, and particularly about the nature of subjective, conscious, and unconscious activity. They are grouped here because of their shared view of the holistic and comprehensive relation between brain activity and mind. Each opposes the cognitive psychology position that mental activity can be considered as a series of computational processes that are separable from the subjective, personal activities of mind. In other words, these "holistic" concepts of mind from philosophy, psychiatry, and neuroscience are consistent with the view that $S = N = M$.

Several experimental results favor the more holistic interpretation of functional imaging experiments. First, the calibration of functional imaging that has been achieved by the recent ^{13}C MRS experiments shows that fractional increases in N during cognitive tasks are less than 10 percent over baseline neuronal activity. These calibrations show that in the resting state, neuronal activity accounts for nearly all of the brain energy consumption. In the computational module viewpoint, brain energy consumption during rest would not include neuronal activity because no computation was being performed. Accordingly, the resting energy consumption, responsible for the signal S, could be subtracted from the signal during the task and yield the difference due to neuronal activity. However, the assumption of constant baseline activities in the differencing method has more uncertainties when the resting state has been shown to have almost the same magnitude of neuronal activity as the stimulated state and to be performing the same neurochemical process of glutamate-glutamine cycling.

The second objection is experimental, coming from imaging science. If the subjective baseline activity were not needed for "mental" activity, then the incremental activity for a mental process should be independent of the baseline. There have been studies in rats in which sensory stimulations were performed at different degrees of anesthesia. As shown previously,[13] neuronal activity of glutamate-glutamine cycling decreases in the anesthetized states, falling monotonically to zero under deep pentobarbital anesthesia. Under certain anesthetics, animals will respond to sensory stimulations such as forepaw electrical stimulation or vibratory sensory stimulation, and studies have reported the incremental rate of glucose consumption, which has been shown to be a direct measure of neuronal activity.[14] If the mental activity needed to perform the task were modular, it should add the *same* incremental signal in the anesthetized and awake states. Starting from the anesthetized state, ΔS should be the same as when stimulated from rest. If, by contrast, the full neuronal activity is needed to perform the task, then the final state during the task should be the same regardless of the initial state, and the increment during the task will be larger under anesthesia. Many animal experiments show that the latter is actually the case.[15] During stimulation, S is observed to rise to approximately the same absolute level, independent of the state. These results support a view of mind in which a particular *magnitude* of neuronal activity is required for a task, not a particular *increment*. Because not all anesthetized states allow the animal to respond, those experiments must be considered as models for cognitive human experiments. Humans with reduced basal activity induced by anesthesia or sleep could be stimulated to perform cognitive tasks. Decisive choices between theories of mind could then be made, as suggested by these rat experiments.

Attempts to evaluate the contributions of conscious activities such as attention to visual responses in the human extrastriate cortex have recently been made by fMRI.[16] The results show that attention to the visual stimulus increases the resting signal as well as the increment, thereby supporting our view that extensive brain activity coexists with a particular response to stimulation.

Where does this present understanding of a large amount of neuronal activity in the absence of stimulation position functional imaging with respect to psychiatry? Both functional imaging and psychoanalysis are presently being used as psychological investigations of mind. However, because their starting assumptions about the mind differ significantly, their findings are incommensurate, and although loosely one may agree with Solms that they study the same "mental apparatus and its function," still on closer examination the present differences in starting assumptions between the imaging and psychoanalysis emphasize their disparities rather than similarities. We suggest that psychiatrists should not do functional imaging experiments based upon hypotheses of cognitive psychology without examining how these hypotheses fundamentally disagree with a more holistic concept of the mind which might more accurately represent their views. Furthermore, we have shown how functional imaging now has the potential to study the mind in biological terms, by taking advantage of the relation between the signals and neurotransmitter activity. The present experimental paradigms are designed to exclude subjective brain activity, which is the essence of the psychoanalytic field. Psychiatrists should base their experiments upon concepts consistent with their own view—a view that embraces the subjective nature of mind.

Notes

1. M. Solms, "What Is Consciousness?" *Journal of the American Psychoanalytic Association* 45 (1997): 681–703.
2. R. G. Shulman et al., "Nuclear Magnetic Resonance Imaging and Spectroscopy of Human Brain Function," *Proceedings of the National Academy of Sciences* 90 (1997): 3127–33; M. E. Raichle, "Behind the Scenes of Functional Brain Imaging: A Historical and Physiological Perspective," *Proceedings of the National Academy of Sciences* 95 (1998): 765–72; M. I. Posner and M. E. Raichle, *Images of Mind* (New York: Scientific American Library, 1994).
3. See sources cited in note 2, above.
4. N. R. Sibson et al., "Stoichiometric Coupling of Brain Glucose Metabolism and Glutamatergic Neuronal Activity," *Proceedings of the National Academy of Sciences* 95 (1998): 316–21; P. Magistretti et al., "Perspective: Neuroscience 'Energy on Demand,'" *Science* 283 (1999): 496–97.
5. F. H. C. Crick, *The Astonishing Hypothesis: The Scientific Search for the Soul* (New York: Charles Scribner's Sons, 1994), 7.
6. Posner and Raichle, *Images of Mind.*
7. R. G. Shulman, "Interview with Robert G. Shulman," *Journal of Cognitive Neuroscience* 8:5 (1996): 474–80; R. G. Shulman and D. L. Rothman, "Interpreting Functional Imaging Studies in Terms of Neurotransmitter Cycling," *Proceedings of the National Academy of Sciences* 95 (1998): 11993–98.
8. Sibson et al., "Stoichiometric Coupling"; Magistretti et al., "Perspective."
9. J. P. Changeux, *Neuronal Man: The Biology of Mind,* translated by L. Garey (Princeton, N.J.: Princeton University Press, 1985).
10. Posner and Raichle, *Images of Mind.*
11. J. R. Searle, *The Rediscovery of the Mind* (Cambridge, Mass.: MIT Press, 1992), 3.
12. G. M. Edelman, *Bright Air, Brilliant Fire* (New York: Basic Books, 1992), 14.
13. Sibson et al., "Stoichiometric Coupling."
14. Ibid.
15. R. G. Shulman et al., "Stimulated Changes in Localized Cerebral Energy Consumption Under Anesthesia," *Proceedings of the National Academy of Sciences* 96 (1999): 3245–50.
16. S. Kastner et al., "Mechanisms of Directed Attention in the Human Extrastriate Cortex as Revealed by Functional MRI," *Science* 282 (1998): 108–11.

The Changing Psychoanalytic Model of the Mind

Arnold M. Cooper, M.D.

A great effort has been made in recent years to achieve some form of integration of mind and brain. If this effort is to succeed, the neurobiologists need as good a model of the mind as is available, and we psychoanalysts, convinced that we possess that most complete and interesting theory of mind, need to begin to frame it in ways that lend themselves to neurobiologic experimentation. We have only just begun to do that.

On the occasion of Freud's eightieth birthday in 1936, Thomas Mann said, "The analytic revelation is a revolutionary force. With it a blithe skepticism has come into the world, a mistrust that unmasks all the schemes and subterfuges of our own souls. Once roused and on alert, it cannot be put to sleep again. It infiltrates life, undermines its raw naïveté, takes from it the strain of its own ignorance."[1] Freud took the view that mental life, the source of all behavior, including conscious and unconscious thoughts and feelings, is lawful, that it can be studied scientifically and understood as we understand other events in the natural world. He never abandoned the idea that studies in neurobiology and chemistry would shed light on the mind. He believed that the greater portion of what we are, what we do and think and feel, is determined outside of awareness, and that we are motivated by desires of which we have no knowledge and may consciously repudiate. This hypothesis of the dynamic unconscious, now evidentially well founded, opened to study large and fascinating realms of human activity. Freud described the baby as a sexual, aggressive, relationship-seeking, imaginative creature that creates its world perhaps even more than it responds to it; and the internalized experiences of babyhood, including the experiences and images of the body and the fantasies of relationships, will enduringly shape adult language and life. He believed that we carry our pleasure-guided motivations within us; we are not stimulus-response machines. We are perpetually in conflict between love and hate, dependency and autonomy, obedience and defiance, fear and desire. These conflicts are universal and unremitting, threatening us with feelings of shame and guilt, and to make our lives tolerable we construct elaborate mental defenses that enable us to achieve some compromise: a final common pathway among our conflicts that will allow us to conduct our lives in reasonably ordinary ways, feeling in charge of ourselves, although consciously ignorant of much of what we think and feel and intend. In this model, every mental action is multiply determined, subject to multiple levels of understanding and interpretation.

In some ways, what Freud did was to deepen, expand, and codify the traditional psychology of everyday life. Ideas such as the child is father to the man, people's motives are often hidden from themselves, we are driven by forces we can neither identify nor control, there is meaning in madness, and so on, are ideas that have forever fueled drama and myth. Freud's achievements were to describe these and other themes systematically; to devise a method—free association and analytic listening—by which we could learn about the individual unconscious mind; to create a theory in terms of some underlying developmental and structural principles that would explain the apparent surface diversity; and to demonstrate the usefulness of his theory when applied to a vast array of human activities whether waking or sleeping, creative or ordinary, intended or not.

This huge arena that psychoanalysis expropriated as within its purview has been sharply challenged in recent years. Much of that challenge has been directed at the basic propositions that Freud enlisted to support his view of the mind within the realm of science. I shall list a few of those propositions as originally understood—primarily by the American ego psychologists—and shall describe some of the alternative understandings that are proposed today, emphasizing that we have moved very far from the reasonably clear and rather dogmatic model that has usually been referred to as "orthodox" or "classical" psychoanalysis toward a multiplicity of competing models that tend to be more open-ended and blurry, acknowledging a greater complexity of development and function than heretofore. It is only within the past several decades that psychoanalysis has acknowledged the diversity of its models and the magnitude of the shift away from what were originally, for Freud, "shibboleths" of psychoanalysis. Psychoanalysts have tended to disguise the extent of change, unlike workers in most other intellectual fields in which part of the game is the competitive fight to establish the primacy of one's own ideas. The terrible early history of analytic schisms, and the overwhelming authority of Freud, frightened people with new ideas into disclaiming originality in favor of compatibility with Freud. The result was what Joseph Sandler has called an elasticity of psychoanalytic terminology, in which the meanings of words change radically without acknowledgment. One result, of course, is that discourse may become difficult as two people using the same term may mean very different things.

There are various ways of attempting to specify the core propositions of Freud's psychoanalytic theory of the mind, and I shall present one rather oversimplified version of that model, indicating where significant changes have occurred or alternative propositions have been put forward.

Psychic determinism. Mental events are not random and can be traced to antecedent causes. This concept is essential for claiming the mind as a field for scientific study, with explanatory principles that can contribute to the understanding of many other disciplines. Freud never abandoned these goals. As in numbers of other sciences, it does not follow, however, that cause-effect prediction is available. Contrary to Freud, a powerful alternative view today would claim psychoanalysis as a hermeneutic discipline, eschewing all scientific claims, and holding that neurobiological findings are of only marginal interest to analysis. The analytic task is one of narrative creation, without any truth claims.

The dynamic unconscious. Major sources of motivation, because they contain painful and unacceptable memories and desires, are maintained out of awareness and cannot be brought to consciousness by an act of will. I believe this is, in the main, uncontested. There are, however, significant debates concerning whether we should credit unconscious affects and whether a good deal of the so-called past unconscious—the earlier, more primitive aspects of unconscious activity—exists in a form that is unavailable to recall or is in the form of something like procedural memory, not subject to symbolic recall. The issue becomes even more blurred if, as Mark Solms has emphasized, one considers that all mental life is originally unconscious, with some portions emerging into consciousness.[2] If this is intended to mean that brain activity and organization of some kind must precede consciousness, the idea is trivial. If intended to convey that formed thought processes have an unconscious existence before consciousness, perhaps in the form of primary process thought, the idea is more interesting, but we must then attend to whether we are only describing processes out of awareness and how this may relate to the dynamic unconscious. Great attention is being directed today toward exploring mechanisms of splitting, disavowal, and denial—alternative techniques for maintaining unacceptable thoughts and desires within consciousness, but not within awareness as part of the self. For some analysts these mental mechanisms are at least as important as repression in coping with conflict.

The motivational point of view. Freud insisted that the body drove the mind to work and that the two basic drives of libido and aggression underlay every form of mental activity. The compass for directing drive energies was supplied by the pleasure-unpleasure principle. Drive energy could be roughly quantified, and affects were an epiphenomenon of the drives. I can only indicate a few of the powerful challenges to Freud's instinct theory. Importantly, the need for safety has been added to the aims of drive satisfaction. Attachment theory postulates that at least an additional, perhaps more fundamental, source of motivation lies in the inherent need for attachment to another, initially of the infant to its mother. Self-psychology would suggest that the innate program to complete a coherent sense of self takes priority over all other needs in the development of mental life. Some interpersonal theorists maintain that the needs for security—and the avoidance of the annihilation anxiety that occurs in the absence of that security—are at the root of all motivated behavior. The place of affects in motivation has radically changed. Far from being an accompaniment of the drives, emotion is seen by many today as primary, inseparable from cognition, and indispensable in motivation. From the vantage of object-relations theory, the organism is motivated to maintain the best fit with its internalized version of the nature of the self and its objects and the expectable transactions between them, often trading pleasure for the safety of familiarity.

Within traditional theory, *psychic conflict* is ubiquitous, a consequence of the two basic drives of aggression and libido that are always active and can be detected in all human actions; any behavior represents a compromise of these competing desires. A number of theorists—perhaps most conspicuously the self-psychologists—hold that conflict arises only when appropriate empathic responsiveness during the course of development has failed. Heinz Kohut, for example, described conflict-free oedipal passage and resolution when both parents are appropriately attuned to the child's developmental needs. For self-psychologists, psychopathology is more likely to be a result of deficit of structure formation rather than conflict.

The genetic point of view, in the main uncontested, asserts that all behavior is part of a series going back to the beginnings of the individual and that the fullest understanding of any behavior requires knowledge of its antecedents. An associated proposition would assert that all behavior is part of an indivisible whole, with any action being a representation of the workings of the entire organism. These propositions fit neatly with Edelman's and Shulman and Rothman's ideas of brain function.[3] Clinically, the derivatives of the genetic point of view have undergone radical change. A foremost aim of the psychoanalytic technique in Freud's earlier work was to reconstruct the actual etiologic past. Freud later shifted toward a construction of a likely past, and in recent years that has given way to an overriding interest in the present behaviors in the transference, with reference to the past occupying at best a secondary confirming role. Analysis today is much more concerned with understanding current experience, bringing to full awareness the internalized object-relational and affective components of current experience, with a significantly diminished interest in the recovery of the repressed past.

Related to these views is the abandonment of *the structural point of view*— the mind understood as consisting of id, ego, and superego—in favor of more holistic versions of the person in action, and increased emphasis on the role of experience and reality on development, rather than on innate timetables or structures.

A few additional words about the theories of therapy, which have changed in accord with the changes I have already described. Fundamental to many of the changes in technique is an altered view of the nature of mind itself. For many, there is no mind that can be examined apart from the interpersonal or object-relational context in which it is being observed. Furthermore, in these views there is no mind that does not have inherent object-representational and interpersonal schemas built into it. Therefore, there can be no outside observer of the mind; rather, there are only forms of participant observation. From this perspective, every action of the analyst, including his or her flow of feelings and attitudes, whether or not conscious, is influencing the patient at every moment. It follows then that there is no such thing as analytic neutrality; enactments of scenarios unconsciously directed by either analyst or patient or both are inevitable, and the analyst can only hope to be as aware as he or she can be of these interactions. This analytic world has forfeited much of its claim to analytic authority, has abandoned a one-person psychology (the analyst examining the patient) for a two-person psychology of intermeshed minds, and has accepted that the subjectivity of the analyst is as much, or almost as much, a part of the analytic material as is the subjectivity of the patient. The analyst's empathic capacity, the role-responsiveness of the analyst, and the use of the analytic encounter as including a corrective emotional experience are now regarded by most analysts as inevitable and, for many, desirable parts of the analytic process. Verbal interpretation of unconscious content in this view is only one of a number of therapeutic actions taking place in analysis. These views represent a vast shift from the standards of practice that were regarded as almost inviolable only a few years ago.

The era of psychoanalytic imperialism is clearly over, but a new era of interdisciplinary work has a glowing future. A major limitation of this venture stems from the failure of psychoanalysis to develop the cadre of researchers that are needed for adequate response and interaction with other disciplines. Brain research will, I believe, appropriately constrain psychoanalytic theories while lending weight to some aspects of practice and opening others to question. But if psychoanalysis is to play its proper role in helping to explore the mind, we will need to cast our ideas and knowledge in forms that are susceptible to investigation or can guide neurobiological investigators toward exploring the interesting questions. We have only just begun to do that.

Notes

1. Thomas Mann, "Freud and the Future" (1936), in *Essays of Three Decades* (New York: Knopf, 1947), 427–28.
2. Mark Solms, "What Is Consciousness?" *Journal of the American Psychoanalytic Association* 45 (1997): 681–703.
3. Gerald M. Edelman, *Bright Air, Brilliant Fire: On the Matter of the Mind* (New York: Basic Books, 1992); Robert G. Shulman and Douglas L. Rothman, "Freud's Theory of the Mind and Modern Functional Imaging Experiments," this volume.

Discussion

David Forrest: I just want to reply to Bob Shulman, briefly. I'm going to ask him if he really thinks what he's saying is true?

Robert Shulman: Yes.

David Forrest: The imaging technology is progressing so fast it's practically every trimester they have to revise what they have. I have a report from *Science* of 20 March 98 which lists all these brand-new, super-fast, ultra-fast MRI, EPI, RARE, SPIRAL, BURST, GRASS, all acronymic techniques, ecoplanner techniques. The point is that the resolution, the speed, and the penetrance into mental process is so great. Don't you think that this enormous wave of imaging that you had so much a part in developing is going to shed light on dynamic processes, too?

Robert Shulman: I think I'm being misinterpreted, though. I'm not hopeless at all; I'm full of hope, actually, about the future of the field. I think the field can give us a lot of information. However, because it is so easy to get these images, you don't have to think before planning an experiment. So people accept the paradigmatic cognitive psychology as a means of getting information about the brain. All I wanted to point out was that the assumptions you make determine the kind of information that you get. Now there are many ways in which that information is extraordinarily valuable. But people should be aware that there are always assumptions.

For example, I've made the point that the increment of the signal is taken as representing the full mental activity. Well, is that correct in your view of the mind? No. I think that in many people's view of the mind it would be the full activity of the brain in that region, which is localized by these methods, that is involved in the mental activity. Say you have a 100 percent signal at rest, and then the signal in that region goes up by a percent to 101 percent. Do you say the mental activity or the neuronal activity has increased by 1 percent? Then you do another experiment and you get 102 percent. Has that increased by 2 percent? Yes. Then what's happened between those two? Well, in one case you have an increment of 1 percent and in the other case an increment of 2 percent. So the second is twice as big as the first. Or is the second merely 102 percent versus 101 percent?

These are very different views about the amount of neuronal activity which is responsible for the activity that has been plotted. And it's easy enough to get this different information from the same experiments. So it's very important to decide how you think the mind is working.

David Forrest: Suppose the cognitive sciences break down the brain into these very, very tiny bits and can interrelate them all dynamically and simultaneously. Then, wouldn't you be happy?

Robert Shulman: No, no, of course not. But what you can do is break the brain up and see activities in different regions of the brain, and then see how they synchronize in their response. People are doing this and testing the connectivities that you spoke about and Mort [Reiser] spoke about. So measuring connectivities between simultaneous or near simultaneous activities in different parts of the brain is a swell thing to do, and the measurements that are being made can do that. No problem. But connectivities is different from what's taking place in a particular region.

Morton Reiser: May I just add one point to that? Because I think one of the most important things in what Shulman presented was the fact that if we don't recognize that, then imaging becomes a new phrenology. You've got the grammar point, the face recognition point, the depression point. And in fact there was a recent article, that I mentioned, about the dreaming brain, which failed to find an increase in activity in the primary visual cortex. And the false conclusion was drawn that the primary visual cortex isn't involved in the imagery of dreams.

Robert Shulman: You just have to look at one of the theories that you mentioned. The idea that there's supposed to be a place in the brain which doesn't recognize faces is an absurdity. That there's going to be a spot in the brain, and if you have trouble or elision there, you're not going to recognize faces. And this therefore is a face recognition point, which actually has a name. That's ridiculous, there's no such thing. I mean if you think that's the way brain works, then it's not ridiculous. I don't think that's the way the brain works. So you have a choice. How do you think the brain works? How are you going to interpret the experiment? Where you start is where you end.

Elise Snyder, Moderator: I'd like to ask a question to all the panel, about the enormous amount of activity which you demonstrated taking place in the brain. And I would like you all to address, if you will, what you think is going on with all that activity. What's that all about?

Arnold Cooper: I don't think it's a question that those large pieces of the brain are not involved in the task. The contemporary view of many at least is that all of the brain, or most of the brain, is involved in every task. One or another piece may be essential for particular tasks—and therefore you can see that the absence of this piece removes the capacity to do that task—but the accomplishment of that task still involves huge chunks of the rest of the brain in a complicated set of networks that we haven't even begun to unravel.

People like to do the math of this. They've done calculations on how the X number of billions and billions of connections in the brain outnumber all the particles in the known universe. So there's a lot going on. And here I think I would disagree with David, we're not going to come up with quantization of all of this. We're going to come up with mappings, some of which will always be qualitative, I believe. Then the question—for those of us who have a more complicated vision of the mind than the cognitive psychologists perhaps have—is: What can we do to help frame questions that enable people like Bob and Mort to start dissecting what tasks are conducted by that other 99 percent of the brain that isn't measured?

David Forrest: According to chaos theory, there's a butterfly effect. If one butterfly flaps its wings it affects all the weather all over the world. True. But you know when Hurricane Hugo hits the South and doesn't hit us, it doesn't make that much difference. In all of this mental activity, there are all kinds of complicated gatings and emphases which can be studied by these techniques, that make sense out of them. It may be true that all of the brain is always lit up, but it isn't all lit up equally as much every time. And the exact amount that each part can be lit up can be measured pixel by pixel. I still think there can be a great deal more specification. Otherwise we're just left with Karl Lashley's cerebral nonlocalization again, that it's all a big mush.

Robert Shulman: I think that Mort and I have a lot in common, and I really enjoyed his talk. We both have a historical sense about brain studies. They're going to go on for a long, long time. And if anything gives you a sense of the historical nature of science, it's working on the brain. Because you know it's going to look so different. Mort proposed ways of comparing two different fields—including Freudian psychology—and maybe devising some sense of communal agreement. I, of course, would concentrate more on *dis*agreement and look for some differences between the two.

The other question that I was fascinated by, more than the bringing together of different fields, was how much energy is needed by the brain. There are experiments which point out that the total activity of the brain is needed in a particular activity, rather than the increment. And I'd be happy to talk about them. But we now need to look for differences where experiments will distinguish one idea from another. And this is a process we're talking about, not the kind of static answer which I'm afraid you were asking for and which of course in my opinion would be premature—static or predictive would be premature.

Morton Reiser: I would just add one thing, if it's adding anything to it at all. And that is again to emphasize that the brain is part of the body, and it's more complicated even than just the networks of the brain. And I think it really will require the kind of intellectual genius of people like Edelman, who see this as a total holistic picture and who are able to begin to model it in different ways than these networks which are pragmatically useful now. I didn't really think it had to be identity from the two sides, but isomorphism. When they start to converge, perhaps, we'll be able to get it. Given all this, I think that attempts to map mind onto brain are premature. We really should do it in modules and stages.

David Forrest: Can I reply to that? You picked, of course, a computer scientist, Edelman, and I'm wondering: do you think that computer science eventually will understand the mind more than departments of English and history and social science and so forth? Because our human minds are very limited and the development of computers is not.

Morton Reiser: But Edelman really is a biologist and not a computer scientist.

David Forrest: Lately he thinks he is.

Morton Reiser: Well, you know—

Arnold Cooper: Let me just interrupt for a moment. I just came, for better or worse, from a two-day conference with Edelman. And he's at great pains to deny that he is a computer scientist, or that computer modeling of the mind will do anything more than help us have a few models. Computational notions of the mind are basically incorrect according to him.

David Forrest: Of course they are. So are all of Freud's models. But it's a step.

Morton Reiser: Well, you know, Edelman has his little machines that run around, Darwin One and Two and so on. They're giant computer models and they can learn to separate configurations from the environment and reach them and move out to them. They can learn but, again, they're just little pieces of the overall picture, it seems to me.

Robert Shulman: Can I take it back to the conference? Throughout the Freudian literature everyone agrees that Freud, of course, was basically a scientist, and basically believed in neuroscience. But the fact of the matter is that Freudian psychiatrists and psychologists have done very, very little about neuroscience. I don't mean to be critical. I tried today to take this modern field of imaging and make the case that if you are really interested in a neuroscientific basis—or biological basis, it's sometimes called—of brain activity, you have to do something like what Mort suggested. Or *something*, if you want to use it to understand a biological basis for Freudian ideas. You have to formulate your hypotheses and put them to work in the experiment. And you have to realize that the paradigm in the field today is different than you assume to be the case.

So if someone tries to explain schizophrenics or schizophrenia by comparing the patient and some normals, and gets them to do a task in cognitive science, some task of finishing words or recognizing faces, you could use that as a symptom of some sort, but it is not approaching the problem of that particular disease in the terms that you would like to start with. And so, don't use a very complex cognitive neuroscientific functional imaging experiment to examine a state of the mind which you don't think can be explained by those sorts of methods.

David Forrest: I think that's a hard sell. I agree with that, having started with schizophrenia myself, but I think it's a hard sell nowadays. The people, the sufferers and families of schizophrenia, want to find a specific deficit and then to build on that. And they say that all the rest of the adjustments and dynamics of psychoanalysis are secondary.

Robert Shulman: I don't think that bad experiments are good for sick people and their families.

Elise Snyder: We will open the discussion to the audience now.

Robert Michels: My question is really addressed to Professor Shulman, but I want some help from the others in pressing him down on this. It seems to me that he's gone a little bit too far. He's presenting the brain sort of as equivalent to the liver or maybe the kidney. And it's somewhat different, in that there is some modularization, some specialization of component function and activity.

It seems to me there's a metaphor that we might use, which is that other repository of information, the genetic system, the genome. The geneticists tell us that single gene effects probably explain 1 or 2 percent of human diseases. And for the genetic determination of others we have to look to various poly and interactive genetic things. There is probably some interesting experimentation to be done with modular cognitive psychology strategies that will pick up 1 or 2 percent of what's interesting about mental activity. A modular model is not worthless in approaching brain and mental functioning. It's simply very weak. But it has the advantage of being easily translatable into experimental strategies, whereas our stronger models are harder to translate into the paradigms we need for correlation with localizing imagery methodologies. So we ought not to discard the technique, we ought to see it as a very primitive stage of using the new methodology.

Robert Shulman: I come here as someone who has worked very hard in this field that I am talking about. And I still do work in it. I do not intend to disregard or to stop experiments in modular. But I think it is very interesting how many assumptions go into the work that one does. And I have been trying to make the argument here that you could take your own assumptions and do your own experiments.

There are experiments which suggest that one could actually show that the amount of brain activity needed to perform a certain task is the full activity in that region. For example, you take an anaesthetized rat and you bring it down to half the activity of rest. And you give it a task to do which normally at rest takes 10 percent of additional energy. So at rest the rat would go from a 100 per-

cent to 110 percent of the signal which we are measuring. Question: The anaesthetized rat down at 50 percent, will he go up by 10 percent, because the additional energy needed to do the task is purely 10 percent modular, or will he have
to go back to a 100 percent and then to 110 percent? Answer: In the rat literature
many, many experiments show he goes back to 110 percent.

This gives a view of what is taking place in the mind. And that's the kind of
thing that I'm here to present. I agree that there is considerable, wonderful information available from the localization that exists. However, these localization
pictures—as has been mentioned several times by David Forrest and as Arnold
[Cooper] also mentioned—show that there is some statistically significant spot
here or there, but there is activity then all throughout the rest of the brain. Do
you want to go on ignoring that activity? What you are espousing here is the majority, almost the exclusive view. I'm taking quite a minority position, suggesting that we can get much more information about it. There is a lot to be done
for localized activities in terms of connectivity, the rapidity of response, measuring blood flow, and measuring energetics and correlating them with what's
taking place. But I'm offering you an opportunity to take advantage of this field,
which has been taken away from you.

Dominick LaCapra: One problem you have raised is the degree to which you
can really localize certain processes, either in parts of the brain or in terms of
certain activities of the brain. And I think that humanists are very interested in
this question. One person who you haven't mentioned, and whose status I think
is somewhat controversial, is Bessel van der Kolk. And Cathy Caruth, among
others, has looked to his work as a way of providing rather graphic and literal
confirmation of some rather intricate theories, his argument being that trauma
is localized in the right side of the brain, as is evidenced by firing picked up by
PET scans.[1] And this is very nice—you can certainly contest it in that all of the
brain is involved in these functions—but if it were true it would be very nice.
Because that would mean you would have an image deposited almost literally,
as an imprint in one side of the brain, that would be inaccessible to verbalization. And the problem of therapy would be to create patterns of translation or
modes of access from this image to verbalization. Now that is an incredibly sim-
plistic idea, but it has great appeal. And humanists, who are usually involved in
very intricate theories, have their knees go weak when they hear scientific facts
that possibly confirm what they're doing. This model of van der Kolk is very
convenient for theories of splitting. And he wants to reject the notion of the un-

conscious. If you accept the notion of repression, a problem would obviously be, how could you approach blockage? Could you in some sense have at least correlative blockage in terms of brain patterns?

Morton Reiser: I just want to start; I can't answer all of that. Most of what we know about right and left brain, and their highly specialized forms, come from studies of patients on whom the connections have been severed between them. In the intact person the two sides are in communication, it's more a matter of emphasis on one side or another. And even some of the split-brain people, if given enough chance, can begin to develop language function on the right side. So it seems to me again, we need to ask how appropriate the model is to the question. And we can't jump to conclusions.

One other thing. There is a psychoanalytic hypothesis of Freud's that something goes into repression when its word label is taken away from it. Well now, with functional imaging it might be possible to do some very sophisticated imaging studies of people who have an aphasia or have a temporary block, and see more clearly whether there is some way that the word does change the total representation of an idea.

David Forrest: In fact, it's fairly easy to subtract the verbal activity because we know where those sites are, and they are fairly localized. And sometimes very tiny lesions can remove—

Morton Reiser: But it's where they connect up with—

David Forrest: And where they connect up is important. But it is possible to do PET and other functional ways of removing those. And also strokes are an enormous area of information. Strokes actually can show you how the human mind categorizes. And some of the categories that seem to be ganged together are rather surprising. There are categories for animals and for tools that you use outside—things that you wouldn't predict, that people can have a specific agnosia, a lack of recognition for. Some of the neurology meetings are very interesting epistemologically.

Question: When Freud formulated his theory of the mind, he did it in relation to different areas of biology. One was neurophysiology—instincts, reflexes, his work on aphasia—but the other was evolutionary psychology, which in his day was Lamarck. And a really crucial part of psychoanalysis is the idea that the mind evolved through millennia of adaptation to the environment, that the instincts themselves evolved, and so forth. This is crucial to a lot of the social and historical dimension of psychoanalysis. Now since Freud, neurophysiological theory has evolved, as we have seen today, in ways that are very promising in relation to psychoanalysis. But no one, of course, can accept Freud's Lamarckianism. So the question that I have is on the evolutionary dimension. The only thing that I know which really resounds with Freud is the idea of the evolution of the emotions that goes back to Darwin's *Expression of the Emotions.*[2] I don't think that sociobiology has anything to offer psychoanalysis. So is there not a gap, a certain half of the biological side, still missing?

Arnold Cooper: Just to comment briefly on that. Any working psychoanalyst or any thoughtful psychoanalyst of course assumes that evolution has made our minds ultimately, if not made our minds up, and that we are a product of it. The problem that exists today is that evolutionary psychology has captured the popular imagination in the way that spot imaging has captured the imagination. And evolutionary psychology, which seeks to understand behavior in terms of the genetic components that have made us, seems to me totally wrong-headed in the light of all that we know about genetic expression. Since, given whatever genetic makeup you want, with very few exceptions in a few extraordinary diseases, the large majority of what goes into the makeup of an individual is experiential, not genetic. Even very strong temperamental events that can be identified in infancy are malleable to degrees that are quite surprising. Not infinitely malleable, but hugely so. So to use evolution as an individual or even mass human explanatory principle would seem to me terribly premature when we barely understand all the rest of the interactions that go on interrelationally.

Robert Jay Lifton: As I heard the panelists, I couldn't help but wonder how Arnie Cooper's presentation related to the other three. And nobody really took that up. So my question is twofold. Is there something now in contemporary neuroscience that shares common features with a certain direction of psychoanalysis: more holistic, less mystified by instincts, more concerned with self and other and self and environment? Is there something in the contemporary intellectual milieu that connects that with brain imaging? The second question is: Does that development in psychoanalysis contribute to studies of brain imaging? Taking what the speakers emphasized about our concepts being crucial to what one finds out from the imaging or any such research.

David Forrest: I was going to ask something like that of Arnie, too, actually. As to whether he thinks that psychoanalysis is actually evolving in a particular direction, or whether it's picking things to emphasize, serially, in all of Freud's grab-bag? Myself, I hate to see any part of analysis abandoned, but I think the self material directly relates to, as I said, the misidentification and other neural structures. But so does the idea of ego agency, and what would be id and affect production. And so would the economic hypothesis.

Arnold Cooper: I think there's no question that there's a direction in which psychoanalysis has been evolving. You've mentioned it. It's evolved from Freud's initial attempts to specify very particular aspects of how the mind ran, very similar in a way to what Bob [Shulman] is describing as the current state of neuroimaging. There's an instinct and there's a set of very nameable things from which one can trace derivatives. It has evolved from this towards much more complex interrelational aspects of human development, in which internal representation plays a much larger role than it initially did in Freud. And in which the role of attachment from early on has to a considerable extent displaced the notion of instinct as providing attachment.

The problem is that at this point all of our data is coming from clinical psychoanalysts who are of schools. The schools have begun to talk to each other, but not adequately. The theorists of various schools are often incomprehensible to theorists of other schools. The languages have only just begun to interpenetrate. And the propositions are still sufficiently broad so that they are not of help to Bob Shulman and people who are doing his work, who would like to be able to investigate the kinds of propositions that we think are interesting, that Mort points to and has begun to indicate pathways towards. But as far as I'm concerned, this is the headiest time in psychoanalysis since the early days of Freud. Ideas are now competing, and ideas are being exchanged. And I think there will be some newer resolution out of this that will last for a while, perhaps providing a basis for other kinds of research.

Notes

1. See Bessel A. van der Kolk and Onno van der Hart, "The Intrusive Past: The Flexibility of Memory and the Engraving of Trauma," in *Trauma: Explorations in Memory,* edited by Cathy Caruth (Baltimore: Johns Hopkins University Press, 1995), 158–82.
2. See Charles Darwin, *The Expression of the Emotions in Man and Animals,* edited by Paul Ekman (Oxford: Oxford University Press, 1998).

Part Six **Psychoanalysis: What Kind of Truth?**

Introduction

Panel Six places philosophical models of truthfulness face to face with the psychoanalytic session. Whereas psychoanalytic theory relies on a horizon of truthfulness, psychoanalytic praxis revolves around an alert attention to the probable fictiveness of the analysand's truth (intentional statements, recovered memories) and the probable truthfulness of his or her fictions (performative acting-out, symbolic transferences). As a comment in the discussion section puts it: "the manifest, apparent story or truth sometimes is only a communication about a hidden more interesting truth"; or as John Forrester more dramatically claims, in psychoanalysis "a 'no' may mean 'yes', and a 'yes' almost certainly does not mean this particular 'yes.'"

What, then, is the relation between the philosophy of truth and the problem of truth and falsehood within the analytic situation? Donald Davidson, the acclaimed language philosopher, poses the question by pointing to the priority of interpretation over evaluation. Davidson highlights the way that for any statement, an interpretive question— what does the statement *mean?*—must precede an evaluation of this statement's truthfulness. Davidson insists that few statements are directly accessible to evaluation: "It is seldom that we use words that literally express what we want to convey to a hearer. Even when we are saying what we believe, with no attempt to exaggerate, deceive, or misrepresent, we often do not mean what we literally say." The distinction he draws between "literal" meaning and "metaphorical" meaning—illustrated through the common idiom that "no man is an island"—establishes a semantic model within which to approach the more complicated divergence between actual and literal meaning posited by psychoanalysis: a divergence that Davidson touches on through an amusing autobiographical story that is literally false but "unknowingly" reveals a truth.

The three other essays all dive into the analytic situation, examining particular experiences between analysts and analysands in order to approach the general question of truth. Richard Wollheim discusses an analytic session led by a psychoanalytic candidate that was itself analyzed in a seminar led by Betty Joseph. Wollheim pays attention both to the different levels of meaning within this material and to the reconstruction of these levels in the analysis *of* the analysis. The session was marked by an *overproduction* of meaning, an "avalanche" of rich material that overwhelmed the analyst. Shifting from what the patient was saying to what she was "doing" by saying so much, the seminar postulates a paradigmatic transference: a reenactment, and transformation, of the patient's childhood relationship to an inaccessible mother. The patient's seemingly disclosing monologue thus actually anticipates the analyst's inability to arrive at the truth of it: making the analyst, like the mother, a person unable to listen or be intimate. Finally, through scrutiny toward the candidate's own free associations about the session, the seminar postulates a third, more aggressive level of meaning—an aggression that has left the candidate quite unsettled, provoking a strong countertransference.

If Wollheim shows how literal truth is embedded within performative contexts of transference and countertransference, Jonathan Lear shows how "truth" can function as a defense within psychoanalysis. Ingeniously using the distinction between the coherence and correspondence theories of truth, Lear specifies two different ways that truth can function to forestall or block psychoanalytic insight. In a version of the correspondence theory of truth, an analysand comes to focus on discovering an "origin" of his or her neurosis, a history to which his or her psychic state will correspond. As Lear writes, "If the analyst were simply to go along with the search for historical reality or the attempt to recover a memory, he or she would in fact be collaborating with the analysand's defenses." Instead of immediately accepting the truth of such a history, the analyst must once again pay attention to what such a history *does,* within the context of the analysis as a whole, rather than only to what it says. Shifting to a coherence theory of truth, Lear finds a parallel obstacle "when an analysand comes into analysis with the hope of constructing an interpretation of his or her life": to build a coherent personality that will circumscribe, and thus control, the byways and paths of the analysis. This kind of defensive truth is particularly threatening because it inevitably plays on the analyst's own desires for a coherent interpretation; as Lear writes, "There is great temptation for the analyst to collaborate with this wish."

John Forrester also shows how statements within psychoanalysis, before they can be evaluated, must be *situated* within the analytic context. Whereas Lear distinguishes between truth "outside" and "inside" psychoanalysis, Forrester analyzes four kinds of statements: looking at the way both an analyst and an analysand make statements that operate within analysis and comment upon analysis. These different perspectives illustrate the complex relation between "performative" and "constative" speech: the way that an analyst's announcement of "truth" might enact the very delusions it aims to dissipate, or the way that what seems like a ludicrously transferential association by the Wolfman— "Jewish swindler he would like to use me from behind and shit on my head,"—*can* be assigned literal truth by a skeptical critic of psychoanalysis.

Notably, and suggestively, Forrester and Lear both do not stop by showing the slippery value of truthfulness within the analytic context; rather, both end by shifting attention to the activity generated in relation to truth. If patients cannot confidently see truth as an endpoint of analysis, they can use the process of truth-seeking to reestablish a proactive and energetic relationship to their own consciousness. We can note similarities in these rich statements, by Forrester and Lear, respectively:

> If one of the classic goals or projects of the patient is to find the truth of their inner life and their history . . . the analytic experience leaves them little of substance to set down for the book-keepers of permanent truths. What they experience instead is the actual drama of their histories, the living of their lies, in the experience of the analytic relation and its process.

> In making the unconscious conscious, it is well known that the analysand gains a certain freedom with respect to what had been an automatic repetition, that new aspects of life are brought under a person's cognitive control; it is also the case that emotional vitality returns to living. . . . When an interpretation is truthful in psychoanalysis, the crucial point, I think, is that it takes up *the very same* emotional-phantastic activity . . . and brings that activity into language. Emotional vividness, a sense of being alive, that this really is who one is starts to pour back into what now seems to have been an empty shell of living.

Psychoanalytical Theory
and Kinds of Truth

Richard Wollheim

I attribute the strange title of this section to the historical fact that people who have become pessimistic about how to connect psychoanalysis with truth, or how to confirm or disconfirm psychoanalytic propositions, whether of a theoretical or an applied kind, have nevertheless continued to hold psychoanalysis in high esteem, and they have thought to resolve the issue by inventing a new value, or virtue, which they still call "truth," but then append to it a qualifier, like "metaphoric," or "narrative." Thus they take away with one hand what they bestow with the other.

One of the reasons for such pessimism is the old positivist conviction that all meaningful propositions come with their method of verification written into them. Once we rid ourselves of this myth, and recognize that it sometimes takes skill, ingenuity, and imagination to devise ways of testing the propositions of science, psychoanalysis may very well turn out to be in no worse a position than its subject-matter necessitates. Human nature makes observation difficult, experiment virtually out of the question, and complexity pervasive.

One area where we might look to test psychoanalytic findings is provided by the psychoanalytic session, so little discussed in this volume: the reason presumingly being that it cannot properly be discussed without some practical experience of the process. In introducing some clinical material that I think is of evidential interest, I shall move away from Freud himself into a less noisy area. The immediate environs of Freud have been made clamorous by the voices of those who totally reject Freud, and by the voices of those who totally accept Lacan. Different voices, but to my ear to the same effect.

Consider a small vignette, based on one meeting of a weekly seminar, in which psychoanalytic candidates would meet, and discuss cases that they were treating with their supervisor. The supervisor was Betty Joseph, a Kleinian analyst working in London, and I owe this very interesting fragment to her book *Psychic Equilibrium and Psychic Change.*

A fairly young candidate was reporting on a patient whom she had had for some time in therapy, and the therapy had had a chequered career. The patient was a woman in her thirties, somewhat difficult, easily aroused to anger, and evidently the daughter of inaccessible parents. In the session being reported on, the patient appeared primed with a great deal of seemingly interesting material, which was rare, and she let it all fall out. It came in an avalanche. The candidate, who was somewhat overwhelmed, did her best, and ventured a correspondingly large number of interpretations, heterogeneous in character, none of which particularly satisfied her. Meanwhile the patient expressed no opinion on any of them, but seemed pleased with the way things were going. Throughout she was blithe.

The other candidates in the seminar tried to improve on the original interpretations, but to no one's satisfaction. Furthermore there was the awareness that, if these new suggestions had actually been offered to the patient as interpretations, the session would have fallen to pieces under the sheer weight of the material. Could it be that this is what the patient wanted?

At this stage the supervisor remarked that it might be profitable to shift attention away from the content of what the patient was saying, and to concentrate instead on what the patient might be doing in saying it.

A plausible proposal along these lines, which thereby established a second level to the session, was that the patient was enacting a certain internal drama, or phantasy. In this phantasy, the patient, now back into her childhood, is saying things of an intimate kind to her distant, or inaccessible, mother, whom the candidate is obliged to enact. The mother is portrayed as willing to listen, but as either unable to do so or unable to comprehend what she hears. The patient notices her mother's failure, and is—and this we may believe to have been the most important part of the phantasy as far as the patient herself was concerned—completely unaffected by it. She expects nothing better, and remains completely happy. She can survive her mother's remoteness.

One thing to note about this second level to the phantasy, or to the process of its enactment, is that the patient is able to bring this off while the first level of the session is strictly maintained. To all appearances, the patient is simply following the first rule of psychoanalysis: in fact, doing so in a particularly conscientious way.

The candidates accepted this as very likely to be true of what was going on, but there was the feeling amongst the candidates that the session was still incompletely described. One thing not accounted for was something that the candidate who presented the case continued to insist was very important, and these were her feelings during, and even more after, the session. She felt bruised from the occasion, and she was convinced that, while the patient was clearly doing something *for herself,* she was just as surely doing something *against her analyst.*

To account for the analyst's feelings, a third level to the analysis was proposed, and the suggestion now was that the patient was prompted, not just by one phantasy, but by two. Whereas the first phantasy was primarily a denial of the patient's inner state—no, she was not unhappy, she was happy—the second phantasy provided a script, or scenario, which, if acted upon, might alter her inner state. For the phantasy promised that, if the patient would only articulate the internal thoughts that were making her unhappy, she might get rid of that part of herself to which these thoughts belonged: she might, the phantasy continued, get rid of it by stuffing it into the listening mother.

Obviously the enactment of the second phantasy has considerable overlap with that of the first phantasy. In both cases, the patient plays a specific aspect of herself, and the candidate plays the mother, and, in both cases, this can be carried out without interference to the first level of the session. Throughout the patient can be the "good" patient. But, this second time through, the younger self that the patient plays is not the long-suffering, misunderstood, but ultimately unaffected, child of the first phantasy. She is an angry, vengeful child, eliminating the bad parts of herself, in a punitive way, into her mother. And, this time, the mother is not just baffled: she is made to suffer. And suffering is precisely what the candidate feels—and now a technical phrase—in the countertransference.

I have introduced a technical phrase for a reason that I shall come to in a moment.

For let us now observe how this small fragment of a session bears out certain psychoanalytical ideas. In the first place, it confirms the general conception of the transference with which applied, or clinical, psychoanalysis works: that is to say, the patient brings into the session, and then projects upon its course, thus diverting it, but appearing not to do so, the principal constituents of his or her character structure. Secondly, in the case of this particular patient, it confirms, through the detail of the transference, material that psychoanalytic theory links with her particular structure: it shows certain desires and certain anxieties, and certain defence mechanisms that are invoked either to curb these desires or to attenuate these anxieties.

But let us at the same time observe that the session can be seen to do all this only if we first do one thing. We must first bring the crucial moments in the session under certain technical categories. We use certain terms of art to describe what the patient is doing. So we recognize her to be *acting out* a certain phantasy. She behaves as if the phantasy were true of the world, in the hope that it will become so. Then, as this fails, and the patient's blitheness in the face of the mother-analyst's incomprehension cannot be sustained, we recognize her to be *projectively identifying* into the mother-analyst the anxieties that she can no longer control. She phantasizes that this is what she is doing, in the hope that this is how it will turn out.

Of course, in redescribing the patient's behavior in this technical language, we are doing more than this. We are offering some kind of explanation of that behavior. And that is because each psychoanalytic category—*acting out,* or *projectively identifying*—contains a reference to a psychological mechanism, triggered by the patient, and this mechanism is a cause of the behavior that the category describes.

I have thought it important to make this last point because it goes against what was said by the first speaker, Fred Crews, who asserted that it was quite wrong to test—that is, try to validate, or invalidate—a given theory against propositions derived from it. There are various ways of taking this assertion, but I thought that the most charitable was to understand it as claiming that it was quite wrong to test a theory against propositions brought under the theory, or cast in terms of it. (I recall the speaker saying that the evidence that is used in support of a theory ought to be expressed in a way that would be comprehensible to someone who was an outsider to the theory, perhaps indeed—though here I may malign him—to the science itself.) Such a claim is clearly a gross exaggeration of anything that science could ask for, as was pointed out by the second speaker, Robert Michels.

On Truth

Donald Davidson

Much that we are tempted to say about truth is false. We think we can explain the truth of the sentences we utter or of what we think by saying they correspond to the facts—we call on the *relation* of correspondence (or, in the case of the early Wittgenstein, the relation of picturing) to explain the *property* of truth. But as an explanation of truth this is empty, not only because if there were such a relation we could never perceive that it holds, but because no one has ever succeeded in giving a viable account of the entities (facts, states of affairs, situations) to which truths are supposed to correspond. The reason for this is that we have no way of specifying the fact that makes the sentence "Lions are nocturnal" true except by saying it is the fact that lions are nocturnal, and this does not go in a circle; it goes nowhere.

The totality of our beliefs might, or so we hope, sometimes turn out to contain no logical inconsistencies. Yet it is obvious that this would not ensure the truth of this coherent corpus of beliefs, as some idealists have held. Truth is not mere coherence. Nor is truth, as William James claimed, what is good in the way of belief, or what it is "good to steer by." It is often useful to know what is true, but not always, so truth cannot be identified with what it is useful to believe; it can be stunningly useful to believe a falsehood.

Richard Rorty has said that as a pragmatist he sees no difference between what we are justified in believing or saying and what is true. There is something to this: it makes no sense to consult all the evidence we can find, check our figures, design and carry out experiments, and then, as a last and additional step, ask whether our hypothesis is true. When we have done all we can to confirm a thesis, the pursuit of truth is not a further chore. So Rorty is right that truth is not a goal or norm in addition to the norms of validation. Every attempt to justify a belief yields more beliefs; beliefs provide the only reasons we can have for beliefs. But beliefs can always be false, and therefore we can be fully justified and yet be wrong. So it is true that as a goal of inquiry, truth does not differ from justification; but it doesn't follow that truth is identical with what is justified.

Nor is truth what science will end up with in the limit, as Charles Sanders Peirce taught (since science may go in a circle), or what the majority of right-thinking people maintain, as Rorty at one time suggested. And so forth. There is no defining truth, as a number of sensible philosophers have held, and Alfred Tarski proved, and there is no short formula that sums up the idea. No wonder those who seek definitions, analyses, or short answers have been frustrated when it comes to the concept of truth.

There is something troubling about the concept. On one hand, truth seems coolly distant from human concerns; we never know for sure that our beliefs are true, and as I just remarked, it isn't sensible to make truth a goal over and above the search for justification. The weight of neutrinos, the beginnings of the universe, the origin of species, the details of what explains how animals develop, whether the universe will go on expanding forever—these truths owe nothing to us. The truth in each of these cases has always been, and always will be, independent of what we believe, independent of our existence.

There is an "on the other hand." On the other hand, nothing in the world would be true or false if it were not for us. Truths may be eternal, but the entities that are true or false are just our states of belief, our utterances, and our scribblings. We talk of sentences and propositions as being true or false, but these are abstractions that would be of no interest if the sentences were never uttered or the propositions never believed or doubted. The magic predicate "true" would have no application if it were not for us.

In a way, it is easy to straighten out the apparent tension between truth as a human creation and truth as almost totally independent of us. Though nothing in this world would be true or false aside from our thoughts and sayings (and writings), *whether* those thoughts or utterances are true is not, in general, up to us. So what's the problem? The complication is this: our utterances are true or false, *given what they mean*. What decides this? Until we know what an utterance or inscription means, or know the propositional content of a belief or other thought, we do not know what is needed even to raise the question of truth. It is here, in the arena of interpretation, that issues concerning "kinds" of truth arise.

They arise, first of all, when we realize that it is seldom that we use words that literally express what we want to convey to a hearer. Even when we are saying what we believe, with no attempt to exaggerate, deceive, or misrepresent, we often do not mean what we literally say. If I say, "No man is an island," what I literally say is no doubt true; an island is a piece of land surrounded by water, and no man is a piece of land surrounded by water. This is what I literally say, and it is something I believe, but it isn't what I mean, or what my utterance means. What I mean, of course, is that no one is entirely isolated from his or her human environment; this is also true, and something I believe. Both truths are relevant to understanding what was said, but in quite different ways. The first is relevant only because we have to know the truth *conditions* of the utterance taken literally if we are to grasp the metaphor. We would not understand the metaphor if we did not know what a man, or an island, was. The truth of the second "meaning," the metaphorical meaning, if we like to talk that way, is the truth of what was meant. We may be uncertain whether what was meant in this sense is actually true, but we can be fairly sure of what the speaker intended us to take as true.

Of course, there are many other ways in which truth may be relevant to an utterance. When I was about to be born, the doctors told my father that they could save the mother or the child, but not both. My father made the sensible choice, and I was discarded. It was only after I loudly protested that measures were taken to see if I, too, could be kept alive. I told this story, believing that my mother had told it to me, until I was forty-some years old, when she informed me that it was completely false and that she had never told the story to me. If you know all this, you will take my story to be literally false, and what I consciously intended to convey by telling it false. My story has the marks of a standard tale of the birth of heroes, so no doubt there was something I hoped to convey beyond the literal meaning; and you, knowing that the story is almost certainly false, will also think there is a truth about me that I unknowingly revealed by telling my tale. (At this point I touch, for the first and last time, on matters that are of direct concern in this volume.)

Understanding anything a speaker says requires that we get the literal meaning, for everything implicated, intentionally or unintentionally suggested, ironically or metaphorically conveyed, is conveyed by way of the literal. But what is the literal meaning? One way to think about it is to reflect on how we learn a first language or, for that matter, a second if we do not have a bilingual speaker or dictionary to prompt us. What we have to go on is the verbal behavior of others. We will first learn one-word sentences, through overt ostension, or the implicit ostension that connects, for the learner, items or episodes in the shared and observed world with sounds. At this stage, there is not even the possibility of error: whatever the learner observes as consistently correlated with a sound provides the content of the utterance. (This can be corrected and refined subsequently, but the point remains: whatever content words have is conferred on them by the observable usage of speakers.)

When the learner becomes a speaker in his or her own right, those who understand him or her will become learners in turn; they will be learning to understand his or her idiolect. The idea of a shared *language* is a myth, a useful myth that allows us to group together people who mean more or less the same thing by the same words. But when we want to evaluate the truth of what speakers say, we cannot count on knowing what they mean except by learning their particular idiolect, and *it* is the product, in the individual, of a social process. In this sense, and in this sense only, truth is a social construct.

Truth in Psychoanalysis

Jonathan Lear

Roughly speaking, there are two ways to approach the concept of truth in psychoanalysis, "from the outside" and "from the inside." In working "from the outside," we bring a conception of truth, developed, say, in philosophy, to psychoanalysis as an object of study. Truth, then, is deployed as a *meta*theoretical concept or predicate, applied to the assertions of psychoanalysis, and allowing us to see the conditions under which those assertions are true. By contrast, when we are working "from the inside," we are concerned with how the issue of truth arises *within* the analytic situation. There is value in each approach, but it is important not to confuse them: for that is ultimately to confuse what is grist with what is mill.

In this essay I want to work "from the inside," and my reflections will draw on my clinical experience. I hasten, therefore, to emphasize that I do not take myself to be making sweeping generalizations, but rather to be giving examples that I think provide illuminating paradigms. I have found that when the concept of truth emerges in the analytic situaiton it is as a resistance. This is so for both of the classical conceptions of truth, truth as correspondence and truth as coherence.

The idea of truth as correspondence emerges in an analysand's concern that he or she is getting historical or psychological reality right. What is the source of this concern? I shall consider the concern for historical reality first. One analysand, who spent the second half of his twenties in analysis, had struggled for the previous twenty years with the fact that he was gay. He had denied it to himself, kept himself in a fog, forced himself to date women, and so on. Only by his early twenties did he begin to admit to himself that he was homosexual, and the analysis was in significant part a further step in coming to accept and enjoy his homosexuality. Throughout the early years of the analysis, there was the recurring theme that maybe he had been abused by his father or uncle when he was a child. It was all very hazy, and he kept expressing the hope that the analysis might help him bring this "memory" to light. Of course, I cannot say what did or did not happen to the person when he was an infant. But I do know that, in this case, the desire to find out the historical truth was the expression of a wish that something external to him would both legitimate and absolve him of his homosexuality. In effect, this analysand had invented his own seduction hypothesis and was using it for the same purpose that Freud used his. At its deepest, the seduction hypothesis is not about seduction per se but about the role reality is to play in psychological explanation. The seduction hypothesis treats the intrusion of external reality as an Archimedian point, an end-of-the-line of psychological explanation. ("I'm gay because I was seduced as a child.") It tacitly assumes that historical truth is the one item within an analysis that is itself exempt from analysis. If the analyst were simply to go along with the search for historical reality or the attempt to recover a memory, he or she would in fact be collaborating with the analysand's defenses. For although the analysis would be proceeding in the name of coming to terms with one's homosexuality, in fact it would be acting out one more evasion of it.

In abandoning the seduction hypothesis one does not abandon the concern for truth—after all, what greater difference could there be, clinically, ethically, psychologically, between an actual and an imagined seduction?—one only abandons the idea that truth comes with its own legitimation and thereby absolves one of the need to analyze its meaning for the analysand. In general, I have found that obsessional patients are scrupulous to describe the events they are talking about accurately. The working assumption seems to be that if the analyst cannot find anything that the analysand can recognize as a distortion, there will be nothing to analyze. In this way, the obsessional concern for truth serves as a remarkably recalcitrant resistance. Precisely because the analysand is so concerned with getting the facts right, he or she cannot see to what use he or she is putting this obsession. In this way the concern for truth as correspondence to reality can serve as a massive obstacle to psychoanalytic understanding.

Similarly with the concern for getting psychological reality right: in one case I listened for a year to a woman talk about her desire to come to terms with her "inner rage," how she did not yet fully understand "the child within" and so on, yet I would get up from each session confused about what was going on. Then one day it dawned on me that I was confused because she was confused: her speech was all Oprah-psychobabble, used defensively to ward off any genuine experience of inner life. This woman's analysis began with her couragous recognition that, really, she had no idea of what her inner life was like. She had grown up in such fear of the power of her wishes that she had managed to confuse herself and keep herself in a fog. She then fastened on women's magazines and talk shows to give her a vocabulary in which to talk about her desires and inner life. There was great concern with getting the facts of her inner life right, with discovering who she really was, and so on, but this concern was itself her way of evading contact with her imaginative life. Again, an analysis that followed her lead would, in the name of discovering psychological reality, be collaborating in the evasion of any such encounter.

The idea of truth as coherence emerges when an analysand comes into analysis with the hope of constructing an interpretation of his or her life. There is, I suspect, a widespread desire that one's life have coherence, meaning, and purpose—and there is a danger that this wish itself will go unanalyzed. For there is great temptation for the analyst to collaborate with this wish. After all, the analytic situation is constructed in such a way that the analyst must endure significant frustration in what he or she says and does. This frustration is made even harder to tolerate by the cultural tide of the past twenty years in which the profession of analysis has been attacked and diminished. It provides relief from that frustration, a sense of professional satisfaction, to join in with the analysand in linking some past event with current experience or behavior. And it is gratifying to see how things fit together. The problem is how to avoid collaborating with the analysand in making things fit together too well. For there is a temptation to enter into a narcissistic collaboration in which both analyst and analysand implicitly congratulate each other on doing a good job. And giving into that temptation is certainly more immediately pleasurable than tolerating the anxiety of not knowing how or if things fit together. As Aristotle recognized, stories tend to have a beginning, a middle, and an end; as Nietzsche recognized, lives often do not. It is precisely the ability to tolerate periods of not knowing that is required for any real psychoanalytic knowing to emerge. In facilitating the construction of a convincing life narrative, one may well be collaborating in the construction of a false self.

Thus far I have been concerned with ways in which the concern for truth as it emerges in analysis can be used as a resistance. But it is part of our life with the concept of truth that truth has a valuable role in our lives. The question is how one might understand the concept of truth within psychoanalysis such that we can see it as a significant psychoanalytic value. When we consider the deployment of the classical conceptions of truth as resistances, we see that they are both concerned with the contents of mental states: whether they correspond to reality or cohere with each other. Perhaps the core conception of truth in psychoanalysis should not be thought of as primarily directed toward contents but rather should be understood as a particular type of mental activity. Truth is a way of living with contents. I should like to suggest that within psychoanalysis, truth should be understood as a certain way of developing fantasy.

Let me give an example from the opening moment of each analytic hour. In my office it begins with analysands either closing or not closing the outer door behind them as they walk in. People tend not to understand how unconscious meanings extend to the tips of their fingers. In the thousands of occasions in which an analysand has come to my office for an appointment, I doubt there has been one in which the physical act of opening or closing the outer door has not been filled with meaning. One analysand, as he entered my office for the beginning of a session, would start to close the outer door behind him but would leave it a fraction of an inch ajar. In the first months of analysis, this was a gesture that officially did not occur. But by the end of the year I realized that I was silently being invited to dance. As his hand let the door handle go, I would see a gesture as delicate as any I have seen in ballet. The next step in the pas de deux was being turned over to me: his fingers *told me* to finish the job and close the door. I, of course, said nothing; but as time passed and the analysand relaxed into his analysis, he eventually became puzzled by this gesture, and here is a small selection of the meanings that began to emerge as he associated to it: He liked getting me to do something, he enjoyed the feeling of control over me, for he knew that I would have to close the door. Leaving the door ajar meant that nothing he was going to say was going to be so important or private that it should not be heard by someone outside. He longed for us both to be working together on a collaborative project, and if we closed the door together, we were a team. Because I noticed he left the door ajar that meant I was sensitive. He was scared of what might happen inside the room and wanted to know that the emergency exit was open and ready for an escape. He was afraid that I might try to rape him from behind and he wanted to be sure people outside could hear his screams. He was hoping that others might accidentally come into my office and then he would get a glimpse of what the rest of my life was like. He was hoping others would come in and he would be the object of their voyeuristic pleasure. He wanted others to know we were a couple. He wanted to be the star in a porno movie. He was teasing me: setting up a game in which he wondered whether I would ever ask him about it. He was testing my analytic resoluteness. Closing the door meant sealing his fate. Closing the door meant there was no escape from facing his own mind. And so on.

It is this kind of elaboration of fantastic-emotional experience that is, I think, the core activity of truth in psychoanalysis. There are a number of points I want to make about this activity, if only in passing: each point really requires an essay of its own. First, one cannot tell simply by looking at the content of the above interpretations whether the activity described is one of "truthification" or one of falsification. As we have seen, it is possible for both analysand and analyst to collaborate in the construction of an ersatz true self. I said that truth was *a certain kind* of elaboration of fantasy, and if I had to give a name to that kind, I would call it "relatively nondefensive," though I am afraid of being misunderstood. The word *defense*, like the word *narcissistic*, has a value neutral use as well as a pejorative use. In the value-neutral use, all mental activity can be viewed as having a defensive function, and in this sense no mental activity is "nondefensive." In the pejorative sense, we are trying to focus on certain pathological rigidities of defense. Truth in psychoanalysis involves the loosening up of those rigidities. In the analytic situation we see this process in the attempt to free associate and in the analysis of the resistances to such association. One might want simply to say that in analysis, truth is free association.

Second, as Freud and Melanie Klein well understood, in psychoanalysis truth emerges from the body. The above interpretations uncovered meanings of fantasies incarnate in the analysand's fingers. Fantasies tend to be expressed, at least in part, in an archaic bodily language: in a gagging reflex, say, when a penis is about to enter a vagina, in difficulty beginning to urinate in a public toilet when one can hear the presence of others, in a nervous cough that can literally break up a thought and clear the mouth of its utterance, in involuntary withholding of feces until one explodes with shit, and in the all-too-familiar heartache, butterflies in the tummy, nausea, and so on. In analysis, these archaic fantasies are taken up again and come to find expression in language. Psychoanalysis began with the recognition of a group of European women at the end of the nineteenth century throwing up, literally as well as figuratively, all over the lives that society and family carved out for them. Anna O., Josef Breuer, and Freud came collectively to shape a method in which physical throwings up were converted into verbal throwings up; and they called this process "catharsis." There have been myriad changes in theory and technique since, but throughout it all, one theme has remained constant: in psychoanalysis, truth is the flesh made word.

A third and related point is that, in psychoanalysis, truth involves the bridging of heterogeneous forms of mental activity. The unconscious is powerful in part because it is constituted by forms of mental activity radically different, and thus split off, from the forms of activity and holistic constraints of preconscious and conscious thought. Analysis brings this heterogeneous activity into some kind of communicative relation with the conscious thoughts and emotional experiences by which it can be understood.

But to understand the nature of this bridging-process we have, finally, to understand truth as a teleological development. In general, I think one needs to maintain a certain skepticism about developmental stories in psychoanalysis because the wishful pull of idealizing myths is difficult to resist. Still, truth does seem to be a developmental process. When I think of the first year of that first split-second of each session when the analysand left the door ajar, I think of an almost-dead ritual. Even the unconscious meanings were all but moribund, floating in a pool of an affectless living. Somehow, in the course of the analysis, the ritual itself started to come to life: there were more variations on a theme, one could feel a heightened intensity and self-awareness as the door was let go. It was as though the ritual itself started to press for its own self-understanding. In making the unconscious conscious, it is well known that the analysand gains a certain freedom with respect to what had been an automatic repetition, that new aspects of life are brought under a person's cognitive control; it is also the case that emotional vitality returns to living. When the infinitely repeated door-leavings were left at that, it was as though they were left to die on the vine. Some emotional development was blocked, and life itself seemed to drain away. Interpreting the door-leavings felt like the resumption of emotional life.

When an interpretation is truthful in psychoanalysis, the crucial point, I think, is that it takes up *the very same* emotional-fantastic activity that had hitherto expressed itself in a door-leaving and brings that activity into language. Emotional vividness, a sense of being alive, that this *really is* who one is starts to pour back into what now seems to have been an empty shell of living. This is what truth as correspondence or coherence misses: The interpretations may well be getting the facts of psychological or historical reality right (correspondence), they may well be forming a compelling narrative with which to understand one's life (coherence), but all of this can be done in a defensive, removed way—as though one were standing outside one's life trying to understand it. The concept of truth in psychoanalysis must be an expression of life itself, not an evasion of it.

Note

I should like to thank Dr. Jean Roiphe for valuable criticisms of a previous draft.

What Kind of Truth?

John Forrester

Mention the word *truth,* and it looks as if one should call in the philosophers. And philosophers themselves do include truth among the standard topics their discipline addresses, along with time, the good, knowledge, and beauty. Yet *truth* is an ordinary word in ordinary use, so it will always be an open question who is in a position to adjudicate on its application and its accomplishment, just as *table* is a word that belongs to all as well as to carpenters, industrial designers, and actuaries. When philosophers are asked to address the question of the kind of truth we can expect from or speak of in relation to psychoanalysis, each of them should bear in mind that there will be others who will have something to say on the topic—principally psychoanalysts and patients—as well as other outside cultural commentators. Yet it would also be foolish not to recognize that philosophers have, since the beginnings of psychoanalysis, taken a great interest in the kind of truth psychoanalysis has generated.

I suspect, however, that most readers up to date with recent commentaries on psychoanalysis will take our question "what kind of truth?" to be, at the very least, an allusion to divisions erected principally by philosophers—between hermeneutic and scientific truth, for instance. First, Wittgenstein and the Oxford philosophers of ordinary language, such as Anthony Flew, Richard Peters, Alisdair MacIntyre, and others, then Jürgen Habermas and Paul Ricoeur, sympathetic critics of psychoanalysis, were the principal proponents of this conceptual dividing up of the territory of truth-saying between the "natural scientific" or "causal" mode of truth enunciation and the "ordinary language" or "interpretative" mode. In the 1980s and 1990s, it then became a habitual if not entirely convincing gesture to "save" psycho-analysis by conceding that it failed to make adequate "natural scientific" truth claims but that it had a privileged position among the hermeneutic or interpre-tative disciplines—alongside history, interpretative sociology, or literary criti-cism. Given that this is an ongoing and consequential debate, there is still room to wonder whether these are the most useful "kinds of truth" that we should continue to consider as providing a habitat for psychoanalysis.

Adolf Grünbaum had the sharp-sightedness to see that a full critique of psy-choanalysis as a purported body of knowledge needs to cut off this line of de-fense. I will not enter into the rights and wrongs of his critique of the hermeneu-tic construal of psychoanalysis, but I will start with his position because, whether he is right or wrong about the relation between reasons and causes, or the speci-ficity of disciplines dealing with "meaning," or the classical debate between un-derstanding and explanation, his position shows us exactly the wrong way to go. And it is, despite his differences with Karl Popper, a wrong way that is preor-dained by the fundamentally positivistic conception of the relationship between the sciences (or, rather, science—since in Grünbaum's vision there can only be one sort of science, conforming to one set of criteria of what constitutes a proper scientific explanation) and truth. Putting it simply, Grünbaum's account of sci-ence conforms entirely to the strategy originally embodied in the classical dis-tinction between sentences that have meaning and sentences that do not—part of the attempt to reserve the term *scientific truth* (the only variety there is) to statements that are meaningful (insofar as they are potentially verifiable or in Popper's version refutable) in the sense that they correspond to "matters of fact."

The reason why Grünbaum's approach leads us down the wrong path is that it assumes an unproblematic answer to the question "true for whom?" The pos-itivists' confident assumption was that there were canons of rationality that were shared by all those competent to discuss the matters under consideration and that therefore there was an unproblematic "subject of scientific knowledge." Whether one regards this subject as unitary and singular—the knower, the scientist, or even the man on the Clapham omnibus, as if we are all on that bus together, for all time—or unitary and collective—the scientific community, the qualified experts, even Gaston Bachelard's "city of savants"—is secondary to the assumption that there is one and only one tribunal of adjudication on matters of truth. With psychoanalysis, alas (or is it, thankfully?), things are not so simple.

In his Introduction, Peter Brooks reminds us that Yale University played a part in the famous visit of Freud to America in 1909. If it is not quite true that the great interest in different circles, medical, academic, and journalistic, stirred by Freud's visit to Worcester, Massachusetts, was the first sign of general, non-professional interest in psychoanalysis, it is certainly true that that visit marked the beginnings of the profound influence of Freud on American life, an influence that is, all journalists and commentators seem to agree, now changing its fundamental character, if not waning entirely. But an event occurred on that trip before Freud set foot in New York that I think captures in microcosm and in a concentrated, purified form what the popular American reception of Freud only repeated. Freud found—one presumes by engaging him in conversation—that his own cabin steward was reading *The Psychopathology of Everyday Life;* it was that discovery that gave Freud his first inkling that he might become more than distinguished; he might become generally famous, indeed popular, even infamous. For me, this meeting was significant because it reveals one of the destinies of psychoanalysis, one that is still in the balance: psychoanalysis will be judged as much by the people—the readers and the long-haul patients, the poets and advertisers, the judges and the filmmakers—as it will be by the experts. And the principal readers of psychoanalysis will always be the people rather than the experts. Freud himself wrote in the preface to the second edition of *The Interpretation of Dreams* in the summer of 1908 that the true market for this "difficult, but in many respects fundamental, work" is not the psychiatrists, philosophers, or small band of enthusiastic followers but "a wider circle of educated and curious-minded readers."[1]

This observation, completely commonplace to anyone who has paid any attention to reader-response theory or to any recent historical work in the history of ideas and intellectual movements, such as Robert Darnton's on the readership of the *Encyclopédie* and the Enlightenment, is the starting point for a broad recognition that there will be a number of different groups, or epistemological subjects, for whom psychoanalysis offers "truths" (or fails to, as the particular fortunes of the case may be). Alongside the philosopher, then, will be the cabin steward, not to speak of the analysts in their capacity as knowledge- and practice-oriented experts, or of their patients, who have a privileged, perhaps *the* privileged relation to the truth of analysis.

So it is possible that there will be different "kinds" of truth for different groups or subjects. One way of getting a clear sense of these differences is to look more closely at the kinds of empirical material that will be considered for their truth-value. An obvious classification for this diverse empirical material arises out of the way that psychoanalysis is organized as a practice for the production of "statements." The analytic dyad produces statements from two sources: from the analyst and from the patient. And each of those two sources produces statements of two kinds: one sort addressed directly to the specific other and a second addressed to those "outside" analysis.[2] So we have four classes of statement, and I shall illustrate the question of the truth of each of these classes with an example of each.

The first example is taken from that class of statements that is the analyst addressing himself to those "outside" analysis—from analytic writing. It is taken from middle Freud, taken almost at random, illustrating many of the registers of his writing all at once—metapsychological, theoretical, and clinical: "If we consider that obsessional neurotics have to develop a super-morality in order to protect their object-love from the hostility lurking behind it, we shall be inclined to regard some degree of this precocity of ego development as typical of human nature and to derive the capacity for the development of morality from the fact that in the order of development hate is the precursor of love."[3] To analyze the truth of this simple sentence would be a hard task indeed. At its core, one might suppose that there is a hypothesis: developmentally, hate is the precursor of love. But arriving at this hypothesis has already involved working from observations of patients that are themselves deeply colored by theoretical principles: that the compulsive behavior displayed by a certain class of behavior can be legitimately regarded as quasi-moral in character (so that, for instance, hand-washing is a meaningful action directed toward keeping something "precious" clean, or undoing an act that has "dirtied" the object, represented symbolically) and that there is evidence of hostility toward an object that is simultaneously loved. In addition, there is a supplementary assumption that the development of morality is linked to the development of the ego—and, indeed, the assumption that charting the development of morality tells us something important about how morality operates. At the same time, we can, with familiarity with other writings of Freud, see the case material from individual patients peeping through the more general and abstract hypothetical construction here. Do we not recognize the Ratman's hostility to his father in this hypothesis, that hostility which was so closely bound to his love and respect for his father that it committed him to his neurosis as to his own private religion?

Most of the questions concerning the truth value of psychoanalysis have been traditionally addressed to statements belonging to this class: statements in writings by psychoanalysts, intended as contributions to knowledge. The truth value can be addressed as if these were straightforward scientific hypotheses and considered by developmental psychologists and have been, from Jean Piaget on. But other scholars might feel they have a stake here—for instance, historians who can analyze the accuracy of the clinical descriptions of Freud's patients. Philosophers might intervene in order to ascertain whether it is a straightforward matter to match a hypothesis drawn from the reconstruction of adult patients' early moral and cognitive development against further such reconstructions with other, different patients or against observations of children (and here further debate might arise from the appropriateness of using interpretations of childrens' play or fantasies in an analytic relationship when compared with so-called direct observation of childrens' behavior). All of these questions are familiar ones in the assessment and adjudication of psychoanalytic hypotheses. And the way these familiar questions can be seen knotted together in the examination of this single sentence from Freud's work reminds us that, as with any other body of knowledge, the examination of an individual statement for its truth value leads us to a network of other statements implicated and consequently under examination in the same way.

The second class of psychoanalytic statements is also spoken by the analyst, but not to a generalized other, as in published writing, but to a specific other— a more specific other than, we might surmise, in any other mode of address: the analytic patient. The first and overriding requirement of such a statement is that it apply to the particular patient in question. Whether it applies to another individual under similar analytic circumstances of the analysis is beside the point. If it doesn't apply to this particular individual, at this moment, then it's not going to count as a truth statement. Direct reports of such statements are, in the nature of things, difficult to come by. The following is taken from a detailed report of an analysis written by the analyst Robert Stoller and reviewed by the patient to whom the interpretation was addressed.

[At this point in the session] I reviewed the many ways she tried to retain control: the sadomasochistic interplay with me; her insistence that she disgusted me with her dirtiness; the defiance that was covered with her "lovely" niceness and gentleness. Most of all—perhaps because I wanted relief after all these years—I emphasized the roots of resistance in her defense against anal attack: you say no, silently and secretively so that I shall not know. "No. I will not hear what you say; no, I will not agree with you; no, I will not speak my thoughts as I think and thus let the shit flow spontaneously;

no, I will not be on time; no, I will not close the door the way I think you want; no, I will not lie down in the manner you want. And even if I say yes, you had better know it is no. No." I ended with this comfort: "I want you to know that I understand you had to do this with me. Yes."[4]

I have not chosen this statement at random; it is what the analyst himself regarded as one of the most important interpretations that he offered in the course of a lengthy analysis, concerning a theme of the first importance to his patient's inner life that had been worked on over many years. I have chosen it in part because it highlights the rhetorical and transferential-countertransferential functioning of the analytic interpretation. What are we to make of the counterpoint of "no, . . . no, . . . no" with the analyst's self-representation as on the side of "yes"? Are we to think of this as a self-conscious echo of the most famous affirmation in English literature—"and yes I said yes I will Yes"?[5]

But it is the more immediately recognizably analytic rhetoric that raises questions about "truth": What are we to make of the analyst's remark concerning his immediate motivations for making this interpretation: "perhaps because I wanted relief after all these years"? What "relief" is he referring to? Immediately afterward we see: "I emphasized the roots of resistance in her defense against anal attack." But this act that gives him such relief after all these years, doesn't this begin to sound like the anal attack that she has been resisting for all these years? And, you might say, he's finally giving it to her with this rather thrusting interpretation. And his knowing that he is symbolically raping her anally with this interpretation—he has finally reached a point where he can reveal her fear to her in enacting the very thing she fears in the guise of an analytic interpretation, the analytic performative of her unconscious dread—is also something to be shared with her.

This knowingness concerning the symbolic meanings of the acts that the patient and the analyst perform upon each other are part of the common language patient and analyst develop. This language has a number of components, sometimes but not always including technical psychoanalytic terms such as *id* or *libido* or *cathexis* (though it would often be about as misleading to call these technical as it would be to think of *black hole* when it appears in a poem or *DNA* when it appears on CNN as technical). If one examines what Stoller actually said to his patient, the closest he came to using a technical term from the psychoanalytic lexicon was the word *shit.* Yet it is absolutely clear that the vocabulary and style of address of patient to analyst and analyst to patient is developed, sophisticated, often telegraphic. And syntax is of fundamental importance: as is well known, the most significant and telling interpretations are often a well placed and operatically toned analytic grunt. How is one to gauge the truth value of grunts, those indispensable media of everyday psychoanalytic communication?

The obvious place to look for some standard by which to judge the accuracy or truth value of interpretations is the patient's response—not necessarily only his or her agreement, since less direct responses may be more trustworthy, just as the change in atmosphere or a shrug of the shoulders may be a more accurate gauge of the end of an argument than a voiced termination such as "Ok, it's over, let's forget it." Stoller looked for some kind of validation of his account of his patient's analysis in the fact that every single line of his book was scrutinized by her, and she had the last word on whether the publication could be printed or not. However, both of them simultaneously knew that this process reenacted her fundamental fantasy, the central focus of those years of analytic work, which was an exhibitionistic, sadomasochistic fantasy. The act of the analyst and his patient publishing this book together was the sublimated version of that masturbation fantasy they had worked on—and in—for so many years. They know all this together, and even many years after the analysis, in the process of validating the clinical data, they are still doing it: "the [fantasy male protagonist] makes Belle reveal her excitement, as a display for an audience. And that, most literally, is what I do with this book."[6] The process of validation is itself a transferential reenactment of the patient's fantasy—with the validating scientist in the role of dirty old man who brings her to orgasm.

But where else can one look than to the patient for validation? A clean and seemingly decisive argument along these lines runs somewhat as follows: "The only person who, when all is said and done, can judge of the truths suggested by the analyst is the person about whom these are meant to be truthful statements—the patient. Without such a vision of the patient as final arbiter, the way is open to an imposition by the analyst of his or her own convictions." However, this argument may have more force as a negative restraint upon the analyst than as a positive condition for the judging of truth within analysis. Grünbaum certainly argues convincingly, contra Habermas, that making the assent or affirmation of the patient the necessary and sufficient condition for the truth of an analytic interpretation is misleading and distorting. But it is also clear that there is no "outside" recourse for such a vantage point from which to judge accuracy or truth. There are at least two important reasons why this is the case: one pertaining to the notion of the unconscious, the other to the nature and manifestations of transference and countertransference. As Freud argued, the unconscious is never done away with, and indeed, the best one can hope for in the lifting of certain key repressions is the entry into consciousness of the repressed material under the form of negation. Stoller's interpretation—"no . . . no . . . no. . . . Yes"—self-consciously reenacts the fundamental position of patient, who can only produce truth under the sign of negation, and of analyst, the only one of the two present for whom affirmation is truly available. How, as scandalized critics from Popper on have declared, can one hope to ascertain the unambiguous data of psychoanalysis when a "no" may mean "yes" and a "yes" almost certainly does not mean this particular "yes"?

Second, any given interpretation and response to the interpretation will be provisional—not just in the sense that it will be subject to later revision in the light of subsequent events and discoveries but also because it is a part of a process that never ceases. Analysis may be represented in textbook form as the discovery of preexisting truths, but the actual process never arrives at a still point of contemplation of such truths. Yet again, we remark that there is never a position "outside" from which the truth value of statements made either by analyst or by patient can be considered. To use J. L. Austin's powerful and illuminating classification scheme, all analytic statements are performative and thus are neither true nor false but, rather, either "successfully perform" or *misfire*. Yet the epistemic function of statements in analysis remains, however much we acknowledge the performative or process-implicated character of analytic speech. So we recognize that analytic statements, in particular analytic interpretations, are simultaneously performative and constative.

The performativity of analytic speech, on both sides, is only accentuated with my third example—a statement the Wolfman made to Freud at the end of his first analytic session, as quoted by Freud in a letter to Sándor Ferenczi written a few days after the session: "Jewish swindler he would like to use me from behind and shit on my head."[7] There is an unfortunate but nonetheless amusing problem in the interpretation of this statement: who exactly is doing what to whom in this scene?[8] Who is using and who is being used, who is shitting and whose head is it? The problem of citation—is Freud citing the exact words, or has he rendered the original "I" into a reported "he"—means that we cannot decide this question. It is, however, in principle decidable. What is less decidable is the weight to attach to the statement once such questions have been cleared up. Freud certainly took it as a classic and analytically useful "transference." The notion of transference, certainly, is a way of bracketing the truth claims of the statement—truth claim here meaning, roughly, that this was the patient's earnestly held view of Freud and his desires concerning him. But the concept of transference includes a promise as to the partial truth claim of the statement—such a statement is "false" on the face of it, but true once displacements, distortions, and transformations have been undone, in accordance with definitely ascertainable processes and mechanisms. But to add to this, we should recognize that a patient's transference is performative in the same way as the analyst's interpretation is: it is the analytic performance par excellence—a performance whose effects are always canceled out by the very rules of the analytic discourse, in particular the act of interpretation. (Freud does not get angry at having his name as a good businessman or an honorable Jew besmirched, nor does he offer himself as a partner for the homosexual or coprophilic acts the patient has proposed to him; he drains them of all possibility of action while retaining their content to be placed elsewhere.)

I do want, however, to remind you of the strange world we live in at the moment, when it comes to psychoanalysis and its truth. In his well-known essay "Withholding the Missing Portion," Stanley Fish says of this statement—"Jewish swindler, he would like to use me from behind and shit on my head"—that the Wolfman got it right. Stanley Fish says that this is the *truth* about psychoanalysis. This is not a jeu d'esprit on Stanley Fish's part. I am a great admirer of Fish's, but this example shows that even this kind of statement can become the exemplary judgment about psychoanalysis and therefore, as it were, the principal truth concerning psychoanalysis. The assigning of ultimate truth value to this statement is also, and this one surely must grant Fish, a rhetorical gesture of great force. This rhetorical gesture is tantamount to saying that the truth of psychoanalysis, the transference, is pure rhetoric.

Finally, I turn to my fourth example. I've switched from the analyst as theoretician writing outside the session to the analyst interpreting in the session and then to the patient talking in the session. And now, symmetrically, we need to hear the patient talking about psychoanalysis outside the session. The following passage from 1988 is taken from a series of interviews with people who had been in analysis:

> I think both the analysts I had were absolutely remarkable people. First of all as human beings. I had total trust in them as responsible individuals. And then I think intellectually they were very, very fine. And I've heard of too many cases where, because it's somehow been the wrong person maybe, it hasn't worked and people have been damaged. I do know some analysts socially and not in a million years would I give any kind of trust to them. I was very lucky. And also the other thing was I never felt I was going to be bound to them forever. With the second one I said I wanted to stop, but there was part of me that knew that she also would know when it was right. A lot of people have said to me, what you will find is the greatest progress you've made is after you finished, and I think that's true.[9]

I doubt if I'm the only one to find this confusing, contradictory, and bland when compared with the three other passages that I have quoted. I did not choose this passage for that reason. In its way, it is striking: we can see the self-contradictions at work. The ex-patient is equally in the grip of idealizations and of generalized suspicion of analysts. It is a self-contradictory final assessment, you might say. In terms of this volume's title, *Whose Freud?* this patient is saying, "Well, my Freud is fine—but yours is ridiculous." But what counted most for me in selecting this passage was that it had a certain ring of truth about it, or, perhaps, to be more modest, it lacked a ring of falsity. And the ring of truth, in part, comes from its contradictoriness. Because one principal strand of my argument has pointed toward the patient's evaluation of the truth of psychoanalysis, we can profitably compare this passage with two others, from a paper written in 1953 and entitled "Was This Analysis a Success?" by the celebrated psychologist and historian of psychology E. G. Boring, about his analysis with Hanns Sachs.[10] That the analysis had an *effect*—that the transference did not misfire—Boring is quite clear: "I had what I think was my share of emotion. I wept. I threw things. And once, right after a session, I found myself quite unmoved by a lecture from a traffic policeman, so much calmer was that usually enraging performance than the analysis."[11] But the judgment as to the overall success of the analysis was entirely unclear:

> It seems strange that a psychologist after his psychoanalysis should not have a message for his colleagues, when there has been so much questioning of psychoanalysis by the orthodox psychologists; and yet it is true that four years after my analysis I still cannot assess with assurance the significance of the experience in my life. . . . I did not know then, nor do I know now, whether my analysis was "successful"; and my analyst himself has never pronounced his judgment. I gathered that he thought it would have been successful if I thought it was; but I needed him to tell me what I should think.[12]

Such judgments as to the ultimate effect, validity, or truth of an analysis nearly always mingle uninformative murkiness with untrustworthy blandness. And with both ex-patients' assessments, the shadow of unresolved transference clouds our trust in their judgments—it is very difficult to judge the self-consciousness of Boring's irony when he declares himself unable to judge on the success of his analysis because his analyst never told him what to think. It is the absence of the ghost of the analyst that may have persuaded Janet Malcolm and, with her, many of her readers, that of the ex-patients of her specimen analyst in *The Impossible Profession* she interviewed, the one whose analysis gave the impression of success was the woman who remembered little and cared less about it. In sum, the last person who seems to be able to stand back and assess the truths discovered by a personal experience of psychoanalysis is the person whose truths these, in the end, are.

What my brief tour of the different classes of psychoanalytic statements leads me to conclude is that both the truths of analysis and what would count as evidence for and against those truths will be manifold and heterogeneous. If one of the classic goals or projects of the patient is to find the truth of his or her inner life and history—in the same sense that Ibsen unravels the drama of the lived lie or that the psychoanalyst-detective of Gladys Mitchell's stories confesses her fascination for the secrets that people keep secret even from themselves—the analytic experience leaves them little of substance to set down for the bookkeepers of permanent truths. What they experience instead is the actual drama of their histories, the living of their lies, in the experience of the analytic relation and its process. Their truth is first and foremost performative, and the analyst, reenacting that anal rape or that suffocating fearfulness of a mother's love, is very much party to that performance. And if the analyst, in the spirit of those who believe in the truth of physics because their plane gets them safely home to Frankfurt, looks to a pragmatic standard by which to gauge the truth of his or her interpretations or theories, he or she may well be doubtful as to the appositeness of the most natural of such pragmatic standards, that of gauging success by the dramatic clarity and aesthetic force of a transference successfully realized and then dissipated (*der Untergang* was the term Freud used to describe the fate of the Oedipus complex, variously translated in the psychoanalytic literature as "passing," "waning," or "dissolution").[13]

That all psychoanalytic truths, even those rendered as far as possible into the constative format of most scientific writing, pass via the performativity of the analytic dialogue is another way of expressing the almost universal conviction of analysts that transference is the central organizing concept and experience in their everyday practices. Yet their particular kind of performativity—a nonperforming performativity, a staging in a Beckettian world of nonaction—is closely linked to the view that the transference is a shadow version of the real, a fictional staging of the patient's truth. If I began by granting the appropriateness of developmental psychologists and neuroscientists appraising psychoanalytic statements in the light of their own research truths, it is as well to close by remembering that the relation of psychoanalytic truth to fiction is and no doubt always will be an intimate one. The fully enacted transference hovers permanently between reality and fiction; and Freud often maintained that the truths of psychoanalysis were clearly stated before him in the works of poets, writers, and artists. Both of these reminders raise the haunting question as to what kind of truth it is that is always presented first in fictional garb, in the garb of illusion, before it is domesticated and disrobed of its excess of the nonreal (if, as a quick and certain critic of psychoanalysis might add at this point, it ever is) and thus rendered into a presentable quasi- or pseudo-scientific truth. It is this perpetual haunting by the ghost of the unreal that makes one wonder if psychoanalysis really does wish to surrender the kind of truth enacted in *Oedipus Rex* for the version that sums it up as being the story of a man who accidentally killed his father and inadvertently married his mother.

Notes

1. Freud, *The Interpretation of Dreams, S.E.* 4: xxv (Preface to 2d edition of 1909). For an extended version of this argument, see my *Dispatches from the Freud Wars: Psychoanalysis and Its Passions* (Cambridge: Harvard University Press, 1997), 138–83.
2. For a similar model, developed in order to discuss the significance of psychoanalytic gossip, see John Forrester, "Psychoanalysis: Gossip, Telepathy, and/or Science?" in Forrester, *The Seductions of Psychoanalysis: Freud, Lacan, and Derrida* (Cambridge: Cambridge University Press, 1990), 243–59.
3. Freud, "The Disposition to Obsessional Neurosis," *S.E.* 12: 325: Stud VII 116–17, translation modified.
4. Robert Stoller, *Sexual Excitement: Dynamics of Erotic Life* (New York: Pantheon, 1979), 107–8.
5. James Joyce, *Ulysses* (Harmondsworth: Penguin, 1971), 704.
6. Stoller, *Sexual Excitement,* 218.
7. *The Correspondence of Sigmund Freud and Sándor Ferenczi,* Vol. 1: *1908–1914,* edited by Eva Brabant, Ernst Falzeder, and Patrizia Giampieri-Deutsch, translated by Peter T. Hoffer, with an introduction by André Haynal (Cambridge: Belknap Press of Harvard University Press, 1994), Freud to Ferenczi, Sunday, February 13, 1910, 138.
8. A fuller extract does not resolve this ambiguity but rather compounds it, in part because of the citation practices that Freud (as a turn-of-the-century German-speaker) employed: "A rich young Russian, whom I took on because of compulsive tendencies, admitted the following transferences to me after the first session: Jewish swindler, he would like to use me from behind and shit on my head. At the age of six he experienced his first symptom cursing against God: pig, dog, etc. When he saw three piles of faeces on the street he became uncomfortable because of the Holy Trinity and anxiously sought a fourth in order to destroy the association."
9. "Ruth," in Rosemary Dinnage, *One to One: The Experience of Psychotherapy* (London: Viking, 1988), 197.
10. E. G. Boring, "Was This Analysis a Success?" in Stanley Rachman, ed., *Critical Essays on Psychoanalysis* (Oxford: Pergamon; New York: Macmillan, 1963), 16–22, reprinted from

E. G. Boring et al., *Psychoanalysis as Seen By Analyzed Psychologists* (Washington, D.C.: American Psychological Association, 1953).

11. Ibid., 18.

12. Ibid., 16–19.

13. Hans Loewald, "The Waning of the Oedipus Complex," *Journal of the American Psychoanalytic Association* 27 (1979): 751–74.

Discussion

Donald Davidson: I thought I'd speak first because I have a similar question for all of the other panelists. It seemed to me that all of them were taking the notion of kinds of truth, at least some of the time, in a different way than I would or than I think it should be taken. Of course, when we observe anything at all—whether it's a person or anything else—there are a great many things that are true. And many of these things we're apt to be right about, and some of them wrong about. But those are not *kinds* of truth in the sense that we have different concepts of truth. We have just one concept of truth but—many truths. And the truths are of different kinds in the sense that they concern different aspects of the situation. Of course, we're not confusing beliefs with truths: some of the things we believe are true and some of them are false. There's plenty of variety of beliefs. But I don't think there's a lot of variety in concepts of truth.

Now the question I have is: Do you agree that the "kinds" doesn't apply to different concepts of truth, different ideas about what truth is, but rather concern different ways of finding it out, different ways of perceiving it, different things that we perceive which are each of them true or false? But with the same notion of truth in each case.

Richard Wollheim: I totally agree with that, and I don't know what I said that might have given rise to thinking that I didn't. At the very beginning I talked about a stratagem which some people pursue who want to attach a value to psychoanalysis and can't see how it can be that of truth. And then they invent these various terms, like "metaphorical truth" or "narrative truth." I didn't say how absurd I thought those maneuvers were because I didn't think that the starting point was justified. So I just left it at that. But I think that's the only thing I said that might have given rise to your suspicion.

Donald Davidson: No, I think there are just two ways of taking these distinctions between, let's say, "narrative" and "historical" truth and "psychological" truth and so forth. We might think those are different concepts of truth that are involved, or just different truths.

Richard Wollheim: I understood these people as saying that we can't really attribute truth to psychoanalytic assertions at all, but we can attribute *something else,* and then they describe that something else honorifically by the notion of truth. But in bad faith.

John Forrester: I'm not clear myself what hangs on whether there is one truth or many—one concept of truth or a number of different concepts. Let me give what might be a parallel: what hangs on the concept of mass being different? We know because of the historical development of the concept of mass that Newton's concept is different from Einstein's concept. And they're mutually contradictory in certain key respects. But they're put together as concepts differently. Now I've often thought that there are basically different kinds of truth we live with. Legal truth is different from scientific truth. And I'm not sure what hangs on saying, "Ah, but the legal concept of truth and the scientific concept of truth will have to fall under one concept," which is, as it were, the larger concept of truth. So a little bit of education for me here might help. My intuition is that the practices by which one establishes truth within a given institution of truth production is where one should look for thinking about truth, rather than the prior concept.

Donald Davidson: Well, in different fields we have different *criteria* for truth. And, of course, with respect to the notion of mass, people may have had different concepts of mass. If they had contradictory views about the same thing, the same phenomenon, then at least one of them must have been false.

What difference does it make which way we talk? It might not make any difference, in some cases. But there's a danger, I think, of falling into the idea that truth really just depends on how you look at things, and it's relative to the speaker or to the discipline, or relative to the age. And that can lead to rather serious difficulties, because it suggests that we don't really have one notion here. I think it's the plainest notion we have. And that's one of the reasons we can't define it in terms of other things. If you can define a concept in terms of other things you can get rid of it in favor of the other notions. Truth is too fundamental to be defined in terms of things that are plainer, simpler, more clear. But we all have a very, very good grip on the ordinary notion. There's water in this cup or there isn't. And we all understand that in a pretty plain way. That doesn't mean we necessarily agree, or even that we agree on how to tell, but as long as we mean the same thing by "water" and "cup" and so forth, it doesn't matter whether you're a lawyer or a psychoanalyst, it's just true or false.

Jonathan Lear: I agree. Throughout my remarks I tried to speak about *the* concept of truth and our life with that concept. I take there to be a concept of truth we live with. I think of our lives with it as a complicated and variegated set of activities that we have to pay attention to. I have a question for you, though. Do you know with confidence what happened to your father?

Donald Davidson: You mean my real father? (Laughter.) "Whose father?" No, the answer to your real question is no.

Peter Gay, Moderator: Do we have any contributions, questions, or argument from the floor?

Peter Brooks: Just really a very simple observation. I was struck by the fact that three of the four speakers—that is, Wollheim, Lear, and Forrester—were all presenting versions not of truth but of the emergence of a truth that had to do with transferential situations, and had to do very much with the dynamics of the transference in dialogic situations between two people. And certainly that would seem to be characteristic of any notion of truth that would be applicable to psychoanalysis or that would emerge from psychoanalysis, which would not necessarily distinguish psychoanalysis from other disciplines, since I suppose it would be true in anthropology, social anthropology, and ethnology as well, but which in some sense, since the transference has been *thought* in psychoanalysis in a way it has not in many other disciplines, would make psychoanalysis paradigmatic for a certain modern understanding of truth as dialogic or transferential.

Richard Wollheim: I think that the case which I talked about is not really such a case. Because here the candidate reported the session to the supervisor, and then the other candidates and the supervisor, between them, arrived at a better understanding of what had gone on in that situation. And simply on the basis of what was reported these people arrived at a better understanding, cooperatively, of what had gone on. What's interesting about this case is that there's nothing here which could be open to the charges which are sometimes raised that there's been some element of suggestion, and that it was from suggestion that there came this kind of congruence of opinion. There's nothing like that in this case, since it's only being discussed after the fact. Of course, we don't really know what went on in the next session, but neither is that relevant. There is simply an understanding of these various processes and defensive measures which were inadequately grasped by the candidate at the time and which, when the whole session is retold, emerge. Nothing dialogic.

Robert Michels: Two comments. It seemed to me that the three clinical vignettes all told how there was an apparent truth that was less interesting than a concealed truth. And it was only after time that the hierarchy of, not truthfulness, but interest, or importance, or relevance of the truths became clear. The initially apparent truth became uninteresting and was seen to be primarily a vehicle for communicating a concealed but more relevant truth. And of course that's the central theme of psychoanalysis, that the manifest, apparent story or truth sometimes is only a communication about a hidden, more interesting truth.

The second comment is addressed to Jonathan [Lear]. If I understood correctly, he suggested that it's possible to have a comprehensive truth which is not true—a comprehensive integration of the facts which is less than true. It's a false self in his words, because it involves defensive processes. And that the test for truth in analysis is not comprehensiveness but nondefensiveness. But I can't imagine a comprehensive version that ignores an account of the defensiveness.

Jonathan Lear: Your first comment seems to me absolutely right in relation to my clinical example, where the door leavings or closings were a vehicle of meaning. And there's something that I think is a deceptively simple point but really bears thinking about, which is that utterances are themselves concrete activities of a sort. Whether they be verbal utterances or the physical act of leaving the door slightly ajar or the mental activity of actually consciously thinking something to oneself. And this is one of the reasons that the body is so important in psychoanalysis. You might say, why is it that fantasy expresses itself in such pervasive and important ways through the body? Well, there are lots of psychoanalytic reasons for that. But one of them is that the body itself can become a concrete vehicle of meaning. The fact that meaning is incarnate, and thus must have a vehicle, is of profound psychoanalytic significance.

The thing that I found myself worrying about in your first comment is the idea that the initial door leavings become uninteresting as other truths about the meaning of that event emerge or are developed. This is not something I would want to agree with. I think the manifest content remains tremendously significant throughout the process of analysis. I don't mind talking about hidden or concealed meanings being revealed in the process. There's a question of what one means by *that* claim. And one of the things I was trying to gesture at in my talk was that one shouldn't conceive of all of these meanings as being fully formed and as having the same shape as the conscious articulation they end up being expressed in. The process of revealing those hidden meanings has to be understood as a more complicated developmental process.

There are two things I want to say about your second comment. When I talked about the construction or the possible construction of a false self, I didn't mean to imply that a fully coherent false self can be constructed. What I meant to suggest is that there's a way of collaborating in the wishful attempt to build such a thing so that the breakdowns in that construction get evaded and avoided and somehow covered over.

Now the final point about defensiveness and nondefensiveness: I think the word *defense* or *defensive*—like *narcissistic,* another word which comes up in psychoanalytic discourse—has both a pejorative use and a value-neutral use. In the case of *narcissistic,* it's both used to describe a pathology of a certain sort and used in ways that are not meant to describe any particular pathology. Similarly, for the word *defensive* or *defense,* there is a use which is pathological—where we're talking about a rigidity in defensiveness, some pathological misformation or fixity of defense—and there's a nonpejorative use of that term, when people claim that all mental activity has a defensive function in it. I was using the term in the pejorative, pathological sense. And the question of what it is to be nondefensive or relatively nondefensive in that sense is an incredibly interesting one. I don't think that the idea of a defense has been conceptualized as deeply as it could be; it's an important area of research. And that's a good place to be looking if you want to think about the concept of truth as it's lived with in psychoanalysis. Rather than looking at issues of correspondence or coherence, it would be very valuable to think about what it is to be defensive or nondefensive.

Robert Jay Lifton: This is a question about psychic truth as opposed to historical or factual truth, and it's stimulated by Jonathan's paper, but certainly the other panelists could address it. Describing the patient who doesn't know whether he was abused, and you don't know whether he's abused, you convinced me that he was using that situation to avoid other issues. But doesn't it matter factually whether he *was* abused? I'm thinking about people who were severely abused, Auschwitz survivors, or people who did the abusing, Nazi doctors. I wanted to know in both cases the psychic truth of what they experienced, in terms of what was done to them or what they did, as well as what they *actually* did and what was actually done to them. And perhaps you didn't have time to emphasize this, but isn't there a tension you want to have between that psychic truth and the importance of the factual truth?

Jonathan Lear: Yes, I did say explicitly that attention to truth matters. And there's a huge difference clinically, experientially, and morally between actual forms of seduction and abuse and, you might say, *merely* fantasized versions. There are important clinical differences that are I think well written about. One place to look is Leonard Shengold's *Soul Murder.*[1]

So I agree. But part of what I was trying to also emphasize is that while in extreme cases extreme differences occur, there's a whole realm where the distinction between whether something is fantasized or real is a false distinction. What it is for parents to unknowingly act in seductive ways—ways that are experienced as seductive and thus *are* seductive—is a real problem of ordinary life. Precisely because the role of fantasy is so powerful in both children and adults, you know, that what counts as an actual seduction and what counts as a merely fantasized one is not always a worthwhile distinction to think about. Precisely because fantasies are so powerful, many gestures in life can be experienced as seductions. In the case of this particular patient, after listening to this person over the course of the analysis, I had in the end no firm view. I did come to think, but tentatively, that some massive form of abuse did not happen. He didn't think this either. But, you know, exactly what did happen in his childhood and what might have been taken up that really was intrusive to him and had real psychic effect on him, I haven't a clue; I just don't know. But what did emerge and became clear over time was the use he was putting that to.

Richard Wollheim: I'm not actually certain that I got the drift of that. Don't you think it's only by initially making the distinction between actual seduction, seductions in actuality, and fantasized seductions that we come to have a sense of the importance that fantasized seductions play? If we didn't make that distinction in the first place, we wouldn't be able to concentrate on fantasized seductions as such and see the role that they have. I think that's really what lies behind and makes interesting Freud's rejection of the seduction hypothesis. Because ultimately it isn't really that he changed his mind so vastly about things, since he incorporated a lot of the material which he had used for the seduction hypothesis within the Oedipus complex. But he came to realize that fantasized seductions could have this enormous place in the life of people. And he could only come to that when he started to recognize that there were a number of these cases where actual seductions hadn't happened.

Robert Jay Lifton: In the work of my wife, Betty Jean Lifton, on adoption, it becomes very important for adopted people to make contact with their actual mother and father if possible, their birth mother in particular. And it's a very great thing to find the literal truth of their origins. It's a slightly different situation, but it raises the question, perhaps more urgently, of the importance in some situations of actual truth. Of course, Freud made the great discovery that fantasy can be the source, but then, as with many things about psychoanalysis, one has to come to some equilibrium in one's judgment and in one's view of truth; an equilibrium that includes the fantasy or the psychic truth and sees something important in the literal process or factual truth that then informs the psychoanalyst or the investigator in the best possible way.

Richard Wollheim: Well, this is of course really a distinction between actuality and fantasy. And truth only comes into it in the sense that truth comes into everything. It doesn't come into it specifically.

John Forrester: I wonder if I can make a comment? I worry a little bit about the problem of the pressure of the real, and I very much agreed with Jonathan's remarks. The idea that psychoanalysis is a kind of forensic inquiry is one that should be treated with great suspicion. And we haven't addressed questions like truth in painting. How would we apply a term like *truth* to painting, to a Cubist painting? And does that question relate to psychoanalysis?—which is, in part, an aesthetic adventure of some sort. The kind of questions about fantasy and reality that we have become preoccupied with certainly don't help us think about questions about aesthetics.

I might mention that one of the drastic solutions that Christopher Bollas and

David Sundelson have in a book called *The New Informants* is the idea of dividing up psychoanalysis into two parts: social psychoanalysis and classical psychoanalysis.[2] And classical psychoanalysis would be dedicated to a very tight, hermetically sealed, confidential, nonforensic inquiry outside the sphere of laws about what is permitted and not permitted to be said. In other words, the idea that free speech and free association are very closely allied. And social psychoanalysis would conform to, say, the laws that require report on a crime to go straight to the police if it happens to come up in a psychoanalytic session. Which is required in certain states in the United States, according to the reading I've done. If someone fantasizes committing a murder in situations that sound relatively realistic, the analyst is obliged to report that to the police. There are probably people here who have personal experience with this.

Now that's the bifurcation which represents the hole that psychoanalysis has got itself into by getting very preoccupied with the fantasy versus reality question. And Bollas has proposed a solution which is not one that analysts are probably going to welcome; but I think its logic is actually impeccable, I'm afraid, given the social and policing functions that psychoanalysis has been called on to make. There is a wonderful sentence in a textbook of biomedical ethics in which the authors—Beauchamp and Childress, I think it is—say: there is a prima facie obligation on a doctor to obey the law, but the obligation is only prima facie.[3] And I think psychoanalysts have to think quite hard about the kinds of problem they are facing vis-à-vis the question of reality and the reporting of fantasy to the police.

Question: I was thinking along somewhat related lines. I was very struck by Professor Davidson's idea that there is only one notion of truth and that this notion is so fundamental that it's almost hard to conceptualize. I think that's right. I just wondered if there wouldn't be a better way to frame the question. Namely, where in psychoanalysis is it necessary or *relevant* to ask the question, "Is this true?" Even in physics it's not always appropriate to ask the question "Is this true?" So where is the question of truth relevant in psychoanalysis and where is it irrelevant?

Peter Gay: Dominick, do you want to have a go at it? Okay, we'll have this as a final comment because the truth is it's a quarter to six.

Dominick LaCapra: I think that, admitting of course the importance of fantasy, there's a concern about whether the actual occurrence of child abuse has an effect upon problems people face in later life or not. It's a significant issue. And

I haven't seen any kind of sustained work on that question, that closely analyzes whether that's the case or whether the fantasy would have very comparable effects of truth claim.

Jonathan Lear: May I respond to the question? I don't mean it to be the final word. I'd want to again mention this book *Soul Murder* by Len Shengold because not only is it an excellent description of the effects of actual violent, intrusive seductions, but it's got a great bibliography of the literature that makes a claim that there is a very, very significant difference between dramatic actual seductions and the ability to fantasize seduction. And one of the dramatic differences it makes is that early massive intrusion actually prohibits the development of the ability to fantasize with the complexity of a narrative of a seduction. And people who have experienced these sorts of massive intrusions in early life remain with very primitive forms of fantasy as the psychological end of the line for them.

Notes

1. Leonard Shengold, *Soul Murder: The Effects of Childhood Abuse and Deprivation* (New Haven and London: Yale University Press, 1989).
2. Christopher Bollas and David Sundelson, *The New Informants: The Betrayal of Confidentiality in Psychoanalysis and Psychotherapy* (Northvale, N.J.: J. Aronson, 1995).
3. Tom L. Beauchamp and James F. Childress, *Principles of Biomedical Ethics,* 4th ed. (Oxford: Oxford University Press, 1994).

Contributors

Leo Bersani is Professor Emeritus in the Department of French at the University of California, Berkeley. His publications include *Caravaggio's Secrets* (1998, with Ulysse Dutoit), *Derek Jarman's Caravaggio* (1999, with Ulysse Dutoit), *Homos* (1995), *The Culture of Redemption* (1990), *The Freudian Body: Psychoanalysis and Art* (1986), and *Baudelaire and Freud* (1979).

Peter Brooks (co-editor) is author of *Reading for the Plot, Psychoanalysis and Storytelling*, and *Troubling Confessions*, among other works. He is Tripp Professor of Humanities and Director of the Whitney Humanities Center, Yale University.

Judith Butler is Maxine Elliot Professor in the Departments of Rhetoric and Comparative Literature at the University of California, Berkeley. Her works include *Gender Trouble: Feminism and the Subversion of Identity* (1999), *Bodies That Matter: On the Discursive Limits of "Sex"* (1993), *The Psychic Life of Power: Theories of Subjection* (1997), and *Excitable Speech* (1997) as well as numerous articles and contributions on philosophy and feminist and queer theory. Her forthcoming work on Antigone and the politics of kinship is entitled *Antigone's Claim: Kinship Between Life and Death*.

Arnold Cooper, M.D., is Stephen P. Tobin and Dr. Arnold M. Cooper Professor of Consultation Liaison Psychiatry at the Weil Medical College of Cornell University and a Training and Supervising Analyst at the Columbia University Psychoanalytic Center. Dr. Cooper is the North American Editor of the *International Journal of Psychoanalysis* and the Deputy Editor of the *American Journal of Psychiatry.*

Frederick Crews is Professor Emeritus of English at the University of California, Berkeley. Among his publications, those that directly address the theme of this book are *Skeptical Engagements* (1986), *The Memory Wars: Freud's Legacy in Dispute* (1995), and the anthology *Unauthorized Freud: Doubters Confront a Legend* (1998).

Hubert Damisch is on the faculty of the Ecole des Hautes Etudes en Sciences Sociales in Paris. He has written widely on philosophy, art history, and aesthetics; his most recently translated works are *The Judgment of Paris* (1996) and *The Origin of Perspec*tive (1994).

Donald Davidson, the Willis S. and Marion Slusser Professor of Philosophy at the University of California, Berkeley, writes mainly about the philosophy of language and the philosophy of action. *The Philosophy of Donald Davidson* in the Library of Living Philosophers has just been published.

David Forrest is Professor of Clinical Psychiatry at Columbia University College of Physicians and Surgeons, where he also serves as Consultation-Liaison Psychiatrist in Neurology and on the Faculty of the Psychoanalytic Center. He was the Founding Editor of SPRING: The Journal of the E.E. Cummings Society, and is a Fellow of the Explorers Club.

John Forrester is Reader in the History and Philosophy of the Sciences at the University of Cambridge. His most recent books are *Dispatches from the Freud Wars: Psychoanalysis and Its Passions* (1997) and *Truth Games: Lies, Money and Psychoanalysis* (1997). The second editions of *Freud's Women* (cowritten with Lisa Appignanesi) and *Language and the Origin of Psychoanalysis* will be published in 2000.

Mary Jacobus, who holds the Anderson Chair of English and Women's Studies at Cornell University and has just become Professor of English at Cambridge University, is working on a book on literature, aesthetics, and British object relations psychoanalysis in the wake of Klein.

Dominick LaCapra is Bryce and Edith M. Bowmar Professor of Humanist Studies at Cornell University and the Associate Director of the School of Criticism and Theory at Cornell. His publications include *History and Memory After Auschwitz* (1998), *Representing the Holocaust* (1994), *History, Politics and the Novel* (1987), *History and Criticism* (1985), and *Rethinking Intellectual History* (1983).

Jonathan Lear is John U. Nef Distinguished Service Professor of Philosophy and a member of the Committee on Social Thought at the University of Chicago. He is a graduate of the Western New England Institute for Psychoanalysis and author of *Open Minded: Working Out the Logic of the Soul* (1998), *Love and Its Place in Nature: A Philosophical Interpretation of Freudian Psychoanalysis* (1990), *Aristotle: The Desire to Understand* (1988), and *Aristotle and Logical Theory* (1980).

Robert Jay Lifton is Distinguished Professor of Psychiatry and Psychology at the City University of New York, John Jay College and the Graduate School. Most recently, he has written *Destroying the World to Save It: Aum Shinrikyo, Apocalyptic Violence, and the New Global Terrorism* (1999). His 1969 book *Death in Life: Survivors in Hiroshima* won a National Book Award. Other publications include *The Protean Self: Human Resilience* *in an Age of Fragmentation* (1993), *The Nazi Doctors: Medical Killing and the Psychology of Genocide* (1986), and *The Broken Connection: On Death and Continuity in Life* (1979).

Peter Loewenberg is Professor of History and Political Psychology at the University of California, Los Angeles. He is the author of *Fantasy and Reality in History* (1995) and *Decoding the Past: The Psychohistorical Approach* (1996). He is a Training and Supervising Analyst and faculty member of the Southern California Psychoanalytic Institute and is Chair of the Committee on Research and Special Training of the American Psychoanalytic Association.

Robert Michels, M.D., is Walsh McDermott University Professor of Medicine and Psychiatry at Cornell University Medical College and a Training and Supervising Analyst at the Columbia University Center for Psychoanalytic Training and Research.

Juliet Mitchell, Lecturer in Gender and Society at Cambridge University, Fellow of Jesus College, and recently Visiting Professor of Comparative Literature at Yale, is the author of *Psychoanalysis and Feminism: Freud, Reich, Laing, and Women* (1975) and *Women, the Longest Revolution: Essays on Feminism, Literature, and Psychoanalysis* (1984). She is the editor of *The Selected Melanie Klein* (1986) and *Who's Afraid of Feminism? Seeing Through the Backlash* (1997, with Ann Oakley). Her new book on hysteria is forthcoming.

Toril Moi is James B. Duke Professor of Literature and Romance Studies at Duke University. She regularly teaches courses on Freud, psychoanalytic theory, and questions in feminist theory. She is the author of *Sexual/Textual Politics: Feminist Literary Theory* (1985), *Simone de Beauvoir: The Making of an Intellectual Woman* (1994), and *What Is a Woman? and Other Essays* (1999). She is also the editor of *The Kristeva Reader* (1986) and *French Feminist Thought* (1987).

Morton Reiser, M.D., is Albert E. Kent Professor Emeritus of Psychiatry at the Yale Medical School. His books include *Mind, Brain, Body: Toward a Convergence of Psychoanalysis and Neurobiology* (1984) and *Memory in Mind and Brain: What Dream Imagery Reveals* (1990).

Paul Robinson is Richard W. Lyman Professor in the Humanities at Stanford University. In addition to numerous articles and essays, his books include *Gay Lives: Homosexual Autobiography from John Addington Symonds to Paul Monette* (1999), *Freud and His Critics* (1993), *Opera and Ideas: From Mozart to Strauss* (1985), *The Modernization of Sex* (1976), and *The Freudian Left* (1969).

Douglas L. Rothman is Associate Professor of Diagnostic Radiology and Director of the Magnetic Resonance Center at Yale University School of Medicine.

Eric L. Santner, the Harriet and Ulrich Meyer Professor in Germanic Studies and Jewish Studies at the University of Chicago, has published *My Own Private Germany: Daniel Paul Schreber's Secret History of Modernity* (1996), *Stranded Objects: Mourning, Memory, and Film in Postwar Germany* (1990), and *Friedrich Hölderlin: Narrative Vigilance and the Poetic Imagination* (1986).

Robert G. Shulman is Sterling Professor of Molecular Biophysics and Biochemistry and former Director of the Magnetic Resonance Center at Yale University School of Medicine.

Kaja Silverman is Chancellor's Professor of Rhetoric and Film at the University of California, Berkeley. She is the author of *World Spectators* (forthcoming), *The Threshold of the Visible World* (1996), *Male Subjectivity at the Margins* (1992), *The Acoustic Mirror: The Female Voice in Psychoanalysis and Cinema* (1988), *The Subject of Semiotics* (1983), and, with Harun Farocki, *Speaking About Godard* (1998).

Meredith Skura, the Libbie Shearn Moody Professor of English at Rice University, is the author of *Shakespeare the Actor and the Purposes of Playing* (1993) and *The Literary Use of the Psychoanalytic Process* (1981), as well as articles on psychoanalysis and early modern writers.

Richard Wollheim is Professor of Philosophy at the University of California, Berkeley. He is the author of *The Mind and Its Depths* (1992), *Painting as an Art* (1987), *The Thread of Life* (1984), *On Art and the Mind* (1972), *Sigmund Freud* (1971), *Art and Its Objects* (1968), and *F. H. Bradley* (1960).

Alex Woloch (co-editor) is Assistant Professor of English at Stanford University. He is completing a book on characterization and realism in the nineteenth-century novel.

Index